The aim of this book is to make more widely available a body of recent research activity that has become known as applied general equilibrium analysis. The central idea underlying this work is to convert the Walrasian general equilibrium structure (formalized in the 1950s by Kenneth Arrow, Gerard Debreu, and others) from an abstract representation of an economy into realistic models of actual economies. Numerical, empirically based general equilibrium models can then be used to evaluate concrete policy options by specifying production and demand parameters and incorporating data reflective of real economies.

In this book, Shoven and Whalley describe all aspects of developing applied general equilibrium models, including developing an appropriate equilibrium structure, calibrating the model, compiling counterfactual equilibria, and interpreting results. The first two parts of the book develop the techniques used to apply general equilibrium theory to policy. The final part presents a number of applications drawn from their previous research work, including international trade, development, regional and environmental economics.

The authors contend that the applied general equilibrium model provides an ideal framework for appraising the effects of policy changes on resource allocation and for assessing who gains and loses, policy impacts not well covered by empirical macro models. The applications in the book illustrate a number of ways in which fresh insights are provided in long-standing policy controversies.

CAMBRIDGE SURVEYS OF ECONOMIC LITERATURE

APPLYING
GENERAL EQUILIBRIUM

CAMBRIDGE SURVEYS OF ECONOMIC LITERATURE

Editor
Professor Mark Perlman, University of Pittsburgh

The literature of economics is expanding rapidly, and many subjects have changed out of recognition within the space of a few years. Perceiving the state of knowledge in fast-developing subjects is difficult for students and time-consuming for professional economists. This series is intended to help with this problem. Each book will be quite brief, giving a clear structure to and balanced overview of the topic, and written at a level intelligible to the senior undergraduate. The books will therefore be useful for teaching but will also provide a mature yet compact presentation of the subject for economists wishing to update their knowledge outside their own specialization.

Other books in the series
E. Roy Weintraub: Microfoundations: The compatibility of microeconomics and macroeconomics
Dennis C. Mueller: Public choice
Robert Clark and Joseph Spengler: The economics of individual and population aging
Edwin Burmeister: Capital theory and dynamics
Mark Blaug: The methodology of economics or how economists explain
Robert Ferber and Werner Z. Hirsch: Social experimentation and economic policy
Anthony C. Fisher: Resource and environmental economics
Morton I. Kamien and Nancy L. Schwartz: Market structure and innovation
Richard E. Caves: Multinational enterprise and economic analysis
Anne O. Krueger: Exchange-rate determination
James W. Friedman: Oligopoly theory
Mark R. Killingsworth: Labor supply
Helmut Frisch: Theories of inflation
Steven M. Sheffrin: Rational expectations
Sanford V. Berg and John Tschirhart: Natural monopoly regulation
Thrainn Eggertsson: Economic behavior and institutions
Jack Hirshleifer and John G. Riley: The analytics of uncertainty and information

Applying
general equilibrium

JOHN B. SHOVEN
Stanford University
and National Bureau of Economic Research

JOHN WHALLEY
University of Western Ontario
and National Bureau of Economic Research

CAMBRIDGE
UNIVERSITY PRESS

Published by the Press Syndicate of the University of Cambridge
The Pitt Building, Trumpington Street, Cambridge CB2 1RP
40 West 20th Street, New York, NY 10011-4211, USA
10 Stamford Road, Oakleigh, Victoria 3166, Australia

First published 1992

Printed in the United States of America

Library of Congress Cataloging-in-Publication Data
Shoven, John B.
Applying general equilibrium / John B. Shoven and John Whalley.
p.   cm. – (Cambridge surveys of economic literature.)
Includes bibliographical references and index.
ISBN 0-521-26655-6 – ISBN 0-521-31986-2 (pbk.)
1. Equilibrium (Economics) – Mathematical models.   I. Whalley,
John.   II. Title.   III. Series.
HB145.S53   1992
339.5 – dc20   91–23007
                                                        CIP

A catalog record of this book is available from the British Library

ISBN 0-521-26655-6 hardback
ISBN 0-521-31986-2 paperback

CONTENTS

Preface   *page* vii

1   Introduction   1

Part I   Techniques
2   General equilibrium theory   9
3   Computing general equilibria   37

Part II   Applying the techniques
4   Designing an applied general equilibrium model   71
5   Using applied general equilibrium models   103
6   A Harberger tax-model application   134
7   A general equilibrium model of U.S. tax policies   153

Part III   Policy applications
8   Global trade models   197
9   Single-country trade modeling   230
10 Analysis of price controls   256

11 Conclusion   279

References   283
Index   291

PREFACE

This volume has its origins in thesis work that the two authors began at Yale in the early 1970s, which then evolved through a number of modeling efforts at both a conceptual and an empirical level in the late 1970s and on into the 1980s. Many individuals have contributed to this effort through direct involvement as coauthors, commentators, thesis supervisors, and graduate students in classes. We are indebted to all of these, and in this preface can only single out a small number of individuals for special comment.

Our primary debt is to Herbert Scarf, our joint thesis supervisor at Yale, whose contribution to equilibrium computation in the late 1960s and 1970s laid the foundation for all the work in this area. His continual support, guidance, and inspiration have been the cornerstone of our efforts in this area.

We are also indebted to our graduate students with whom we have worked over the years on various equilibrium computation projects. These include Don Fullerton, Larry Goulder, Charles Ballard, Alfredo Pereira, and Karl Scholz at Stanford; and John Piggott, Ashan Mansur, Trien Nguyen, Randy Wigle, Gordon Lenjosek, Chia Ngee-Choon, and Bob Hamilton at Western. In addition, secretarial support from Karen Prindle, Connie Nevill, and Lucy Steffler is gratefully acknowledged, as is logistical support from Leigh MacDonald. Extraordinarily detailed comments on an earlier draft by Hiroshi Kodaira greatly improved the quality and clarity of the draft. To all of them, we are grateful.

Finally, we would like to dedicate this volume to the next generation of Shoven–Whalley friendships: our children, Jimmy Shoven and Tim and Alex Whalley.

1

Introduction

The aim of this book is to make more widely available a body of recent research activity that has become known as applied general equilibrium analysis. The central idea underlying this work is to convert the Walrasian general equilibrium structure (formalized in the 1950s by Kenneth Arrow, Gerard Debreu, and others) from an abstract representation of an economy into realistic models of actual economies. Numerical, empirically based general equilibrium models can then be used to evaluate concrete policy options by specifying production and demand parameters and incorporating data reflective of real economies.

We have earlier summarized a number of these modeling efforts in a survey article (Shoven and Whalley 1984). Here we try to go one stage further and give readers more of a sense of how to do their own modeling, including developing an appropriate equilibrium structure, calibrating their model, compiling counterfactual equilibria, and interpreting results. The first part of the book develops the techniques required to apply general equilibrium theory to policy evaluations. The second part presents a number of applications we have made in our previous research.

The Walrasian general equilibrium model provides an ideal framework for appraising the effects of policy changes on resource allocation and for assessing who gains and loses, policy impacts that are not well covered by empirical macro models. In this volume, we outline a number of ways in which applied versions of this model are providing fresh insights into long-standing policy controversies.

Our use of the term "general equilibrium" corresponds to the well-known Arrow–Debreu model, elaborated in Arrow and Hahn (1971). The number of consumers in the model is specified. Each consumer has an initial endowment of the N commodities and a set of preferences, resulting in demand functions for each commodity. Market demands are the sum of each consumer's demands. Commodity market demands depend on all prices, and are continuous, nonnegative, homogeneous of degree zero (i.e., no money illusion), and satisfy Walras's law (i.e., that at any set of prices, the total value of consumer expenditures equals consumer incomes. On the production side, technology is described by either constant-returns-to-scale activities or nonincreasing-returns-to-scale production functions. Producers maximize profits. The zero homogeneity of demand functions and the linear homogeneity of profits in prices (i.e., doubling all prices doubles money profits) imply that only relative prices are of any significance in such a model. The absolute price level has no impact on the equilibrium outcome.

Equilibrium in this model is characterized by a set of prices and levels of production in each industry such that the market demand equals supply for all commodities (including disposals if any commodity is a free good). Since producers are assumed to maximize profits, this implies that in the constant-returns-to-scale case, no activity (or cost-minimizing technique for production functions) does any better than break even at the equilibrium prices.

Most contemporary applied general equilibrium models are numerical analogs of traditional two-sector general equilibrium models popularized by James Meade, Harry Johnson, Arnold Harberger, and others in the 1950s and 1960s. Earlier analytic work with these models has examined the distortionary effects of taxes, tariffs, and other policies, along with functional incidence questions. More recent applied models, including those discussed here, provide numerical estimates of efficiency and distributional effects within the same framework.

The value of these computational general equilibrium models is that numerical simulation removes the need to work in small dimensions, and much more detail and complexity can be incorporated than in simple analytic models. For instance, tax-policy models can simultaneously accommodate several taxes. This is important even when evaluating changes in only one tax because taxes compound in effect with other taxes. Also, use of a tax-policy model permits an evaluation of comprehensive tax-reform proposals such as those debated in the United States during the 1984–6 period. Likewise, the complexities of the issues handled in trade negotiations in the General Agreement on Tariffs and Trade (GATT), such as simultaneous tariff reductions in several countries or codes to limit the use of nontariff barriers, cannot be analyzed in ways useful to policy makers other than through numerical techniques. Models involving 30 or more sectors and industries are commonly employed, providing substantial detail for policy makers concerned with feedback effects of policy initiatives directed at specific products or industries.

In the next chapter we briefly review the theory of general equilibrium relevant for applied general equilibrium analysis. We sketch proofs of existence, and discuss in detail the inclusion of such policy instruments as taxes and tariffs for which a modeling of government behavior is also required. The applied models that follow in later chapters are consistent with the Arrow–Debreu theoretical structure, reflecting the attempt in applied general equilibrium work to make that structure relevant to policy.

The techniques and models described in this book have been applied to a range of policy questions in a number of economic fields over the last ten or so years. These include public finance and taxation issues, international trade-policy questions, evaluations of alternative development strategies, the implications of energy policies, regional questions, and even issues in macroeconomic policy.

Policy makers daily confront the need to make decisions on all manner of both major and minor policy matters that affect such issues as the intersectoral allocation of resources and the distribution of income. Some form of numerical model is implicit in the actions of any policy maker. Techniques such as those presented here can, in our opinion, help policy makers by making explicit the implications of alternative courses of action within a framework broadly consistent with that currently accepted by many microeconomic theorists. Although model results are not precise owing to data and other problems, they nonetheless provide a vehicle for generating initial null hypotheses on the impacts of policy changes where none previously existed. They also yield assessments of the impacts of policies, which may challenge the received wisdom that guides policy making. We emphasize the large elements of subjective judgment involved both in building and in using these models, and also their large potential for generating fresh insights on policy issues of the day.

We hope that the insights gained from particular models will become clearer as the reader proceeds with the description of the various models, but some examples may be helpful at this stage. One result of applied general equilibrium tax models' use has been a reassessment of the importance of the efficiency costs of taxes relative to their equity consequences. Twenty years ago it was commonly believed that the resource misallocation costs of taxes were relatively small (perhaps 1% of GNP), and that the tax system in total did little to redistribute income. The applied models have challenged this view by producing estimates of combined welfare costs from distortions in the tax system of 8%–10% of GNP, and estimates of their marginal welfare costs as large as $0.50 per additional dollar of revenue raised. These models have also indicated that there are more significant redistribution effects caused by the tax system than had previously been believed. The models have also been used to provide a ranking of various tax-policy alternatives, and have showed how interactions among the various parts of the tax system can affect the evaluation of tax-reform alternatives.

Applied general equilibrium trade models that assume constant returns to scale have in the main suggested that the welfare costs of trade distortions are smaller than those of tax distortions, confirming the suggestions made by previous partial equilibrium calculations. Such trade models have, however, found a significantly different geographical pattern in results owing to terms-of-trade effects. When increasing returns to scale are incorporated along with market structure features, larger effects are discovered.

Further insights have been gained in cases involving more specific analyses. For instance, in analyzing the impacts of regional trade agreements, results suggest that the more important effects arise from the elimination of trade barriers in partner countries and the benefits from improved access abroad, rather than from the internal trade creation and trade diversion effects discussed in the theoretical literature. Analyses of the impact of protection in the North on developing countries have put the annual costs to the South at about the value of the aid flow from the North, suggesting that these aid and trade effects roughly cancel out. (See Section 8.4.)

Another example of a model-generated insight concerns the international trade dimensions of the basis used for indirect taxes by American trading partners. Given that these taxes are heavier on manufactures than nonmanufactures, model results have shown that a destination basis abroad (taxes on imports, but not on exports) may be better for the United States than an origin basis (taxes on exports, but not on imports). This follows if the United States is a net importer of manufactures in its trade with the country involved. This suggests that an origin basis abroad need not be in the U.S. interest, as is often assumed; nor should the United States push for the same basis in all its trading partners.

These and other insights could, no doubt, have been obtained in other ways, but the virtue of using applied general equilibrium models is that, once constructed, they yield a facile tool for analyzing a wide range of possible policy changes. Such analyses generate results that either yield an initial null hypothesis, or challenge the prevailing view. It may be that subsequently the conclusions from the model are rejected as inappropriate; the assumptions may be considered unrealistic, errors may be unearthed, or other factors may undermine confidence in the results. But there will be situations in which the modeler and those involved in the policy decision process will have gained new perspectives as a result of using the model. In our opinion, this is the virtue of the approach, and is the reason why we believe its use in the policy process will spread further than the applications we report.

Applied general equilibrium analysis is not without its own problems. As the development of applied general equilibrium models has progressed from merely demonstrating the feasibility of model construction and ·solution to serious policy applications, a variety of issues has arisen. Most modelers recognize the difficulties of parameter specification and the necessity for (possibly contentious) assumptions. Elasticity and other key parameter values play a pivotal role in all model outcomes, and no consensus exists regarding numerical values for most of the important elasticities. The choice of elasticity values is frequently based on scant empirical evidence, and what evidence exists is often contradictory. This limits the degree of confidence with which model results can be held. On the other hand, there are no clearly superior alternative models available to policy makers who base their decisions on efficiency and distributional consequences of alternative policy changes. Whether partial equilibrium, general equilibrium, or back-of-the-envelope quantification is used, key parameter values must be selected, yet current econometric literature in so many of the areas involved is not particularly helpful.

Modelers have also been forced to confront the problem of model preselection: the need to specify key assumptions underlying the particular applied model to be used before any model calculations can begin. Both theoretical and applied modelers have long recognized the need to use particular assumptions in building general equilibrium models, assumptions such as full employment and perfect competition. There are also other equally important assumptions that enter these analyses. One example involves international factor flows. In tax models, the incidence effects of capital income taxes are substantially affected by the choice of this assumption: If capital is internationally mobile, capital owners will not bear the burden of income taxes; in a closed economy, however, domestic capital owners may well be affected. Another example is the treatment of time. In a static model, a tax on consumption may appear distorting since capital goods are tax free, but this effect will be absent when the tax is analyzed from an intertemporal viewpoint.

A further difficulty with general equilibrium analysis is how the policies themselves are represented in applied models. Taxes must be represented in model-equivalent form, and yet for each tax there is substantial disagreement in the literature as to the appropriate treatment. In the case of the corporate tax, for instance, the original treatment adopted by Harberger (1962) of assuming average and marginal tax rates on capital income by industry to be the same can bias results. Recent literature has emphasized that this tax could be viewed as applying to only the equity return on capital rather than to the total return, that is, as a tax on one financing instrument available to firms. This view has been used by Stiglitz (1973) to argue that the tax is a lump-sum tax; more recently, Gordon (1981) has argued that the corporate tax is in effect a benefit-related risk-sharing tax. Similar difficulties arise in other areas of application. With trade models, for instance, the modeling of nontariff barriers is an especially difficult and contentious issue.

A final and somewhat broader issue is that most of the applied general equilibrium models are not tested in any meaningful statistical sense. Parameter specification usually proceeds using deterministic calibration (often to one year's data), and there is no statistical test of the model specification (see Mansur and Whalley 1984). In determining parameter values by calibrating to a single data observation, equilibrium features in the data are emphasized. A purely deterministic equilibrium model in which consumers maximize utility and producers maximize profits is thus constructed in a manner consistent with the observed economy. With enough flexibility in choosing the form of the deterministic model, one can always choose a model so as to fit the data exactly. Econometricians, who are more accustomed to thinking in terms of models whose economic structure is simple but whose statistical structure is complex (rather than vice versa), frequently find this a source of discomfort.

PART I

Techniques

2

General equilibrium theory

2.1 Introduction

Applying general equilibrium analysis to policy issues requires a basic understanding of general equilibrium theory, which we attempt to provide in this chapter. A general equilibrium model of an economy can be best understood as one in which there are markets for each of N commodities, and consistent optimization occurs as part of equilibrium. Consumers maximize utility subject to their budget constraint, leading to the demand-side specification of the model. Producers maximize profits, leading to the production-side specification. In equilibrium, market prices are such that the required equilibrium conditions hold. Demand equals supply for all commodities, and in the constant-returns-to-scale case zero-profit conditions are satisfied for each industry.

A number of basic elements can be identified in general equilibrium models. In a pure exchange economy, consumers have endowments and demand functions (usually derived from utility maximization). In the two-consumer–two-good case, this leads to the well-known Edgeworth box analysis of general equilibrium of exchange. In the case of an economy with production, endowments and demands are once again specified, but production sets also need to be incorporated into the analysis.

2.2 Structure of general equilibrium models

The simple pure trade general equilibrium model can be represented as one in which there are N commodities, $1, \ldots, N$, each of which has a nonnegative price $p_i \geq 0$. Market prices are denoted by the vector $\mathbf{p} = p_1, \ldots, p_N$. The term W_i represents the nonnegative economywide endowment of commodity i owned by consumers, assumed to be strictly positive for at least one i; $\xi_i(\mathbf{p})$ are the market demand functions, which

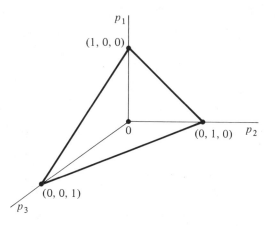

Figure 2.1. A 3-dimensional unit price simplex.

are nonnegative, continuous, and homogeneous of degree zero in **p**. The latter assumption implies that doubling all prices doubles incomes and hence the physical quantities demanded are unchanged.

Because the demand functions are assumed to be homogeneous of degree zero in prices, an arbitrary normalization of prices can be used; we will ordinarily set

$$\sum_{i=1}^{N} p_i = 1. \tag{2.1}$$

The prices of the N commodities lie on a unit simplex. The case where $N = 3$ is depicted in Figure 2.1.

A key further assumption usually made on the market demands is that they satisfy Walras's law. Walras's law states that the value of market demands equals the value of the economy's endowments, that is,

$$\sum_{i=1}^{N} p_i \xi_i(\mathbf{p}) = \sum_{i=1}^{N} p_i W_i, \tag{2.2}$$

or the value of market excess demands equals zero at all prices,

$$\sum_{i=1}^{N} p_i(\xi_i(\mathbf{p}) - W_i) = 0. \tag{2.3}$$

This condition must hold for any set of prices, whether or not they are equilibrium prices. Walras's law is an important basic check on any equilibrium system; if it does not hold, a misspecification is usually present

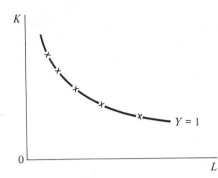

Figure 2.2. Approximating a unit isoquant by a series of linear activities.

since the model of the economy in question violates the sum of individual budget constraints.

A general equilibrium in this system is a set of prices p_i^* such that

$$\xi_i(\mathbf{p}^*) - W_i \le 0, \qquad (2.4)$$

with equality if $p_i^* > 0$. Equilibrium prices, therefore, clear markets.

A general equilibrium model with production is similar, but would also include a specification of a production technology. One representation of production has a finite number K of constant-returns-to-scale activities or methods of production. Each activity is described by coefficients a_{ij} denoting the use of good i in activity j when the activity is operated at unit intensity. A negative sign indicates an input and a positive sign an output.

These activities can be displayed in the nonsquare matrix A, which lists the many possible ways of producing commodities and can be used in any nonnegative linear combination:

$$A = \begin{bmatrix} -1 & 0 & 0 & a_{1,N+1} & \cdots & a_{1,j} & \cdots & a_{1,K} \\ 0 & -1 & 0 & \cdot & & \cdot & & \cdot \\ \cdot & 0 & \cdots & \cdot & \cdot & & & \cdot \\ \cdot & \cdot & 0 & \cdot & & \cdot & & \cdot \\ 0 & \cdot & -1 & a_{N,N+1} & \cdots & a_{N,j} & \cdots & a_{N,K} \end{bmatrix}. \qquad (2.5)$$

The first N activities are "slack" activities reflecting the possibility of free disposal of each commodity. In the case of only two inputs (capital and labor) and one output, these technology activities can be thought of as approximating a unit isoquant through a series of activities giving linear facet isoquants, as shown in Figure 2.2.

Activities are assumed to be nonreversible; that is, it is not possible to produce inputs from outputs. The vector $\mathbf{X} = X_1, \ldots, X_K$ denotes levels of intensity of operation associated with each activity and is nonnegative. Production is assumed to be bounded; that is, infinite amounts of outputs from finite inputs are ruled out. This corresponds to the often-made "no free lunch" assumption. In technical terms, this assumption implies that the set of $\mathbf{X}$ such that

$$\sum_{j=1}^{K} a_{ij} X_j + W_i \geq 0 \quad \text{for all } i \tag{2.6}$$

is contained within a bounded set.

A general equilibrium for this model is given by a set of prices p_i^* and activity levels X_j^* such that:

(i) demands equal supplies,

$$\xi_i(\mathbf{p}^*) = \sum_{j=1}^{K} a_{ij} X_j^* + W_i \quad \text{for all } i = 1, \ldots, N; \tag{2.7}$$

and

(ii) no production activity makes positive profits, whereas those in use break even,

$$\sum_{i=1}^{N} p_i^* a_{ij} \leq 0 \quad (=0 \text{ if } X_j^* > 0) \quad \text{for all } j = 1, \ldots, K. \tag{2.8}$$

In contrast to the pure exchange equilibrium model, no complementary slackness condition appears in equilibrium condition (i) because of the incorporation of the disposal activities in the technology matrix A. If there is excess supply of any commodity, disposal occurs through the use of a disposal activity.

2.3 Existence of a general equilibrium

The major result of postwar mathematical general equilibrium theory has been to demonstrate the existence of such an equilibrium by showing the applicability of mathematical fixed point theorems to economic models. This is the essential contribution of Arrow and Debreu (1954), which has been expanded upon in Debreu (1959), Arrow and Hahn (1971), and elsewhere. Since applying general equilibrium models to policy issues involves computing equilibria, these fixed point theorems are important: It is essential to know that an equilibrium exists for a given model before attempting to compute that equilibrium.

Fixed point theorems involve continuous mappings of the unit simplex into itself. That is, if S denotes the set of vectors $\mathbf{X}$ on the unit simplex

$$\sum_{i=1}^{N} X_i = 1, \quad X_i \geq 0, \tag{2.9}$$

then the mapping $F(\mathbf{X})$ is such that

$$\sum_{i=1}^{N} F_i(\mathbf{X}) = 1, \quad F_i(\mathbf{X}) \geq 0, \tag{2.10}$$

and F satisfies continuity properties. Two different types of mappings are usually considered: point-to-point mappings (i.e., $F(\mathbf{X})$ is a point on the unit simplex), and point-to-set mappings (i.e., $F(\mathbf{X})$ is a set on the unit simplex). These are displayed in Figure 2.3, where fixed points under each type of mappings are also presented.

The two basic fixed point theorems used in general equilibrium theory are the Brouwer fixed point theorem for point-to-point mappings, and the Kakutani fixed point theorem for point-to-set mappings. These are discussed by Scarf (1973, p. 28), who states them as follows:

> *Brouwer's theorem:* Let $Y = F(\mathbf{X})$ be a continuous function mapping the simplex into itself; then there exists a fixed point of the mapping, that is, a vector such that $\mathbf{X}^* = F(\mathbf{X}^*)$.
>
> *Kakutani's theorem:* Let the point-to-set mapping $\mathbf{X} \to \phi(\mathbf{X})$ of the simplex S into itself be upper semicontinuous. Assume that for each $\mathbf{X}$, $\phi(\mathbf{X})$ is a nonempty, closed, convex set. Then there exists a fixed point $\hat{\mathbf{X}} \in \phi(\hat{\mathbf{X}})$.

The concept of upper semicontinuity in Kakutani's fixed point theorem is as follows: A point-to-set mapping $\mathbf{X} \to \phi(\mathbf{X})$ is upper semicontinuous if the following condition is satisfied. Let $\mathbf{X}^1, \mathbf{X}^2, \ldots, \mathbf{X}^j$ converge to $\mathbf{X}$. Let $\theta^1 \in \phi(\mathbf{X}^1), \theta^2 \in \phi(\mathbf{X}^2), \ldots$ and assume that the sequence $\theta^1, \theta^2, \ldots, \theta^j, \ldots$ converges to θ. Then $\theta \in \phi(\mathbf{X})$. The importance of the continuity property can be depicted diagrammatically by considering a mapping of the unit interval into itself, as in Figure 2.4. Provided the mapping is continuous, a fixed point must exist. However, if a discontinuity occurs in the mapping, a fixed point need not exist. In this simple case, a continuous mapping must cross the 45° line for a fixed point to exist. The existence of more than one fixed point is illustrated in Figure 2.5.

An example of a continuous mapping of the unit simplex into itself would transform each point x on the unit simplex into the midpoint of the line segment connecting x to the center of the simplex; that is,

$$y_i = \frac{x_i + 1/n}{2} \quad \text{for all } i. \tag{2.11}$$

The fixed point in this case is clearly the center of the simplex. A second example is to let A be an $N \times N$ nonnegative matrix whose column and

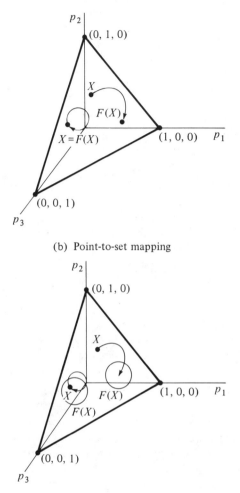

(a) Point-to-point mapping

(b) Point-to-set mapping

Figure 2.3. Point-to-point and point-to-set mappings of the unit simplex into itself.

row sums equal unity. The equation $y = Ax$ maps the simplex into itself. In both of these cases, appealing to the Brouwer fixed point theorem establishes the existence of a fixed point.

A further example, important to general equilibrium models, is one due to Gale (1955) and Nikaido (1956) that transforms the excess demand

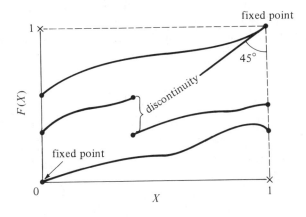

Figure 2.4. A mapping of unit interval into itself.

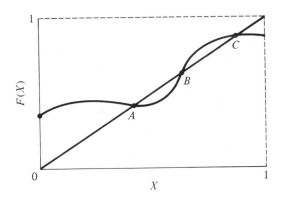

Figure 2.5. Existence of multiple fixed points.

functions of the pure exchange model into a mapping of the unit simplex into itself, to which the Brouwer fixed point theorem may be applied. A fixed point of this mapping can then be shown to imply that the equilibrium conditions of the pure exchange model must hold.

This mapping works as follows: An equilibrium for the pure exchange model is a vector of prices $\mathbf{p}^*$ such that $\xi_i(\mathbf{p}^*) - W_i \le 0$ for all i, with strict equality holding if $p_i^* > 0$. Defining the excess demand functions $g_i(\mathbf{p}) = \xi_i(\mathbf{p}) - W_i$, the Gale–Nikaido mapping is

$$y_i = \frac{p_i + \max[0, g_i(\mathbf{p})]}{1 + \sum_{i=1}^{N} \max[0, g_i(\mathbf{p})]} \quad \text{for all } i = 1, \dots, N. \tag{2.12}$$

Because $\sum_{i=1}^{N} y_i = 1$, $y_i \geq 0$, and $g_i(\mathbf{p})$ is continuous (since the demand functions $\xi_i(\mathbf{p})$ are assumed continuous), (2.12) provides a continuous mapping of the unit simplex into itself. By Brouwer's theorem there must exist a fixed point, that is, a vector $\mathbf{p}^*$ such that

$$p_i^* = \frac{p_i^* + \max[0, g_i(\mathbf{p}^*)]}{1 + \sum_{i=1}^{N} \max[0, g_i(\mathbf{p}^*)]} \quad \text{for all } i = 1, \ldots, N. \tag{2.13}$$

To show that $\mathbf{p}^*$ corresponds to an equilibrium for this model, we define $c = 1 + \sum_{i=1}^{N} \max[0, g_i(\mathbf{p}^*)]$. Equation (2.13) can then be rewritten as

$$cp_i^* = p_i^* + \max[0, g_i(\mathbf{p}^*)] \quad \text{for all } i. \tag{2.14}$$

Thus, if $c > 1$,

$$(c-1)p_i^* = \max[0, g_i(\mathbf{p}^*)] \quad \text{for all } i. \tag{2.15}$$

If $p_i^* > 0$, this implies $g_i(\mathbf{p}^*) > 0$. However, by Walras's law we know that

$$\sum_{i=1}^{N} p_i^* g_i(\mathbf{p}^*) = 0. \tag{2.16}$$

Since $p_i^* > 0$ implies $g_i(\mathbf{p}^*) > 0$ for the case where $c > 1$, it must be true that $\sum_{i=1}^{N} p_i^* g_i(\mathbf{p}^*) > 0$; that is, Walras's law is violated. Thus, $c > 1$ implies a contradiction. By definition $c \geq 1$, and hence c must equal 1. From (2.13) this implies that $g_i(\mathbf{p}^*) \leq 0$ for all i, and this together with Walras's law means that all of the conditions for equilibrium hold at the fixed point $\mathbf{p}^*$.

The demonstration of the existence of equilibria is more complicated when production activities are included in the model. If these exhibit decreasing returns to scale and the technology is such that there is a unique profit-maximizing output level for each commodity for any vector of prices, then the Gale–Nikaido mapping just presented can again be used. However, if constant returns to scale are assumed, or if several production plans are equally profitable, then there is not a unique vector of production in response to any set of prices.

This situation is most easily handled by applying the Kakutani fixed point theorem for point-to-set mappings as discussed in Debreu (1959). Here we present an outline of the full general equilibrium existence proof. Many of the intermediate assertions are not rigorously proven, since they can be found in Debreu (1959) for the cases without taxes and in Shoven (1974) for the cases with taxes.

In a general equilibrium model with production, we assume that the role of producers is to choose and carry out a production plan. Such a plan is characterized by the specification of all of the producer's inputs, represented by negative numbers, and outputs, given as positive numbers. Hence, a production plan can be represented as a point in N-dimensional Euclidean space.

The economy is assumed to consist of L producers, each of which (say, the lth) has an associated feasible production set Y^l. The assumptions made with regard to Y^l for each l are as follows.

(A.2.1) Y^l is convex (i.e., if $y^1 \in Y^l$ and $y^2 \in Y^l$, then $\alpha y^1 + (1-\alpha) y^2 \in Y^l$ for $0 \le \alpha \le 1$).

(A.2.2) $0 \in Y^l$ (i.e., inactivity is feasible).

(A.2.3) Y^l is closed (i.e., if $y^n \in Y^l$ and $y^n \to y^0$, then $y^0 \in Y^l$).

(A.2.4) Y^l is bounded from above (i.e., for some B, $y \le B$ for all $y \in Y^l$).

Assumptions (A.2.1) and (A.2.2) imply that the production possibility set Y is convex and contains the origin. Existence proofs can be produced with somewhat more general assumptions, particularly with respect to (A.2.4), but the general methodology still follows that presented here.

We assume that each producer l maximizes profit subject to the production set Y^l. Thus, for a price vector $\mathbf{p} = (p_1, \dots, p_N)$, the producer finds those activities $y^* \in Y^l$ such that

$$\sum_{i=1}^{N} p_i y_i^* \ge \sum_{i=1}^{N} p_i y_i \quad \text{for all } y \in Y^l. \tag{2.17}$$

Let $Y^l(\mathbf{p})$ be the point-to-set supply response of the producer, defined as

$$Y^l(\mathbf{p}) = \left\{ y^* \,\middle|\, y^* \in Y^l, \ \sum_{i=1}^{N} p_i y_i^* \ge \sum_{i=1}^{N} p_i y_i \text{ for all } y \in Y^l \right\}. \tag{2.18}$$

Thus, $Y^l(\mathbf{p})$ is the set of all profit-maximizing responses for producer l to the price vector $\mathbf{p}$. Debreu (1959) shows that (A.2.1)–(A.2.4) imply that the set $Y^l(\mathbf{p})$ is nonnull, convex, and closed, and further that the mapping $Y^l(\mathbf{p})$ is upper semicontinuous. The market production response $Y(\mathbf{p})$ is defined as the sum of the individual production responses

$$Y(\mathbf{p}) = \sum_{l=1}^{L} Y^l(\mathbf{p}), \tag{2.19}$$

and retains all of the properties of the individual production response sets $Y^l(\mathbf{p})$.

If we define π_l as the profit of the lth producer,

$$\pi_l(\mathbf{p}) \equiv \max_{y \in Y^l} \sum_{i=1}^{N} p_i y_i, \tag{2.20}$$

it can further be demonstrated that, under (A.2.1)–(A.2.4), $\pi_l(\mathbf{p})$ is a continuous, nonnegative function of prices $\mathbf{p}$, as are total profits in the economy $\pi(\mathbf{p}) = \sum_{l=1}^{L} \pi_l(\mathbf{p})$.

The consumer side of this model is the same as in the pure exchange model just presented. However, in this case formal assumptions analogous to our treatment of production are required. We assume that there are M consumers, who may be thought of as individuals, households, or even classes of individuals. The consumption of each consumer is represented by an N-dimensional vector, and the set of all possible consumption vectors for the mth consumer is denoted by X^m.

We let x_i^m denote the consumption of commodity i by consumer m. Leisure is treated as a consumed good rather than as a factor of production, so that X^m is a nonnegative set (i.e., $x_i^m \geq 0$, $i = 1, ..., N$, $m = 1, ..., M$). In addition, $0 \in X^m$, so that the consumer chooses from a set bounded from below by the origin. We also specify a utility function $U^m(\mathbf{x}^m)$ for each individual.

The assumptions for the consumer side of the model are as follows.

(A.2.5) X^m is convex and closed.

(A.2.6) $U^m(\mathbf{x}^m)$ is continuous and semistrictly quasiconcave (i.e., the "at least as desired as" set is convex). If $\mathbf{x}^1$ is preferred to $\mathbf{x}^2$, then $[\alpha\mathbf{x}^1 + (1-\alpha)\mathbf{x}^2]$, $0 < \alpha \leq 1$, is also preferred to $\mathbf{x}^2$.

(A.2.7) Individual m's income is given by the value of m's initial endowments, plus m's share of production profits.

That is,

$$I^m(\mathbf{p}) = \sum_{i=1}^{N} p_i w_i^m + \mu^m(\mathbf{p}), \qquad (2.21)$$

where w_i^m is individual m's initial endowment of commodity i and $\mu^m(\mathbf{p})$ is the amount of profits distributed to m. The function $\mu^m(\mathbf{p})$ is assumed to be nonnegative, continuous, and homogeneous of degree one in $\mathbf{p}$, so $\mu^m(\mathbf{p})$ represents nominal profits and doubles should all prices double. All profits are disbursed to consumers; that is,

$$\sum_{m=1}^{M} \mu^m(\mathbf{p}) = \pi(\mathbf{p}) = \sum_{l=1}^{L} \pi_l(\mathbf{p}). \qquad (2.22)$$

The sum of the initial endowments of individual consumers equals the economy's endowment. That is,

$$\sum_{m=1}^{M} w_i^m = W_i \quad \text{for } i = 1, ..., N. \qquad (2.23)$$

We also make the assumptions

(A.2.8) $w^m > \xi^m$ for some $\xi^m \in X^m$

and

(A.2.9) X^m is bounded[1] (i.e., no individual can consume more than some given finite amount of each commodity).

---

[1] The boundedness assumption (A.2.9) can also be replaced by a nonsatiation assumption.

Using (A.2.5)–(A.2.9), we can define consumer m's demand correspondence as

$$X^m(\mathbf{p}) \equiv \{\mathbf{x}^m \,|\, \mathbf{x}^m \text{ maximizes } U^m(\mathbf{x}^m)$$
$$\text{subject to } C^m(\mathbf{x}^m, \mathbf{p}) \le I^m(\mathbf{p}), \, \mathbf{x}^m \in X^m\}, \qquad (2.24)$$

where

$$C^m(\mathbf{x}^m, \mathbf{p}) = \sum_{i=1}^{N} p_i x_i^m \qquad (2.25)$$

is the cost of the consumption vector $\mathbf{x}^m$ at prices $\mathbf{p}$. It can be shown that for any $\mathbf{p}$, $X^m(\mathbf{p})$ is a nonnull, closed, convex, and bounded set, and that the mapping $X^m(\mathbf{p})$ is upper semicontinuous. The market demand response $X(\mathbf{p})$, defined as the sum of the individual demand responses, is given by

$$X(\mathbf{p}) = \sum_{m=1}^{M} X^m(\mathbf{p}), \qquad (2.26)$$

which also has the same properties as the individual responses.

To prove that there exists an equilibrium price vector for this model, we first define the market excess demand mapping (or correspondence) as

$$Z(\mathbf{p}) = X(\mathbf{p}) - Y(\mathbf{p}) - W. \qquad (2.27)$$

The vector $\mathbf{p}^*$ then defines an equilibrium set of prices if there is a $z \in Z(\mathbf{p}^*)$ such that

$$z_i \le 0 \quad \text{for all } i = 1, \ldots, N. \qquad (2.28)$$

That is, there are demand and supply responses consistent with $\mathbf{p}^*$ for which all markets clear. Walras's law implies that $z_i < 0$ only when $p_i^* = 0$.

In order to prove the existence of an equilibrium price vector $\mathbf{p}^*$, the first step is to establish that $Z(\mathbf{p})$ is nonnull, closed, convex, and bounded for any $\mathbf{p}$, and that $Z(\mathbf{p})$ is an upper semicontinuous correspondence. These properties are all implied by the corresponding properties of $X(\mathbf{p})$ and $Y(\mathbf{p})$.

Now let Z be a closed, convex, and bounded set that contains all of the sets $Z(\mathbf{p})$, where $\mathbf{p}$ is on the unit simplex. In order to use Kakutani's theorem to prove the existence of an equilibrium, we must use a higher-dimensional product space than that represented by the unit simplex. If we let S be the set of points lying on the unit simplex, we consider the product set $S \times Z$. This set is closed, convex, and bounded, and meets the required conditions for Kakutani's theorem. What we need to do is describe an upper semicontinuous point-to-set mapping of this set into itself, such that a fixed point is an economic equilibrium.

Consider the mapping of each point $(\mathbf{p}, \mathbf{z})$ in the product space $S \times Z$ that operates in the following manner:

$$\begin{pmatrix} \mathbf{p} \\ \mathbf{z} \end{pmatrix} \times \begin{pmatrix} \mathbf{p(z)} \\ Z(\mathbf{p}) \end{pmatrix}. \qquad (2.29)$$

The first N elements of $(\mathbf{p}, \mathbf{z})$ are the N prices, the corresponding set for which (the last N elements of the image set) is the market excess demand correspondence $Z(\mathbf{p})$ just described. The vector $\mathbf{z}$, which contains the last N elements of the vector $(\mathbf{p}, \mathbf{z})$, are market excess demands.

The image set for $\mathbf{z}$ is the set of price vectors $\mathbf{p(z)}$ that maximize the value of the market excess demands. That is, they form the solution set to the problem

$$\max \sum_{i=1}^{N} p_i z_i, \quad \text{where} \quad \sum_{i=1}^{N} p_i = 1, \ p_i \geq 0. \qquad (2.30)$$

The product mapping $(\mathbf{p}, \mathbf{z}) \to (\mathbf{p(z)}, Z(\mathbf{p}))$ is an upper semicontinuous mapping of $S \times Z$ into itself, and thus by Kakutani's theorem there is a fixed point. That is, there is a vector $(\mathbf{p}^*, \mathbf{z}^*)$, where $\mathbf{p}^* \in \mathbf{p(z}^*)$ and $\mathbf{z}^* \in Z(\mathbf{p}^*)$.

The remaining task in demonstrating the existence of equilibrium is to show that $\mathbf{p}^*$ represents an equilibrium price vector. To do so, we recall that Walras's law can be written

$$\sum_{i=1}^{N} p_i^* z_i^* = 0. \qquad (2.31)$$

However, since $\mathbf{p}^* \in \mathbf{p(z}^*)$, we know that

$$0 = \sum_{i=1}^{N} p_i^* z_i^* \geq \sum_{i=1}^{N} p_i z_i^* \quad \text{for} \ \mathbf{p} \in S, \qquad (2.32)$$

where S is the unit simplex. This inequality must hold for all $\mathbf{p} \in S$, including the cases where $\mathbf{p}$ has all its coordinates equal to zero except for the kth, which is equal to unity. For this $\mathbf{p}$, we have

$$z_k^* \leq 0. \qquad (2.33)$$

But since this argument is valid for all k between 1 and N, we see that all excess demands must be nonpositive, the very equilibrium condition we were seeking. This completes the sketch of the proof of the existence of an equilibrium in a model with production.

The application of fixed point theorems to show the existence of an equilibrium for pure exchange models and those with production were important in the 1950s and 1960s in demonstrating the consistency of general equilibrium models. They provide the logical support for the subsequent use of this framework for policy analysis.

The weakness of such applications is twofold. First, they provide nonconstructive rather than constructive proofs of the existence of equilibrium; that is, they show that equilibria exist but do not provide techniques by which equilibria can actually be determined. Second, existence per se has no policy significance. Policy makers are interested in how the economy will behave when policy or other variables change; their interest is in comparative statics rather than existence. Thus, fixed point theorems are only relevant in testing the logical consistency of models prior to the models' use in comparative static policy analysis; such theorems do not provide insights as to how economic behavior will actually change when policies change. They can only be employed in this way if they can be made constructive (i.e., be used to find actual equilibria). The extension of the Brouwer and Kakutani fixed point theorems in this direction is what underlies the work of Scarf (1967, 1973) on fixed point algorithms, which we describe in the next chapter.

2.4 Extending existence proofs to models with taxes and tariffs

Section 2.3 outlined existence proofs for the conventional Arrow–Debreu model in which no government policy interventions occur. Because of the central role of policy analysis in recent applications of general equilibrium techniques, we now turn to adding taxes, tariffs, and trade restrictions to this model in order to make it more appropriate for the kind of governmental-policy evaluations we are seeking. As taxes and tariffs are important institutional realities of real-world economies, their inclusion in a general equilibrium framework is of some importance. The existence property is reassuring in the sense that without it one cannot seriously contemplate developing general algorithms for the computation of such equilibria that can in turn be useful for economic analyses.

We will first discuss taxes. The inclusion of taxes necessitates the introduction of a government into the traditional general equilibrium model. The role of the government is to be interpreted as solely that of a tax-collecting and revenue-dispersing agency. It may, however, disperse some of the revenue to itself (i.e., retain it) in order to buy goods and services, but the issues involving the derivation of a government utility function, which determines government purchases, are not dealt with here. For simplicity, we discuss the case where all government revenue is distributed to consumers as transfer payments. Each consumer's disbursement is a function of total government revenue, and this is what makes the inclusion of taxes into the general equilibrium model a nontrivial extension of the basic Arrow–Debreu model. The individual agents are now interdependent since incomes are partially determined by government revenue, which in turn is a function of every agent's decisions. Prices no longer convey enough information for an individual consumer to determine his or her demands, as consumer income is dependent not only on prices but also on the demands of all other consumers and the production of all producers. It is this feature – not the additional notational complexity caused by having different agents face different effective (i.e., after-tax) prices – that makes the problem interesting. The solution involves working in a space of slightly higher dimensionality than is customary, with more information than simply prices being communicated between agents.

Rather than repeat the logical sequence of the proof sketched in Section 2.3, we will merely indicate how taxes modify the basic existence argument. Since we have already characterized the problem posed by taxes as one where prices no longer convey sufficient information, the nature of the solution – namely, to augment the N-dimensional price vector $\mathbf{p}$ – should not be surprising. The added variable in the case where there is one government (the national government) is total government revenue R, generating an $(N+1)$-dimensional simplex containing vectors $\bar{\mathbf{p}}$, $\bar{\mathbf{p}} = (p_1, ..., p_N, R)$.

Since taxes drive a wedge between the prices that buyers pay and what sellers receive, it is important to clarify what the announced prices signify. We take them to be the prices faced by consumers before consumer taxes. They can be thought of as "consumer selling prices": the prices consumers receive for their initial endowments when they sell to producers or other consumers. Thus, these are the prices producers pay for inputs before any taxes that may apply, and the prices at which they sell their outputs (including any producer-output taxes). If a producer faces taxes on both inputs and outputs, that producer will pay more than the corresponding p_i if good i is an input and receive (net) less than the price p_i if good i is an output. Likewise, if consumers face consumption taxes, they must pay more than p_i for the ith good. As before, we are searching for an equilibrium vector, although in this case it is the augmented price vector $\bar{\mathbf{p}}^*$. As both the demand and supply correspondences to be defined are homogeneous of degree zero in $\bar{\mathbf{p}}$, the search for $\bar{\mathbf{p}}^*$ will be confined to

$$\bar{S} \equiv \left\{ \bar{\mathbf{p}} \,\middle|\, \sum_{i=1}^{N} p_i = 1,\ 0 \le R \le \bar{R} \right\}, \tag{2.34}$$

where $\bar{R}$ is a large number the magnitude of which is discussed later. Alternatively, the search could take place on the surface of an $(N+1)$-dimensional unit simplex with the units of revenue chosen in such a way as to make it somewhat comparable in magnitude to the commodity prices.

Each of the L producers has associated with it a given set of *ad valorem* tax rates $t^l = (t_1^l, ..., t_N^l)$ on its production activity. The assumptions regarding the set of feasible production activities Y^l are the same as for the no-tax case, that is, assumptions (A.2.1)–(A.2.4) with one additional assumption as follows:

(A.2.10) For any i where $t_i^l > 0$, if $y_i^l < 0$ and $\mathbf{y}^l \in Y^l$ then there is no $\mathbf{y} \in Y^l$ with $y_i > 0$.

This assumption simply rules out the case where there are two activities in the production set Y^l, one of which produces a taxed commodity as an output while the other uses the same commodity as an input, and eliminates the possibility of avoiding taxation through vertical integration. Producers may be defined more narrowly here (i.e., for tax purposes) than in other contexts.

It is assumed that each producer l maximizes profit subject to the production set Y^l. Thus, for a given augmented price vector $\bar{\mathbf{p}} = (p_1, \ldots, p_N, R)$ a producer finds those activities $\mathbf{y}^* \in Y^l$ such that

$$\sum_{i=1}^{N} p_i(y_i^* - t_i^l |y_i^*|) \geq \sum_{i=1}^{N} p_i(y_i - t_i^l |y_i|) \quad \text{for all } \mathbf{y} \in Y^l. \tag{2.35}$$

Let $Y^l(\bar{\mathbf{p}})$ be the supply response of the firm, defined as

$$Y^l(\bar{\mathbf{p}}) \equiv \left\{ \mathbf{y}^* \,\middle|\, \mathbf{y}^* \in Y^l, \; \sum_{i=1}^{N} p_i(y_i^* - t_i^l |y_i^*|) \geq \sum_{i=1}^{N} p_i(y_i - t_i^l |y_i|) \text{ for all } \mathbf{y} \in Y^l \right\}. \tag{2.36}$$

In Shoven (1974) it is shown that $Y^l(\bar{\mathbf{p}})$ is nonnull, convex, closed, and bounded for any fixed $\bar{\mathbf{p}}$, and also that the mapping $Y(\bar{\mathbf{p}})$ is upper semicontinuous. The proofs follow closely those in Debreu (1959). An $(N+1)$-dimensional set $\bar{Y}^l(\bar{\mathbf{p}})$, termed the *tax-augmented production response* of the lth producer, can be defined as

$$\bar{Y}^l(\bar{\mathbf{p}}) = \left\{ (\mathbf{y}, \tau) \,\middle|\, \mathbf{y} \in Y^l(\bar{\mathbf{p}}), \; \tau = -\sum_{i=1}^{N} p_i t_i^l |y_i| \right\}. \tag{2.37}$$

That is, each $\mathbf{y} \in Y^l(\bar{\mathbf{p}})$ is augmented by the negative of the amount of tax the lth producer pays given $\mathbf{y}$ and $\bar{\mathbf{p}}$. With assumptions (A.2.1)–(A.2.4) and (A.2.10), $\bar{Y}^l(\bar{\mathbf{p}})$ is also nonnull, convex, closed, and bounded for each $\bar{\mathbf{p}}$, and $\bar{Y}^l(\bar{\mathbf{p}})$ is a bounded upper semicontinuous mapping.

The *market-augmented production correspondence* is defined as the sum of the individual augmented production responses. That is,

$$\bar{Y}(\bar{\mathbf{p}}) = \sum_{l=1}^{L} \bar{Y}^l(\bar{\mathbf{p}}). \tag{2.38}$$

Under (A.2.1)–(A.2.4) and (A.2.10), $\bar{Y}(\bar{\mathbf{p}})$ has all of the properties of $\bar{Y}^l(\bar{\mathbf{p}})$.

The profit of the lth producer is given by

$$\pi_l(\bar{\mathbf{p}}) \equiv \max_{\mathbf{y} \in Y^l} \sum_{i=1}^{N} p_i(y_i - t_i^l |y_i|). \tag{2.39}$$

As in the case without taxes, $\pi_l(\bar{\mathbf{p}})$ is a continuous and nonnegative function, as is the function giving total profits in the economy $\pi(\bar{\mathbf{p}}) = \sum_{l=1}^{L} \pi_l(\bar{\mathbf{p}})$.

The consumer side of the model also needs relatively slight modification for the inclusion of taxes. As with producers, we allow each of the consumers to face a different set of commodity tax rates, $\mathbf{s}^m = (s_1^m, \ldots, s_N^m)$. The assumptions dealing with consumption (A.2.5)–(A.2.9) are left unchanged except that individual m's income is now given by

$$I^m(\bar{\mathbf{p}}) = \sum_{i=1}^{N} p_i w_i^m + \mu^m(\bar{\mathbf{p}}) + r^m(\bar{\mathbf{p}}), \qquad (2.40)$$

where the new third term is the amount of government revenue distributed to m as transfer payments. The $r^m(\bar{\mathbf{p}})$ function is assumed to be nonnegative, continuous, and homogeneous of degree one. We also assume that

$$\sum_{m=1}^{M} r^m(\bar{\mathbf{p}}) = R. \qquad (2.41)$$

The consumer's demand correspondence $X^m(\bar{\mathbf{p}})$ is as without taxes (i.e., m finds the sets of feasible consumption bundles that maximize utility), except that the cost of $\mathbf{x}^m$ for consumer m at prices $\mathbf{p}$ is given by

$$C^m(\mathbf{x}^m, \mathbf{p}) = \sum_{i=1}^{N} p_i x_i^m + S^m(\mathbf{x}^m, \mathbf{p}), \qquad (2.42)$$

where

$$S^m(\mathbf{x}^m, \mathbf{p}) = \sum_{i=1}^{N} p_i s_i^m x_i^m \qquad (2.43)$$

is the total purchase taxes paid by consumer m. The correspondence $X^m(\bar{\mathbf{p}})$ retains all of the properties of the no-tax $X^m(\mathbf{p})$.

The tax-augmented demand response is an $(N+1)$-dimensional set $\bar{X}^m(\bar{\mathbf{p}})$ defined as

$$\bar{X}^m(\bar{\mathbf{p}}) \equiv \{(\mathbf{x}, \gamma) \mid \mathbf{x} \in X^m(\bar{\mathbf{p}}), \ \gamma = S^m(\mathbf{x}, \mathbf{p})\}. \qquad (2.44)$$

The market-augmented demand response is the sum of the individual $\bar{X}^m$ sets, and both the market-augmented response $\bar{X}(\bar{\mathbf{p}})$ and the individual augmented responses $\bar{X}^m(\bar{\mathbf{p}})$ are nonnull, closed, convex, and bounded, and are upper semicontinuous mappings.

Equilibrium in this case has the properties that

$$\sum_{m=1}^{M} \mathbf{x}^{m*} \leq \sum_{l=1}^{L} \mathbf{y}^{l*} + W \qquad (2.45)$$

and

$$\sum_{m=1}^{M} S^m(\mathbf{x}^{m^*}, \mathbf{p}^*) + \sum_{l=1}^{L} \sum_{i=1}^{N} p_i^* t_i^l |y_i^{l^*}| = R^* \tag{2.46}$$

for some $\mathbf{x}^{m^*} \in X^m(\bar{\mathbf{p}}^*)$ for all m, and for some $\mathbf{y}^{l^*} \in Y(\bar{\mathbf{p}})$ for all l. That is, in addition to excess demands being nonnegative, in equilibrium revenue collections match the announced government revenue R^*.

With this structure, the proof of existence is straightforward. Let $\bar{W}$ be the augmented vector of the economy's endowments,

$$\bar{W} \equiv (W_1, \dots, W_N, 0), \tag{2.47}$$

and let $\bar{Z}(\bar{\mathbf{p}})$ be the market-augmented excess demand correspondence

$$\bar{Z}(\bar{\mathbf{p}}) \equiv \bar{X}(\bar{\mathbf{p}}) - \bar{Y}(\bar{\mathbf{p}}) - \bar{W}; \tag{2.48}$$

$\bar{Z}$ retains the nonnull, closed, convex, and bounded properties of $\bar{X}(\bar{\mathbf{p}})$ and $\bar{Y}(\bar{\mathbf{p}})$, and is an upper semicontinuous mapping.

To prove the existence of an equilibrium in an economy such as this, one gain resorts to a product space. Let $\bar{Z}$ be a closed, convex, and bounded set that contains all of the sets $\bar{Z}(\bar{\mathbf{p}})$, $\bar{\mathbf{p}} \in \bar{S}$. Then we show that a fixed point of a mapping of the product space $\bar{S} \times \bar{Z}$ into itself will define an economic equilibrium. The map can be pictured as

$$\begin{pmatrix} \bar{\mathbf{p}} \\ \bar{z} \end{pmatrix} \times \begin{pmatrix} \bar{\mathbf{p}}(\bar{z}) \\ \bar{Z}(\bar{\mathbf{p}}) \end{pmatrix}, \tag{2.49}$$

where we have just developed the $\bar{Z}(\bar{\mathbf{p}})$ correspondence. The first N components of the $\bar{\mathbf{p}}(\bar{z})$ correspondence represent the set of price vectors that maximize the value of market excess demands, as in the no-tax case. The last component of $\bar{\mathbf{p}}(\bar{z})$ is equal to $\bar{z}_{N+1}$. That is, the last dimension of the $\bar{\mathbf{p}}(\bar{z})$ correspondence is simply the identity function.

This mapping of the $\bar{S} \times \bar{Z}$ space into itself meets all of the conditions of Kakutani's theorem, and thus there exists some $(\bar{\mathbf{p}}^*, \bar{z}^*)$ such that

$$\bar{\mathbf{p}}^* \in \bar{\mathbf{p}}(\bar{z}^*) \quad \text{and} \quad \bar{z}^* \in \bar{Z}(\bar{\mathbf{p}}^*). \tag{2.50}$$

The fact that $\mathbf{p}^* \in \bar{\mathbf{p}}(\bar{z}^*)$ implies that, for the last dimension, we have

$$p_{N+1}^* = R^* = z_{N+1}^* = \sum_{m=1}^{M} S^m(\mathbf{x}^{m^*}, \mathbf{p}^*) + \sum_{l=1}^{L} \sum_{i=1}^{N} p_i^* t_i^l |y_i|; \tag{2.51}$$

that is, the second condition for an equilibrium holds. The argument that all market excess demands are nonpositive is completely analogous to the no-tax case of Section 2.3. Therefore, there exists an equilibrium for an economy with both consumers and producers facing arbitrary and differentiated tax vectors.

The above arguments can easily be extended to cover a model in which there are a number, say K, of governments. This model can be interpreted either as an international trade model where several countries trade with each other, or as a model with tiered governments (e.g., federal/state/local). In fact, the two interpretations can be merged to yield a model with several countries each of which has governments within governments. Again, government is considered to be simply a tax-collecting and revenue-distributing agent.

With several governments, say K, the system of prices must be augmented by K revenue terms and may be represented by $\bar{p} = (p_1, \dots, p_N, R_1, \dots, R_K)$. Similar goods in different locations are treated as separate commodities. The definition of location can be as narrow as necessary. That is, if any agent is taxed by any government at different tax rates on two physically identical commodities because of their location, then these two items are treated as different commodities. As before, it is assumed that there are a total of N commodities, M consumers, and L producers in the model (i.e., the "world").

Each of the M consumers is assigned a claim on one or more of the K revenue terms in such a way that

$$\sum_{m=1}^{M} r_k^m(\bar{p}) = R_k \quad \text{for} \quad k = 1, \dots, K, \tag{2.52}$$

where $r_k^m(\bar{p})$ is a continuous, linear, homogeneous function representing individual m's distribution from government k. A special case would be where each individual has claim to the revenue of only one government; in this case, the mth consumer's income is given by

$$I^m(\bar{p}) = \sum_{i=1}^{N} p_i w_i^m + \mu^m(\bar{p}) + \sum_{k=1}^{K} r_k^m(\bar{p}). \tag{2.53}$$

Each consumer faces a set of tax rates $s^m = (s_1^m, \dots, s_N^m)$, as before. It makes no difference to the consumer whether part or all of these taxes are termed tariffs. Further, the consumer is indifferent as to which government or combination of governments is imposing these taxes. The mechanics of the existence proof allow complete generality in that each of the K governments could tax individual m on purchases of each of the N goods (of course, realism may dictate that many of these tax rates are zero). The individual tax vectors imposed on individual m sum to a total tax vector; that is,

$$s_i^m = \sum_{k=1}^{K} {}^k s_i^m \quad \text{for} \quad m = 1, \dots, M, \ i = 1, \dots, N, \tag{2.54}$$

where ${}^k s_i^m$ is the tax rate imposed by the kth government on the mth consumer's purchases of the ith commodity.

Let $^k s^m(\mathbf{x}^m, \mathbf{p})$, the taxes the mth consumer pays to the kth government for consumption $\mathbf{x}^m$ at prices $\mathbf{p}$, be defined as

$$^k s^m(\mathbf{x}^m, \mathbf{p}) = \sum_{i=1}^{N} p_i {}^k s_i^m p_i^* s_i^m x_i^m. \tag{2.55}$$

The set $\bar{X}^m(\bar{\mathbf{p}})$, consumer m's augmented demand response, is then redefined as the $(N+K)$-dimensional set

$$\bar{X}^m(\bar{\mathbf{p}}) \equiv \{(\mathbf{x}, \gamma_1, \ldots, \gamma_K) \mid \mathbf{x} \in X^m(\bar{\mathbf{p}}), \; \gamma_k = {}^k s^m(\mathbf{x}, \mathbf{p}); \; k = 1, \ldots, K\}. \tag{2.56}$$

With the same assumptions as before, $\bar{X}^m(\bar{\mathbf{p}})$ is nonnull, closed, convex, and bounded for any $\bar{\mathbf{p}}$, and $\bar{X}^m(\bar{\mathbf{p}})$ is an upper semicontinuous mapping. The market-augmented demand response is defined as

$$\bar{X}(\bar{\mathbf{p}}) \equiv \sum_{m=1}^{M} \bar{X}^m(\bar{\mathbf{p}}). \tag{2.57}$$

The analysis on the production side is quite symmetrical to that on the consumer side. Each producer, say the lth, faces a vector of tax rates $\mathbf{t} = (t_1^l, \ldots, t_N^l)$, which is the sum of the vectors of tax rates imposed on producer activity by the K governments. That is,

$$t_i^l = \sum_{k=1}^{K} {}^k t_i^l \quad \text{for } l = 1, \ldots, L, \; i = 1, \ldots, N, \tag{2.58}$$

where $^k t_i^l$ is the tax rate imposed by the kth government on the use of the ith commodity by the lth producer. Naturally, there are special cases where many of the tax rates are zero.

The set $\bar{Y}^l(\bar{\mathbf{p}})$, producer l's augmented production correspondence, is redefined as the $(N+K)$-dimensional set

$$\bar{Y}^l(\bar{\mathbf{p}}) \equiv \left\{(\mathbf{y}, \tau_1, \ldots, \tau_K) \,\middle|\, \mathbf{y} \in Y^l(\bar{\mathbf{p}}), \; \tau_k = -\sum_{i=1}^{N} p_i {}^k t_i^l |y_i|; \; k = 1, \ldots, K\right\}. \tag{2.59}$$

As redefined, $\bar{Y}^l(\bar{\mathbf{p}})$ retains all of its properties of the one-government case. The market-augmented production correspondence is again defined as

$$\bar{Y}(\bar{\mathbf{p}}) \equiv \sum_{l=1}^{L} \bar{Y}^l(\bar{\mathbf{p}}). \tag{2.60}$$

Letting $\bar{W}$ be an $(N+K)$-dimensional vector

$$\bar{W} = (w_1, \ldots, w_N, 0, \ldots, 0), \tag{2.61}$$

$\bar{Z}(\bar{\mathbf{p}})$ is then defined as

$$\bar{Z}(\bar{\mathbf{p}}) \equiv \bar{X}(\bar{\mathbf{p}}) - \bar{Y}(\bar{\mathbf{p}}) - \bar{W}. \tag{2.62}$$

An equilibrium in this model is a $\bar{\mathbf{p}}^*$ such that there exists an $\mathbf{x}^{m^*} \in X^m(\bar{\mathbf{p}}^*)$ and a $\mathbf{y}^* \in Y(\bar{\mathbf{p}}^*)$ with the properties

$$\sum_{m=1}^{M} \mathbf{x}^{m^*} \le \sum_{l=1}^{L} \mathbf{y}^{l^*} + W \tag{2.63}$$

and

$$\sum_{m=1}^{M} {}^k S^m(\mathbf{x}^{m^*}, \mathbf{p}^*) + \sum_{l=1}^{L} \sum_{i=1}^{N} p_i^* \, {}^k t_i^l |y_i^{l^*}| = R_k^*, \quad k = 1, \dots, K. \tag{2.64}$$

That is, at $\mathbf{x}^{m^*}$ ($m = 1, \dots, M$); $\mathbf{y}^{l^*}$ ($l = 1, \dots, L$); and $\bar{\mathbf{p}}^*$, demand is less than supply for all N commodities and tax collections equal revenue distributed for each of the K governments.

The proof of existence for the multigovernment case is very similar to the one-government case. Both $\bar{S}$ and $\bar{Z}$ are now $(N+K)$-dimensional, and the last K dimensions of the $(N+K)$-dimensional correspondence $\bar{\mathbf{p}}(\bar{\mathbf{z}})$ have K identity functions. The result is an equilibrium where all excess demands are nonpositive and all governments have balanced budgets.

Trade policy, price-control schemes, additional taxes, or other policy interventions can be incorporated into the general equilibrium model and existence demonstrated. Wealth taxes and profit taxes are added in Shoven (1974). It would also be simple to incorporate Social Security and payroll taxes. Quotas and other quantity restrictions can also be added. A particularly easy way to do this is to create an artificial commodity, termed "tickets," which must be purchased when consuming or using the quantity-constrained commodity, as discussed in Shoven and Whalley (1972). The fact that these tickets must be allocated as endowments and may have a positive value simply reflects the fact that real rents are created if a government agency creates an artificial scarcity. Price-control schemes are closely related to tax schemes, as noted by Imam and Whalley (1982). In this case, controlling consumer prices while allowing producer prices to be endogenously determined means that the wedge between them is not prespecified as in the tax case.

2.5 Two-sector general equilibrium models

A more specific form of general equilibrium model, widely used in the applied fields of taxation and international trade, is the two-sector general equilibrium model (see the discussion in Ch. 8 of Atkinson and Stiglitz 1980, and Jones 1965). This model is used where the focus is on comparative static analysis for policy evaluation, rather than on existence. Since much of the theoretical literature in applied policy fields uses two-sector models, it is natural for numerical modelers to use a similar structure, so results can be checked against theoretical work. Also, much of the data available for use with applied models (such as national accounts data, input–output data, and other sources) fits a two-sector modeling approach.

Considerable simplification of equilibrium solutions can also be gained in applications by exploiting the special structure of two-sector models, since factors are not produced and commodities are not initially owned. It is possible to compute an equilibrium solution for these models by searching only in the space of factor prices and using zero-profit conditions to determine goods prices. In effect, an equilibrium in these models can be found by working with derived factor excess demands alone. Existence can also be shown using these functions. Even though two-sector models involve production, these simplifications allow Brouwer's theorem to be used in the proof of existence. Such dimension-reducing techniques are also important for the discussion of computational methods in the next chapter.

Following Uzawa (1963), the two-sector model, based on an assumption of constant returns to scale in each industry, can be defined by a five-equation system.

Production functions in each sector:

$$Y_i = F_i(K_i, L_i) = L_i f_i(k_i) \quad (i = 1, 2). \tag{2.65}$$

Value of marginal factor products equalized across sectors:

$$\frac{P_i}{P_j} = P = \frac{f_j'}{f_i'} = \frac{f_j - k_j f_j'}{f_i - k_i f_i'} \quad (i = 1, 2, \; j \neq i). \tag{2.66}$$

Wage–rentals ratio equals the ratio of marginal factor products in each sector:

$$\omega = \frac{f_i}{f_i'} - k_i \quad (i = 1, 2). \tag{2.67}$$

Cost-minimizing factor input ratio in each sector as a function of the wage–rentals ratio:

$$\frac{\partial k_i}{\partial \omega} = \frac{-(f_i')^2}{f_i f_i''} > 0 \quad (i = 1, 2). \tag{2.68}$$

Cost-covering commodity price ratio as a function of the wage–rentals ratio:

$$\frac{1}{P} \cdot \frac{\partial P}{\partial \omega} = \left(\frac{1}{k_i + \omega} - \frac{1}{k_j + \omega} \right) \quad (i = 1, 2, \; j \neq i). \tag{2.69}$$

Equations (2.65) define constant-returns-to-scale, two-input production functions in each industry. Using these, the marginal products of factors can be written in terms of the intensive-form production function $(f(k) = F(K/L, 1))$ as

$$\frac{\partial F_i}{\partial K_i} = f_i'(k_i), \quad \frac{\partial F_i}{\partial L_i} = f_i(k) - k_i f_i' \quad (i = 1, 2). \tag{2.70}$$

Equation (2.66) thus gives the relative cost-covering commodity prices consistent with competitive goods and factor markets, and (2.67) is the equilibrium condition that factor prices in each of the two sectors equal the ratio of marginal factor products. Equation (2.68) describes the behavior of the cost-minimizing capital–labor ratio for each sector with respect to the wage–rentals ratio, and (2.69) describes how competitive output prices change as factor prices change. Demand conditions in the algebraic statement in this model are usually not explicitly specified, although when used for numerical computation (as will be seen later) the precise demand conditions assumed determine the particular equilibrium attained.

Of these five equations, the first three require no explanation, but (2.68) and (2.69) involve some manipulation to derive them. The derivations proceed as follows.

Derivation of equation (2.68): From (2.67),

$$\omega = \frac{f_i - k_i f_i'}{f_i'} \quad (i = 1, 2); \tag{2.71}$$

$$\frac{\partial \omega}{\partial k_i} = \frac{f_i' - f_i' - k_i f_i''}{f_i'} - \frac{(f_i - k_i f_i')f_i''}{(f_i')^2} = \frac{-f_i f_i''}{(f_i')^2} \quad (i = 1, 2). \tag{2.72}$$

Thus we have (2.68):

$$\frac{\partial k_i}{\partial \omega} = \frac{-(f_i')^2}{f_i f_i''} > 0 \quad (i = 1, 2). \tag{2.73}$$

Derivation of equation (2.69): From (2.66),

$$P = \frac{P_i}{P_j} = \frac{f_j'}{f_i'} \quad (i = 1, 2, j \neq i). \tag{2.74}$$

Thus

$$\frac{\partial P}{\partial \omega} = \left(f_j'' \frac{\partial k_j}{\partial \omega} f_i' - f_j' f_i'' \frac{\partial k_i}{\partial \omega} \right) \bigg/ (f_i')^2 \quad (i = 1, 2, j \neq i) \tag{2.75}$$

$$= \left(\frac{-(f_j')^2}{f_j} \cdot f_i' + \frac{f_j'(f_i')^2}{f_i} \right) \bigg/ (f_i')^2 \quad (i = 1, 2, j \neq i) \tag{2.76}$$

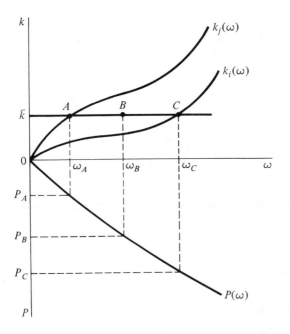

Figure 2.6. Equilibrium in a two-sector model $(P = P_i/P_j)$.

$$= \left[\left(\frac{-f_j'}{f_j}\right)+\left(\frac{f_i'}{f_i}\right)\right]\cdot\frac{f_j'}{f_i'} \quad (i=1, 2, \ j \neq i). \tag{2.77}$$

Thus, since $P = f_j'/f_i'$, $f_i'/f_i = 1/(k_i+\omega)$, and $f_j'/f_j = 1/(k_j+\omega)$,

$$\frac{\partial P}{\partial \omega} = P\left(\frac{1}{k_i+\omega} - \frac{1}{k_j+\omega}\right) \quad (i=1, 2, \ j \neq i), \tag{2.78}$$

which yields (2.69):

$$\frac{1}{P}\cdot\frac{\partial P}{\partial \omega} = \left(\frac{1}{k_i+\omega} - \frac{1}{k_j+\omega}\right) \quad (i=1, 2, \ j \neq i). \tag{2.79}$$

The manner in which competitive equilibria are characterized by this model can be displayed using (2.68) and (2.69). In Figure 2.6, $k_i(\omega)$ and $k_j(\omega)$ reflect the cost-minimizing capital intensities of the two sectors for any wage–rentals ratio ω. From (2.68), these intensities are upward sloping. Since $k_j(\omega) > k_i(\omega)$ for all values of ω, sector j is the capital-intensive sector. The ratio P_i/P_j is increasing in ω owing to (2.69), since j is capital intensive.

The economywide capital–labor ratio $\bar{k}$ is given by the initial factor endowments $\bar{K}$ and $\bar{L}$, and full employment of both factors implies that

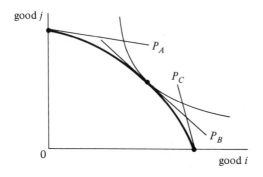

Figure 2.7. Production possibility frontier corresponding to Figure 2.6.

$$\bar{k} = \frac{K_i}{L_i} \cdot \frac{L_i}{\bar{L}} + \frac{K_j}{L_j} \cdot \frac{L_j}{\bar{L}} \tag{2.80}$$

or

$$\bar{k} = k_i l_i + k_j l_j, \quad \text{where } l_i + l_j = 1. \tag{2.81}$$

The terms l_i and l_j define the shares of labor in each of the two sectors.

Equation (2.81) thus defines a region of potential equilibrium values of ω, and through (2.69) a region of potential equilibrium values for P. At the wage–rentals ratio ω_A the cost-minimizing capital–labor ratio in sector j equals $\bar{k}$, while in sector i it is below $\bar{k}$. Thus, for (2.81) to hold, the economy must be completely specialized in the production of good j. By a similar argument, at the wage–rentals ratio ω_C, the economy will be completely specialized in the production of good i. The line segment AC thus defines a range of potential equilibria as the economy moves from complete specialization in j to complete specialization in i. The corresponding price ratios P_A and P_C define the slopes of the production possibility frontier at its terminal points, as shown in Figure 2.7. The particular equilibrium in this range that actually occurs will depend on demand conditions, which need to be specified to complete the model. For a simple one-consumer economy, such an equilibrium is depicted as point B in Figures 2.6 and 2.7. Figure 2.8 depicts factor price equalization occurring in a two-country, two-sector model.

In applying the two-sector model to the analysis of policy issues, the ability to reduce the effective dimensionality of the model when solving it is also important. This enables the two-sector model of production and exchange to be converted to a pure exchange model in factor space, which in turn makes the model easier to solve, as outlined in Figure 2.9.

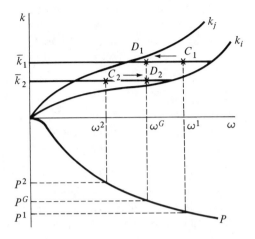

Figure 2.8. Factor price equalization in a two-country trade model.

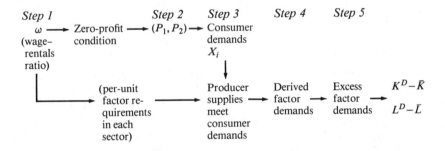

Figure 2.9. Schematic outline of dimension-reducing techniques used in solving two-sector models.

This dimension reduction works as follows. The basic two-factor, two-good model has four prices (P_L, P_K, P_1, P_2). However, an equilibrium may be characterized by (P_L, P_K) only, and the model solved using a one-dimensional unit simplex. Using the zero-profit conditions for each sector, cost-covering commodity prices (P_1, P_2) can be calculated (step 2). This enables commodity demands X_i to be calculated from consumer utility maximization (step 3). If production in each sector is set to meet commodity demands, then derived factor demand functions can be calculated (step 4), and excess factor demands determined (step 5). Since Walras's law applies to the commodity demand functions, and since the calculation of commodity prices directly imposes zero-profit conditions on the model solution, Walras's law must also apply to the excess factor demands. Because of this, and because zero-profit conditions and demand–supply equalities in goods markets are directly imposed, an equilibrium in this model can be characterized by factor prices (P_L^*, P_K^*) so that the derived factor excess demands are zero; that is,

$$K^D(P_L^*, P_K^*) - \bar{K} = 0 \quad \text{and} \quad L^D(P_L^*, P_K^*) - \bar{L} = 0. \tag{2.82}$$

If these conditions are met then an equilibrium will have been determined for the whole model, including goods markets and zero-profit conditions. As shown in Chapter 3, this same approach can also be used for goods and factors models with more than two sectors.

2.6 The normative content of general equilibrium analysis

General equilibrium analysis is widely used in modern economics in large part because it provides a wide-ranging framework that captures interactions between markets in economies. It is important, however, to note that equilibrium analysis also has a strong normative content.

This normative content is reflected in the two fundamental theorems of welfare economics (Arrow 1951), which state that any competitive equilibrium is Pareto optimal and that any Pareto optimal allocation can be supported as a competitive equilibrium with appropriate lump-sum transfers. The implication of these two theorems is that government intervention in the economy that distorts relative commodity prices will have a social cost when analyzed using a general equilibrium model. Policies such as taxes or tariffs will move the economy away from a Pareto optimal allocation and will cause a deadweight loss. In trade models this can still be nationally beneficial owing to a terms-of-trade improvement, but will remain costly from a global point of view. These theorems also imply that concerns over income-distribution effects of policy interventions should be separated from efficiency concerns; redistribution in kind, which distorts relative prices, should be resisted in favor of redistribution through lump-sum transfers.

The first of these theorems can be demonstrated with relative ease for the general equilibrium model, using an activity analysis specification of production presented earlier in the chapter. For any competitive equilibrium $(\mathbf{p}^*, X^*)$ there is an associated allocation of goods $\xi_i^m(\mathbf{p}^*)$ between M individuals, where the superscript m refers to individuals and the subscript i to commodities. Suppose that we consider an alternative allocation of goods ξ_i^m, which is superior to $\xi_i^m(\mathbf{p}^*)$ in the sense that at least one individual prefers the allocation ξ_i^m and no individual prefers the allocation $\xi_i^m(\mathbf{p}^*)$. If ξ_i^m is preferred to $\xi_i^m(\mathbf{p}^*)$ then

$$\sum_{i=1}^{N} p_i^* \xi_i^m \geq \sum_{i=1}^{N} p_i^* \xi_i^m(\mathbf{p}^*), \tag{2.83}$$

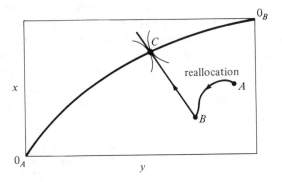

Figure 2.10. Supporting a Pareto optimal allocation as a competitive equilibrium with appropriate lump-sum transfers.

with strict inequality holding for at least one m. Thus, by Walras's law,

$$\sum_{i=1}^{N} p_i^* \xi_i > \sum_{i=1}^{N} p_i^* \xi_i(\mathbf{p}^*) = \sum_{i=1}^{N} p_i^* W_i, \tag{2.84}$$

where

$$\xi_i = \sum_{m=1}^{M} \xi_i^m \quad \text{and} \quad \xi_i(\mathbf{p}^*) = \sum_{m=1}^{M} \xi_i^m(\mathbf{p}^*). \tag{2.85}$$

This, however, is a contradiction; if ξ_i^m can be associated with $(\mathbf{p}^*, X^*)$ as an alternative general equilibrium, then multiplying both through the demand–supply equilibrium conditions by p_i^* and summing and through the zero-profit conditions by X_i^* and summing gives

$$\sum_{i=1}^{N} p_i^* \xi_i = \sum_{i=1}^{N} p_i^* W_i + \sum_{i=1}^{N} \sum_{j=1}^{K} p_i^* a_{ij} X_j^* \tag{2.86}$$

and

$$\sum_{i=1}^{N} \sum_{j=1}^{K} p_i^* a_{ij} X_j = 0. \tag{2.87}$$

However, by Walras's law,

$$\sum_{i=1}^{N} p_i^* \xi_i = \sum_{i=1}^{N} p_i^* W_i = \sum_{i=1}^{N} p_i^* \xi_i(\mathbf{p}^*), \tag{2.88}$$

which contradicts (2.84). Thus, such a general equilibrium must be Pareto optimal.

The second of the theorems follows directly, since lump-sum transfers between individuals in the pure exchange case can be used to achieve a particular competitive equilibrium outcome, even if the initial allocation of endowments is not compatible with the desired equilibrium. This is shown in Figure 2.10.

These two theorems are also usually cited as justification for reliance on the price mechanism for making resource-allocation decisions.[2] These theorems suggest that distorting policies will always have social costs when analyzed using applied general equilibrium techniques because of the deviations from conditions required for Pareto optimality. In turn, the social costs of such policies as taxes will be determined by comparing prechange and postchange equilibria, where distorting policies are replaced by allocationally neutral alternatives.

[2] However, the results due to Debreu and Scarf (1963) on the convergence to competitive equilibria of allocations in the core of an economy suggest an equivalence between political and market processes. They show that, in a pure exchange economy with a specified number of agents, increasing the number of identical agents of each type shrinks the set of core allocations, collapsing in the limit to the same allocation of resources as achieved in a competitive equilibrium. This equilibrium is not reached using any price-allocation mechanism, but relies on a procedure of proposals and blocking by coalitions.

3

Computing general equilibria

COAUTHORED BY WOLFGANG WIEGARD

In order to use general equilibrium models for counterfactual policy analysis, it is necessary to solve models for the general equilibrium associated with policy or other changes. Counterfactual equilibria are typically computed in applied models, since data generated in the presence of existing policies provide a direct observation on the initial equilibrium situation. Applied models are usually calibrated in such a way that they exactly replicate the initial equilibrium data in the presence of existing policies. This chapter outlines the procedures employed in computing counterfactual equilibria. The techniques used to calibrate applied models so that they replicate initial equilibrium data are discussed in Chapter 5.

3.1 An introduction to computing equilibria in general equilibrium models

Much of the recent literature on computation of general equilibria in economic systems derives from the work of Scarf (1967, 1973), which contained the first description of an algorithm to find a general equilibrium that was guaranteed to converge. Subsequent contributions have both refined Scarf's original algorithm, to increase its speed and flexibility, and developed alternative methods that seem to work well in practice, even though the guaranteed convergence property of Scarf's algorithm is often not present. Typically, these are variants on the well-known Newton method for solving systems of nonlinear equations.

To illustrate what is involved in computing a general equilibrium, it is convenient to consider the simple two-person pure exchange general equilibrium model presented in Section 2.2 and displayed in Figure 3.1. In

The material in this coauthored chapter draws heavily on a paper by Wolfgang Wiegard (1984).

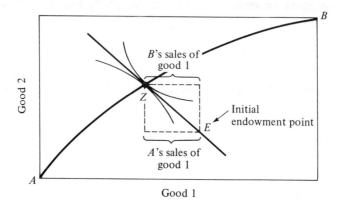

Figure 3.1. Simple pure exchange general equilibrium model.

this model, two individuals are specified by their preferences and endowments. From the initial endowments of the two goods among the individuals (point E), the economywide endowments (the dimensions of the Edgeworth box) are known. From the preferences, the contract curve is determined as the locus of tangencies of indifference surfaces. At all points on the contract curve the net trades of the two individuals balance at the price line tangent to both indifference surfaces. The initial endowment point must also be on this price line if the point on the contract curve is a competitive equilibrium.

This situation is represented by the equilibrium point Z in Figure 3.1, where the desired net trades of the two individuals at the equilibrium price ratio balance and the market excess demand functions for the two goods are zero. Computing general equilibria thus implies finding a set of prices corresponding to zero market excess demands for both goods.

To find an equilibrium, a number of procedures could be considered. A simple one would be to write down the market excess demand functions generated by the preferences and endowments, then conduct a line search of alternative price ratios P_1/P_2. Such excess demand functions are represented in Figure 3.2 as $g_1(P_1, P_2)$ and $g_2(P_1, P_2)$. If one market is in equilibrium, then by Walras's law the other market must be also, since the value of excess demands across both goods must always be zero. To find an equilibrium, it is therefore necessary to search for a zero value of only one of the two excess demand functions. Clearly, the difficulty with such a procedure is that, as the number of dimensions increases beyond two, carrying out such searches rapidly becomes prohibitively expensive.

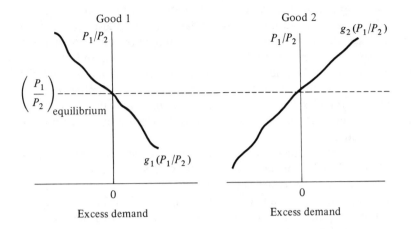

Figure 3.2. Excess demand functions for a simple general equilibrium model.

An alternative procedure in making such a search is to use a process of price adjustment. Under this approach, trial price ratios are used for which excess demands are calculated, with prices adjusted according to the size of excess demands or supplies. Prices are raised for commodities with positive excess demands, and are lowered for commodities with excess supplies. The size of the change in any price will typically depend on the magnitude of the excess demand or supply involved.

Although this procedure may work for simple two-commodity examples, difficulties can easily arise for higher-dimensional cases. There are no guarantees that such procedures will converge because the excess demand functions may have local inflection points, changes in slope, or both. Thus, determining prices corresponding to zero excess demands is usually more complex than these simple diagrams suggest; whence our need for a more elaborate computational method of finding counterfactual equilibria.

An early paper by Scarf (1960) illustrates these difficulties by showing how relatively easy it is to construct examples of global *in*stability using simple price-adjustment procedures in simple general equilibrium models. In the examples he presents, attempts to calculate a general equilibrium using such a price-adjustment rule are unsuccessful because prices continually diverge from their equilibrium values.

Because of this, in the 1960s Scarf began to work on methods for the determination of general equilibria that were based on earlier applications by Lemke and Howson (1964) of pivoting theory (from linear programming) to two-person, non–zero sum games. Lemke and Howson devised a computational procedure for the determination of a Nash equilibrium for a two-person, non–zero sum game that is guaranteed to converge. In essence, the procedure involves examining possible combinations of strategies for players until a Nash equilibrium is found, and considering each of these combinations in such a way that no combination already examined can be returned to. Because there are a finite number of combinations of strategies, the procedure can only terminate at a Nash equilibrium, and such an equilibrium will always be found by the computational procedure.

This no-cycling argument due to Lemke and Howson is used in Scarf's algorithm (1967, 1973) for the computation of a general equilibrium. His algorithm applies a procedure similar to that in Lemke and Howson to the problem of computing a fixed point of a mapping of the unit simplex into itself, a mapping whose existence is established by either the Brouwer or the Kakutani fixed point theorem.

As discussed in Chapter 2, a continuous mapping of the unit simplex into itself provides an image $F(\mathbf{X})$ for each N-dimensional vector $\mathbf{X}$ such that the components of both vectors $\mathbf{X}$ and $F(\mathbf{X})$ are nonnegative and sum to unity:

$$\sum_{i=1}^{N} X_i \equiv \sum_{i=1}^{N} F_i(\mathbf{X}) \equiv 1 \quad (X_i \geq 0, F_i(\mathbf{X}) \geq 0). \tag{3.1}$$

A fixed point of this mapping is given by a vector $\hat{\mathbf{X}}$ that is identical to its image $F(\hat{\mathbf{X}})$, that is, $F(\hat{\mathbf{X}}) = \hat{\mathbf{X}}$. Equilibrium in a model of exchange can be shown to be equivalent to finding a fixed point of a mapping of the unit simplex into itself generated using the Gale–Nikaido mapping discussed in Chapter 2. Thus, if a fixed point of the appropriate mapping can be found, an equilibrium for the corresponding general equilibrium model will also have been found.

In using Scarf's algorithm to find such a fixed point, the unit simplex is divided into a finite number of smaller simplices, each defined by N vertices that are each associated with a label. These labels are chosen from the set of integers that define the dimensionality of the general equilibrium problem (i.e., $1, \ldots, N$, if N is the dimensionality of the problem). The labels are chosen in such a way that if a simplex can be found whose vertices have a complete set of labels (from 1 to N) associated with them, then this implies that a close approximation to a general equilibrium must have been found.

The algorithm operates by moving through adjacent simplices, deleting and adding vertices. The starting point and each continuation step in the algorithm are such that, prior to finding an approximate equilibria, the algorithm always considers simplices whose vertices have all but one label present, with one label appearing as a duplicate. The procedure involves deleting a vertex with a duplicate label and replacing it with a new vertex; it then moves to an adjacent simplex. The replacement procedure is such that no simplex once examined can ever be returned to. Because of the finiteness of the number of simplices, and the inability to terminate the procedure other than at a close approximation to an equilibrium, the procedure is guaranteed to find an approximation to an equilibrium. In the limiting process where the number of simplices considered becomes infinite, this approximation will be exact. A point-to-point mapping corresponds to the case in which the Brouwer fixed point theorem applies. A point-to-set mapping, corresponding to the Kakutani fixed point theorem, uses slightly more complex vector labels.

The no-cycling argument used in Scarf's algorithm attracted a lot of interest when it first emerged in the late 1960s, because it provided a constructive proof of the existence of a general equilibrium – that is, a method guaranteed to terminate at an equilibrium solution for any properly specified general equilibrium model. However, the original version of Scarf's algorithm suffered from two drawbacks that made it inefficient as a solution procedure. First, in order to refine the initial equilibrium approximation in a way that would maintain the no-cycling argument, there was no alternative but to discard the initial calculations and begin again. Any information obtained in the first set of calculations had to be ignored in recomputation. Second, the algorithm always began in the corner of the unit simplex so that the no-cycling argument would apply. It was thus impossible, in computing equilibria with this procedure, to use prior information in the form of an initial guess. Typically, a large amount of time would be spent moving through regions of the unit simplex where it was known a priori that a low probability existed of finding the equilibrium solution.

These two problems were overcome in Merrill's (1972) algorithm, which made it possible to start the computational procedure on the face of the unit simplex, make an initial calculation, and then – if not within the desired tolerance – begin again at the last solution. As developed by Merrill, this procedure allowed for choice in the initial starting point, while preserving the no-cycling argument contained in Scarf's original algorithm. This "restart" algorithm was further refined by a number of contributors including Van der Laan and Talman (1979), who used a more sophisticated way of performing the restart procedure without requiring, as in Merrill's algorithm, that an extra dimension be added.

Scarf's algorithm and its subsequent refinements have an elegance in their no-cycling arguments that have appealed to many mathematical economists. But alternative and somewhat more traditional approaches (such as Newton's) to solving systems of nonlinear equations, while not being guaranteed to converge, have nonetheless been widely used in solving applied general equilibrium models. Methods that cannot be guaranteed to converge can still perform well in practice, and these alternative methods can be computationally faster. This was recognized in early work on general equilibrium analysis of tax systems by Whalley (1973); a similar theme appears in Ginsburgh and Waelbroeck (1981), Adelman and Robinson (1978), and the work of several other authors.

Most of these modelers use variants on Newton's method for the solution of a system of nonlinear equations. This method considers a series of local linearizations of the nonlinear equation system characterizing the model, for which a zero is sought for an equilibrium solution. The linear equation system is solved, with the linearization revised as solution proceeds. The major variations in the application of this procedure arise from the alternatives available for the calculation of the Newton steps. For instance, in Ginsburgh and Waelbroeck (1981) each linearization step involves calculating a Jacobian matrix of the excess demand functions. The procedure used by Dixon et al. (1982), and implicit in the earlier Johansen (1960) work on general equilibrium, is to linearize the system of demands and solve a derived system of linear equations. This linear approximation can then be further refined, as in Dixon et al.

Therefore, something of a divide currently exists between the theory and application of computational general equilibrium techniques. In theoretical work, primary stress is placed on computational procedures that are guaranteed to converge. In applications, the no-cycling convergence argument is often dispensed with in favor of computational procedures that are typically faster and require less execution time. Where difficulties are encountered with solution, resort may then be made to one of a number of fixed point methods, but this does not always occur.

3.2 Using fixed point algorithms to solve a two-factor model

In this and following sections we outline how an equilibrium can be computed using the algorithms of Scarf and Merrill for a general equilibrium model with M consumers, N commodities, and two factors of production (capital and labor), illustrating these procedures for the two-good–two-factor case. This specific model is chosen because it is close to the form that commonly used applied models take.

We assume that commodity demands for mth consumer $(m = 1, ..., M)$, $X_i^m = X_i^m(p_1, ..., p_N, r, w)$ $(i = 1, ..., N)$, can be derived from the first-order conditions of the utility-maximization problem

$$\max U^m(X_1^m, ..., X_N^m) \quad \text{s.t.} \quad \sum_{i=1}^{N} p_i X_i^m = wL^m + rK^m, \tag{3.2}$$

where X_i^m, L^m, K^m denote commodity demand and factor endowments for the mth consumer; p_i, w, r are the corresponding commodity and factor prices. Assuming that the utility function $U^m(\cdot)$ is strictly quasiconcave and differentiable implies that the solutions to (3.2) are homogeneous of degree zero in prices.

On the production side we consider N industries, each with linear homogeneous production functions

$$Q^j = Q^j(L^j, K^j) \quad (j = 1, \ldots, N). \tag{3.3}$$

Cost-minimizing behavior yields factor demands

$$L^j = L^j(r, w, Q^j) \quad \text{and} \quad K^j = K^j(r, w, Q^j), \tag{3.4}$$

which are homogeneous of degree zero in factor prices.

In this simple model, an equilibrium is characterized by a set of goods and factor prices for which excess demands for both goods and factors are less than or equal to zero:

$$\sum_{m=1}^{M} X_j^m(p_1, \ldots, p_N, r, w) - Q^j \leq 0 \quad (j = 1, \ldots, N),$$

$$\sum_{j=1}^{N} L^j(r, w, Q^j) - \sum_{m=1}^{M} L^m \leq 0, \tag{3.5}$$

$$\sum_{j=1}^{N} K^j(r, w, Q^j) - \sum_{m=1}^{M} K^m \leq 0,$$

where industry outputs Q^j are given by (3.3).

In addition, if the output of industry j is positive then zero-profit conditions prevail; that is,

$$p_j Q^j = wL^j(r, w, Q^j) + rK^j(r, w, Q^j). \tag{3.6}$$

Walras's law in this case can be written as

$$\sum_{j=1}^{N} p_j \left[Q^j - \sum_{m=1}^{M} X_j^m \right] + w \left[\sum_{j=1}^{N} L^j - \sum_{m=1}^{M} L^m \right] + r \left[\sum_{j=1}^{N} K^j - \sum_{m=1}^{M} K^m \right] = 0, \tag{3.7}$$

and the homogeneity properties of demand functions imply that we can normalize prices as in Chapter 2.

The dimensionality of the solution space in this model can be reduced to the number of factors of production, as indicated in Chapter 2. The steps involved are as follows.

    1. Determine cost-minimizing factor demands per unit of output j. Given factor prices r, w,

$$\frac{L^j}{Q_j} = l^j(r, w, 1), \quad \frac{K^j}{Q_j} = k^j(r, w, 1) \quad (j = 1, \ldots, N). \tag{3.8}$$

2. Compute commodity prices as functions of r and w using the zero-profit conditions:

$$p_j(r, w) = wl^j(r, w, 1) + rk^j(r, w, 1) \quad (j = 1, ..., N). \tag{3.9}$$

3. Once the N commodity prices are known, individual commodity demands can then be evaluated as

$$X_j^m(r, w) = X_j^m(p_1(r, w), ..., p_N(r, w), r, w)$$
$$(j = 1, ..., N, m = 1, ..., M). \tag{3.10}$$

4. Calculate output quantities that meet market demands,

$$Q^j(r, w) = \sum_{m=1}^{M} X_j^m(r, w) \quad (j = 1, ..., N), \tag{3.11}$$

and calculate derived factor demands as

$$L^j(r, w) = l^j(r, w, 1) \cdot Q^j(r, w) \quad (j = 1, ..., N),$$
$$K^j(r, w) = k^j(r, w, 1) \cdot Q^j(r, w) \quad (j = 1, ..., N). \tag{3.12}$$

5. Aggregate excess factor demands are given as

$$\rho_k(r, w) = \sum_{j=1}^{N} K^j(r, w) - \sum_{m=1}^{M} K^m;$$
$$\rho_l(r, w) = \sum_{j=1}^{N} L^j(r, w) - \sum_{m=1}^{M} L^m. \tag{3.13}$$

For arbitrarily given (positive) factor prices r, w, the values of ρ_k, ρ_l will generally be nonzero. Walras's law guarantees that the value of the sum of the two excess factor demands is zero. An equilibrium is given by values of r and w for which ρ_k and ρ_l are both zero.

3.3 An example

Before describing how the algorithms of Scarf and Merrill can be used to compute equilibria in factor price space, a small-dimensional numerical example illustrating the model structure just described may prove useful. We consider an example used by Shoven and Whalley (1984) that has two final goods (manufacturing and nonmanufacturing), two factors of production (capital and labor), and two classes of consumers.

The structure of the model and the parameters used are summarized in Table 3.1. Consumers have initial endowments of factors but no initial endowments of goods. The "rich" consumer group (R) owns all of the capital, while the "poor" group (P) owns all of the labor. Production of each good takes place according to a constant elasticity of substitution

Table 3.1. *Parameters and functional forms for the numerical examples of a 2-function, 2-sector general equilibrium model presented in Shoven and Whalley (1984)*

A. Demand

Utility functions	Parameter values	Demand functions
$U^m = \left(\sum_{i=1}^{2} (\alpha_i^m)^{1/\mu^m} (x_i^m)^{(\mu^m-1)/\mu^m} \right)^{\mu^m/(\mu^m-1)}$ $(m = R, P)$	$(\alpha_1^R, \alpha_2^R) = (0.5, 0.5)$ $(\alpha_2^P, \alpha_2^P) = (0.3, 0.7)$ $(\mu^R, \mu^P) = (1.5, 0.75)$ $(\bar{K}^R, \bar{K}^P) = (25, 0)$ $(\bar{L}^R, \bar{L}^P) = (0, 60)$	$x_i^m = \dfrac{\alpha_i^m (w\bar{L}^m + r\bar{K}^m)}{P_i^{\mu^m}\left(\sum_{i=1}^{2} \alpha_i^m p_i^{(1-\mu^m)}\right)}$ $(m = R, P, \ i = 1, 2)$

B. Production

Production functions	Parameter values	Factor demand functions
$Q^j = \Phi^j \left(\delta^j L_j^{(\sigma^j-1)/\sigma^j} + (1-\delta^j) K^{j(\sigma^j-1)/\sigma^j} \right)^{\sigma^j/(\sigma^j-1)}$ $(j = 1, 2)$	$(\Phi^1, \Phi^2) = (1.5, 2.0)$ $(\delta^1, \delta^2) = (0.6, 0.7)$ $(\sigma^1, \sigma^2) = (2.0, 0.5)$	$L^j = \dfrac{1}{\Phi^j} Q^j \left[\delta^j + (1-\delta^j)\left(\dfrac{\delta^j r}{(1-\delta^j)w} \right)^{(1-\sigma^j)} \right]^{\sigma^j/(1-\sigma^j)}$ $K^j = \dfrac{1}{\Phi^j} Q^j \left[\delta^j\left(\dfrac{(1-\delta^j)w}{\delta^j r} \right)^{(1-\sigma^j)} + (1-\delta^j) \right]^{\sigma^j/(1-\sigma^j)}$

Note: Sector 1 is manufacturing, sector 2 is nonmanufacturing.

(CES) production function, and each consumer class has demands that are derived from maximizing a CES utility function subject to a budget constraint.

The α variables are consumer share parameters, the μ's are elasticities of substitution in consumption, and $\bar{L}$ and $\bar{K}$ are household endowments. For production, the ϕ parameters are scale factors, the δ's are factor weighting parameters, and the σ's are elasticities of factor substitution.

The equilibrium solution for this example is given in Table 3.2, where prices have been normalized so that the price of labor equals unity. In equilibrium, total demand for each output exactly matches the amount produced, and producer revenues equal consumer expenditures. The labor and capital endowments are fully employed and consumer factor incomes equal producer factor costs. The cost per unit of output in each sector matches its price, meaning that economic profits are zero. The expenditure of each household exhausts its income.

3.4 Background concepts for fixed point algorithms

The solution to the numerical example given in Table 3.1 can be obtained using a fixed point algorithm such as those due to Scarf (1967, 1973) or Merrill (1972), both of which are numerical methods for approximating a fixed point of a continuous mapping of the unit simplex into itself. Before turning to these algorithms, we present some of the basic mathematical concepts that are required.

We define an m-dimensional simplex S as the convex hull of $m+1$ linearly independent vectors of integers $\mathbf{b}^1, \ldots, \mathbf{b}^{m+1}$, that is, the set of points of the form

$$X = \sum_{j=1}^{m+1} \alpha_j \mathbf{b}^j, \quad \text{with} \quad \alpha_j \geq 0 \quad \text{and} \quad \sum_{j=1}^{m+1} \alpha_j = 1. \tag{3.14}$$

Vectors $\mathbf{b}^1, \ldots, \mathbf{b}^{m+1}$ are referred to as *vertices* of the simplex. Each $m-1$ simplex S' is called a *face* of S if the m vertices of S' are a subset of $\{\mathbf{b}^1, \ldots, \mathbf{b}^{m+1}\}$. If vectors $\mathbf{b}^1, \ldots, \mathbf{b}^{m+1}$ are the $m+1$ unit vectors then S is called the *unit simplex*. A point $x \in S$ is a *fixed point* of a continuous mapping $f: S \to S$ if $x = f(x)$. A set of simplices $S^1, \ldots, S^k$ is called a *simplicial subdivision* (or *triangulation*) of S if (a) S is contained in the union of the simplices $S^1, \ldots, S^k$ and (b) the intersection of any two simplices S^e, S^m is either empty or a common face of both of them.

In order to effectively implement fixed point algorithms on a computer, a simple and efficient triangulation is required. A widely used and convenient triangulation is that due to Hansen (1969) and Kuhn and McKinnon (1975), characterized as follows: Let $\mathbf{b}^1 \in I^{n+1}$ be called a *base point* whose

Table 3.2. *Equilibrium solution for Shoven and Whalley's example given in Table 3.1*

Equilibrium prices

Manufacturing output	1.399
Nonmanufacturing output	1.093
Capital	1.373
Labor	1.000

A. Production

	Quantity	Revenue	Capital	Capital cost	Labor	Labor cost	Total cost	Cost per unit of output
Manufacturing	24.992	34.898	6.212	8.532	26.366	26.366	34.898	1.399
Nonmanufacturing	54.378	59.439	18.788	25.805	33.634	33.634	59.439	1.093
Total		94.337	25.000	34.337	60.000	60.000	94.337	

B. Demand

	Manufacturing	Non-manufacturing	Expenditure	Labor income	Capital income	Total income
Rich households	11.514	16.674	34.337	0	34.337	34.337
Poor households	13.428	37.704	60.000	60	0	60.000
Total	24.942	54.378	94.337	60	34.337	94.337

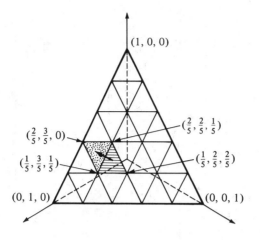

Figure 3.3. A subdivision of a 2-dimensional unit simplex.

coordinates can be represented by $(b_1^1/D, \dots, b_{n+1}^1/D)$, with $b_1^1, \dots, b_{n+1}^1$ nonnegative integers summing to D.

We define $\mathbf{e}^1, \dots, \mathbf{e}^n$ as n vectors, each $(n+1)$-dimensional, given by

$$\mathbf{e}^1 = (1, -1, 0, \dots, 0)$$
$$\mathbf{e}^2 = (0, 1, -1, \dots, 0)$$
$$\vdots$$
$$\mathbf{e}^n = (0, 0, 0, \dots, 1, -1),$$

(3.15)

so that $\mathbf{e}^j$ has a 1 in the jth coordinate and a -1 in the $(j+1)$th coordinate. Let $\phi = (\phi_1, \dots, \phi_n)$ be a permutation of the set of integers $(1, \dots, n)$. Then the $n+1$ vertices of a typical simplex in the subdivision are given by

$$\mathbf{b}^1 = \frac{\mathbf{e}^{\phi_1}}{D} \quad \text{and} \quad \mathbf{b}^{j+1} = \mathbf{b}^j + \frac{\mathbf{e}^{\phi_j}}{D} \quad \text{for } j = 1, \dots, n.$$

(3.16)

A simplicial subdivision is then a collection of vectors with vertices given by (3.16), where the factor D determines the *grid size* $(1/D)$ of the triangulation. Figure 3.3 illustrates a simplicial subdivision of the 2-dimensional unit simplex for $D = 5$. For base point $\mathbf{b}^1 = (1/5, 2/5, 2/5)$ and permutation $\phi = (2, 1)$, equation (3.16) gives the vertices $\mathbf{b}^2 = (1/5, 3/5, 1/5)$ and $\mathbf{b}^3 = (2/5, 2/5, 1/5)$, which together with $\mathbf{b}^1$ define the hatched simplex in Figure 3.3.

The algorithms due to Scarf and Merrill work by moving through a sequence of adjacent simplices until a solution is found, using the Lemke–Howson argument to guarantee that the algorithm cannot cycle. The

Hansen–Kuhn subdivisions allow the new vertex to be calculated as soon as the vertex to be replaced is known, using a remarkably simple rule that is especially easy to program. The $n+1$ vertices of an n-simplex can be represented as columns of an $(n+1)\times(n+1)$ matrix, with the jth column $(j=1,...,n+1)$ corresponding to the jth vertex of the simplex. If the vertices of a simplex in the subdivision are given by $\mathbf{b}^1,...,\mathbf{b}^{n+1}$, the replacement rule for an arbitrary vector $\mathbf{b}^j$ is then

$$\mathbf{b}^{j+1}+\mathbf{b}^{j-1}-\mathbf{b}^j, \tag{3.17}$$

with the interpretation that columns 1 and $n+1$ are adjacent.

To illustrate how this works, suppose that vertex $(1/5, 2/5, 2/5)$ of the hatched subsimplex is to be replaced, where we store the numerators of the coordinates of the three vertices characterizing the simplices as columns in a 3×3 matrix, that is,

$$\begin{bmatrix} 1 & 1 & 2 \\ 2 & 3 & 2 \\ 2 & 1 & 1 \end{bmatrix}. \tag{3.18}$$

Using the replacement rule (3.17) above, the new vertex is given by

$$\begin{bmatrix} 1 \\ 3 \\ 1 \end{bmatrix} + \begin{bmatrix} 2 \\ 2 \\ 1 \end{bmatrix} - \begin{bmatrix} 1 \\ 2 \\ 2 \end{bmatrix} = \begin{bmatrix} 2 \\ 3 \\ 0 \end{bmatrix}. \tag{3.19}$$

The vertex itself is given by $\mathbf{b}=(2/5, 3/5, 0)$; the new simplex is shown in Figure 3.3.

3.5 Scarf's algorithm

We use the numerical example presented in Section 3.3 to show how Scarf's algorithm works. Since commodity demand functions and derived factor excess demand functions are homogeneous of degree zero, we will normalize the factor prices so that they lie on the unit simplex; that is,

$$r+w=1. \tag{3.20}$$

Figure 3.4 displays this 1-dimensional unit simplex with a triangulation for a grid size of 10. The rental price of capital, r, and the wage rate w are on the axes.

Each vertex of a simplex has associated with it a specific label generated according to a general label rule. Under this rule, a vertex lying on the boundary of a n-dimensional unit simplex is assigned an integer i, where i is the index for the first coordinate that is equal to zero. Otherwise, a vertex receives an integer label j $(1 \le j \le n+1)$, where j corresponds to the index of the first commodity whose excess demand is positive.

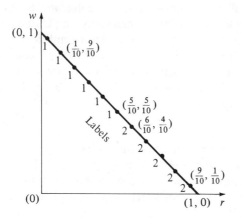

Figure 3.4. A *l*-dimensional unit simplex used in solving the numerical example presented in Table 3.1.

Applying this rule to the 1-dimensional unit simplex in Figure 3.4, the vertices $(0, 1)$ and $(1, 0)$ are assigned integers 1 and 2, respectively. The interior vertices receive the label 1 or 2, depending upon whether the first or second excess factor demand is positive (i.e., $\rho_k(\cdot)$ or $\rho_l(\cdot)$). Here, "first" or "second" refers to the excess factor demands corresponding to the first (r) and second (w) factor price coordinate. If both excess factor demands are zero at some vertex, the corresponding factor price combination is an equilibrium price vector. Otherwise, Scarf's algorithm continues the search for a completely labeled simplex (i.e., for a simplex with differently labeled vertices) since, by Walras's law and continuity of the excess demand functions, such a completely labeled simplex must be an approximate equilibrium.

As can be seen from Figure 3.4, such a solution clearly exists and (for a finite grid size D) is found using Scarf's algorithm after a finite number of steps. Each point on a completely labeled simplex represents an *approximate equilibrium* price vector (r^*, w^*) in the sense that

$$\max \rho_i(r^*, w^*) < \epsilon \quad (i = l, k), \tag{3.21}$$

where ϵ is determined by the behavior of the functions ρ_l, ρ_K and the grid size used in the triangulation (3.16). For given excess demand functions, the approximation can be improved by selecting a smaller grid size, that is, a larger D.

Scarf's algorithm always starts at the *initial simplex,* a subsimplex that contains one of the vertices of the unit simplex, and uses the following steps.

Steps in applying Scarf's algorithm:
1. Select an initial simplex (given by one of the vertices of the unit simplex) and a grid size D for the triangulation (3.16).
2. Calculate the labels of the vertices of the initial simplex by applying the labeling rule.
3. If the simplex is completely labeled, go to step 5; otherwise, go to step 4.
4. Since the simplex is not completely labeled, the labels of two of the vertices must be the same. If it is the initial simplex, then remove the vertex of the unit simplex and generate the new vertex by applying the replacement rule (3.17). Calculate the label of the new vertex; go back to step 3. If it is not the initial simplex, then remove that vertex with a duplicate label that was not introduced in the previous step, and generate a new vertex using the replacement rule (3.17). Determine the label of the new vertex, and go back to step 3.
5. Since the vertex is completely labeled, an approximation to a competitive equilibrium has been found. Select any point in the completely labeled simplex and calculate the vector of all excess factor demands. If the approximation is close enough, the algorithm terminates. Otherwise, select a larger D and a new initial simplex as described in step 1; proceed to step 2.

Scarf's algorithm is guaranteed to converge because at any stage of the calculation there are two duplicate labels, and one label is missing. By consistently using a continuation that involves replacing the vertex originally associated with the simplex having a duplicate label, no position once entered can be returned to. There are a finite number of positions and the computational procedure cannot exit from the face of the unit simplex. It must therefore terminate, and can do so only by finding a completely labeled simplex in the subdivision.

The different steps taken by Scarf's algorithm can be illustrated using the numerical example from Table 3.1. Our interest here centers on the solution procedure, not on the solution itself. Table 3.3 presents the steps taken by the algorithm for a grid size of 10. The algorithm starts in the corner of the unit simplex, in this case the line segment between the two vertices $(10/10, 0)$ and $(9/10, 1/10)$, where the first coordinate is r and the second w. This starting simplex is shown in Table 3.3. The algorithm proceeds to move across the unit simplex until it reaches the simplex defined by the vertices $(6/10, 4/10)$ and $(5/10, 5/10)$. That simplex is fully labeled, and the procedure is terminated.

The solution is also illustrated in Figure 3.5, where the factor excess demands $\rho_k(\cdot)$, $\rho_l(\cdot)$ for the example are presented. The interval $[0, 1]$ is

Table 3.3. *Scarf's algorithm applied to the numerical example presented in Table 3.1*

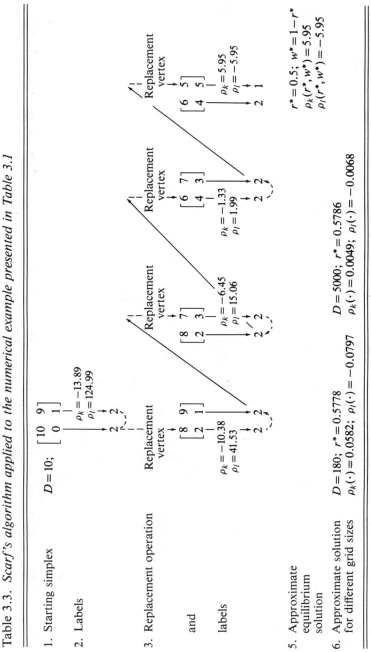

1. Starting simplex $\quad D = 10; \quad \begin{bmatrix} 10 & 9 \\ 0 & 1 \end{bmatrix}$

2. Labels
$$\rho_k = -13.89$$
$$\rho_l = 124.99$$

3. Replacement operation

and

Replacement vertex $\begin{bmatrix} 8 & 9 \\ 2 & 1 \end{bmatrix}$

labels
$$\rho_k = -10.38$$
$$\rho_l = 41.53$$

Replacement vertex $\begin{bmatrix} 8 & 7 \\ 2 & 3 \end{bmatrix}$
$$\rho_k = -6.45$$
$$\rho_l = 15.06$$

Replacement vertex $\begin{bmatrix} 6 & 7 \\ 4 & 3 \end{bmatrix}$
$$\rho_k = -1.33$$
$$\rho_l = 1.99$$

Replacement vertex $\begin{bmatrix} 6 & 5 \\ 4 & 5 \end{bmatrix}$
$$\rho_k = 5.95$$
$$\rho_l = -5.95$$

$$r^* = 0.5; \quad w^* = 1 - r^*$$
$$\rho_k(r^*, w^*) = 5.95$$
$$\rho_l(r^*, w^*) = -5.95$$

5. Approximate equilibrium solution

6. Approximate solution for different grid sizes

$D = 180; \quad r^* = 0.5778$
$\rho_k(\cdot) = 0.0582; \quad \rho_l(\cdot) = -0.0797$

$D = 5000; \quad r^* = 0.5786$
$\rho_k(\cdot) = 0.0049; \quad \rho_l(\cdot) = -0.0068$

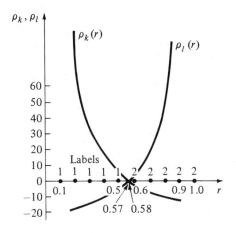

Figure 3.5. Excess factor demands for the numerical example presented in Table 3.1.

subdivided so that it corresponds to the triangulation of the unit simplex in Figure 3.4. One of the labels 1 or 2 is associated with each of the interval points, depending upon whether the excess demand of capital or labor is positive. If ρ_l and ρ_k are continuous and strictly decreasing or increasing, the equilibrium price vector must be in an interval with differently labeled vertices. Scarf's algorithm locates such a simplex. It is clear from Figure 3.5 and Table 3.3 that the equilibrium solution found in this way will be approximate: For the final simplex obtained using a grid of 10, the relative price of capital to labor ranges from 1.0 to 1.5 across the vertices, whereas from Table 3.2 the true equilibrium factor price ratio is 1.373. It may be instructive to note that only relative prices have real consequences in this model. In Table 3.2 we used the arbitrary assumption that $w = 1.0$, whereas in Table 3.3 we assumed that $r + w = 1.0$. Such normalizations are made for convenience, but are inconsequential in terms of the model's results concerning quantities and welfare.

Reducing the grid size of the triangulation improves the approximation, but raises computing costs. The reason is that Scarf's algorithm must be repeatedly restarted at one of the vertices of the unit simplex. The major drawback of Scarf's algorithm is that such restarting is required when the approximation is too poor, and that prior information cannot be used in choosing a good starting point. Existing information is completely discarded when the grid is refined. Figure 3.5 suggests an obvious improvement. Having found a completely labeled simplex for a given grid

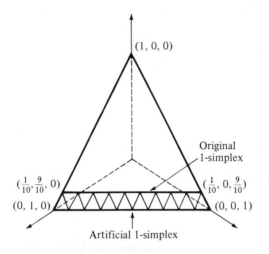

Figure 3.6. Triangulation of the 2-dimensional unit simplex used in applying Merrill's algorithm to the numerical example of Table 3.1.

size, computing costs could be reduced if the algorithm could be restarted for a finer grid at one of the vertices of the previous solution simplex. This is the approach taken in Merrill's algor‌hm.

3.6 Merrill's algorithm

The major modification of Merrill's procedure to Scarf's algorithm is the addition of a dimension to the solution space. In solving the numerical example in Table 3.1, instead of using a 1-dimensional unit simplex, Merrill's algorithm moves through a triangulation of a 2-dimensional unit simplex, or (more precisely) through a part of this triangulation. The 1-dimensional unit simplex of Figure 3.4 with a grid size of 10 is represented in Figure 3.6 by the lower boundary of the 2-dimensional unit simplex. Merrill's procedure introduces an additional (artificial) 1-dimensional simplex with grid size $D-1$, and subdivides the resulting 2-dimensional "sandwich" figure. This 2-dimensional figure can be interpreted as part of the triangulation of a 2-dimensional unit simplex with grid size 10 (see (3.16)). The numerators of the first coordinate of the different vertices are either 0 or 1, depending upon whether they are on the original or the artificial 1-dimensional simplex. The two remaining coordinates correspond to normalized factor prices r and w.

Merrill's algorithm starts with the *initial vertex,* an arbitrary interior vertex on the original (lower) 1-dimensional simplex, which – after adding the two appropriate vertices on the artificial (upper) 1-dimensional simplex – defines a unique 2-dimensional simplex, the so-called initial simplex. If the coordinates of the initial vertex are given by $(0, b_1, b_2)$ then the corresponding vertices on the artificial 1-dimensional simplex are uniquely determined by $(1, b_1 - 1, b_2)$ and $(1, b_1, b_2 - 1)$, where only the numerators are specified here.

Like Scarf's algorithm, Merrill's associates labels with the vertices on the relevant 2-simplices, according to a general labeling rule. For any vertex on the original 1-simplex (where the numerator of the first coordinate is zero), the same labeling rule is used as in Scarf's algorithm (ignoring the first coordinate). Any vertex on the artificial 1-simplex (where the numerator of the first coordinate is 1) is assigned an integer i, where i is the index for the first of the remaining vertex coordinates that is smaller than the corresponding value of the initial vertex **b**.

For a given grid size, Merrill's algorithm then moves through a sequence of adjacent 2-simplices until a completely labeled 1-simplex is found on the 1-simplex (i.e., on the boundary of the 2-unit simplex). The movement from one 2-simplex to the other is accomplished by using the replacement rule (3.17). The algorithm has a unique starting position that, unlike Scarf's algorithm, is characterized by a complete collection of labels. The problem is that all the labels are associated with vertices on the artificial level. The algorithm then continues as in Scarf's algorithm, with movements between adjacent simplices, until a complete collection of labels is obtained on the original level and the vertex to be replaced is on the artificial level. The starting point is unique and cannot be returned to; the continuation always involves removing the vertex originally in the simplex with a duplicate label. Any position typically has N distinct labels and one duplicate, and hence the same no-cycling argument as used in Scarf's algorithm applies.

If the accuracy of the solution is not adequate, any of the vertices of the final simplex can be taken as the initial vertex of a new calculation with a finer grid size. This new grid size can be chosen in any way, such as by multiplying $1/D$ by a factor β $(0 < \beta < 1)$. The algorithm terminates if the approximation to an equilibrium satisfies a given criterion, usually a sufficiently small value of ϵ in (3.21). Figure 3.7 illustrates such a refinement of Figure 3.6 for $\beta = 1/2$.

Merrill's procedure can be stated more formally as follows.

Steps in applying Merrill's algorithm:
1. Select a grid size and a refinement factor $0 < \beta < 1$; fix the approximation criterion ϵ; choose a starting vector $\mathbf{b} \in I^{n+1}$.
2. The initial simplex is given by the following matrix:

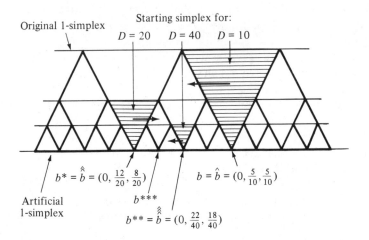

Figure 3.7. Progressive refinements of the solution obtained in applying Merrill's algorithm to the numerical example of Table 3.1.

$$
\begin{bmatrix}
0 & 1 & 1 & 1 \\
b_1 & b_1-1 & b_1 & b_1 \\
b_2 & b_2 & b_2-1 & b_2 \\
\cdot & \cdots & \cdots & \cdot \\
b_n & b_n & b_n & b_n-1
\end{bmatrix}.
$$

3. Calculate the labels of the initial simplex by applying the labeling rule described previously.
4. Replace that vertex on the artificial $(n-1)$-simplex whose label is equal to that of the initial vertex; compute the new vertex using the replacement rule (3.17) and determine the label of the newly added vertex.
5. If all but one of the $n+1$ vertices of the n-simplex are on the original $(n-1)$-simplex, and if the simplex is completely labeled, then go to step 7; otherwise, go to step 6.
6. Remove that vertex of the n-simplex whose label is the same as that of the newly added vertex. Find the label for the new vertex. Go to step 5.
7. Take any point from the solution simplex and compute the relevant excess demands. Terminate if a desired approximation criterion is fulfilled, that is, if

$$\max|\rho_i(\cdot)| < \epsilon. \tag{3.22}$$

Otherwise, multiply the given grid size by a refinement factor; set $b = b^*$ (i.e., use the approximate equilibrium b^* just found as the initial simplex b in the new calculation). Go to step 2.

Table 3.4 presents the steps followed in applying Merrill's algorithm to the example of the two-sector general equilibrium model presented in Table 3.1. Other refinements of Scarf's original algorithm also allow for restart on the face of the simplex, and in the case of the Van der Laan and Talman (1979) algorithm, dispense with the need for the extra dimension required by Merrill's algorithm. The superiority of Merrill's algorithm over Scarf's algorithm is clear from a comparison of execution times.

3.7 Modifying solution algorithms for the presence of taxes

The previous sections show how to solve a two-factor general equilibrium model by applying Scarf's or Merrill's algorithm. In this section we show how to further modify the algorithms for policy-evaluation work. These modifications cover the inclusion of taxes in two-sector models, and are due to Shoven and Whalley (1972, 1973, 1977).

A two-sector general equilibrium model can be extended to include a wide range of taxes. Sales taxes can be considered that apply to each of the commodities $1, \ldots, N$ at different rates. The tax base is the net-of-tax price. If p_j denotes the producer price of commodity j, with q_j the consumer's price and τ_j the commodity tax rate, then

$$q_j = p_j(1 + \tau_j). \tag{3.23}$$

Factor taxes can also be incorporated. If τ_l is the payroll tax rate,[1] then the corresponding user price of factors for producers is $w(1 + \tau_l)$. If there are sector-specific capital income taxes at rates τ_k^j $(j = 1, \ldots, N)$, then the gross-of-tax price of capital in sector j is $r(1 + \tau_k^j)$.

A variety of income-tax schemes can also be considered, but for simplicity we restrict ourselves here to a linear tax function. If τ_y denotes the marginal tax rate and F a real personal exemption (assumed to be equal for all households), then the tax liability of the mth household is given by

$$\tau_y(wL^m + rK^m - F), \tag{3.24}$$

where L^m and K^m denote the ownership of labor and capital by the mth household. We also simplify our analysis by assuming that tax revenues are distributed in a lump sum to consumers. Transfers T^m, received by household m, are thus given by

---

[1] The labor tax rate could also vary by industry.

Table 3.4. *Merrill's algorithm applied to the numerical example of Table 3.1*

1. Parameter specification

$D = 10$; $\beta = 1/3$; $\epsilon = 0.001$; $\hat{b} = (0, 5/10, 5/10)$

2. Starting simplex

$$\begin{bmatrix} 0 & 1 & 1 \\ 5 & 4 & 5 \\ 5 & 5 & 4 \end{bmatrix}$$

3. Labels

$\rho_k = 5.95$
$\rho_l = -5.95$

$$\begin{array}{ccc} 1 \\ 1 & 2 & 2 \end{array} \rightarrow 2$$

4. Replacement operation

Replacement vertex

$$\begin{bmatrix} 0 & 0 & 1 \\ 5 & 6 & 5 \\ 5 & 4 & 4 \end{bmatrix}$$

and

$\rho_k = -1.33$
$\rho_l = 1.99$

labels

$$\begin{array}{c} 1 \\ 2 \rightarrow 2 \\ 1 \rightarrow 2 \end{array}$$

$r^* = 0.6$
$\rho_k, \rho_l > \epsilon$
$\hat{b} = (0, 18/30, 12/30)$

$$\begin{bmatrix} 0 & 1 & 1 \\ 18 & 17 & 18 \\ 12 & 12 & 11 \end{bmatrix}$$

$\rho_k = -1.33$
$\rho_l = 1.99$

$$\begin{array}{c} \rightarrow 2 \\ \rightarrow 1 \\ \rightarrow 2 \end{array} \rightarrow 2$$

Replacement vertex

$$\begin{bmatrix} 0 & 1 & 0 \\ 18 & 17 & 17 \\ 12 & 12 & 13 \end{bmatrix}$$

$\rho_k = 0.80$
$\rho_l = -1.04$

$$\begin{array}{c} \rightarrow 1 \\ \rightarrow 1 \\ \rightarrow 1 \end{array}$$

$r^* = 0.57$
$\rho_k, \rho_l > \epsilon$
$\hat{b} = (0, 51/90, 39/90)$

$$\begin{bmatrix} 0 & 1 & 1 \\ 51 & 50 & 51 \\ 39 & 39 & 38 \end{bmatrix}$$

· · · · · ·

$$\begin{bmatrix} 1 & 0 & 0 \\ 37966 & 37966 & 37967 \\ 27643 & 27644 & 27643 \end{bmatrix}$$

$\rho_k = -0.0001$
$\rho_l = 0.0001$

$$\begin{array}{c} \rightarrow 2 \\ \rightarrow 1 \\ \rightarrow 2 \end{array}$$

5. Is the approximation close enough?

$r^* = 0.5787$
$\rho_k, \rho_l < \epsilon$
(Execution time: 0.105 CP seconds)

$$T^m = \gamma^m T, \quad \text{with} \quad \sum_{m=1}^{M} T^m = T,$$ (3.25)

where γ^m is a constant and $\sum_{m=1}^{M} \gamma^m = 1$.

The two-factor model given by equations (3.8)–(3.13) must be modified as follows:

$$\frac{L^j}{Q^j} = l^j(r(1+\tau_k^j), w(1+\tau_l), 1), \qquad \frac{K^j}{Q^j} = k^j(\cdot),$$ (3.8′)

$$p_j(\cdot) = w(1+\tau_l) \cdot l^j(\cdot) + r(1+\tau_k^j) k^j(\cdot),$$ (3.9′)

$$X_j^m(\cdot) = X_j^m((1+\tau_1)p_1(\cdot), \ldots, (1+\tau_N)p_N(\cdot), r, w, \tau_y, F, T^m).$$ (3.10′)

Equations (3.11)–(3.13) remain unchanged except for modifications to the arguments of functions to reflect the use of gross-of-tax rather than net-of-tax prices. The model must be changed, however, to include a government budget imbalance equation. This reflects the fact that tax revenues and transfers generally do not coincide in disequilibrium:

$$\rho_G(\cdot) = \sum_{j=1}^{N} \sum_{m=1}^{M} \tau_j p_j X_j^m + \tau_l \sum_{j=1}^{N} wL^j + \sum_{j=1}^{N} \tau_k^j rK^j$$
$$+ \sum_{m=1}^{M} \tau_y(wL^m + rK^m - F) - \sum_{m=1}^{M} T^m.$$ (3.26)

With this specification of government activity, Walras's law can now be written (in abbreviated notation) as

$$w\rho_l + r\rho_k + \rho_G = 0.$$ (3.27)

Demand and supply functions are now homogeneous of degree zero in factor prices and tax revenue. An equilibrium is therefore characterized by a vector (r^*, w^*, T^*) such that excess demand functions ρ_k, ρ_l, ρ_G are zero.

To illustrate this extension to the basic model, we consider a change of one (or more) of the exogenously given tax rates. We first describe the modifications required for Scarf's algorithm; the changes needed for Merrill's algorithm follow directly.

Since demand and supply functions are homogeneous of degree zero in r, w, and T, we replace the price normalization (3.20) by

$$r + w + T = 1.$$ (3.20′)

Scarf's algorithm thus becomes a search process on a 2-dimensional unit simplex (see Figure 3.8), whereas Merrill's algorithm works on part of a 3-dimensional unit simplex.

Given the (r, w, T) coordinates for vertices of any simplex, consumers and producers can solve their respective optimization problems. In

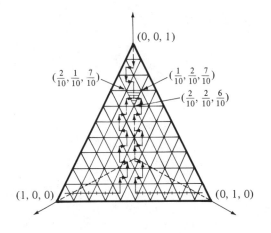

Figure 3.8. Solution using Scarf's algorithm applied to the numerical example of Table 3.1, with a 50% tax on capital income added. A grid size of 10 is assumed.

calculating the government budget imbalance ρ_G, T (and hence T^m for each household) is given by the coordinate of the vertices of the different simplices, while actual tax revenues collected are determined endogenously.

Figure 3.8 illustrates three different paths to an approximate equilibrium using Scarf's algorithm for $D = 10$. We start at the three vertices of the 2-unit simplex for the case where a 50% capital income tax in sector 1 and a 10% commodity sales tax are both introduced into the numerical example presented in Table 3.1. Tax revenues are distributed to consumers using the shares $\gamma^R = 0.4$ and $\gamma^P = 0.6$. Table 3.5 gives the same equilibrium solution after applying Merrill's algorithm to the example. If Merrill's algorithm is used then the simplex must be augmented by an additional coordinate. In this case the initial vertex is $(0, b_1, b_2, b_3)$, the initial simplex being calculated as in step 2 of Merrill's algorithm.

An alternative approach to general equilibrium tax-policy analysis is to consider tax alternatives of equal yield, as in Shoven and Whalley (1977), rather than equilibria in which taxes increase. This approach is often termed *differential tax incidence,* following Musgrave (1959). Here we also describe how to perform differential incidence analysis in a computational context.

Differential incidence analysis supposes that an existing tax system results in revenue R^0, and that the government wants to substitute one tax for another while maintaining revenues. It is not at all obvious, however, when and in what sense two tax revenues R^0 and R^1 are equal. Here we

Table 3.5. *Equilibrium solution using Merrill's algorithm for the numerical example of Table 3.1 with taxes added*

Model	Parameters and functional forms from Table 3.1
	Tax parameters
	$\tau_k^1 = 0.5$ (50% capital tax in manufacturing)
	$\tau_1 = \tau_2 = 0.1$ (10% consumer taxes)
	$\delta^R = 0.4$, $\delta^P = 0.6$ (revenue-distribution shares among consumers)
Algorithm	Merrill
	Specification: $D = 30$; $\beta = 1/3$; $\epsilon = 0.001$;
	$\hat{b} = (0, 10/30, 10/30, 10/30)$
Equilibrium[a] prices	$r = 1.126$; $w = 1.000$; $p_1 = 1.466$; $p_2 = 1.005$
Equilibrium[a] quantity	*Demands* *Production*
	$x_1^R = 9.181$ $x_1^P = 13.261$ $Q^1 = 22.442$ $Q^2 = 57.236$
	$x_2^R = 16.170$ $x_2^P = 41.066$ $L^1 = 26.049$ $L^2 = 33.950$
	$K^1 = 4.057$ $K^2 = 20.943$
Taxes and transfers	$T = 11.328$; $T^R = 4.531$; $T^P = 6.797$
Excess demands	$\rho_k = 0.002$; $\rho_l = -0.0006$; $\rho_G = 0.0004$

[a] All prices are denominated in terms of labor.

assume that new taxes are required, so that revenue R^1 corrected by a Laspeyeres price index

$$Q_L = \frac{\sum_{i=1}^N q_i^1 \sum_{m=1}^M x_i^{m0}}{\sum_{i=1}^N q_i^0 \sum_{m=1}^M x_i^{m0}} \qquad (3.28)$$

is equal to R^0 in real terms. In Q_L, the x_i^{m0} terms are the base period consumption of good i by household m, and q_i^0 and q_i^1 refer to base prices and revised-case prices of commodity i, respectively. For equal-yield tax alternatives, one may require that

$$R^1 = R^0 \cdot Q_L. \qquad (3.29)$$

Since the equilibrium values of base period 0 are known, tax revenue R^1 for given consumer prices $q_1^1, \ldots, q_N^1$ can be calculated using (3.29).

Using this equilibrium specification, tax revenue R^1 no longer corresponds to any additional dimension of the unit simplex. Rather, one wants to calculate that tax rate τ that produces equal revenue for the replacement tax system. This might be a uniform-rate sales tax, for instance.

However, this tax rate cannot itself be the additional coordinate of the unit simplex because, from (3.29), R^1 is linearly homogeneous in consumer prices $q_1^1, \ldots, q_N^1$. For given tax rates, commodity demand functions are also homogeneous of degree zero in factor prices. Suppose τ were a coordinate of an augmented unit simplex and (r^*, w^*, τ^*) were an exact equilibrium solution that coincided with an interior vertex of the 2-unit simplex. The vector $(kr^*, kw^*, k\tau^*)$ gives different evaluation demands, owing to the homogeneity properties just mentioned. This is clearly inappropriate.

We therefore use an auxiliary variable z to compute such an equilibrium, and normalize

$$r + w + z = 1. \tag{3.20''}$$

Using this formulation, the tax rate τ is a linearly homogeneous function of the variables on the unit simplex. The tax rate can be determined as

$$\tau = \frac{z}{r + w}. \tag{3.30}$$

The application of either Scarf's or Merrill's algorithm remains unchanged; the only modification needed is in calculating excess demand functions ρ_k, ρ_l, ρ_G.

To illustrate this, we again use the numerical example outlined in Table 3.1. In comparing equilibria we have used the arithmetic sum of Hicksian equivalent variations (HEV) as an aggregate measure of welfare. Let I^0, I^1 denote the income of consumers in periods 0 and 1, respectively, and let $E(q, U)$ be the expenditure function. Then

$$\text{HEV} = I^1 - I^0 - [E(q^1, U^1) - E(q^0, U^1)]. \tag{3.31}$$

If utility functions are homothetic then this measure simplifies to

$$\text{HEV} = \frac{U^1 - U^0}{U^0} I^0. \tag{3.32}$$

In our first example, we assume a 30% payroll tax and that differentiated commodity taxes are initially levied. We consider the case where the government abolishes the payroll tax and replaces it by an equal-yield change in commodity taxes. We consider both multiplicative and additive changes in tax rates. Table 3.6 displays the results.

The second example reports the effects of replacing a 30% proportional income tax by an equal-yield sales tax with a differentiated rate structure $(\tau_1 = 2\tau_2)$. With constant labor supply, an income tax has no effects on resource allocation, and thus welfare losses can be expected as a result of

Table 3.6. *Differential tax incidence analysis using the numerical example of Table 3.1: equal-yield tax substitution of commodity taxes for payroll taxes*

	Case 0	Case 1	
Model	Payroll taxes: $\tau_1^1 = \tau_1^2 = 0.3$ Commodity taxes: $\tau_1 = 0.2$ $\tau_2 = 0.1$	New payroll taxes: $\tau_1^1 = \tau_1^2 = 0.0$ New commodity taxes (endogenously determined):	
		Multiplicative	*Additive*
		$q_1 = p_1(1+\tau)$ $q_2 = p_2(1+0.5\tau)$	$q_i = p_i(1+\tau_i+\tau)$
Equilibrium prices	$r = 1.806 \quad w = 1.0$ $p_1 = 1.824 \quad p_2 = 1.428$	$r = 1.426 \quad w = 1.0$ $p_1 = 1.412 \quad p_2 = 1.111$	$r = 1.393 \quad w = 1.0$ $p_1 = 1.404 \quad p_2 = 1.100$
Equilibrium quantities	$x_1^R = 12.369 \quad x_1^P = 11.733$ $x_2^R = 20.343 \quad x_2^P = 35.109$ $Q^1 = 24.102 \quad Q^2 = 55.452$ $L^1 = 25.617 \quad L^2 = 34.383$ $K^1 = 5.901 \quad K^2 = 19.099$	$x_1^R = 10.216 \quad x_1^P = 12.044$ $x_2^R = 19.237 \quad x_2^P = 38.563$ $Q^1 = 22.260 \quad Q^2 = 57.801$ $L^1 = 23.957 \quad L^2 = 36.044$ $K^1 = 5.239 \quad K^2 = 19.762$	$x_1^R = 11.130 \quad x_1^P = 12.753$ $x_2^R = 17.946 \quad x_2^P = 37.786$ $Q^1 = 23.883 \quad Q^2 = 55.732$ $L^1 = 25.421 \quad L^2 = 34.579$ $K^1 = 5.821 \quad K^2 = 19.179$
Taxes	$T = 34.709$	$\tau = 0.5$	$\tau = 0.195$
Welfare effects		$\text{HEV}^R = -6.52945$ $\text{HEV}^P = 6.04880$ $\text{HEV} = -0.48064$	$\text{HEV}^R = -6.47947$ $\text{HEV}^P = 6.43596$ $\text{HEV} = -0.04351$

Table 3.7. *Differential tax incidence analysis using the example of Table 3.5: equal-yield tax substitution of indirect for direct taxes*

	Benchmark equilibrium		Counterfactual equilibrium	
Model	Income tax rates: $\tau_y^R = \tau_y^P = 0.3$		Differentiated consumer tax rates: $q_1 = p_1(1+\tau)$; $q_2 = p_2(1+0.5\tau)$	
Equilibrium prices	$r = 1.372$	$w = 1.0$	$r = 1.438$	$w = 1.0$
	$p_1 = 1.399$	$p_2 = 1.092$	$p_1 = 1.415$	$p_2 = 1.115$
Equilibrium quantities	$x_1^R = 11.846$	$x_1^P = 13.203$	$x_1^R = 9.931$	$x_1^P = 11.763$
	$x_2^R = 17.162$	$x_2^P = 37.079$	$x_2^R = 19.783$	$x_2^P = 38.737$
	$Q^1 = 25.049$	$Q^2 = 54.241$	$Q^1 = 21.693$	$Q^2 = 58.519$
	$L^1 = 26.460$	$L^2 = 33.539$	$L^1 = 23.441$	$L^2 = 36.560$
	$K^1 = 6.252$	$K^2 = 18.748$	$K^1 = 5.040$	$K^2 = 19.960$
Taxes	$T = 28.286$		$\tau = 0.66$	
Welfare effects			$\text{HEV}^R = -0.10857$ $\text{HEV}^P = -0.41310$ $\text{HEV} = -0.52168$	

the change. Replacing a proportional income tax by a general sales tax thus does not have any effects. Table 3.7 presents the results for these cases.

3.8 Van der Laan and Talman's algorithm

The previous sections illustrate how Scarf's and Merrill's algorithms can be used to solve two-factor general equilibrium models. In this section[2] we briefly describe an algorithm of Van der Laan and Talman (1979) that, like Merrill's algorithm, can start from any arbitrary point on the N-unit simplex, but avoids Merrill's requirement of an additional dimension.

For this algorithm, some additional terminology needs to be introduced. We define a t-dimensional simplex $\sigma = \sigma(\mathbf{y}^1, \ldots, \mathbf{y}^{t+1})$ as the convex hull of $t+1$ linearly independent vectors $\mathbf{y}^1, \ldots, \mathbf{y}^{t+1}$ in R^N ($t < N$). The standard unit simplex S is simply an $(N-1)$-dimensional simplex $\sigma(\mathbf{e}^1, \ldots, \mathbf{e}^N)$, with each vertex $\mathbf{e}^j$ ($j = 1, \ldots, N$) being the jth unit vector in R^N (i.e., the jth component of $\mathbf{e}^j$ is unity and the remaining components of $\mathbf{e}^j$ are zero). A t_1-dimensional simplex σ_1 is a face of a t_2-dimensional simplex

---

[2] This section draws on unpublished notes on fixed point algorithms prepared by Trien Nguyen of the University of Waterloo.

σ_2 ($t_1 \leq t_2$) if all the vertices of σ_1 are also vertices of σ_2. If $t_1 = t_2 - 1$ then σ_1 is called a *facet* of σ_2. The simplices σ_1 and σ_2 are said to be *adjacent* if they share a common facet or if one of them is a facet of the other.

A standard triangulation with grid size D of the unit simplex S is a collection of $(N-1)$-dimensional simplices $\sigma(\mathbf{y}^1, \ldots, \mathbf{y}^N)$ such that

(i) each coordinate of the vertex $\mathbf{y}^1$ is a multiple of $(1/D)$, and

(ii) the remaining vertices $\mathbf{y}^2, \ldots, \mathbf{y}^N$ are defined recursively by

$$\mathbf{y}^{j+1} = \mathbf{y}^j + (1/D)\mathbf{q}(\pi_j) \quad (j = 1, \ldots, N-1),$$

where $\pi = (\pi_1, \ldots, \pi_{N-1})$ is a permutation of the set of integers $\{1, \ldots, N-1\}$, each vector $\mathbf{q}(j) = \mathbf{e}^{j+1} - \mathbf{e}^j$ for $j = 1, \ldots, N-1$, and $\mathbf{q}(N) = \mathbf{e}^1 - \mathbf{e}^N$. The simplex $\sigma(\mathbf{y}^1, \ldots, \mathbf{y}^N)$ is thus defined by the first vertex $\mathbf{y}^1$ and the permutation π. We denote this by $\sigma(\mathbf{y}^1, \pi)$.

The Van der Laan–Talman restart algorithm begins at an arbitrary point s in S and generates a path of adjacent simplices of variable dimension until a completely labeled, full-dimensional simplex is found. If a new label is obtained, a simplex of higher dimension is constructed by attaching a new vertex to the current simplex; one of lower dimension is constructed by dropping a label and a vertex from the current simplex. These replacements are unique and, as with Scarf's and Merrill's algorithms, it can be shown that the algorithm will terminate after a finite number of iterations.

Let T denote the set of integers $\{1, \ldots, t\}$, where $1 \leq t \leq N-1$, and let $\pi(T) = (\pi_1, \ldots, \pi_t)$ denote a permutation on T. An arbitrary point s in S is the starting point for the algorithm. For any current simplex $\sigma(\mathbf{y}^1, \pi(T))$ in a triangulation of S with grid size $(1/D)$, the relationship between the vertex $\mathbf{y}^1$ and the starting point s is given by a vector $\mathbf{r} = (r_1, \ldots, r_N)$ of nonnegative integers such that

$$\mathbf{y}^1 = s + \frac{1}{D} \sum_{j=1}^{N} r_j \mathbf{q}(j). \tag{3.33}$$

Van der Laan and Talman's algorithm can be described by the following steps.

Steps in applying Van der Laan and Talman's algorithm:

1. Initialize the algorithm by setting

$$T = \phi \text{ (the empty set)}, \qquad t = 0,$$

$$\mathbf{y}^1 = s, \qquad \bar{\mathbf{y}} = s,$$

$$\sigma = \sigma(\mathbf{y}^1, \pi(T)) = \{s\}, \qquad \mathbf{r} = 0.$$

The starting simplex σ thus consists of only one point: the starting point s. The dimension of σ is zero.

2. Calculate the label $l(\bar{\mathbf{y}})$ according to the labeling rules described previously. If the calculated label $l(\bar{\mathbf{y}})$ does not belong to the set T, go to step 4. On the other hand, if the calculated label $l(\bar{\mathbf{y}})$ does belong to the set T then there is exactly one vertex (say, $\mathbf{y}^k$) of the current simplex σ that has the same integer label as $\bar{\mathbf{y}}$; that is, $l(\mathbf{y}^k) = l(\bar{\mathbf{y}}) \in T$ and $\mathbf{y}^k \neq \bar{\mathbf{y}}$.

3. Note that the current simplex $\sigma = \sigma(\mathbf{y}^1, \pi(T))$ has $t+1$ vertices $\mathbf{y}^1, \ldots,$ $\mathbf{y}^{t+1}$, defined recursively by $\mathbf{y}^{j+1} = \mathbf{y}^j + (1/D)\mathbf{q}(\pi_j)$ for $j = 1, \ldots, N-1$. If the vertex $\mathbf{y}^k$ in step 2 is the last vertex $\mathbf{y}^{t+1}$ of the current simplex σ (i.e., $k = t+1$), and if $r_{\pi_t} = 0$, then go to step 5. Otherwise, replace the vertex $\mathbf{y}^k$, the current simplex σ, and the vector $\mathbf{r}$ according to the following rules:

  (i) If $k = 1$: replace the vertex $\mathbf{y}^1$ by $\mathbf{y}^1 + (1/D)\mathbf{q}(\pi_1)$; replace the permutation $\pi(T) = (\pi_1, \ldots, \pi_2)$ by $(\pi_2, \ldots, \pi_t, \pi_1)$; and replace the vector $\mathbf{r} = (r_1, \ldots, r_n)$ by $\mathbf{r} + \mathbf{e}^{\pi_1}$.

  (ii) If $k = 2, \ldots, t$: replace only the permutation $\pi(T)$ by

$$(\pi_1, \ldots, \pi_{k-2}, \pi_k, \pi_{k-1}, \pi_{k+1}, \ldots, \pi_t).$$

  (iii) If $k = t+1$: replace the vertex $\mathbf{y}^1$ by $\mathbf{y}^1 - (1/D)\mathbf{q}(\pi_t)$; replace the permutation $\pi(T)$ by $(\pi_t, \pi_1, \ldots, \pi_{t-1})$; and replace the vector $\mathbf{r}$ by $\mathbf{r} - \mathbf{e}^{\pi_1}$.

Now set $\bar{\mathbf{y}}$ equal to the new vertex of $\sigma(\mathbf{y}^1, \pi(T))$ and return to step 1.

4. If $t = N-1$, then the current simplex $\sigma(\mathbf{y}^1, \pi(T))$ is completely labeled and the algorithm is terminated. Otherwise, increase the dimension of $\sigma(\mathbf{y}^1, \pi(T))$ by replacing T by $T \cup \{(l\bar{\mathbf{y}})\}$ and replacing $\pi(T)$ by $(\pi(T), (\bar{\mathbf{y}}))$. Note that t becomes $t+1$. Set $\bar{\mathbf{y}}$ equal to $\mathbf{y}^{t+1}$ and return to step 2.

5. Decrease the dimension of $\sigma(\mathbf{y}^1, \pi(T))$, replacing T by $T/\{(l\bar{\mathbf{y}})\}$ and $\pi(T)$ by $(\pi_1, \ldots, \pi_{t-1})$. Note that t becomes $t-1$. Set $\mathbf{y}^k$ equal to the vertex of $\sigma(\mathbf{y}^1, \pi(T))$ that has a label equal to the deleted integer π_t, and return to step 3.

As van der Laan and Talman (1979) demonstrate, their algorithm enables significant computational savings over Merrill's algorithm, although the coding involved is slightly more complex.

3.9 Using Newton methods to solve general equilibrium models

Despite the detail with which we have presented fixed point solution techniques for solving general equilibrium models, Newton methods are used in several recent applied general equilibrium models to compute counterfactual equilibria associated with changes in policies.[3] These

---

[3] An illustration of these Newton methods is in Piggott (1988).

procedures determine an equilibrium where all goods and factor markets clear for the whole economy, and where zero imbalances exist between government expenditures and revenues raised through taxes.

These methods solve the systems of nonlinear equations characterizing equilibrium by using successive linear approximations to the nonlinear system. Each approximation is solved until a true equilibrium solution is obtained. The equation system that characterizes equilibrium in a two-factor or other general equilibrium model cannot typically be written in closed form, since market demands are the sum of individual agent demands. As a result, point estimates of derivatives of market excess demand functions (contained in the Jacobian matrix of own- and cross-price derivatives of market demand functions) are repeatedly calculated and used to estimate successive adjustments to the initial guess of the equilibrium prices. These Newton steps allow large initial adjustments to the starting vector of prices. When necessary, the Jacobian matrix can be recalculated as computation proceeds. The weakness of Newton methods is that no general argument is available for convergence, but applied modelers who have used them seem not to have encountered nonconvergence difficulties.

Applying a Newton procedure to the solution of a two-factor general equilibrium model involves solving for a zero of excess factor demands and government imbalances. This can be represented as a special case of the more general problem of finding a zero for a system of N excess demand functions:

$$G_i = G_i(P_1, \ldots, P_N) \quad (i = 1, \ldots, N). \tag{3.34}$$

The Jacobian matrix J contains the derivatives of the excess demand functions with respect to the prices:

$$J = \left[\frac{\partial G_i}{\partial P_j} \right] \quad (i = 1, \ldots, N, \ j = 1, \ldots, N). \tag{3.35}$$

At any trial set of prices, $\mathbf{P}$, the excess demand functions $G_i(\mathbf{P})$ can be evaluated. Using the elements of the Jacobian matrix, the changes in each price, ΔP_i^*, required to eliminate the excess demand $G_i(\mathbf{P})$ can be calculated:

$$\Delta P_i^* = \sum_{j=1}^{N} \frac{\partial P_i}{\partial G_j} \cdot G_j(\mathbf{P}) \quad (i = 1, \ldots, N). \tag{3.36}$$

Some multiple $k\Delta P_i^*$ is added to the price P_i to give a further trial solution $\hat{P}_i = P_i + k\Delta P_i^*$ for each commodity, with the $\hat{P}_i$ renormalized to sum to unity. This results in a new evaluation of the excess demand functions, a further application of derivatives appearing in the Jacobian matrix, and a continuation of the procedure. The procedure terminates when all $G_i(\mathbf{P})$ are within a desired criterion of closeness to zero. The adjustment factor k is typically determined on a trial-and-error basis.

In practice, the choice of the initial starting value and the adjustment factors used in such methods is very important to their successful implementation. In solving applied models, the benchmark equilibrium is typically used as the starting value. An issue affecting the speed of solution is the number of times one must recalculate the Jacobian matrix. In practice, a flexible procedure seems to be most commonly followed. With an initial Jacobian matrix, if convergence is found to be slow or if successive adjustments produce divergence rather than convergence in solution, further calculation of the Jacobian matrix takes place. Calculating a Jacobian matrix requires N function evaluations, and recalculation at each step is avoided as much as possible.

Computational experience with these procedures by applied modelers has generally been good. If the Jacobian matrix in the neighborhood of the benchmark equilibrium is already known, and if relatively small policy changes are being considered, full equilibrium solutions can be obtained in a small number of evaluations of the excess demand functions $G_i(\mathbf{P})$. Where larger changes are involved, more function evaluations may be necessary and, in addition, several new Jacobian matrices may be required, which increases costs. Execution costs thus change from equilibrium solution to equilibrium solution.

PART II

Applying the techniques

4

Designing an applied general equilibrium model

In applying general equilibrium analysis to policy questions, a series of further issues typically arises, not concerned so much with the broad theoretical framework as with how to implement a model that captures the features of the policy being analyzed. This chapter discusses some of the design issues that have been encountered in the models built thus far, and that would also likely be encountered in any modeling work with which the reader may subsequently become involved.

4.1 Some examples of applied general equilibrium models

The applied general equilibrium models in operation today differ substantially from one another. Some are large-scale multipurpose models; others, small-scale issue-specific models. They vary in their country of application, use of functional forms, and treatment of such issues as time, foreign trade, and the government sector. Their use of data and parameter values also varies. In this section we describe some of the more prominent models in the areas of taxation and international trade, drawing upon the presentation in Shoven and Whalley (1984), so as to provide more focus to the subsequent discussion of design issues in specifying models.

Tax models

The main characteristics of some applied general equilibrium tax models are presented in Table 4.1; the data used in these models is given in Table 4.2; and some of the more significant features of their results are reported in Table 4.3.

In these models, taxes are all treated in *ad valorem*–equivalent form, and the government budget is balanced in equilibrium. The taxes that appear as part of a typical modern tax system (income, corporate, property,

71

Table 4.1. *Main features of some applied general equilibrium tax models*

| Model | Country | Demand side | | Production side | |
		Demand functions	Disaggregation	Production functions	Disaggregation
Ballard, Fullerton, Shoven, and Whalley (1985)	United States	Derived from nested CES/Cobb–Douglas utility functions	12 consumer income groups	CES or Cobb–Douglas production functions; fixed-coefficient use of intermediate inputs	19 industries 16 final demand categories
Ballentine and Thirsk (1979)	Canada	Differential equations giving quantity changes in terms of elasticities	12 income classes	Differential equations giving quantity changes in terms of elasticities	12 production sectors 7 final production categories
Keller (1980)	Netherlands	Derived from nested CES utility functions	4 demand sectors: skilled and unskilled labor, public, foreign	Nested CES production functions	4 industries
Piggott (1980)	Australia	Derived from nested CES utility functions	12 socioeconomic household groups, plus government, foreign, and corporate sectors	CES value-added production functions with intermediate production structure allowing substitutability between domestic and foreign inputs	18 domestic industries 14 foreign industries
Piggott and Whalley (1985)	United Kingdom	Derived from nested CES utility functions	100 socioeconomic household groups, plus public, investment, and external sectors	CES value-added production functions; fixed-coefficient use of intermediate goods	33 industries

72

Study	Country	Demand side	Consumer groups	Production	Industries
Serra-Puche (1984)	Mexico	Derived from Cobb–Douglas utility functions	10 rural/urban income groups, plus government, plus the rest of the world	Cobb–Douglas production functions	14 industries producing 15 final consumption goods
Shoven and Whalley (1972)	United States	Derived from Cobb–Douglas utility functions	2 income groups	CES production functions	2 industries: corporate and noncorporate
Slemrod (1983)	United States	Derived from Cobb–Douglas utility functions	9 income groups	Cobb–Douglas production functions	4 industries 6 income-generating assets
Whalley (1975)	United Kingdom	Derived from CES utility functions	7 income groups	CES production functions	9 industries

Table 4.2. *Sources for data and elasticities in the tax models of Table 4.1*

Model	Base year for data	Extraneous use of elasticities	Production data	Demand data	Taxes incorporated in the model
Ballard, Fullerton, Shoven, and Whalley (1985)	1973	Labor supply; savings (literature search); production elasticities of substitution between capital and labor (literature search)	National accounts; input–output tables	Consumer expenditure survey; taxation statistics	All existing U.S. taxes including corporate, income, social security, sales, and property taxes
Ballentine and Thirsk (1979)	1969	Factor substitution; price and income demand elasticities (literature search)	Input–output tables; national accounts data	Budget share	Corporate, property, and income taxes
Keller (1980)	1973	Income elasticities of demand (from survey data); elasticities of substitution in production and consumption (best guess)	National accounts; input–output tables	National accounts; personal income distribution survey; budget survey; savings survey	Taxes on consumer goods and services, on capital goods, imports, labor, capital, and corporate income; lump-sum taxes
Piggott (1980)	1972–3	Elasticities of substitution in production (literature search); elasticities of substitution in demand (literature search and best guess)	National income and expenditure accounts; input–output tables	National income and expenditure accounts; household expenditure survey	All existing Australian taxes and subsidies including income and sales taxes, production taxes and subsidies, and factor taxes and subsidies

Study	Year	Elasticities	Data source	Data source	Taxes
Piggott and Whalley (1985)	1973	Elasticities of substitution in demand and production (literature search)	National accounts; input–output tables	National accounts; family expenditure survey	All major U.K. taxes and subsidies including income, corporate, property, excise, social security, and value-added taxes and housing and agricultural subsidies
Serra-Puche (1984)	1977	Unitary substitution elasticities in demand and production	Input–output tables	Survey of family income and expenditure	All existing Mexican taxes, including turnover taxes, special taxes, income taxes, tariffs, and export taxes
Shoven and Whalley (1972)	1953–9 (average)	Elasticities of substitution in production (various specifications)	Literature source	Literature source	Taxes on income from capital
Slemrod (1983)	1977	Unitary substitution elasticities in demand and production	Extraneously specified Cobb–Douglas exponents	Survey of financial characteristics of consumers; income and expenditure data	Corporate and property taxes
Whalley (1975)	1968–70 (average)	Elasticities of substitution in production and demand (best guess and literature search)	National accounts	National accounts	Major U.K. taxes including purchase and excise taxes, income taxes, corporation taxes, rates (property tax), and national insurance (social security)

Table 4.3. *Major policy findings from tax models listed in Table 4.1*

Model	Policy interventions incorporated	Policy data used	Policy conclusions
Ballard, Fullerton, Shoven, and Whalley (1985)	Integration analysis: four alternative plans for corporate and personal income tax integrations. Consumption tax alternatives: change in the tax treatment of savings.	U.S. personal and corporate income taxes	Total integration of personal and corporate income taxes yields gains whose discounted present value is $500 billion or 1% of national income. Total integration with scaling to preserve tax yields leads to a progressive change in income distribution even though every class is better off. Consumption tax alternatives yield gains of $650 billion in present-value terms.
Ballentine and Thirsk (1979)	Changes in local government expenditures, corporate and property income taxes, federal income taxes, and housing subsidies	Tax and expenditure data	Personal income taxes markedly progressive while property and corporate income taxes have a more mixed incidence pattern. Incidence effects of different expenditure programs small.
Keller (1980)	Changes in marginal tax rates in various production and consumption sectors	Major taxes in the Netherlands (value-added, corporate, social security, and income)	Efficiency effects of taxes generally small (excepting corporate income tax); only small amounts of tax shifting
Piggott (1980)	Total and sectoral abolition of taxes and subsidies under various model parameter specifications	Existing Australian sectoral taxes and subsidies	Replacing all taxes and subsidies with an equal-yield replacement tax leads to decrease in total domestic final demand: demand for imports rises modestly and world demand for Australian exports rises dramatically. Replacing all taxes and subsidies with an equal-yield export tax leads to total welfare gain of 3.5% of Australian NDP.

Piggott and Whalley (1985)	Variations in U.K. taxes and subsidies	Existing U.K. taxes and subsidies	Existing U.K. tax system yields distorting losses of 6%–9% of NNP per year. Subsidies to local authority housing area are a significant source of welfare loss. Significant redistributive effects of taxes.
Serra-Puche (1984)	Replacement of indirect turnover taxes with consumption value-added tax (as instituted in Mexico in 1981)	Existing Mexican turnover taxes, specific goods taxes, income taxes, tariffs, and export taxes	Resource allocation moved in favor of the government target sectors (agriculture and foodstuffs); income distribution improved, reducing differentials between urban and rural households.
Shoven and Whalley (1972)	Imposition and removal of existing taxes on income from capital under various model parameter specifications	Existing U.S. capital income taxes (corporate, property, and personal income, including capital gains)	In 6 of the 12 cases examined, capital bears more than the full burden of the surtax; in the remaining 6 cases, labor shares in the burden
Slemrod (1983)	Complete indexation of U.S. tax system for inflation	Existing U.S. corporate and property taxes	Indexing the U.S. tax system leads to aggregate efficiency gains, with the lowest income groups experiencing slight losses and the highest income groups receiving substantial gains.
Whalley (1975)	1973 U.K. tax reform	1973 U.K. taxation changes represented in model-equivalent form	Welfare gain from 1973 U.K. tax changes found to be small and in some cases may be negative. Replacement of purchase tax and SET by VAT appears to yield welfare losses, while changes made to income-tax systems may yield gains.

77

sales, excise, and social security taxes) have all been analyzed. For instance, corporate and property taxes are usually treated as part of a larger system of taxes on capital income, with rates varying across industries. An emphasis on the twin issues of efficiency and distributional impacts of taxes appears in most of the work.

Shoven and Whalley (1972, 1973) were the first to analyze taxes using a full general equilibrium computational procedure. In their 1972 paper, an artificial commodity is used to incorporate the tax distortions, which effectively limits the applicability of the analysis to one tax at a time. In 1973, they developed a procedure to deal with several simultaneous tax distortions without using artificial commodities. Scarf's algorithm enables the existence of a tax equilibrium to be shown, and also provides a method through which such equilibria can be computed.

This method of simultaneously incorporating several tax distortions was used by Whalley (1975) to examine the impact of 1973 tax changes in the United Kingdom, and this work was further developed by Piggott and Whalley (1977, 1985) into a 33-product and 100-household-type model that has been used to evaluate structural characteristics of the United Kingdom's tax/subsidy system.

Two models closely related to the Shoven–Whalley work are those by Piggott (1980) on Australia and Serra-Puche (1984) on Mexico. Piggott's model differs from the other tax models in using two-stage CES (constant elasticity of substitution) production functions with differing types of capital and labor. At one stage, different types of labor "produce" the aggregate labor input and, correspondingly, different types of capital services "produce" the aggregate capital input. At the second stage, aggregate labor and capital combine to produce value added. Serra-Puche analyzes tax incidence in Mexico in a model with three factors. Subsequent work by Kehoe and Serra-Puche (1983) has used a similar approach to analyze the 1980 fiscal reform in Mexico, incorporating unemployment generated by an exogenously specified, downward-rigid real wage.

Keller's (1980) tax model of Holland differs from the Shoven–Whalley work in using a local linearization procedure to solve for the tax-change equilibria. Four groups of agents on the demand side are incorporated. Government and the foreign sector are separately identified, along with low-income/unskilled-labor and high-income/skilled-labor groups. Keller's incidence analysis concentrates on distributional effects between these two latter groups.

Ballentine and Thirsk (1979) also use a local linearization approach in their general equilibrium tax work on Canada. Their main concern is incidence analysis of changes in financing arrangements (including intergovernmental transfers) for local government expenditures, such as increases in federal, personal, or corporate taxes to finance increased municipal expenditures. No explicit functional forms for demand and production are used, but are implied by the configuration of elasticities adopted. On the demand side, for instance, they are careful to ensure that Engel and Slutsky aggregation conditions are satisfied by the elasticities chosen. Total differentials through the equilibrium conditions yield approximate estimates of changes between equilibria. An especially interesting departure in this model is the attempt to incorporate a degree of factor mobility, both domestically among regions and internationally.

The main departures from the basic general equilibrium structure outlined in Chapter 2 appear where the modeling of time and the treatment of financial assets are addressed. The 1985 Ballard, Fullerton, Shoven, and Whalley (BFSW) model of the United States incorporates all major distorting taxes as in earlier work, but differs from other models in the incorporation of time through dynamic sequencing of single-period equilibria. In the BFSW model, a number of commodities and industries appear as in the static models, but saving decisions in any period are made by households based on myopic expectations regarding the future rate of return to capital. Household savings determine the demand for capital goods produced in the period; this treatment allows each period's equilibrium to be computed without requiring information on future periods' prices.

Savings result in an increase in the capital stock, and affect intertemporal behavior through changed consumption possibilities in future periods. Calibration is made to an assumed steady-state growth path in the presence of existing tax policies, rather than to a single benchmark equilibrium. A change in policy displaces the economy from the balanced growth path. After a transition period,[1] the economy settles on a new growth path with an alternative capital–labor ratio. The pairwise comparison between equilibria in static models is replaced by a pairwise comparison between the equilibrium sequences under the alternative policy regimes. The restrictive assumption of myopic expectations can be replaced by a perfect-foresight approach (or a limited-foresight specification), as shown by Ballard and Goulder (1982a, b), although significantly more computation costs are involved. Bovenberg and Keller (1983) have also extended Keller's model to analyze tax incidence over time by adding dynamic features similar to those introduced by BFSW.

The treatment of financial assets has been addressed in Slemrod's (1983) model of the United States, which differs from earlier models in incorporating endogenous financial behavior of both households and firms into the general equilibrium approach. His work is motivated by the extensive

---

[1] The economy does not jump instantaneously to the new balanced growth path, because changes in the capital stock cannot exceed domestic savings in the model. As long as savings cause the capital stock to grow at a rate different from the labor growth rate, factor prices will be changing along the transitional path.

literature on modeling the corporate tax as a tax on all capital income originating in the corporate sector. The rate of tax on capital income depends not only on the sector of origin, but also on the financial arrangements that accompany the flow of income. Slemrod introduces uncertainty into his model through stochastic production function parameters. A risk-aversion parameter is introduced into the preference functions, which are defined over both expected consumption and the variance of income. Both risky and riskless assets yield capital income, resulting in a portfolio-allocation problem for households in addition to the usual budget problem generating consumption demands. Household commodity and asset demands are based on maximization of a two-stage preference function, the first stage incorporating the risk-aversion parameter. Market clearing for all goods and assets is incorporated in the model. The supply response in financial assets is based on an extraneous elasticity that determines the response of the firm's debt–equity ratio to changes in the relative tax costs of debt and equity. The model is parameterized to represent a "stylized" economy, rather than calibrated to an exact benchmark equilibrium as in the other models.

Trade models

Applied trade models differ from tax models in that they are based on a more varied heritage and have a more diffuse focus. Some are multi-country models designed to analyze global issues. Other, single-country models investigate how developments abroad affect individual economies. Some models are oriented exclusively to trade-policy questions; others are general-purpose modeling efforts, with only one part providing the capability to analyze trade questions. Some are models of developed economies, while others analyze developing economies where trade-policy issues are often quite different.

We also display the details of some of these models in tabular form, drawing upon the presentation in Shoven and Whalley (1984). Tables 4.4 and 4.5 summarize the main characteristics of the models, along with sources for data and elasticity values. Table 4.6 presents summaries of the major policy implications of results obtained thus far. To aid presentation in the tables, we separate the models into multicountry and single-country groups. Some of the design issues raised by these models are discussed in Chapters 8 and 9.

These applied trade models are based on the traditional framework emphasized in pure trade theory: Countries export commodities in which they have a comparative advantage. The differences among models reflect the ways in which comparative advantage is incorporated, as well as the modeling of the policy regimes.

The most prevalent approach in modern trade theory is that associated with Heckscher (1949) and Ohlin (1933). Within this framework, each country involved in trade has production functions and demand functions; in "strong" versions, identical production and demand parameters are assumed across countries. Trade is determined by the factor intensities of production and by the relative factor abundance among countries.

In contrast, the multicountry models listed in Tables 4.4 and 4.6 are not assumed to have identical production and demand parameters. Thus trade is determined on the basis of more than just differences in relative factor endowments. A further characteristic common to most of the multicountry and single-country models is the use of the so-called Armington assumption, which treats products produced in different regions as qualitatively different (i.e., heterogeneous rather than homogeneous) across countries, as in a traditional Heckscher–Ohlin model.

The reasons for this treatment are multifold, revealing the compromises that empirical modelers often have to make. In addition to the problems created by the presence of "crosshauling" in trade data, some of the early trade models encountered the difficulty that unrealistically strong specialization effects were produced when a change in trade policy occurred. This reflected the use of homogeneous products and production possibility frontiers that were close to linear, so that a small change in trade policy resulted in large moves toward specialization. The Armington treatment avoids these difficulties.

Also, the key empirical parameters to which many of the models are calibrated are import- and export-demand elasticities; in a model with homogeneous products, there is no simple import-demand elasticity unless the economy is completely specialized. Unless the Armington assumption is used, calibration becomes difficult because there is only a demand for the imported commodity (some of which is also domestically produced).

A major difference between the multicountry and single-country models is the way in which the determinants of trade are modeled. In the multicountry models, there is a specification of production and demand for all of the countries participating in trade. This is not the case for single-country models, whose focus on the implications of trade policy for a single country entails adoption of a cruder modeling for the rest of the world. Usually a "closing rule" is adopted for trade with the rest of the world (i.e., a simple specification of the import-supply and export-demand functions). This may be complemented by a specification of capital flows and other external-sector characteristics. The use of such external-sector closing rules in these models can be quite important, as emphasized by Whalley and Yeung (1984). Another major difference between the multicountry and single-country models is the capability of the multicountry

Table 4.4. *Main features of some applied general equilibrium trade models*

Model	Countries	Demand side		Production side	
		Demand functions	Disaggregation	Production functions	Disaggregation
Multicountry models					
Gunning, Carrin, and Waelbroeck (1982)	11 groups of less developed countries and the rest of the world	Demand for CES import–export composite goods modeled as Extended Linear Expenditure System (ELES) for each consumer group	2 consumer groups (rural, urban) for each region, plus a rudimentary rest of the world	CES value-added functions plus fixed-coefficient intermediate use of composite goods in the urban sectors; linear production functions in the rural sectors	6 production sectors (2 rural, 4 urban) in each regional model
Deardorff and Stern (1981)	18 major industrialized countries, 16 major developing countries, and the rest of the world	Cobb–Douglas utility functions; CES between home and imported goods in the same industry	34 countries plus the rest of the world	CES value-added functions; fixed-coefficient intermediate use of CES composites of home and imported goods[a]	22 tradable and 7 nontradable industries for each of the 34 countries, plus a residual rest of the world
Manne and Preckel (1983)	3 regions: industrialized countries; oil-exporting developing countries; oil-importing developing countries	Demand for energy and nonenergy imports derived from CES production functions	3 regions: industrialized countries; oil-exporting developing countries; oil-importing developing countries	Nested CES	Energy and aggregated nonenergy commodities for each region

Study	Countries/regions	Demand derivation	Consumers	Production	Commodities
Miller and Spencer (1977)	4 "countries": U.K.; (6-member) EEC; Australia and New Zealand; rest of the world	Derived from 2-stage CES utility functions	4 "countries": U.K.; (6-member) EEC; Australia and New Zealand; rest of the world	Cobb–Douglas	2 commodities per country (agriculture and nonagriculture)
Whalley (1982)	EEC, U.S., Japan, rest of the world	Derived from nested CES utility functions	41 consuming groups comprising households, government, investment (stratified by income in U.S. and Japan and by region in EEC)	CES value-added functions; fixed-coefficient intermediate use of CES domestic-import composites	33 commodities in each of 4 regions
Whalley (1985)	7 trade blocs: U.S.; EEC; Japan; other developed countries; OPEC; newly industrialized countries; less developed countries	Derived from nested CES–LES utility functions	7 trade blocs	Nested CES value-added functions; fixed-coefficient intermediate use of composite inputs	6 commodities in each of 7 trade blocs
Single-country models					
Boadway and Treddenick (1978)	Canada	Domestic final demand for each CES composite good is unit-price and income elastic; import supply and export demand own-price–dependent only (constant elasticity)	Domestic demand for final goods; world demand for domestic exports	3 alternate specifications: fixed intermediate coefficients with Cobb–Douglas functions for labor and capital; fixed intermediate coefficients with CES functions for labor and capital; variable coefficients with Cobb–Douglas functions	2 alternate aggregations of industries: (1) 16 groups, and (2) 56 groups
Dervis, de Melo, and Robinson (1982)	Turkey	Constant expenditure proportions for import-export composite goods	One aggregate household[b]	2-level CES production functions; fixed coefficient use of intermediate goods	19 industries 3 labor types

Table 4.4 (cont.)

| Model | Countries | Demand side | | Production side | |
		Demand functions	Disaggregation	Production functions	Disaggregation
Dixon, Parmenter, Sutton, and Vincent (1982)	Australia	Derived from Klein–Rubin utility functions with CES aggregation of comparable imported and domestic goods	Effectively one household	4-level input functions: (1) Leontief between inputs of composite products, (2) CES between imported and domestic products, (3) CRESH between primary factors, (4) CRESH between labor inputs; CRESH output functions	114 commodities (112 industries)

[a] Alternative assumptions are used in other versions of this model.
[b] In Ch. 13 of Dervis et al., the model is disaggregated to include 7 socioeconomic household groups in order to study income distribution effects.

Table 4.5. *Sources for data and elasticities in the trade models of Table 4.4*

Model	Base year	Base-year data	Extraneous use of elasticities	Production data	Demand data	Trade data
Multicountry models						
Gunning, Carrin, and Waelbroeck (1982)	1978	From World Bank data for 1978	Elasticity of substitution between domestic goods and imports; export demand elasticity; elasticity of substitution between capital and labor in urban sectors	World Bank data	World Bank data	World Bank data
Deardorff and Stern (1981)	1976	Derived from various sources	Import demand and production function elasticities; elasticity of substitution between home and imported goods (literature search)	UN industrial data, OECD labor force statistics, and national accounts data	OECD national accounts data	UN trade data
Manne and Preckel (1983)	1980 (with projection to 1990 and 2000)	Based on 1980 World Bank data	Elasticities of substitution between domestic and imported commodities (various specifications)	World Bank regional data on GNP and energy production; Royal Dutch/Shell supply forecasts	World Bank regional data on GNP and energy consumption	World Bank data
Miller and Spencer (1977)	1960 (Production) 1968 (Demand)	Based on data from various sources	Production elasticities (literature search); elasticities of substitution between domestic and imported goods, and between goods from each production sector	Derived principally from Denison (1967)	Derived principally from OECD foreign trade statistics	OECD foreign trade statistics

Table 4.5 *(cont.)*

Model	Base year	Base-year data	Extraneous use of elasticities	Production data	Demand data	Trade data
Whalley (1982)	1973	Constructed international benchmark data set	Elasticities of substitution between home and imported goods and within product categories (best guess); elasticity of substitution in production (literature search)	Input–output plus value-added data (capital and labor return) for each region	Household expenditure data disaggregated across traded goods using foreign trade data	OECD trade statistics; balance-of-payments accounts
Whalley (1985)	1977	Constructed benchmark data set	Production elasticities of substitution; demand elasticities of substitution within good categories, between categories, and between imported and domestic goods (literature search, central case, and various specifications)	UN national accounts data	Calculated as a residual	UN, UNCTAD, and OECD trade statistics
Single-country models						
Boadway and Treddenick (1978)	1966	1966 input–output table	Production elasticities of substitution (literature search); world elasticities of supply of imports and demand for exports; domestic elasticities of substitution between domestic and imported goods (various specifications)	Input–output table	Input–output table	Input–output table

Dervis, de Melo, and Robinson (1982)	1973	Constructed benchmark data set, with some parameters adjusted to fit dynamic (1973–6) trends	Elasticities of substitution in production; elasticities of substitution between domestic and imported goods; export demand elasticities (various specifications)	Input–output table; Census of Manufacturing Industries data	Input–output table; population census data	Input–output table
Dixon, Parmenter, Sutton, and Vincent (1982)	1968–9	Constructed 1968–9 input–output data base from government and agricultural statistics	Extensive elasticities file (literature search and best guess)	Constructed input–output table	Constructed input–output table	Constructed input–output table

Source: From Denison (1967), used by permission of The Brookings Institution.

Table 4.6. *Major policy findings from trade models listed in Table 4.4*

Model	Policy interventions incorporated	Policy data used	Policy conclusions
Multicountry models Gunning, Carrin, and Waelbroeck (1982)	8 simulation experiments to evaluate the impact on LCDs of changes in (1) RoW growth; (2) capital flows to LDCs; (3) oil prices; (4) RoW's income elasticity of imports	Simulation experiments; no data required	Impact on LDCs of exogenous changes is limited: suggests that LDC growth is less sensitive to RoW growth rate than earlier fixed-price models would indicate
Deardorff and Stern (1981)	Tokyo Round changes in tariff and nontariff barriers (agricultural quota concessions, government procurement liberalization)	Post-Kennedy Round base-rate tariffs; Tokyo Round offer-rate tariffs; quantification of nontariff barriers	Economic welfare will increase in all industrialized countries except Australia, New Zealand and the Netherlands. Welfare will decrease in most of the developing countries
Manne and Preckel (1983)	Alternative scenarios incorporating: 2 assumptions on energy supply; 2 assumptions on energy demand; 2 assumptions on capital flows	Alternative energy supply and demand scenarios	Increases in world oil prices have very little effect on GDP growth in industrialized countries, but could have a major (negative) impact on the terms of trade of oil-importing developing countries, inducing GDP growth substantially.
Miller and Spencer (1977)	Removal of U.K.–EEC tariffs and U.K.–Commonwealth preferences	U.K.–EEC and U.K.–Commonwealth tariffs and transfers	U.K. entry into EEC increases U.K. imports of EEC-manufactured goods by 50%, but increases U.K. income by only 1/6 of 1%; with transfer to EEC of 1.5% of income, U.K. net loss is 1.8% of national income.

Whalley (1982)	Changes in tariffs, nontariff barriers, and taxes in the EEC, U.S., and Japan	World welfare gain from tariff cuts no greater than 0.1% of world GNP; EEC and Japan gain proportionally more than U.S. or RoW, but this could be offset by proposed changes in nontariff barriers.
Whalley (1985)	Abolition of tariff and nontariff barriers in the North, the South, and in both regions simultaneously	Abolition of tariff and nontariff barriers in: (1) the North results in annual welfare gains of $21 billion, the majority of which accrues to the LDCs and NICs; (2) the South leads to annual gains of $17 billion, but with a $65 billion gain to the North and a $48 billion loss to the South; (3) both North and South yields world welfare gain of $30 billion, with gains accruing to the North and losses to the South.
Single-country models		
Boadway and Treddenick (1978)	Elimination of tariffs; elimination of tariffs along with taxes (commodity and capital income)	Similar results for all cases studied (excepting variations in export demand elasticity): when tariffs are removed, the welfare index falls by 1.16% (when export demand elasticity = 1) and rises by 0.06% when export demand elasticity = 25; when taxes and tariffs are removed, the welfare index falls by 2.63% with unit export demand elasticity and rises by 0.27% with export demand elasticity of 25.

89

Table 4.6 (cont.)

Model	Policy interventions incorporated	Policy data used	Policy conclusions
Dervis, de Melo, and Robinson (1982)	Setting a 50% tariff on imports; giving a 50% subsidy to exports; examining 1977 Turkish foreign exchange crisis	Simulation experiments and actual events; no data required	Imposing a 50% tariff in one sector at a time produces small short-run allocational effects, with no sector experiencing more than a 5% change in output. A 50% export subsidy has greater effect on domestic output than does the 50% tariff: the home country is more sensitive to export-side than import-side disturbances. Causes of the 1977 foreign exchange crisis in Turkey were principally differential domestic inflation and increases in oil prices.
Dixon, Parmenter, Sutton, and Vincent (1982)	A 25% across-the-board increase in Australian import tariffs	Simulation experiment; no data required	A 25% increase in all protection rates leads to a 0.21% fall in total employment, an increased deficit in the balance of trade, and increases in consumer and capital goods prices.

models to analyze multilateral trade policy issues such as those involved with customs unions, trade liberalization under the GATT, or any other trade policy change simultaneously involving a number of countries. Single-country models are typically inappropriate for analyzing this class of policy issues.

The models also use different approaches in their treatments of trade-protection policies. Most models incorporate tariffs, but varying attempts have been made to incorporate nontariff barriers. A simple way to incorporate nontariff barriers is through *ad valorem*-equivalent tariffs, but this can be inappropriate in a number of cases. For example, the effect of a quantity constraint is such that the *ad valorem*-equivalent tariff would not remain unchanged as prices change in a model. In turn, nontariff barriers in developed and developing countries are quite different. Developing countries typically have import licensing, usually accompanied by foreign-exchange rationing, and – as is evident from the Dervis–de Melo–Robinson (1982) work on Turkey and other countries – a careful modeling of these policies is crucial to an understanding of the policy issues involved.

A further issue that emerges in more recent work concerns modeling the production side. Although not summarized in the tables, recent work by Harris (1984) has emphasized how both scale economies and industrial organization features, stressed in some of the recent international trade–theory literature, can have important implications for numerical results of the impacts of trade-policy changes. Harris emphasizes that if scale economies are large enough and the trade-policy issues involve countries of different size, as is true in the U.S.–Canadian case, then incorporating scale economies can substantially change estimates of the impact of trade policies. A similar theme appears in earlier work by Dixon (1978).

Another issue with these models concerns the role of exchange rates and the related issue of international capital flows, since the traditional pure theory of international trade produces no real effects from exchange-rate changes. If a monetized extension of a classical general equilibrium model (in which a money-demand function by region along with specified levels of national money stocks) were used to analyze trade policy changes, neutrality would prevail in the sense that the real and financial behavior of the system would be entirely independent. Once real behavior is known, specifying national money stocks in each of the regions simply serves to determine domestic price levels and exchange rates. Alternatively, should a fixed-exchange-rate regime be analyzed, one can calculate the national money stocks necessary to support the equilibrium and achieve the desired exchange rates.

The models summarized in Tables 4.4 and 4.6 do not all follow this classical approach to neutrality. This is especially the case with the single-country models where, in a number of instances, exchange rates appear in the formulation. In some cases these exchange-rate terms refer to the real exchange rate between traded and nontraded goods; however, in a number of models, results are reported for changes in exchange rates with the appearance that these changes have real effects. This can make the interpretation of results difficult from a theoretical point of view.

The approach in most models is to exclude international capital flows; where capital flows are present, countries are typically modeled as takers of rental rates on world capital markets and therefore face perfectly elastic capital-supply functions. This issue has been analyzed for tax models by Goulder, Shoven, and Whalley (1983), who have shown how the treatment of international capital flows can significantly affect results. Intuitively, a similar conclusion could apply for analysis of trade policy.

4.2 Choosing the model structure in designing an application

Although the general equilibrium model appropriate for any particular application depends largely on the policy issues being addressed, most applied models currently in use have a similar form. They are typically variants of static, two-factor models that have long been employed in public finance and international trade, and are associated with the work of Heckscher, Ohlin, Samuelson, Meade, Johnson, and Harberger. Most models involve more than two goods, while aggregating the factors of production into two broad types – capital and labor. In some models, these composite factors are disaggregated into subgroups (e.g., skilled versus nonskilled labor). Intermediate transactions are also usually incorporated, either through fixed- or flexible-coefficient input–output matrices.

It seems reasonable to ask why most models have evolved in this way when it is possible to use more general specifications, possibly involving joint production[2] and more primary inputs than simply the composite factors of capital and labor. Although it is possible that richer structures will gradually appear in future work, at present three reasons seem to account for the popularity of the basic two-factor structure.

First, many policy issues have already been analyzed theoretically using this framework. If the major contribution of numerical work is to advance from qualitative to quantitative analysis, it is clearly natural to retain the same basic theoretical structure. In this way, researchers can use the intuition gleaned from theoretical work to guide numerical investigations of policy alternatives.

Second, most data on which numerical specifications are based comes in a form consistent with two-factor models. For instance, national ac-

---

[2] The ORANI model of Dixon et al. (1982) incorporates joint production with empirically estimated transformation frontiers.

counts data identifies wages and salaries and operating surpluses as major cost components; this suggests using models with capital and labor as inputs. Input–output data provides intermediate transaction data, with value added broken down in a similar way.

Finally, the partition between goods and factors can be used in applied models to simplify computation and significantly reduce the costs of repeated equilibrium solution. In Chapter 3 it was shown how factor prices can generate cost-covering goods prices, which in turn can be used to evaluate consumer demands and finally the derived demands for factors (i.e., those amounts needed to meet consumer demands). In this way, even a model with large numbers of goods can be solved by working with a system of excess factor demands only. This simplification not only reduces execution costs, but also makes feasible the incorporation of a larger number of commodities and more detail in the treatment of households.

However, elaborations on the basic two-factor structure can and have been used. In some cases, static equilibrium models have been sequenced through time to reflect changes in the economy's capital stock due to net savings. Models with this structure have been used to analyze intertemporal issues in tax policy, such as the efficiency advantages of a move from an income tax to a consumption tax (under which savings are less heavily taxed). A consumption tax will also cause lowered consumption in the initial years, with an eventual higher consumption level due to the larger capital stock.

Under the sequenced equilibrium approach, a series of single-period equilibria are linked through savings decisions that change the capital stock of the economy through time. Savings depend on the expected future return to assets acquired in the current period, with myopic expectations frequently assumed to simplify computations (i.e., expected future returns on assets are assumed to equal current returns). In each period a general equilibrium is computed in which all markets clear, including the market for newly produced capital goods.

Other aspects of model design include the treatment of investment and government expenditures. Investment in closed-economy models usually reflects household savings decisions (broadly defined to include corporate retentions), which are based either on constant expenditure shares in static models or on intertemporal utility maximization in dynamic formulations. Government expenditures are usually broken down into transfers and real expenditures. The latter are frequently determined from utility-maximizing behavior for government: that is, the government is treated as a separate consuming agent that buys public goods and services. Usually the derivation of the demand for public goods is not dealt with, although in a few cases models have been used with public goods in household utility functions.

A further set of issues are raised by model preselection (i.e., the necessity to decide on a particular model structure before the policy analysis proceeds). A good way of illustrating this problem is to consider the classic Harberger (1959) analysis of the impacts of corporate tax. Using the standard assumption (in static models) of a closed economy with a fixed amount of capital, Harberger concludes that capital bears the burden of the corporate tax. Clearly, if the economy in question is viewed as a participant in an international capital market and as a taker of rental rates on world capital markets, then policy conclusions would change. In this case, it is impossible for capital to bear the burden of a capital tax, because the effect of the tax would simply be to cause capital to leave the country until the net-of-tax return is equal to that prevailing on the world markets. Model preselection can thus strongly affect the conclusions reached from the model, no matter what functional forms, level of aggregation, or data is used.

The fundamental difficulty is that there are many alternative theoretical models in the literature, each applicable to the policy question at hand and each yielding different policy implications. Applied general equilibrium analysis does not provide a way of discriminating between alternative models, because no form of hypothesis testing is involved. For example, the effects of a tariff are different in models with or without international factor mobility, and in models with or without a downward-rigid real wage. Conflicts among alternative economic theories cannot be resolved merely by putting numerical values on parameters in specified functional forms, and some degree of summary judgment by modelers in selecting the particular theoretical structure to be used seems inevitable.

4.3 Choosing functional forms

Another issue in model design is choice of functional forms. The major constraints on the specification of demand and production functions in applied models is that they be consistent with the theoretical approach and be analytically tractable. The first constraint involves choosing functions that satisfy the restrictions listed in Section 2.2, such as Walras's law for demand functions. The second constraint requires that the demand and supply responses from the economy be reasonably easy to evaluate for any price vector considered as a candidate equilibrium solution for the economy. This largely explains why the functional forms used are so often restricted to the family of "convenient" forms (Cobb–Douglas; constant elasticity of substitution (CES); linear expenditure system (LES);

Table 4.7. *Functional forms commonly used in applied general equilibrium models*

(1) Cobb–Douglas (C.D.)	$\prod_i X_i^{\alpha_i}$	$\sum_i \alpha_i = 1$
(2) CES	$\left[\sum_i \alpha_i^{1/\sigma} X_i^{(\sigma-1)/\sigma}\right]^{\sigma/(\sigma-1)}$	$\sum_i \alpha_i^{1/\sigma} = 1$
(3) LES (C.D.)	$\prod_i (X_i - C_i)^{\alpha_i}$	$\sum_i \alpha_i = 1$
(4) LES (CES)	$\left[\sum_i \alpha_i^{1/\sigma} (X_i - C_i)^{(\sigma-1)/\sigma}\right]^{\sigma/(\sigma-1)}$	$\sum_i \alpha_i^{1/\sigma} = 1$

Notes: For the Cobb–Douglas function, the terms α_i are expenditure shares in demand functions. For the CES function, σ is the elasticity of substitution in preferences between any pair of goods i, j. For the LES function, C_i are minimum requirements of each commodity in demand functions.

constant ratios of elasticities of substitution, homothetic (CRESH); translog; and others). The main functional forms used are listed in Table 4.7, and the associated demand and other functions in Tables 4.8–4.10.

The specific form chosen typically depends upon how elasticities are to be used in the model. This point is best illustrated by considering the demand side of models. Demands derived from Cobb–Douglas utility functions are easy to work with, but have the restrictions of unitary-income and uncompensated own-price elasticities, and zero uncompensated cross-price elasticities. These restrictions are typically implausible, given empirical estimates of elasticities applicable to any particular model, but can only be relaxed by using more general functional forms. With CES functions, unitary own-price elasticities no longer apply. However, if all expenditure shares are small, the compensated own-price elasticities equal the elasticity of substitution in preferences, and it may be unacceptable to model all commodities as having essentially the same compensated own-price elasticities. The unitary-income–elasticity feature of Cobb–Douglas and CES functions can also be relaxed; one way is to use LES functions with a displaced origin, but then the origin displacements need to be specified.

The general approach adopted by most modelers is to select the functional form that best allows key parameter values (e.g., income and price elasticities) to be incorporated, while retaining tractability. On the production side, CES value-added functions are usually used to allow for

Table 4.8. *Properties of Cobb–Douglas functions*[a]

Demand functions	$X_i = \dfrac{\alpha_i I}{P_i}$
Own-price (uncompensated) elasticity	$= -1$
Own-price (compensated) elasticity[b]	$= -(1-\alpha_i)$
Income elasticity	$= 1$
Cross-price (uncompensated) elasticities $= 0$	
Indirect utility function	$U = I \cdot \prod_i \left(\dfrac{\alpha_i}{P_i}\right)^{\alpha_i}$
Expenditure function (true cost-of-living index)	$E = \prod_i \left(\dfrac{P_i}{\alpha_i}\right)^{\alpha_i}$

[a] Utility maximization implies (max $U = \prod_i x_i^{\alpha_i}$ s.t. $\sum_i P_i X_i = I$).
[b] The relationship between compensated (η_i^c) and uncompensated (η_i^u) elasticities follows directly from the Slutsky equation $\eta_i^c = \eta_i^u + S_i \eta_i^I$, where S_i is the expenditure share on good i and η_i^I is the income elasticity of demand.

Table 4.9. *Properties of CES functions*[a]

Demand functions	$X_i = \dfrac{\alpha_i I}{P_i^\sigma \cdot \sum_j \alpha_j P_j^{(1-\sigma)}}$
Own-price (uncompensated) elasticity	$= -\sigma - (1-\sigma)\alpha_i P_i \gamma^{-1}$
Own-price (compensated) elasticity[b]	$= -\sigma(1 - \sigma_i P_i^{(1-\sigma)} \cdot \gamma^{-1})$, where $\gamma = \sum_j \alpha_j P_j C_j$
Income elasticity	$= 1$
Cross-price (uncompensated) elasticities $= -(1-\sigma)\alpha_j P_j^{(1-\sigma)} \gamma^{-1}$	
Indirect utility function	$U = I \cdot \left(\sum_j \alpha_j P_j^{(1-\sigma)}\right)$
Expenditure function (true cost-of-living index)	$E = \left(\sum_j \alpha_j P_j^{(1-\sigma)}\right)^{(1-\sigma)}$

[a] Utility maximization implies (max $U = [\sum_i \alpha_i^{1/\sigma} X_i^{(\sigma-1)/\sigma}]^{\sigma/(\sigma-1)}$ s.t. $\sum_i P_i X_i = I$).
[b] If the share parameters α_i are small, both compensated and uncompensated elasticities will be the same (as for the Cobb–Douglas case).

Table 4.10. *Properties of LES functions*

Demand functions	$X_i = C_i + \dfrac{\alpha_i(I - \Sigma_j P_j C_j)}{P_i}$
Own-price (uncompensated) elasticity	$= -1 - \alpha_i \dfrac{P_i C_i}{(P_i C_i + \alpha_i(I - \gamma)}$,
	where $\gamma = \sum_j P_j C_j$
Income elasticity	$= \dfrac{\alpha_i I}{P_i(C_i + \alpha_i(I - \gamma))}$
Indirect utility function	$U = (I - \gamma) \prod_i \left(\dfrac{\alpha_i}{P_i}\right)^{\alpha_i}$
Expenditure function (true cost-of-living index)	$E = \prod_i \left(\dfrac{P_i}{\alpha_i}\right)^{\alpha_i}$

substitution between primary factors. The intermediate production functions are sometimes modeled as fixed coefficients; on other occasions, some intermediate substitutability is allowed. A common specification used in international trade models is to allow fixed coefficients in terms of composite goods, but with substitution among the components of the composite. By way of example, a fixed steel requirement per car may be specified, but with substitution between imported and domestic steel represented by CES functions. This may be necessary because of the large amount of trade in intermediate products and the unrealistically low import-price elasticities that fixed-coefficient intermediate production would imply if the Armington treatment of differentiating products by country were used.

A further device widely employed in applied models is to use hierarchical (or nested) functions. Under this approach CES (or Cobb–Douglas) functions can be contained within CES functions, and many layers of hierarchy can be employed. The benefit of this approach is that it greatly expands the number of elasticity parameters that can be used to calibrate to estimates in the literature.

Examples of this are provided in Figures 4.1 and 4.2. Figure 4.1 displays the nesting structure for preferences used by Hamilton and Whalley (1985) in their analysis of tax treatment of housing. Their model uses a four-level nesting structure in specifying preference functions. At level one, the elasticity of substitution between current and future consumption appears; level two involves substitution between housing and nonhousing consumption services in each period; level three involves substitution

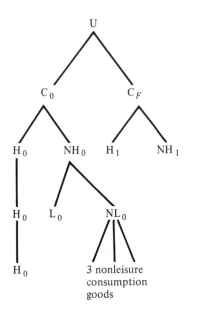

Level 1 (intertemporal substitutic

Level 2 (housing/nonhousing
choice in each period)

Level 3 (leisure/nonleisure
consumption choice)

Level 4 (substitution between
nonleisure goods)

Figure 4.1. Nesting structure in preferences used by Hamilton and Whalley (1985) (dynamic sequenced general equilibrium model, benchmarked to 1972 Canadian data set and balanced growth assumptions). *Source:* Redrawn from Hamilton and Whalley (1985), used by permission of Elsevier Science Publishing Company.

between leisure and nonleisure in each period; and level four involves substitution between nonleisure goods. While at any level the elasticity of demand functions is affected by elasticities at other levels, the dominant influence is the elasticity specified at the level in question. Thus, level-one elasticities are chosen to calibrate to estimates of the elasticity of savings with respect to real (net-of-tax) rates of return on capital, level two to calibrate to the price elasticity of demand for housing, and level three to estimates of labor-supply elasticities.

Figure 4.2 summarizes the nesting structure used in Whalley's (1985) seven-region international trade model. In this model the key elements in the nesting structure are those affecting substitution between commodities produced in different regions, since trade-related policies such as tariffs discriminate between such commodities. The effects of these policies depend in turn on the import-demand elasticities that prevail within regions

Figure 4.2. Nesting structure used in Whalley's (1985) seven-region international trade model. *Source:* Redrawn from Whalley (1985), © 1985 by the Massachusetts Institute of Technology, used by permission.

PRODUCTION

Value-added functions
Each industry in each region has a CES value-added function with capital and labor services as primary inputs.

Intermediate substitution
Fixed-coefficient intermediate requirements technology, but with each fixed coefficient expressed in terms of composites only (i.e. a fixed machinery requirement per unit of manufacturing).

Each fixed-coefficient input requirement met by cost-minimizing bundle of domestic and import composites obtained from CES substitution functions.

CES hierarchy
(For each fixed coefficient in terms of composites; e.g., machinery requirement per unit of manufacture.)

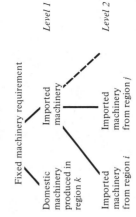

DEMAND

Final demand functions
In each region, 1 4-level CES/LES functional form is used.

CES hierarchy

Level 1
Substitution between categories (e.g., energy/non-energy)

Level 2
Substitution within categories among composite goods (e.g., among components of non-energy)

Level 3
Substitution between domestic and import composites (e.g., between domestic and imported food)

Level 4
Substitution between import types in import composites (e.g., between imported food from regions k and j)

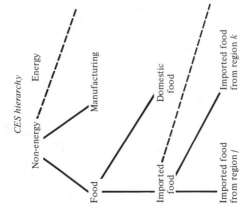

LES hierarchy

Minimum requirements for each import composite at Level 3 used. These allow income elasticities for import demands to differ from unity.

and the export-demand elasticities they face. This explains the choice of the nesting structure, particularly at levels three and four in demands and at levels one and two in intermediate production.

Once specified, nesting structures are relatively easy to work with (although sometimes tedious to implement in computer code). Beginning at the bottom level of the nesting structure, one first moves up the hierarchy by constructing price indexes for each of the composites at each level. With all these indexes constructed, one then moves back down the hierarchy in solving for quantities at each level. Quantities at the higher level need to be determined before quantities at the next level can be calculated. Moving down the hierarchy in this way, one arrives at the bottom level, where the disaggregated quantity responses from optimizing behavior are determined.

4.4 Choosing the level of aggregation

Choice of the level of aggregation for an applied model is one of the more difficult design issues that any prospective modeler must confront. On the one hand, there is the natural desire to make the model as detailed as possible in the belief that this will increase its realism. On the other hand, more detail is not always beneficial; much of it may prove superfluous to the issues at hand. Excessive detail can be costly in terms of data gathering, and large-dimensional models are both computationally expensive to solve and clumsy and time-consuming to manipulate. In practice, three considerations enter the choice of aggregation level in applied models: the need to accurately capture the main discriminatory features involved in the policy issues under discussion; the limits of data availability; and the need to constrain computer costs by using a model structure that can be manipulated with relative ease.

The levels of aggregation used in practice are also heavily influenced by the orientation of the model: whether it is designed as an issue-specific model or whether a general-purpose capability is intended. The level of detail among general-purpose models varies, with 114 industries and commodities in the ORANI model of Australia (Dixon et al. 1982), 33 industries and commodities in the U.K. tax model of Piggott and Whalley (1985), and 19 industries and 16 commodities in the U.S. tax model of Ballard et al. (1985). Among issue-specific models, dimensions tend to be smaller. Hamilton and Whalley (1985) use six industries and commodities; Lenjosek and Whalley (1986) use only three.

To provide readers with a sense of the levels of aggregation that may be involved in a typical model application, Table 4.11 reports the industry, commodity, and household classifications used by Ballard et al. (1985) in their U.S. tax model. On the demand side, the level of aggregation is

Table 4.11. *Classification of industries, consumer expenditures, and consumer groups in the U.S. tax model due to Ballard, Fullerton, Shoven, and Whalley (1985)*

Industries	Consumer expenditures
1. Agriculture, forestry, and fisheries	1. Food
2. Mining	2. Alcoholic beverages
3. Crude petroleum and gas	3. Tobacco
4. Contract construction	4. Utilities
5. Food and tobacco	5. Housing
6. Textiles, apparel, and leather products	6. Furnishings
7. Paper and printing	7. Appliances
8. Petroleum refining	8. Clothing and jewelry
9. Chemicals and rubber	9. Transportation
10. Lumber, furniture, stone, clay, and glass	10. Motor vehicles, tires, and auto repair
11. Metals, machinery, miscellaneous manufacturing	11. Services
12. Transportation equipment	12. Financial services
13. Motor vehicles	13. Reading, recreation, miscellaneous
14. Transportation, communications, and utilities	14. Nondurable and nonfood household items
15. Trade	15. Gasoline and other fuels
16. Finance and insurance	
17. Real estate	
18. Services	
19. Government enterprise	

Consumer groups[a]

1. 0–3	5. 6–7	9. 12–15
2. 3–4	6. 7–8	10. 15–20
3. 4–5	7. 8–10	11. 20–25
4. 5–6	8. 10–12	12. 25+

[a] Households classified by gross income in thousands of 1973 dollars.
Source: From Ballard et al. (1985), © 1985 by the University of Chicago, used by permission.

very much a function of the focus of the modeling effort. If the main issues are efficiency issues, it may be quite acceptable to aggregate households into one single consumer group, a procedure used in a number of applied models. If, however, distributional issues are at the heart of the analysis, detail on the demand side becomes crucial. Generally speaking, applied models are not very detailed on the demand side. The most detailed model is the U.K. tax model of Piggott and Whalley (1985), which has 100 household groups stratified by income, occupation, and family characteristics.

A trend appearing in some recent modeling efforts is to use different levels of aggregation applied to the same data set, and then code for different phases of model development and use. In initial model development, a highly aggregated data set can be used to reduce execution costs and simplify model manipulations. For first model runs, where only initial broad indications of results are desired, an intermediate level of aggregation can be used. Only when the modeler is sure that all development problems in designing the modeling system have been resolved will more detailed calculations be made. In turn, depending upon the issues to be analyzed, some portions of the model may be highly aggregated (such as a single manufacturing industry if, say, agricultural policies are the issue) while others are more disaggregated. Flexible aggregation of this type is often the best accommodation to these competing concerns. Rather than thinking in terms of a single model, a modeler may think in terms of developing a more general modeling capability into which several alternative levels of aggregation, and even different model variants, will fit.

5

Using applied general equilibrium models

In this chapter we outline how applied general equilibrium models are specified and how results from them are used in arriving at policy judgments.

5.1 Specifying and using applied models

In determining results of policy simulations generated by any applied model, parameter values for the functional forms are crucial. The procedure most commonly used to select parameter values has come to be labeled "calibration" (Mansur and Whalley 1984).

Steps commonly used in both constructing and using applied models are summarized in Figure 5.1. The economy under consideration is assumed to be in equilibrium, a so-called benchmark equilibrium. The parameters of the model are chosen through a calibration procedure, which has the property that, once specified, the model will reproduce this data set as an equilibrium solution.[1] The parameter values thus generated can then be used to solve for the alternative equilibrium associated with any changed policy regime. These are usually termed "counterfactual" or "policy-replacement" equilibria. Policy appraisal then proceeds on the basis of pairwise comparisons of counterfactual and benchmark equilibria.

Calibration is most easily understood as the requirement that the entire model specification be capable of generating a base-year equilibrium observation as a model solution. In effect, the model is solved from equilibrium data for its parameter values, rather than vice versa as discussed in Chapter 3. Only when the model is used to analyze counterfactual equilibria are computational methods used to derive such equilibria.

---

[1] This is the replication check referred to in Figure 5.1, which serves as an important accuracy test of computer code. If the replication check fails, then a programming error has been discovered and the coding must be investigated further.

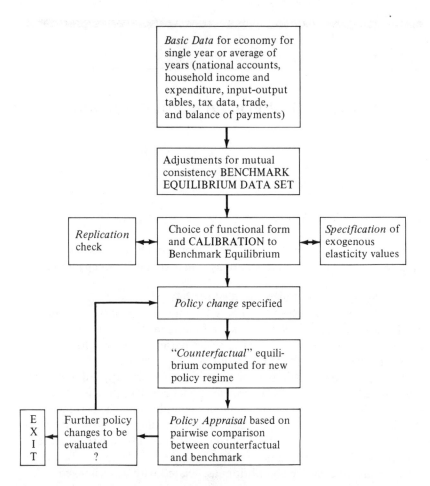

Figure 5.1. Flow chart outlining calibration procedures and model use in typical applied general equilibrium model.

If the model is specified as having Cobb–Douglas functions, these calibration procedures will uniquely determine the parameter values required, as indicated later in the chapter. If CES or LES functions are used, exogenously specified elasticity values (usually based on literature estimates) are required, because the benchmark data only give price and quantity observations associated with a single equilibrium observation.

In practice, the benchmark equilibria or benchmark data sets used in calibration are constructed from national accounts and other government data sources. In general, in published form this data is inconsistent with general equilibrium conditions (e.g., payments to labor from firms will not equal labor income received by households), and a number of adjustments are required to ensure that equilibrium conditions hold. Some data is taken as correct and other data is adjusted to be consistent in the process of generating a benchmark data set. The construction of data sets of this type is described in Dervis et al. (1982), St-Hilaire and Whalley (1983), Piggott and Whalley (1985), Ballard et al. (1985), and later in this chapter.

Furthermore, because benchmark data is usually produced in value terms, units must be chosen for goods and factors so that separate price and quantity observations are obtained. A commonly used units convention, originally adopted by Harberger (1959, 1962), is to choose units for both goods and factors so that they have a price of unity in the benchmark equilibrium.

Typically, calibration involves only one year's data, or a single observation represented as an average over a number of years. Because of the reliance on a single observation, benchmark data typically does not identify a unique set of values for the parameters in any model. Particular values for the relevant elasticities are usually required, and are specified on the basis of other research. These serve, along with the equilibrium observation, to uniquely identify the other parameters of the model. This typically places major reliance on literature surveys of elasticities; as many modelers have observed in discussing their own work, it is surprising how sparse (and sometimes contradictory) the literature is on some key elasticity values. Also, although this procedure might sound straightforward, it is often exceedingly difficult because each study is different from every other.

The specification of elasticities in calibration is most easily thought of as determining the curvature of isoquants and indifference surfaces, with their position given by the benchmark equilibrium data and their slope by the unit's convention. For Cobb–Douglas demand or production functions, a single price and quantity observation is sufficient to uniquely determine the parameters of the function. For CES functions, extraneous values of substitution elasticities are required, because the curvature of indifference curves and isoquants (given by the single elasticity parameter) cannot be inferred from the benchmark data. Similarly, for LES demand functions, income elasticities are determined once the original coordinates for utility measurement are known.

A prominent feature of calibration is that no statistical test of the model specification is used, because a deterministic procedure of calculating parameter values from the equilibrium observation is employed. The procedure thus uses the key assumption that the benchmark data represents an equilibrium for the economy under investigation. In contrast to econometric work, which often simplifies the structure of the economic model to allow for substantial richness in statistical specification, here the procedure is quite the opposite. The richness of the economic structure allows only for a much cruder statistical model that, in the case of calibration to a single year's data, becomes deterministic.

Once the calibration procedure is complete, a fully specified numerical model is available that can be used for policy analysis. As indicated in Figure 5.1, a policy change can be considered and a counterfactual equilibrium computed for the new policy regime. Policy appraisal then proceeds on the basis of pairwise comparisons of counterfactual and benchmark equilibria.

Because of the use of deterministic calibration rather than stochastic estimation, the parameter specification methods used in these models are often troubling to econometricians. It is therefore worthwhile to outline some of the reasons why this calibration approach is so widely used.

First, in some applied models many thousands of parameters are involved, and to estimate simultaneously all of the model parameters using the time-series methods would require either unrealistically large numbers of observations or overly severe identifying restrictions. Although partitioning models into submodels (such as a demand and a production system) may reduce or overcome this problem, partitioning does not fully incorporate all the equilibrium restrictions that are emphasized in calibration. Second, as mentioned previously, benchmark data sets are formulated in value terms, and their decomposition into separate price and quantity observations makes it difficult to sequence equilibrium observations with consistent units through time, as would be required for time-series estimation.

Thus far, these problems have largely excluded complete econometric estimation of general equilibrium systems in applied work, although some progress in this direction has been made in work by Clements (1980), Mansur (1980), and Jorgenson (1984). Mansur, for instance, notes the difficulties in formulating a maximum-likelihood procedure incorporating equilibrium restrictions. Allingham (1973) has also worked on estimation of general equilibrium systems, but for a linear system of demand and supply functions rather than preferences and production functions. Jorgenson provides estimates for an economywide system of cost functions.

5.2 Building benchmark equilibrium data sets

Calibration relies on the prior construction of a benchmark equilibrium data set for the applied model under investigation. Constructing such a data set involves the assumption of an "observable" equilibrium, a data set that meets the equilibrium conditions for the general equilibrium model being studied.

The detailed information presented in most national accounts, although clearly of enormous value to economists, is nonetheless largely a byproduct of the process of assembling macro-aggregates and typically does not aim at consistency in the various areas of detail that general equilibrium analysis requires. If equilibrium is to be reflected in an assembled set of accounts, demands must equal market supplies for all commodities, and supplies and demands must be separately disaggregated by agent. Each agent, in turn, has incomes and expenditures consistent with his (or her) budget constraint.

Four major sets of equilibrium conditions are satisfied by most of the constructed benchmark equilibrium data sets:

   (i) demands equal supplies for all commodities;
   (ii) nonpositive profits are made in all industries;
   (iii) all domestic agents (including the government) have demands that satisfy their budget constraints; and
   (iv) the economy is in external sector balance.

These conditions are not all satisfied in intermediate transactions accounts (input–output data) and other data published by agencies producing national accounts data. With input–output data, sector income and outlay accounts are not made explicit, nor is an external-sector balance condition satisfied. Household expenditure data is usually inconsistent with production data; classifications differ and totals do not agree.

In constructing benchmark data sets for use in applied general equilibrium models, various adjustments are necessary to blocks of data that are available separately but are not arranged on a micro-consistent basis. The nature of these adjustments varies from case to case, as alternate sets of benchmark accounts are constructed to fit alternative models.

In practice, differences in measurement concepts from national accounts frequently arise for particular items. One example is the measurement of input use by industry, since unadjusted national accounts measures of the use of capital by industry are inappropriate for use in general equilibrium models. This is because national accounts record capital income in the industry of capital ownership rather than in the industry of capital use. Problems arise in cases such as airlines leasing planes owned by insurance companies; another example arises with the imputation of retained earnings as household savings.

Further difficulties arise with differences in classifications among inconsistent data sets. One example is the incompatibility between consumers' expenditure categories in family expenditure data, and the classification of industry products in gross domestic product (GDP) accounts by which final consumer expenditures (by product) are recorded in input–output data. A further difficulty is that producer-output classifications refer to measures of the value of output net of transportation costs and on the basis of net-of-retail and wholesale margins, whereas consumer-expenditure classifications are on a gross basis. Classification difficulties also arise with tax data and other data that is collected on an administrative rather than a statistical basis.

Further adjustments arise with the need to guarantee mutual consistency between inconsistent data. Most benchmark data sets rely heavily on the RAS adjustment method[2] for these modifications. This technique is applied, for example, where household demands for individual products do not equal the supplies of firms, where costs of industries are not equal to sales (after modifications to published intermediate transactions accounts), and where household incomes do not equal expenditures.

In Table 5.1 we provide a numerical example presented in Piggott and Whalley (1985) of interlocking benchmark accounts for an artificial economy with four industries, four goods, and three consumer groups. In this micro-consistent set of accounts, the value of GNP (gross national product) at market prices is 29, GNP at factor cost is 22, and the total value of production is 49. Zero-profit conditions are satisfied for each industry, as is an external-sector balance condition. On the right-hand side of the table we highlight the equilibrium consistency conditions satisfied by the data.

The data sets used in the applied models typically contain much more detail than this example. Data is usually for a single year, although some averaging across years is performed in constructing portions of those data sets where substantial volatility occurs. The documentation of both the data sources and adjustments used in specifying particular general equilibrium models is often both incomplete and scattered. Complex and detailed modifications are often involved, modifications that authors are continually revising.

The paper by St-Hilaire and Whalley (1983) is a good illustration of what is involved in building benchmark data sets, since it is solely concerned with describing data modifications and procedures used in the construction of a 1972 benchmark data set for Canadian tax-policy analysis. The Canadian System of National Accounts and its related data sets provide the starting point for this micro-consistent 1972 data set. In Table 5.2 we outline the sequences of calculations involved and their relation to the national accounts and other data from which St-Hilaire and Whalley start.

In essence, the procedure followed to produce the data set involves extensions, modifications, and redefinitions of concepts for portions of the national accounts data; the addition of further detail to this system; and

[2] RAS refers to the row-and-column sum method; see Bacharach (1971).

final adjustments between blocks of data in order to restore mutual consistency. After these modifications and adjustments are complete, a reconciliation of the major aggregates in the data set with published national accounts aggregates is made in order to quantify the size of the adjustments involved in ensuring mutual consistency.

The Canadian input–output tables contain the most detailed information on separate industries and products available in the present national accounting system, and provide their starting point for data assembly. The tables expand the input–output data to incorporate demands and incomes of individual household groups consistent with production accounts, incorporate financial transactions, impute corporate sector investment via retained earnings as household savings, redefine factor payments and incomes data using more acceptable definitions, and explicitly incorporate an external-sector balance condition that is not present in input–output data. Because their ultimate aim is general equilibrium tax-policy analysis, they incorporate substantially more detail on taxes than exists in the input–output tables or the income and expenditure accounts.

The level of commodity detail in the data set is the maximum level of detail contained in the small level of aggregation in the Canadian input-output tables, which they assume provides sufficient industrial and commodity differentiation for the desired analysis. The remaining data is accommodated to this level of detail as far as is possible. The classification of consumer expenditure in Canadian family-expenditure survey data is quite different from the industry classification used for production data, and for this reason the data set simultaneously uses two classifications with a linking concordance. The detail among household groups is an aggregated version of that appearing in family expenditure survey data.

The major adjustments made in each of the blocks of data may be summarized as follows.

External-sector data

From the input–output tables, St-Hilaire and Whalley reconcile the export and import (net of customs duties) of goods and services with merchandise and service receipts and payments reported in balance-of-payments accounts. The external-sector accounts are then completed by incorporating data on capital transactions. Import data is disaggregated further by industry and by sector, and is used to disaggregate intermediate transactions and final demands in order to separately distinguish demands for domestic and imported products.

Indirect tax data

Commodity indirect taxes on final and intermediate demand from the input–output tables are disaggregated by commodity and by type of

110

Table 5.1. Simple example of a benchmark equilibrium data set

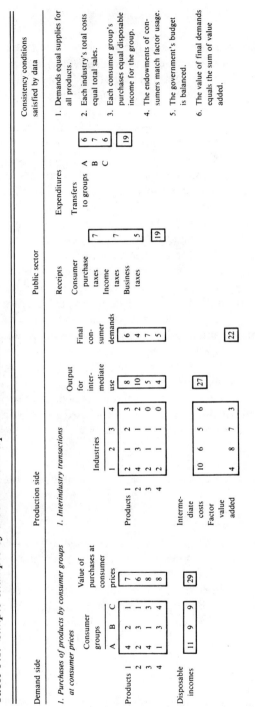

Demand side

1. Purchases of products by consumer groups at consumer prices

	Consumer groups A	B	C	Value of purchases at consumer prices
Products 1	4	2	1	7
2	2	3	1	6
3	4	1	3	8
4	1	3	4	8
Disposable incomes	11	9	9	29

Production side

1. Interindustry transactions

	Industries 1	2	3	4	Output for intermediate use	Final consumer demands
Products 1	2	1	2	3	8	6
2	4	3	1	2	10	4
3	2	1	1	0	5	7
4	2	1	1	0	4	5
Intermediate costs	10	6	5	6	27	
Factor value added	4	8	7	3		22

Public sector

Receipts		Expenditures	
Consumer purchase taxes	7	Transfers to groups A	6
Income taxes	7	B	7
Business taxes	5	C	6
	19		19

Consistency conditions satisfied by data

1. Demands equal supplies for all products.
2. Each industry's total costs equal total sales.
3. Each consumer group's purchases equal disposable income for the group.
4. The endowments of consumers match factor usage.
5. The government's budget is balanced.
6. The value of final demands equals the sum of value added.

2. *Consumer disposable incomes*

| | Consumer groups | | | |
	A	B	C	Total
Income from capital	5	1	1	7
Labor income	3	3	4	10
Transfers received	6	7	6	19
less income tax paid	3	2	2	7
Disposable incomes	11	9	9	29

2. *Composition of value added by industry*

	1	2	3	4	Total
Capital service usage	1	2	3	1	7
Labor service usage	2	4	3	1	10
Indirect business taxes	1	2	1	1	5
Total	4	8	7	3	22

3. *Consumer taxes paid*

	Value of purchases at consumer prices	Consumer taxes	Value of purchases at producer prices
Products 1	7	1	6
2	6	2	4
3	8	1	7
4	8	3	5
Total	29	7	22

Note: A number of features not included in this example must be incorporated into the data set used in the model, such as: (1) real government expenditures; (2) foreign trade; (3) consumer savings; (4) investments by business, consumers, and government; (5) depreciation; (6) inventory accumulation; (7) financial transactions between the personal business, public, and external sectors; (8) more complex taxation and subsidy arrangements (e.g., a value-added tax).
Source: Piggott and Whalley (1985).

Table 5.2. *Basic data sources and adjustments for the St-Hilaire and Whalley (1972) benchmark equilibrium data set for Canada*

INPUT-OUTPUT STRUCTURE

(Industries)

MAKE MATRIX
(Output)

USE MATRIX
(Input)

Indirect Taxes

Value Added

C G I X M

FINAL DEMAND MATRIX

Indirect Taxes

Value Added

EXTERNAL-SECTOR DATA

Reconciliation of the 1-O trade data with balance-of-payments estimates, incorporating: (1) zero-trade-balance condition; and (2) complete transactions with non-residents.

INDIRECT-TAX DATA

Extension of tax data into matrices reporting indirect taxes on: (1) intermediate demand for domestic products; (2) intermediate demand for imported products; (3) final demand for domestic products; (4) final demand for imported products; as well as (5) taxes on production (net of subsidies).

Extension of trade data into matrices differentiating between domestically produced and imported products. This produces matrices reporting: (1) the use of domestic products by industry; (2) the use of imported products by industry; (3) the final demand for domestic products by sector; and (4) the final demand for imported products by sector.

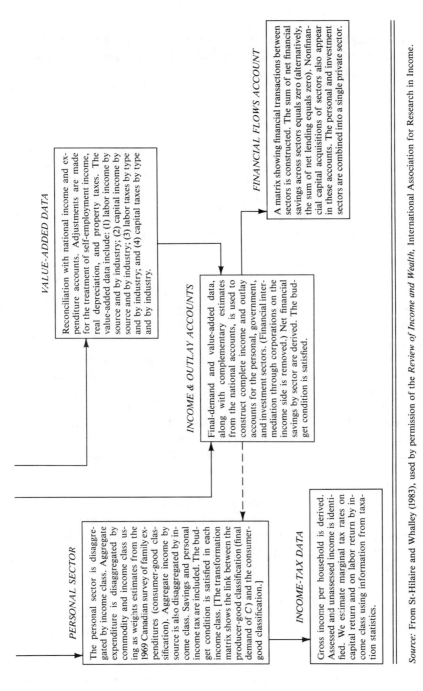

VALUE-ADDED DATA

Reconciliation with national income and expenditure accounts. Adjustments are made for the treatment of self-employment income, real depreciation, and property taxes. The value-added data include: (1) labor income by source and by industry; (2) capital income by source and by industry; (3) labor taxes by type and by industry; and (4) capital taxes by type and by industry.

FINANCIAL FLOWS ACCOUNT

A matrix showing financial transactions between sectors is constructed. The sum of net financial savings across sectors equals zero (alternatively, the sum of net lending equals zero). Nonfinancial capital acquisitions of sectors also appear in these accounts. The personal and investment sectors are combined into a single private sector.

INCOME & OUTLAY ACCOUNTS

Final-demand and value-added data, along with complementary estimates from the national accounts, is used to construct complete income and outlay accounts for the personal, government, and investment sectors. (Financial intermediation through corporations on the income side is removed.) Net financial savings by sector are derived. The budget condition is satisfied.

PERSONAL SECTOR

The personal sector is disaggregated by income class. Aggregate expenditure is disaggregated by commodity and income class using as weights estimates from the 1969 Canadian survey of family expenditures (consumer-good classification). Aggregate income by source is also disaggregated by income class. Savings and personal income tax are included. The budget condition is satisfied in each income class. [The transformation matrix shows the link between the producer-good classification (final demand of C) and the consumer-good classification.]

INCOME-TAX DATA

Gross income per household is derived. Assessed and unassessed income is identified. We estimate marginal tax rates on capital return and on labor return by income class using information from taxation statistics.

Source: From St-Hilaire and Whalley (1983), used by permission of the *Review of Income and Wealth*, International Association for Research in Income.

demand (for domestic or imported products) using distributions from the corresponding demand matrices. Customs duties deducted from the value of imports are also disaggregated in this way, and are incorporated into the matrices of indirect taxes on the demand for imports. Property taxes are deducted from "other indirect taxes" and included as a tax on capital.

Household incomes and expenditures by income range

The income and outlay account of the personal sector is further disaggregated into detailed accounts by income range, using the classification found in 1969 family-expenditure survey data. Expenditure estimates in this data are reported on a consumer-good classification that coincides with that of the personal expenditure from the national income and expenditure accounts, as opposed to the producer-good classification used for final demands. To accommodate the different expenditure category classifications in this data, a transformation matrix is constructed linking the two. Estimates of personal expenditures on consumer goods from the 1972 income and expenditure accounts are then reconciled with total final demand of consumers at consumer prices (gross of taxes and margins). The family-expenditure survey data are used for the allocation by income range.

Considerable care is devoted to the allocation of the various income sources (e.g., transfers, retained earnings, imputed rent, self-employment income) by income range, since significant differences occur between measurement concepts in the benchmark data set and the survey, particularly in the definition of capital income. Disposable income by income range is estimated by deducting personal income tax and net savings from the sum of labor, capital, and transfer income by income range.

Income-tax data

Because of the focus of the data set on eventual tax-policy analysis, St-Hilaire and Whalley also estimate a number of income-tax characteristics by household,[3] in particular average rates and marginal rates on components of income (i.e., labor and capital). This also includes estimating the unassessed portion of capital income.

RAS adjustments

After the adjustments, modifications, and additions just listed are complete, the remaining inconsistencies in the data set involve major data blocks that need to be realigned so as to satisfy (or restore in certain

---

[3] The Canadian income tax applies to individual tax filers rather than to households.

cases) equilibrium conditions. For example, in the case of the matrix of intermediate transactions, modifications to estimates of value added by industry require that an adjustment be made so as to restore demand–supply equalities by commodity, as well as the zero-profit conditions by industry. In the household sector, expenditures should equal the value of final demands, and each household's expenditures must equal its disposable income. Comparable adjustments must be made to other matrices and a RAS (row-and-column sum) procedure is used for this purpose.

In the RAS procedure, a nonnegative matrix that does not initially meet prescribed row-and-column sum constraints is restored to a situation of consistency through a sequence of alternating operations on rows and columns of the matrix. First row constraints are satisfied, then column constraints, then row constraints, and so on until a consistent matrix is achieved. The sums of prespecified row-and-column constraints must be the same since they both provide the matrix sum. If the matrix is everywhere dense, convergence is assured.

St-Hilaire and Whalley apply the RAS procedure to four matrices in the construction of their benchmark data set. The largest adjustments occur with the "use" matrix (intermediate transactions) for domestic products, where the sum of the absolute value of deviations between initial and terminal matrices is on the order of 20%. The large size of this adjustment is accounted for mainly by the fact that real depreciation is deducted from both capital return and capital expenditure, and therefore appears as an intermediate cost of industries in the data set. The adjustments in the other matrices are not of this magnitude, and are explained mostly by the reallocations of row and column constraints.

5.3 Determining parameter values through calibration

Calibration involves a deterministic approach to specifying parameter values to be used in an applied general equilibrium model. The assumption made is that there is an equilibrium observed in the economy under consideration in the presence of existing policies. The first task in applying general equilibrium analysis is not to solve for an equilibrium, but rather to use the observed equilibrium to solve for model parameters consistent with that observation.

In two-factor models, physical units for factors of production are taken as the amount that earns a reward of one currency unit ($1) in equilibrium, net of taxes and before receipt of subsidies in any of its alternative uses. Units for commodities are similarly defined as those amounts that sell for $1 net of all consumer taxes and subsidies in equilibrium. The assumption that (in equilibrium) marginal revenue products of factors are equalized in all uses permits factor payments data by industry to be used directly as observations of physical quantities of factors in the determination of model parameters.

Using this data, it is possible to calculate production function parameters from the benchmark equilibrium observations of the use of capital and labor services in each industry. We illustrate this approach by considering CES value-added functions for each of N industries in a two-factor general equilibrium tax model. These functions are given by

$$Y_j = \gamma_j[\delta_j K_j^{-\rho_j} + (1-\delta_j)L_j^{-\rho_j}]^{-1/\rho_j} \quad (j=1,...,N), \tag{5.1}$$

where γ_j is a constant defining units of measurement, δ_j is a weighting parameter, $\sigma_j = 1/(1+\rho_j)$ is the elasticity of substitution, K_j and L_j are capital and labor service inputs, and Y_j is the industries' value added.

From the benchmark equilibrium data, values for K_j and L_j can be obtained and (in the case of tax model) factor tax rates t_j^K and t_j^L calculated. As units are chosen for factors such that $P_K = P_L = 1$ (where P_K and P_L refer to the net-of-tax factor prices) at the benchmark equilibrium, prices associated with the equilibrium quantities are known.

Once the elasticity parameter σ_j is selected for each industry, the values of the share parameters δ_j are given by

$$\delta_j = \left[\frac{K_j^{1/\sigma_j}(1+t_j^K)}{L_j^{1/\sigma_j}(1+t_j^L)}\right] \Big/ \left[1 + \left[\frac{K_j^{1/\sigma_j}(1+t_j^K)}{L_j^{1/\sigma_j}(1+t_j^L)}\right]\right]. \tag{5.2}$$

Values for γ_j are then derived from the zero-profit conditions for each industry, given the units definition for outputs. Thus, although (5.1) appears to be a three-parameter function, the requirement that the function be consistent with the benchmark data and units implies that, given ρ_j, the other two parameters can be determined.

Parameters for household demand functions are determined in a similar manner from benchmark equilibrium data on purchases of commodities by households. The procedure is analogous to that for production functions, except that individual consumer demand functions rather than first-order conditions from cost minimization are used.

Taking a two-nested variant of CES consumer demand functions, the ratio of expenditures by household q on any two commodities i, j within the same nest gives an equation involving the bottom-level weighting parameters in each household utility function,

$$\frac{(p_i^q)^{\sigma_l}X_i^q}{(p_j^q)^{\sigma_l}X_j^q} = \frac{(b_i^q)^{1/\sigma_l}}{(b_j^q)^{1/\sigma_l}}, \tag{5.3}$$

where the X_i^q represent benchmark demands, the b_i^q are weighting parameters of the lower-level CES utility function, and σ_l is the value of the elasticity of substitution within the nest l. Using the elasticity value, the ratios of the coefficients b_i^q, b_j^q can be calculated. A normalization of the coefficients within the nest is then typically made.

For top-level utility function weighting parameters, the benchmark data on the sum of expenditures on components of the nest can be used. If $P_l X_l^q$ is the expenditure by household q on the nest, the ratio of expenditures on any two nests l, l' yields a similar equation involving top-level weighting parameters,

$$\frac{P_l X_l^q}{P_{l'} X_{l'}^q} = \frac{(b_l^1)^{1/\sigma}}{(b_{l'}^q)^{1/\sigma}} \cdot \frac{(p_l^q)^\sigma}{(P_{l'}^q)^\sigma}. \tag{5.4}$$

A value for σ (the elasticity of substitution across nests) is selected, and the coefficients b_l^q are calculated as for lower-level nests. This same procedure can be extended to three- or higher-level nested CES functions.

A further component of these procedures is the calibration of point estimates for own-price elasticities of model demand functions at the benchmark equilibrium. In this way, substitution elasticities in the model functions can be related to elasticity estimates in the literature. This can be illustrated in the case of a single-stage CES demand function. The N-commodity demand functions derived from maximization of a single-stage CES utility function, subject to a household budget constraint, are

$$X_i = \frac{b_i I}{p_i^\sigma \cdot \Sigma_j b_j p_j^{1-\sigma}} \quad (I = 1, \dots, N), \tag{5.5}$$

where I is household income, b_i are weighting parameters, σ is the elasticity of substitution, and p_i is the price of good i.

Taking derivatives through the demand function yields

$$\frac{\partial X_i}{\partial p_i} = -\sigma b_i I p_i^{-\sigma-1} \cdot \left(\sum_j b_j p_j^{1-\sigma}\right)^{-1} - b_i I p_i^{-\sigma} \left(\sum_j b_j p_j^{1-\sigma}\right)^{-2} \cdot (1-\sigma) b_i p_i^{-\sigma}, \tag{5.6}$$

which yields the following expression for the uncompensated own-price elasticity:

$$\frac{\partial X_i}{\partial p_i} \cdot \frac{p_i}{X_i} = -\sigma - \frac{b_i \cdot (1-\sigma)}{p_i^{(\sigma-1)} \cdot \Sigma_j b_j p_j^{(1-\sigma)}}. \tag{5.7}$$

The (uncompensated) cross-price elasticities can be shown to be

$$\frac{\partial X_i}{\partial p_k} \cdot \frac{p_k}{X_i} = \frac{b_k(1-\sigma)}{p_k^{(\sigma-1)} \cdot \Sigma_j b_j p_j^{(1-\sigma)}}. \tag{5.8}$$

At the benchmark equilibrium, producer prices are equal to unity because of the units definition adopted for outputs. Consumer prices may not exactly equal unity if there are consumer taxes. However, if the prices are assumed (for simplicity) to equal unity, and if the b_i are chosen such that $\Sigma_j\, b_j = 1$, then

$$\frac{\partial X_i}{\partial p_i} \cdot \frac{p_i}{X_i} = -\sigma - b_i(1-\sigma) \tag{5.9}$$

and

$$\frac{\partial X_i}{\partial p_k} \cdot \frac{p_k}{X_i} = -b_k(1-\sigma). \tag{5.10}$$

In those cases where weighting parameters are small (and σ is not too different from unity), it follows that

$$\frac{\partial X_i}{\partial p_i} \cdot \frac{p_i}{X_i} \approx -\sigma, \qquad \frac{\partial X_i}{\partial p_k} \cdot \frac{p_k}{X_i} \approx 0. \tag{5.11}$$

For two-level CES functions, the uncompensated own-price elasticity at the benchmark equilibrium is approximately

$$\frac{\partial X_i}{\partial p_i} \cdot \frac{p_i}{X_i} \approx -\sigma_k. \tag{5.12}$$

Under these approximations, the own-price elasticity of a commodity or composite of commodities is determined primarily by the elasticity of substitution in the lowest level of the nesting in which it appears. Similar but more complex expressions can be obtained for three-level staged CES functions. In all these cases expressions such as those derived here are used to calibrate model substitution elasticity values to those appearing in the literature.

5.4 Specifying extraneous elasticity values

CES functions are in widespread use in current applied models. Heavy reliance is typically placed on literature searches for elasticity values (or extraneous estimation of elasticities of substitution) in production and demand functions. Here we review how such estimates from the literature are used.

Production function elasticities

Most models incorporate CES value-added functions for each industry. For each industry in the model, it is therefore necessary to specify a separate value for the elasticity of substitution between capital and labor.

Since the introduction of the CES function in the early 1960s, there has been a continuing debate as to whether the elasticity of substitution for manufacturing is approximately unity. If unity is a correct value, the more complex CES form can be replaced by the simpler Cobb–Douglas form that has a unitary elasticity of substitution. This debate has concentrated primarily on substitution elasticities for aggregate manufacturing, rather than for the component industries specified in these models.

Early estimation of the elasticity of substitution in manufacturing industry by Arrow et al. (1961) involved a pooled cross-country data set of observations on wage rates and output per worker. The same production function was assumed to apply in all countries, and the first-order condition from the industry cost-minimization problem equating the marginal product of labor to the wage rate was used to estimate the elasticity of substitution. Results indicated that the elasticity of substitution was below unity, but that the difference between the estimated coefficient and unity was not significant at a 90% level. This was used as support for the position that Cobb–Douglas production functions are a reasonable specification of aggregate production functions.

Following Arrow et al. (1961), a number of econometric studies have estimated substitution elasticities for manufacturing industry (primarily in the United States) by a variety of methods, producing results with substantial disagreement. Cross-section studies (many of which use statewide data) produce estimates that are close to unity, but time-series studies produce lower estimates, typically differing from cross-section studies by a factor of about 2. Also, estimates of substitution elasticities appear to vary systematically with the choice of estimating equation. Using the equation for marginal product of capital produces lower estimates than using that for marginal product of labor.

A number of explanations for this difference have been offered, such as lagged adjustment, technical change, problems in measurement of inputs, serial correlation in time-series data, and cyclical variations in utilization rates. At present, no single explanation is widely accepted. An attempt by Berndt (1976) to reconcile alternative elasticity estimates used six different functional forms, five alternate measures of capital prices, and two estimation methods. His main finding was that estimates of substitution elasticities "are extremely sensitive to differences in measurement and data construction," and he concurred with an earlier remark of Nerlove (1967) that "even slight variations in the period or concepts tend to produce drastically different estimates of the elasticity." Given this degree of uncertainty over estimates for manufacturing in aggregate, obtaining estimates for individual industries is indeed hazardous.

A common procedure is to construct "central tendency" tables for elasticity estimates (by industry) drawn from the literature. A catalog of industry estimates of substitution elasticities has been compiled by Caddy (1976) in connection with the IMPACT project. Table 5.3 was constructed

Table 5.3. *Central tendency estimates of elasticities of substitution by industry used by Piggott and Whalley (1985) in their U.K. tax model*

Industry	Central tendency value (plus number of estimates used and their variance)		
	Overall	Cross section	Time series
Agriculture and fishing	0.607 (29, .13)	0.809 (17, .10)	0.322 (12, .03)
Food	0.789 (58, .17)	0.937 (14, .13)	0.433 (17, .08)
Drink	0.657 (30, .15)	0.879 (17, .11)	0.368 (13, .06)
Tobacco	0.848 (12, .24)	1.309 (3, .24)	0.694 (9, .13)
Mineral oils	0.827 (24, .17)	1.002 (13, .15)	0.621 (11, .13)
Chemicals	0.827 (42, .16)	1.009 (26, .11)	0.531 (16, .12)
Metals	0.806 (79, .16)	0.967 (51, .09)	0.511 (28, .14)
Mech. engineering	0.587 (35, .11)	0.663 (21, .11)	0.451 (14, .09)
Instr. engineering	0.893 (16, .14)	1.053 (10, .12)	0.627 (6, .06)
Elec. engineering	0.750 (32, .13)	0.811 (24, .11)	0.568 (8, .17)
Shipbuilding	0.808 (21, .35)	1.043 (14, .33)	0.341 (7, .04)
Vehicles	0.810 (25, .31)	1.040 (15, .33)	0.471 (9, .08)
Textiles	0.914 (67, .18)	1.093 (46, .11)	0.520 (21, .11)
Clothing	1.106 (25, .17)	1.221 (20, .14)	0.649 (5, .05)
Leather, fur, etc.	0.940 (50, .13)	1.058 (35, .09)	0.664 (15, .08)
Timber, furniture, etc.	0.843 (76, .13)	0.974 (56, .07)	0.475 (20, .10)
Paper, printing, and publishing	0.908 (65, .14)	1.057 (48, .08)	0.489 (17, .08)
Other manufacturing	0.944 (76, .17)	1.067 (54, .11)	0.641 (22, .196)

Source: Piggott and Whalley (1985), based on estimates from Caddy (1976).

by Piggott and Whalley (1985) for use in their model of the U.K. economy and tax system. This table was compiled for all estimates in a given industry, and separately for cross-section and time-series estimates. In building the table, a small number of estimates were rejected as being implausible (owing to a wrong sign, for instance), and the remainder classified according to the industries used in the model. An important point to note is that, for some of the industries used in the applied models, no estimates exist in the literature because of the problems of measurement of outputs (such as financial services, government, and other service industries).

Demand function elasticities

Household demand functions derived from staged CES utility functions are commonly used in applied models. These functions specify constant substitution elasticities between subgroups from the list of commodities. Few econometric estimates exist of substitution elasticities for CES demand functions of the staged variety, and few (if any) demand function systems are separately estimated by household type. Therefore, a set of indirect procedures has been used in the applied models to obtain elasticity values that have some claim to plausibility. These procedures involve collection of central tendency estimates from a literature survey of (both compensated and uncompensated) own-price elasticities of demand, by product, for aggregate household-sector demand functions. Substitution elasticities are then chosen for the various levels of nests, in order to approximately calibrate to these central tendency estimates as point estimates of the model demand functions at the benchmark equilibrium.

The elasticity values used by Piggott and Whalley (1985) in their U.K. model are shown in Table 5.4. The majority of estimates reported in the literature are point estimates at sample means. These central tendency estimates are therefore differentiated by estimating equations. Moreover, these estimates relate to aggregate rather than to household demand functions. Most estimates are based on time-series rather than cross-section data, in contrast to production function estimates.

Other elasticities
Depending upon the orientation of the particular applied model, additional elasticities may also be important elements of the parameter set, and are treated in a similar way: literature search followed by some form of calibration, as needed. In international trade models, for instance, import- and export-demand price elasticities are critical parameters. The compendium of estimates from Stern, Francis, and Schumacher (1976) is widely used. In some trade modeling, income elasticities of import-demand functions are also important; LES variants of CES forms are used, with calibration of intercept LES parameters to income elasticities in the literature.

In tax models, two important parameters are labor-supply and savings elasticities. In analysis of labor-supply taxation issues, the common procedure is to define utility functions over leisure and goods, choosing a value for the leisure–goods substitution elasticity consistent with literature estimates of labor-supply elasticities with respect to the net-of-tax wage. Literature estimates on this elasticity vary sharply by the group involved, with prime-age males having low (if not negative) elasticities and secondary and older workers having higher elasticities (around 0.5). Fullerton, Shoven, and Whalley (1983) use an elasticity of 0.15 for the entire workforce.

With intertemporal taxation issues, the elasticity of savings with respect to the real net-of-tax rate of return becomes important. The approach in Fullerton et al. (1983) is to consider a sequence of equilibria through time, with savings decisions depending on expected rates of return. Savings

Table 5.4. *Central tendency values for own-price elasticities of household demand functions used by Piggott and Whalley (1985) in their U.K. tax model*

Industry	LES estimates	Log-linear demand estimates	Other	Total
Agriculture and fishing	0.334 (17, .03)	0.420 (25, .05)	0.562 (44, .08)	0.468 (86, .07)
Coal mining	—	0.321 (1, 0)	1.265 (2, .01)	0.950 (3, .76)
Other mining and quarrying	0.425 (1, 0)	0.905 (3, .06)	0.257 (2, .01)	0.609 (6, .13)
Food	0.353 (15, .03)	0.580 (30, .19)	0.476 (27, .08)	0.494 (72, .13)
Drink	0.617 (5, .07)	0.780 (12, .25)	0.464 (15, .06)	0.607 (32, .16)
Tobacco	—	0.611 (8, .15)	0.431 (11, .04)	0.507 (19, .10)
Mineral oils	0.425 (1, 0)	0.905 (3, .07)	0.257 (2, .01)	0.609 (6, .13)
Other coal and petroleum products	1.283 (2, .01)	1.404 (3, .80)	1.978 (3, 1.41)	1.589 (8, .90)
Chemicals	0.685 (1, 0)	0.890 (1, 0)	0.680 (3, .07)	0.724 (5, .05)
Metals	—	1.522 (19, .42)	0.989 (18, .40)	1.083 (51, .48)
Mech. engineering	—	1.296 (16, .61)	1.068 (15, .43)	1.005 (45, .48)
Instr. engineering	0.606 (14, .15)	1.099 (17, .57)	1.240 (11, .54)	0.972 (42, .49)
Elec. engineering	—	1.388 (19, .377)	1.049 (17, .410)	1.060 (50, .44)
Vehicles	0.606 (14, .15)	1.137 (19, .55)	1.099 (18, .40)	0.985 (51, .44)
Clothing	0.277 (16, .03)	0.491 (26, .16)	0.564 (19, .15)	0.458 (61, .18)
Timber, furniture, etc.	0.570 (14, .09)	1.258 (19, .23)	0.974 (20, .39)	0.969 (53, .33)
Paper, printing, and publishing	0.191 (1, 0)	0.343 (5, .02)	0.416 (5, .02)	0.362 (11, .02)
Other manufacturing	0.578 (14, .02)	0.527 (7, .11)	0.626 (17, .12)	0.592 (38, .09)
Gas, electricity, and water	1.203 (1, 0)	0.921 (9, .02)	0.369 (10, .01)	0.659 (20, .10)
Transport	0.761 (4, .23)	1.027 (14, .26)	0.994 (10, .16)	0.977 (28, .23)
Banking and insurance	—	0.559 (3, .02)	0.894 (1, 0)	0.642 (4, .04)
Housing services (private)	0.461 (15, .11)	0.550 (29, .45)	0.434 (9, .09)	0.505 (53, .29)
Professional services, other services	0.488 (7, .08)	1.090 (16, .39)	0.946 (16, .39)	0.961 (50, .48)

Note: All uncompensated own-price elasticity estimates; figures in parentheses refer to the number of studies included and the variance of estimate.
Source: Piggott and Whalley (1985).

today augment the capital stock in all future periods. Fullerton et al. place substantial reliance on Boskin's (1978) estimated elasticity of 0.4.

Critical elasticities also arise in other areas. In energy modeling, a major issue is the substitutability (or complementarity) between energy, capital, and labor. Regional features are sometimes incorporated in development models, and the elasticity of outward migration from rural areas becomes important.

5.5 Evaluating results from models

Typically, applied general equilibrium models are used to provide analyses of counterfactual or unobservable equilibria that are then compared to benchmark equilibrium observations. The information generated in the process of computing counterfactual equilibria provides data on all prices and quantities, utility levels of consumers, factors employed by industry, and other characteristics of the unobservable equilibrium.

In using this approach to evaluate the possible impacts of policy changes, the common procedure is to compare the counterfactual and benchmark equilibria. Who has gained or who has lost from the policy change? Is the change an improvement from a social point of view? Has the distributional situation worsened or improved? How large are the adjustments between equilibria? Answering these questions requires the use of various indexes, which form the basis for comparisons between equilibria.

Individual welfare measures

As in most theoretical literature on the effects of policy changes, applied general equilibrium models typically focus on welfare measures of the impacts of policy change. Generally speaking, these models are not constructed to answer macro questions (such as the impact on unemployment, inflation, or growth performance), but are best understood as extensions of existing theoretical analysis with a numerical specification provided. It is therefore natural that the focus of these models be on welfare measures.

Measuring the welfare impacts of public policies has been discussed by economists for decades. From Dupuit (1844) to the present day, there has been substantial discussion of consumer surplus measures of welfare impacts of policy changes. Consumer surplus measures, however, are only an approximation device for appraising the impacts of policies. For instance, it is often assumed in such analyses that linear demand functions characterize behavior in the economy.

In using applied general equilibrium models there is no need to rely on such approximations. The characteristics of a new equilibrium are computed exactly, and all its associated features are determined as part of the

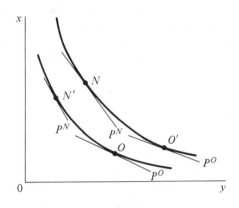

Figure 5.2. Equivalent and compensating variations.

equilibrium solution. In the applied general equilibrium literature, welfare measures focus not on an approximation of what may happen in the event of a policy change, but rather on exact comparisons between equilibria.

There are many possible indexes that can be constructed to provide a measure of welfare change. In Hicks's (1939) well-known work on welfare comparisons, four separate measures of welfare impacts between equilibria were identified: equivalent and compensating variations, and equivalent and compensating surpluses.

The compensating variation involves looking at the utility levels that consumers achieve in each of the two equilibria and at the prices they face when purchasing commodities, asking the question: How much money would be required to compensate someone for the price changes that have occurred? This can be written as

$$CV = E(U^N, P^N) - E(U^O, P^N), \tag{5.13}$$

where $E(U^N, P^N)$ is the expenditure necessary to achieve utility level U^N with prices P^N. This measure is illustrated in Figure 5.2. The consumer's consumption bundle associated with the old equilibrium is at O. The relative prices faced in the original equilibrium are given by the slope of the price line, P^O. The new equilibrium, as a result of a policy or other induced change, moves the consumer to a preferred consumption point N. Associated with consumption at point N is a different set of equilibrium prices P^N.

The compensating variation asks: By how much is it necessary to compensate the individual for the change that has occurred? In this case the consumer is now better off, and calculation of the compensating variation begins at point N. The consumer's budget constraint is shifted (parallel) from point N until a tangency point N' is reached with the original indifference curve. The compensating variation is the distance between the budget constraints tangent to points N and N', using the prices P^N.

In contrast, the equivalent variation asks: How much money is a particular change (that has taken place between equilibria) equivalent to? This can be written as follows:

$$EV = E(U^N, P^O) - E(U^O, P^O). \tag{5.14}$$

In Figure 5.2 this is given by the distance between the budget constraints tangent to points O and O', each constructed using the prices P^O. Point O' corresponds to the consumption point on the indifference curve achieved by the individual in the new equilibrium, and is associated with a price line that is parallel to the budget constraint faced in the original equilibrium. A comparison between these budget constraints (through points O and O'), each of whose slope is given by the price line P^O, illustrates how much the equilibrium change is equivalent to for this consumer. It also follows that the equivalent variation when moving from the original equilibrium to the new equilibrium is equal to the negative of the compensating variation when moving from the new equilibrium to the original equilibrium.

The difference between the compensating and equivalent variation is the initial point of reference. With the compensating variation, the point of reference is the consumption point in the new equilibrium; with the equivalent variation, the point of reference is consumption in the old equilibrium.

In using applied models, a convenient property of compensating equivalent variations can be exploited for the case where preferences are linear homogeneous. This is represented in Figure 5.3. In this case, since all indifference surfaces are radial projections of all other surfaces, a comparison between the points N, N' and O, O' can be represented simply by the radial projections associated with these indifference surfaces. In this case, the percentage change in utility associated with the movement between the indifference curves equals the percentage change along the radial projection through the corresponding consumption points. As a result, the compensating and equivalent variations can be written as:

$$CV = \frac{U^N - U^O}{U^N} \cdot I^N; \tag{5.15}$$

$$EV = \frac{U^N - U^O}{U^O} \cdot I^O. \tag{5.16}$$

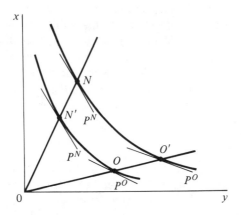

Figure 5.3. Equivalent and compensating variations in the linear homogeneous case.

The equivalent and compensating variations are perhaps the most widely used of the measures associated with comparisons between equilibria, but – as indicated in the literature – they also have the problem of implicitly involving a path between equilibria (see Burns 1973, Silberberg 1972, and Willig 1976). This is recognized in literature that formulates equivalent and compensating variational measures in a somewhat different way: using the so-called money-metric approach.

Since $I^N = E(U^N, P^N)$ and $I^O = E(U^O, P^O)$, (5.13) can be rewritten as

$$CV = I^N - I^O + E(U^O, P^O) - E(U^O, P^N). \tag{5.17}$$

This implies that

$$CV = \gamma I + \int_{P^N}^{P^O} \sum_{i=1}^{N} \frac{\partial E}{\partial P_i}(U^O, P) \, dP_i, \tag{5.18}$$

which implies

$$CV = \gamma I + \int_{P^N}^{P^O} \sum_{i=1}^{N} X_i^D(U^O, P) \, dP_i, \tag{5.19}$$

where X_i^D are compensated demands (by Roy's identity). Thus, it is possible to represent the compensating variation as the change in income between equilibria, along with the integral over prices of the change in compensated demands evaluated at the utility level associated with the original equilibrium.

In addition to compensating and equivalent variations, another approach to welfare measurement (also associated with the work of Hicks)

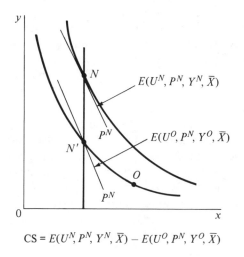

$$CS = E(U^N, P^N, Y^N, \overline{X}) - E(U^O, P^N, Y^O, \overline{X})$$

Figure 5.4. Compensating surplus.

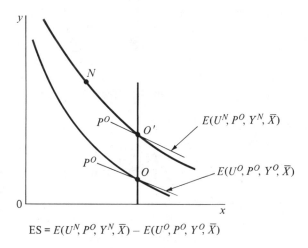

$$ES = E(U^N, P^O, Y^N, \overline{X}) - E(U^O, P^O, Y^O, \overline{X})$$

Figure 5.5. Equivalent surplus.

involves equivalent and compensating surpluses. In the case of compensating surplus, represented in Figure 5.4, one takes the prices associated with the new equilibrium and asks: With how much money must one compensate an individual so that the individual buys the same amount of one good (in this case, good X) and receives the utility level associated with the original equilibrium? The equivalent surplus, shown in Figure 5.5, makes the same calculation, except that old rather than new prices are used. The difference, then, between equivalent and compensating surpluses and equivalent and compensating variations is that, with the former, price lines shift to maintain tangency to a new indifference curve whereas, with the latter, price lines shift so that the quantity of one particular commodity consumed remains unchanged.

Although equivalent and compensating variations are used to calculate welfare indexes in most applied general equilibrium models, this approach is not sufficient to provide measures of aggregate improvement or worsening resulting from policy changes. Multiple consumers are specified in most models, and as a result comparisons between consumers must be made. The procedure typically followed is to use an arithmetic sum of compensating or equivalent variations, summed across all consumer groups; this procedure is also widely used in cost–benefit analysis. Problems inherent in such procedures have been noted by Boadway (1974), and are discussed more fully in Boadway and Bruce (1984).

Welfare measures in dynamic models

Some models that we describe later deviate from the traditional static general equilibrium model in using an explicit dynamic formulation of the economy. For such models it is therefore important to construct dynamic welfare measures. The most commonly used approach in dynamic models is to use a utility function on which to base consumer consumption and savings behavior. This can be represented as follows:

$$\max U = \int_0^T e^{-\rho t} U(C_t)\, dt \quad \text{s.t.} \quad W = \int_0^T e^{-rt} C_t\, dt, \tag{5.20}$$

where ρ is the rate of a consumer's time preference, $U(C_t)$ is a time-separable utility-of-consumption function, r is the rate of return on assets, and W is the consumer's wealth.

This utility-maximization problem defines the intertemporal consumption path that individuals wish to follow. If a static general equilibrium model is expanded to a dynamic setting with all markets clearing at one point in time, the same approach of calculating compensating or equivalent variations can simply be applied. However, in most applied dynamic general equilibrium models, the assumption of market clearing at a single point in time is replaced by sequential market clearing. This reflects a fundamental difference in model structure relative to an Arrow–Debreu model. In these dynamic models, the Arrow–Debreu structure of complete market clearing is replaced by a sequential process in which individuals make decisions in each period on the basis of expectations of future events. Typically these are decisions on consumption today and expected incremental future consumption.

This process can be represented as

$$\max U(C_0, C_E^F) \quad \text{s.t.} \quad I = p_0 C_0 + p_S S, \tag{5.21}$$

where C_0 represents consumption today, C_E^F represents expected future consumption as a result of current-period savings, p_S represents the acquisition price of capital goods, p_0 the price of current consumption, and S the quantity of capital goods purchased. Saving is therefore represented by the term $p_S S$, and income is divided between current and future consumption, with decisions on future consumption being based on an expectations mechanism.

As written, equation (5.21) is not soluble because the arguments of the utility function do not correspond to the comparable arguments in the budget constraint. It is therefore necessary to adopt an expectations mechanism in order to make this formulation tractable; this is typically accomplished by assuming myopic expectations.

In the dynamic-sequence general equilibrium tax model of Ballard et al. (1985), it is assumed that a unit of capital goods bought today will yield a flow of capital service units γ that can be sold at a price of P_K in the future, where P_K is the rental price of capital prevailing in the current period. It is also assumed that the price of consumption goods, P_0, prevailing today will also prevail in the future. This gives an expectations mechanism, which under myopic expectations can be written as

$$C_F = \frac{P_K \gamma S}{P_0}. \tag{5.22}$$

Substituting (5.22) into (5.21) yields:

$$\max U(C_0, C_F) \quad \text{s.t.} \quad I = p_0 C_0 + \frac{P_S P_C}{P_K \gamma} C_F. \tag{5.23}$$

However, use of this utility function in welfare evaluations across sequences of equilibria is misleading, owing to the sequential nature of decision making in this dynamic-sequence equilibrium approach. The utility function U reflects both current-period utility from consumption and expected future utility. If this utility function is used directly for the calculation of Hicksian compensating or equivalent variations, double counting arises. Utility accrues not only in the first period as a result of the expectation of consumption in the future, but also in following periods as a result of utility when consumption is undertaken.

In applying the Hicksian compensating or equivalent variation criteria in a dynamic setting, changes must therefore be made. The change adopted by Ballard et al. (1985) is to take the subfunction C_0 as the utility of consumption in the current period, making calculations of Hicksian equivalent

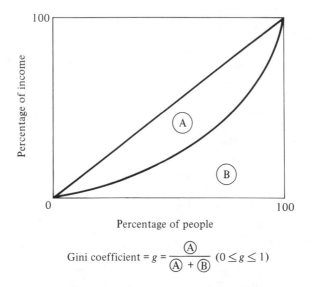

Gini coefficient = $g = \dfrac{Ⓐ}{Ⓐ + Ⓑ}$ $(0 \leq g \leq 1)$

Figure 5.6. Lorenz curve of income distribution.

and compensating variations in each period on this basis. The discounted present value of either equivalent or compensating variations then provides their welfare measure.

Distributional measures

In addition to measures analyzing the efficiency impacts of policy changes, other measures widely used in applied general equilibrium models are those that reflect the impact of policy changes on the distribution of income. These may be constructed simply as percentile shares of income by income ranges, where individuals are ranked according to income and cumulative percentile shares are reported. Alternatively, welfare impacts for each of the various consumer groups identified in the model may be calculated, and the results reported by income range and other characteristics.

However, in assessing distributional impacts it is also necessary to construct measures of distributional changes. Typically, reference is made to the literature on distributional measures of policy change. In Figure 5.6 we indicate how a Gini coefficient can be calculated using a Lorenz curve. Here we rank individuals by increasing income across the population, and plot the percentage of people against the percentage of income. In an economy where the distribution of income is perfectly equal, the Lorenz curve corresponds to the diagonal of the figure represented in Figure 5.6. In the case of an economy that is completely unequal, the Lorenz curve would correspond to the lower and right sides of this figure.

A particular income distribution will yield a Lorenz curve that lies in the lower triangular segment, as shown; the issue is then to construct measures of income distributions. The commonly used measure is the Gini coefficient g, defined in terms of the areas shown in the diagram as the ratio of area A to areas $A + B$. By construction, g lies between 0 and 1; where g is equal to 0, a situation of complete equality prevails; where g is equal to 1, a situation of complete inequality prevails. Calculating how g changes in response to varying policies provides an indication of how unequal the income distribution is. If g increases as the result of a policy change then this indicates a move toward increased inequality. If g decreases, this suggests a move toward increased equality.

This measure must, however, be used with caution, as it is well known that the Gini coefficient provides only a partial ordering among income distributions. For instance, it is possible to have two Lorenz curves that cross and that also have identical values for the Gini coefficient. In this case, the Gini coefficient would be unable to distinguish between these two income distributions, and no comparison between them could be based on such an index. Only where Lorenz curves do not cross can unambiguous measures based on a Gini coefficient be constructed.

A further measure of the distributional impact of policy changes is provided by the Atkinson measure of inequality (see Atkinson 1970), as represented in Figure 5.7. This calculates the potential saving that could be achieved in an economy's total income if the existing distribution of income were replaced by one where all individuals received exactly the same income, as at B. This involves imputing a social-welfare function over the incomes received by individuals, as shown in Figure 5.7.

Price and quantity measures

In addition to analyzing efficiency and distributional impacts of policy changes, calculations are also made of the size of adjustments between equilibria. This typically involves constructing price and quantity indexes, or simply calculating the percentage change in outputs by industry, consumption by product, and other magnitudes.

The simplest indexes are Laspeyres and Paasche price and quantity indexes. These can be represented as follows.

Laspeyres price index:

$$L^D = \frac{\sum_{i=1}^{N} P_i^N X_i^O}{\sum_{i=1}^{N} P_i^O X_i^O}. \tag{5.24}$$

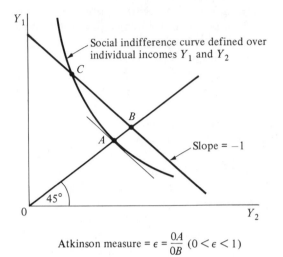

Atkinson measure $= \epsilon = \dfrac{0A}{0B}$ $(0 < \epsilon < 1)$

Figure 5.7. Atkinson's measure of income inequality.

Laspeyres quantity index:

$$L^Q = \frac{\sum_{i=1}^{N} P_i^O X_i^N}{\sum_{i=1}^{N} P_i^O X_i^O}. \tag{5.25}$$

Paasche price index:

$$P^P = \frac{\sum_{i=1}^{N} P_i^N X_i^N}{\sum_{i=1}^{N} P_i^O X_i^N}. \tag{5.26}$$

Paasche quantity index:

$$P^Q = \frac{\sum_{i=1}^{N} P_i^N X_i^N}{\sum_{i=1}^{N} P_i^N X_i^O}. \tag{5.27}$$

In all of these equations, the superscript N refers to the new equilibrium and the superscript O to the original equilibrium, P's are prices, and X's are quantities.

In addition, given the utility functions used in any particular model, it is also possible to construct true cost-of-living indexes. In the CES case this can be represented as follows.

True cost-of-living index (CES case):

$$\bar{P} = \left[\sum_{i=1}^{N} a_i P_i^{1-\sigma} \right]^{1/(1-\sigma)}. \tag{5.28}$$

These indexes provide measures of the impact of changes in prices, either in aggregate or by individual consumer income range. These can be used, for instance, to calculate the impact on different income ranges of changes in relative prices, where preferences differ between individuals.

6

A Harberger tax-model application

6.1 Introduction

In this chapter we illustrate the application of applied general equilibrium techniques by focusing on early small-dimensional general equilibrium tax modeling by Shoven and Whalley (1972) and Shoven (1976). We discuss the distortions introduced into the U.S. economy by the differential tax rates applied to income from capital originating in various sectors of the economy. These modeling analyses were a continuation of earlier work in three seminal articles by Harberger (1959, 1962, 1966).

The earlier Harberger model, as detailed in his 1959 and 1962 articles and in several subsequent studies, is a two-factor, two-sector, general equilibrium model in which a tax applies to the use of one factor (capital) in one sector. Unlike more recent general equilibrium modeling work, however, Harberger solves his model using a series of approximations and local linearization assumptions.

In Harberger's model, an empirical distinction is made between heavily and lightly taxed sectors. He assumes that each sector employs two factors, capital services and labor, in the production of homogeneous outputs. These sectors are sometimes also referred to as the "corporate" and "noncorporate" sectors, owing to the major role played by the corporation income tax in causing these differential tax rates. This sectoral division does not, however, exactly correspond to the legal distinction between incorporated and unincorporated enterprises.

In order to estimate the efficiency loss due to differential taxation of the return to capital, Harberger applies a form of welfare analysis in the tradition of Marshallian producer surplus. He assumes that each sector's schedule of marginal product of capital is linear, as shown in Figure 6.1. Units for outputs are chosen so that both commodity prices are unity,

134

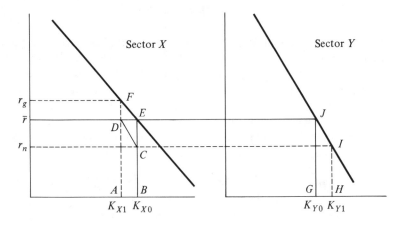

Figure 6.1. Diagrammatic representation of Harberger's local approximation technique used in solving his general equilibrium tax model.

and therefore the schedules in Figure 6.1 can be thought of as marginal revenue product schedules. The total quantity of both capital and labor in the economy is assumed to be fixed and always fully employed. Under these assumptions, the changes in capital allocation by sector can be used to generate a measure of the social waste associated with these distortions. In the absence of any taxes, capital will allocate itself such that the rate of return $\bar{r}$ is equal in the two sectors and the capital endowment is fully employed. Upon the imposition of a tax on capital income in sector X, the gross rate of return r_g in that sector must be such that the net rate of return r_n is equalized across sectors and capital is again fully employed. The difference between r_g and r_n is by definition the tax T per unit of capital utilized in sector X.

In Figure 6.1, the area $ABEF$ can be interpreted as the value of the lost output in sector X when K_X decreases from K_{X0} to K_{X1} upon the imposition of the tax. Analogously, $GHIJ$ is the value of increase in output in sector Y. Since we know that capital is fully employed both in the presence and absence of the tax, it must be true that $K_{X0}-K_{X1}=K_{Y1}-K_{Y0}$. The area $FECD$ represents the social loss of the tax ($ABEF-GHIJ$) and is given by

$$\tfrac{1}{2}(r_g-\bar{r})(K_{X0}-K_{X1})+\tfrac{1}{2}(\bar{r}-r_n)(K_{Y1}-K_{Y0})=-\tfrac{1}{2}T\Delta K_X, \qquad (6.1)$$

where $\Delta K_X = K_{X1}-K_{X0}=K_{Y0}-K_{Y1}$ and $T=r_g-r_n$.

Estimating the magnitude of the social efficiency loss requires an expression for ΔK_X. In order to obtain such a solution, Harberger uses a static, two-sector, two-factor, general equilibrium model. Local or "small-change" assumptions are made repeatedly in this analysis. For example, in calculating the efficiency loss from differential taxation, it is assumed that the marginal product of capital varies linearly with the amount of capital in each of the sectors. In addition, either the labor allocation must be assumed to be unaltered, or the marginal product of capital must be taken as independent of the amount of labor employed in each sector.

In the appendix to this chapter we present the equations used by Harberger (1962) in solving his model. Following is the solution for ΔK_X, the change in capital use in the taxed sector:

$$\Delta K_X = K_X T \frac{-E[g_K S_X (L_X/L_Y) + f_K S_Y] - S_X S_Y f_L}{E(g_K - f_K)[(K_X/K_Y) - (L_X/L_Y)]}, \qquad (6.2)$$
$$-S_Y - S_X[f_L(K_X/K_Y) + f_K(L_X/L_Y)]$$

where

E = compensated price elasticity of demand for X,
$S_X(S_Y)$ = elasticity of factor substitution in sector $X(Y)$,
$f_K(g_K)$ = share of capital in sector $X(Y)$, and
$f_L(g_L)$ = share of labor in sector $X(Y)$.

As one would expect, the capital shift between sectors attributable to the tax depends on the various elasticities and factor intensities and is also proportional to T. Along with (6.1), this implies that the social cost of the tax distortion varies with the square of the tax rate.

Harberger similarly solves his linearized system for the change in the net price of capital (i.e., $\Delta P_K = r_n - \bar{r}$), and obtains

$$\Delta P_K = T \frac{E f_K [(K_X/K_Y) - (L_X/L_Y)] + S_X[f_L(K_X/K_Y) + f_K(L_X/L_Y)]}{E(g_K - f_K)[(K_X/K_Y) - (L_X/L_Y)]},$$
$$-S_Y - S_X[f_L(K_X/K_Y) + f_K(L_X/L_Y)]$$

$$(6.3)$$

Harberger uses this to evaluate the incidence of these taxes, reasoning as follows. If $\Delta P_K = -(TK_X)/(K_X + K_Y)$ then capital could be said to bear the full burden of the tax, in that its gross return would be unchanged; if $\Delta P_K = 0$ then both net factor prices would be unaffected, and thus the share of national income going to capital and labor would remain constant.

6.2 An applied general equilibrium version of Harberger's model

To implement an applied general equilibrium variant of Harberger's original analysis, the approach (outlined in previous chapters) of calibration and counterfactual equilibrium analysis is used both by

Shoven and Whalley (1972) and Shoven (1976). In calibrating, data on factor inputs, tax rates, and elasticities is needed. Table 6.1 contains the factor input and capital tax data from Shoven (1976) for both a 2- and a 12-sector level of aggregation for averaged data for the United States for the period 1953–9. The capital income and tax data is drawn from Rosenberg (1969), and the "Other capital tax adjustments" column is constructed using assumptions similar to those employed by Harberger. The labor data is derived from national income and product accounts. The capital data, which defines a unit of capital as that amount earning an average flow of \$1.00 net of all taxes, indicates that $K_Y = \$26,878$ million and $K_X = \$34,244$ million. The data in this table corrects for two errors in Harberger's original study; these corrections are discussed in more detail in Shoven (1976).

Harberger uses data similar to that in Table 6.1, augmented with labor data,[1] to estimate ΔK_X and $-\frac{1}{2}T\Delta K_X$ for several different elasticities of factor substitution (S_X and S_Y), and for two different compensated elasticities of demand for the "corporate" product X. The two demand elasticities E are based on the elasticity of substitution V between X and Y, which is assigned values of 1 and $\frac{1}{2}$, respectively. The relationship between V and the compensated demand for X is

$$E = Vr_Y, \tag{6.4}$$

where r_Y is the share of national income spent on Y. Thus the case $V = 1$ is consistent with demands derived from a Cobb–Douglas utility function. Harberger takes r_Y as 0.17, although column (3) of Table 6.1 suggests that r_Y is just slightly under 0.15. Harberger considers several combinations of S_X and S_Y. Table 6.2 contains Harberger's published results, appropriately qualified as only rough estimates, for the elasticities examined.

Using data from Table 6.1, Shoven recomputes the efficiency cost of the distortionary taxation of capital income using Merrill's algorithm as described in Chapter 3. In most cases the assumptions of Harberger are used, although the models are, of course, not strictly comparable. Production functions are assumed to be of the CES form, while both CES and Cobb–Douglas utility functions are analyzed for consumers. Two classes of consumers are incorporated: one representing the top 10% of income recipients in the United States, the other the bottom 90%. The model is solved both with and without the inclusion of a labor–leisure choice, although detailed results are presented only for the fixed–labor-supply case.

---

[1] Harberger takes L_X to be \$200 billion and L_Y to be \$20 billion. Column 1 of Table 6.1 agrees very closely with his L_X figure, but shows L_Y to be only \$17,471 billion (or units).

Table 6.1. *U.S. factor payments and capital income taxes by major sectors (annual averages, 1953–9, in $ million)*

Sector	Total return to labor (1)	Total return to capital (2)	Total factor return (1)+(2) (3)	Property and corporate income tax (4)	Other capital tax adjustments (5)	Total capital tax (4)+(5) (6)	Net return to capital (2)−(6) (7)	Capital tax as a fraction of total return to capital (6)/(2) (8)	Capital tax as a fraction of net return to capital (6)/(7) (9)
Noncorporate	17,471	26,878	44,349	6,639	1,724	8,363	18,515	0.31	0.45
Agriculture	8,800	7,481	16,281	1,302	927	2,229	5,252	0.30	0.42
Real estate	6,869	18,429	25,298	5,140	797	5,937	12,492	0.32	0.48
Crude oil and gas	1,802	968	2,770	197	—	197	771	0.20	0.26
Corporate	199,871	52,394	252,265	22,907	5,898	28,805	23,589	0.55	1.22
Mining[a]	2,528	688	3,216	305	77	382	306	0.56	1.25
Contract construction	16,670	1,195	17,865	435	152	587	608	0.49	0.97
Manufacturing[b]	79,626	24,665	104,291	12,488	2,435	14,923	9,742	0.61	1.53
Lumber and wood products	2,426	718	3,144	206	102	308	410	0.43	0.75
Petroleum and coal products	1,846	3,028	4,874	770	452	1,222	1,806	0.40	0.68
Trade	43,590	10,897	54,487	3,493	1,481	4,974	5,923	0.46	0.84
Transportation	14,078	2,683	16,761	1,230	291	1,521	1,162	0.57	1.31
Communication and public utilities	7,394	6,489	13,883	3,290	640	3,930	2,559	0.61	1.54
Services	31,713	2,031	33,744	690	268	958	1,073	0.47	0.89
Total	217,342	79,272	296,614	29,546	7,622	37,168	42,104	0.47	0.88

[a] Other than crude oil and gas.   [b] Other than lumber and wood products and petroleum and coal products.
Source: From Imam and Whalley (1982), © 1976 by the University of Chicago, used by permission.

Table 6.2. *Harberger's (1966) estimates of the social efficiency cost of distortionary taxes on income from capital (1953-9)*

Case	S_X (1)	S_Y (2)	V (3)	ΔK_X (4)[a]	$-(1/2)T\Delta K_X$ (5)[b]
1	−1.0	−1.0	−1.0	−6.9	2.9
2	−1.0	−0.5	−1.0	−5.9	2.5
3	−0.5	−1.0	−1.0	−5.2	2.2
4	−0.5	−0.5	−1.0	−4.8	2.0
5	−1.0	0.0	−1.0	−4.7	2.0
6	−0.5	0.0	−1.0	−3.9	1.7
7	−1.0	−1.0	−0.5	−5.3	2.3
8	−1.0	−0.5	−0.5	−4.2	1.8
9	−0.5	−1.0	−0.5	−4.1	1.7
10	−0.5	−0.5	−0.5	−3.5	1.5
11	−1.0	0.0	−0.5	−5.0	2.1
12	−0.5	0.0	−0.5	−2.4	1.0

Note: S_X (resp., S_Y) are elasticities of substitution in corporate (resp., noncorporate) sector; V are elasticities of substitution between products X and Y.
[a] In billions.   [b] In \$ billion.
Source: Reprinted from "Efficiency Effects of Taxes on Income from Capital" by A. C. Harberger, in M. Krzyzaniak (ed.), *Effects of Corporation Income Tax,* © 1966 by Wayne State University Press, Detroit, Michigan 48202, used by permission.

On the production side of the economy, each sector's technological production possibilities are characterized by a CES production function such as

$$Q_i = \gamma_i [\alpha_i L_i^{-\rho_i} + (1-\alpha_i) K_i^{-\rho_i}]^{-1/\rho_i}. \tag{6.5}$$

Shoven considers seven different combinations of elasticities of substitution: three in line with Harberger, and four others.

Case	S_X	S_Y
1	−1.00	−1.00
2	−1.00	−0.50
3	−1.00	−0.25
4	−0.75	−0.25
5	−0.50	−0.50
6	−0.50	−0.25
7	−0.25	−0.25

The higher-income consumer is endowed with approximately 23% of the economy's labor (corresponding to the observed share of labor income going to the top 10% of income receivers) and 40% of total stock of capital (both figures from Projector and Weiss 1966). This latter figure roughly corresponds to the share of capital income going to the top 10% of income receivers, although it is much lower than the share of capital income going to the top 10% of wealth holders. Endowing the high-income receivers with more than 10% of the labor yields an equal endowment of labor in natural units but a disproportionate endowment in efficiency units.

Each consumer's CES demand functions are of the form

$$x_{ij} = \frac{b_{ij} I_j}{P_i^{(\sigma_j)} \sum_{k=1}^{n} b_{kj} P_K^{(1-\sigma_j)}}, \tag{6.6}$$

where x_{ij} is consumer j's demand for commodity i, b_{ij} is the share parameters for commodity i, P_i is the price of the ith good, σ_j is individual j's elasticity of substitution between commodities, and I_j is j's income, given by

$$I_j = \sum_{i=1}^{n} P_i w_{ij} + \alpha_j R, \tag{6.7}$$

where the w_{ij} are j's initial asset holdings (including labor) and α_j is the jth consumer's share in government revenue R.

In Shoven's computations, two values of consumer elasticities of substitution (i.e., the σ_j's) are examined: 1.0 and 0.5. With σ_j equal to 1.0, the demand functions (6.6) are of the familiar Cobb–Douglas type.

Using the demand functions (6.6) permits one to impose the observed aggregate 5.69/1.00 expenditure ratio for the outputs of the heavily and lightly taxed sectors. Table 6.1 indicates that the total expenditure on corporate products was $252.265 billion; $44.349 billion was spent on output of the noncorporate sector. If each individual's tastes were such that $b_{1j} = 5.69 b_{2j}$ ($j = 1, 2$), where the corporate product is labeled commodity 1 and the noncorporate product commodity 2, then expenditure ratios of the model would exactly correspond to 5.69/1.00 with unitary prices. However, in the case investigated, lower-income individuals were assumed to place a relatively higher weight on the output of the lightly taxed sector than higher-income individuals. This is consistent with observed higher budget shares allocated to food expenditures (agricultural output) by lower-income people. The ratios used for b_{1j}/b_{2j} were 7.00 for the higher-income consumer and 5.30 for the lower-income consumer.

The total endowments of the economy were also taken from Table 6.1. We need, however, to clarify the units conventions adopted by Shoven. The approach taken is to analyze all capital income taxes, and not simply the surtax. This implies taking as a unit of capital that amount earning

$1.00 net of all taxes (Harberger's original units). In the absence of a labor–leisure choice, the total labor endowment is taken to be 217.342 billion units, while the capital-services endowment is 42.104 billion units. In the presence of the surtax, 199.871 billion units of labor and 23.589 billion units of capital are allocated to the corporate sector (Table 6.1, columns 1 and 7). To focus solely on the impact of the tax, the fraction of government tax proceeds returned to each consumption class is assumed equal to that class's fraction of the total capital endowment; redistributive effects are not considered here.

Table 6.3 contains a summary of the social loss and incidence results for the case of two production sectors. Efficiency-loss estimates in Shoven's analysis are based on changes in the value of national product, not on calculations using the Hicksian equivalent and compensating variation measures typical of later applied general equilibrium work. The comparison in Table 6.3 is between the observed equilibrium (in the presence of distortionary capital income taxes) and the equilibrium that would prevail in the absence of distortionary taxes (i.e., in the absence of what Harberger refers to as the surtax). Also reported are the equilibrium prices and the capital tax rate (on net income) that would prevail if the replacement were a flat tax designed to have the same real yield occurring in the case of distortionary taxes. A Paasche price index is used to determine real rather than nominal revenue equivalence; the technique of determining this equal-yield tax rate is described in Chapter 3 and in Shoven and Whalley (1977).

Table 6.3 also presents a "shift factor" that gives some indication of the incidence of distortionary capital taxation with respect to the functional distribution of income. The shift factor is defined as $1 + (\Delta P_K K)/(\Delta R)$, where K is the total endowment of capital, ΔP_K is the change in the net price of capital in moving from the nondistortionary to the distortionary tax regime (thus this term is negative in all cases), and ΔR is the change in nominal government revenue (which is of course positive). If the shift factor is zero, the decrease in the net return to capital is equal to the increase in government revenue due to the distortionary surtax, and in this sense capital may be said to bear the full burden. A negative value for the shift factor indicates that capital bears more than 100% of the burden of the surtax; a positive value indicates that labor is sharing in its costs.

Part A of Table 6.3 presents results for those cases where both consumer classes have demand elasticities of substitution (σ_j's) equal to 1. As one would expect, the removal of the surtax involves a decrease in the price of X, the corporate output, and an increase in the price of Y (owing to the increase in the net price of capital). These price changes tend to benefit the higher-income more than the lower-income consumer class, as the former spends a larger fraction of its income on products (i.e., X)

Table 6.3. *Summary of 2-sector results presented by Shoven (1976) in his analysis of distortionary capital income taxation*

	Observed equilibrium	Case[a]						
		1	2	3	4	5	6	7
S_X	—	−1.00	−1.00	−1.00	−0.75	−0.50	−0.50	−0.25
S_Y	—	−1.00	−0.50	−0.25	−0.25	−0.50	−0.25	−0.25

A. Consumer demand elasticities = 1.0; fixed factor supplies

	Observed equilibrium	1	2	3	4	5	6	7
Surtax removal:								
P_X	1.00	0.97	0.97	0.97	0.97	0.96	0.96	0.94
P_Y	1.00	1.17	1.19	1.21	1.18	1.13	1.14	1.08
P_L	1.00	1.00	1.00	1.00	1.00	1.00	1.00	1.0
P_K	1.00	1.30	1.33	1.35	1.31	1.22	1.24	1.12
R	37.17	24.67	25.30	25.66	24.86	23.21	23.61	21.39
X^b	252.27	261.07	261.50	261.74	261.07	259.67	259.97	257.88
Y^b	44.35	37.88	37.37	37.08	37.54	38.61	38.31	39.62
$K_X{}^b$	23.60	27.83	27.32	27.04	26.82	26.59	26.43	25.67
$K_Y{}^b$	18.52	14.28	14.79	15.06	15.29	15.52	15.67	16.44
$L_X{}^b$	199.87	199.87	201.25	202.03	201.92	201.17	201.73	201.37
$L_Y{}^b$	17.47	17.47	16.09	15.32	15.43	16.18	15.61	15.98
Shift factor	—	0.00	−0.17	−0.28	−0.05	0.34	0.25	0.67
Relative share of rich	0.27	0.27	0.27	0.28	0.27	0.27	0.27	0.27
ΔNNP[c]	—	0.94	0.63	0.45	0.47	0.59	0.48	0.44
ΔNNP[d]	—	2.34	2.26	2.21	2.00	1.67	1.67	1.09

Equal-yield replacement:

P_X	1.00	0.97	0.97	0.97	0.97	0.96	0.96	0.94
P_Y	1.00	1.17	1.19	1.21	1.18	1.13	1.14	1.08
P_L	1.00	1.00	1.00	1.00	1.00	1.00	1.00	1.0
P_K	1.00	1.01	1.05	1.07	1.02	0.91	0.93	0.78
R	37.17	36.88	37.14	37.29	37.00	36.38	36.54	35.72
Tax rate	1.22/0.45	0.87	0.84	0.83	0.86	0.95	0.93	1.08

B. Consumer demand elasticities = 0.5; fixed factor supplies

S_X	—	−1.00	−1.00	−1.00	−0.75	−0.50	−0.50	−0.25
S_Y	—	−1.00	−0.50	−0.25	−0.25	−0.50	−0.25	−0.25

Surtax removal:

P_X	1.00	0.97	0.98	0.98	0.98	0.97	0.97	0.96
P_Y	1.00	1.19	1.22	1.24	1.22	1.17	1.19	1.13
P_L	1.00	1.00	1.00	1.00	1.00	1.00	1.00	1.00
P_K	1.00	1.33	1.38	1.40	1.37	1.28	1.32	1.21
R	37.17	25.34	26.2	26.70	26.09	24.40	25.06	23.00
X^b	252.27	257.43	257.62	257.74	257.46	256.76	256.98	255.97
Y^b	44.35	40.88	40.50	40.28	40.46	41.04	40.78	41.47
K_X^b	23.59	26.86	26.18	25.80	25.69	25.76	25.51	25.10
K_Y^b	18.52	15.24	15.92	16.30	16.41	16.34	16.60	17.01
L_X^b	199.87	198.18	199.71	200.60	200.58	199.87	200.56	200.51
L_Y^b	17.47	19.16	17.64	16.75	16.76	17.47	16.78	16.83
Shift factor	—	−0.18	−0.45	−0.62	−0.41	0.07	−0.10	0.38
Relative share of rich	0.27	0.27	0.28	0.28	0.28	0.27	0.27	0.27
ΔNNP^c	—	0.89	0.54	0.33	0.33	0.49	0.33	0.31
ΔNNP^d	—	1.69	1.51	1.41	1.31	1.19	1.15	0.83

Table 6.3 (cont.)

	Observed equilibrium	Case[a]						
		1	2	3	4	5	6	7
Equal-yield replacement:								
P_X	1.00	0.97	0.98	0.98	0.98	0.97	0.97	0.96
P_Y	1.00	1.19	1.22	1.24	1.22	1.17	1.19	1.13
P_L	1.00	1.00	1.00	1.00	1.00	1.00	1.00	1.00
P_K	1.00	1.05	1.11	1.14	1.10	0.99	1.03	0.89
R	37.17	37.04	37.59	37.81	37.58	36.91	37.18	36.40
Tax rate	1.22/0.45	0.84	0.81	0.79	0.81	0.89	0.86	0.97

[a] These cases differ in the specification of production side elasticity values; see Section 6.2.
[b] Billions of units.
[c] $ billion; calculated at new (i.e., nondistortionary) prices.
[d] $ billion; calculated at old (i.e., observed) prices.
Source: From Shoven (1976), © 1976 by the University of Chicago, used by permission.

that decrease in price. As in Harberger's work, labor is taken as the numeraire commodity and thus always has a price of unity. The rows of Table 6.3 labeled X and Y show that the output of sector X increases by 2%–3% while the output of sector Y decreases by as much as 15%. Factor substitution does occur, and the corporate sector switches to a more capital-intensive technology with the removal of the surtax while the lightly taxed sector becomes more labor intensive.

One interesting aspect of the data underlying these calculations is that the sector whose capital income is heavily taxed is relatively labor intensive. This raises the possibility that labor may bear a large fraction of the burden of the surtax, particularly in cases with low elasticities of factor substitution. Indeed, in Table 6.3 the "shift factor" row of part A shows that labor's share of the burden is significant in cases 5, 6, and 7. In fact, in case 7 the relative share of the rich consumer class (whose assets are capital intensive) is 0.4% higher in the presence of the distortionary tax than in its absence. Efficiency-loss estimates are sensitive to specification of the production parameters, and range between $0.435 billion and $2.344 billion. These figures amount to 2.8%–18.7% of the revenue generated by the surtax. For each specification, two loss estimates (of changes in NNP)[2] are given: one evaluated at the observed prices and one at the new, nondistortionary prices.

As capital services are fixed (by assumption) in aggregate supply, any flat-rate tax on capital income is nondistortionary, and capital fully bears the burden of such a tax. Further, since tax proceeds are distributed according to ownership of capital, the distribution of income is unaffected by flat-rate capital income taxes. It is for these reasons that the net price of capital is the only price that changes when moving from a flat 45.2% tax (surtax-removal cases) to a flat tax at an equal-yield rate. For each of the seven production parameterizations, the new net price of capital and the equal-yield tax rate applying to net capital income are shown in the "P_K" and "tax rate" rows, respectively.

Part B of Table 6.3 presents the same seven cases of factor elasticity, where now the consumers' elasticities of substitution are specified as 0.5. As shown, the efficiency-loss estimates are reduced by 10%–40% and the shift factors are substantially lower, indicating that labor bears a smaller share of the burden of the surtax. The sensitivity of the functional distribution incidence of this distortion to different parameterizations seems to be far greater than expected or indicated by Harberger.

---

[2] NNP (net national product) refers to the value of the product of the two (or twelve) sectors. The efficiency loss is the value of the change in production. Ideally, Hicksian equivalent or compensating variations (described in Chapter 5) should be computed, but these were omitted in early applied modeling calculations.

In order to evaluate the impact of disaggregation, the 12-sector data of Table 6.1 was also analyzed by Shoven using the applied general equilibrium approach. Results for a subset of the cases with 12 production sectors are presented in Table 6.4. As intermediate products are not explicitly incorporated in these early models, it is necessary to interpret consumers as demanding value added from each of the 12 sectors. Table 6.4 compares the current tax situation (each of the 12 sectors facing the different effective tax rates shown in column 9 of Table 6.1) with a flat-tax regime, with the tax rate set at 45.2% (for comparability with the two-sector results presented in Table 6.3).

As before, the equal-yield tax rate and the corresponding net price of capital were computed. Compared with the two-sector results, the loss estimates for these 12-sector cases are 10%–70% higher; the efficiency cost as a percentage of the surtax yield now runs as high as 24.4%. The restrictiveness of a two-sector treatment of production is seen by noting that, in the 12-sector treatment, large relative price differentials develop between sectors previously aggregated together in the corporate sector. In particular, the price of petroleum and coal products is shown to rise as much as 24% relative to the price of communication and public utilities with the switch to neutral capital income taxation. Although the two-sector results indicate that the corporate sector's output prices would fall, Table 6.4 shows the price of some components of that sector rising relative to the price of labor. The added detail of this disaggregated analysis thus yields an alternative picture that may be valuable in the making of policy decisions.

Tables 6.3 and 6.4 show that a change in tax rates causes a vector of changes in outputs that must be aggregated to arrive at a single-number deadweight loss estimate. Table 6.4 includes the Paasche and Laspeyres measures of the inefficiency (change in NNP) resulting from distortionary taxation of capital income in the 1953–9 U.S. economy. Nonetheless, policy makers often want a single number and not a range of numbers. One technique of combining the Paasche and Laspeyres indexes into a single loss estimate is to form the Fisher "ideal" index (Fisher 1927), which is the square root of their product. The results of such a procedure for the cases shown in part A of Tables 6.3 and 6.4 are shown in Table 6.5: the Fisher index shows a loss of $1.47 billion, or 11.9% of the surtax revenue.

While demonstrating the applicability of the applied general equilibrium approach, this analysis nonetheless uses a relatively simple model. The model is static, and its basic form incorporates only two sectors and analyzes only one tax distortion. More complex and comprehensive applied general equilibrium tax models were developed subsequent to this work, and are discussed in the next chapter.

Table 6.4. *Selective summary of Shoven's 12-sector results on an analysis of distortionary U.S. capital income taxation*

	Observed equilibrium	Case 1	Case 2	Case 3
A. Consumer demand elasticities = 1.0; fixed factor supplies				
$S_{1,2,3}$	—	−1.00	−0.75	−0.25
S_{4-12}	—	−1.00	−0.25	−0.25
Surtax removal:				
P_1/Y_1	1.00/ 16.28	1.14/ 14.32	1.15/ 14.20	1.07/ 14.68
P_2/Y_2	1.00/ 25.30	1.19/ 21.18	1.20/ 21.03	1.09/ 22.49
P_3/Y_3	1.00/ 2.77	1.15/ 2.40	1.17/ 2.37	1.11/ 2.42
P_4/X_4	1.00/ 3.22	0.96/ 3.34	0.96/ 3.34	0.94/ 3.30
P_5/X_5	1.00/ 17.87	0.10/ 17.92	1.00/ 17.94	0.99/ 17.48
P_6/X_6	1.00/104.29	0.93/111.86	0.94/111.67	0.92/110.31
P_7/X_7	1.00/ 3.14	1.02/ 3.09	1.02/ 3.09	0.99/ 3.08
P_8/X_8	1.00/ 4.87	1.07/ 4.54	1.08/ 4.52	0.99/ 4.75
P_9/X_9	1.00/ 54.49	1.00/ 54.24	1.01/ 54.26	0.98/ 53.82
P_{10}/X_{10}	1.00/ 16.76	0.97/ 17.32	0.97/ 17.32	0.95/ 17.02
P_{11}/X_{11}	1.00/ 13.88	0.87/ 15.96	0.87/ 15.90	0.83/ 16.12
P_{12}/X_{12}	1.00/ 33.74	1.00/ 33.76	1.00/ 33.80	0.99/ 32.92
P_L	1.00	1.00	1.00	1.00
P_K	1.00	1.30	1.30	1.14
R	37.17	24.67	24.81	21.73
Shift factor	—	0.00	−0.04	0.61
ΔNNP[a] (Paasche)	—	1.34	0.77	0.48
ΔNNP[b] (Laspeyres)	—	3.30	2.81	1.76
Equal yield:				
P_K	1.00	1.01	1.02	0.81
R	37.17	36.76	36.88	35.77
Tax rate	—	0.86	0.86	1.05
B. Consumer demand elasticities = 0.5; fixed factor supplies				
$S_{1,2,3}$	—	−1.00	−0.75	−0.25
S_{4-12}	—	−1.00	−0.25	−0.25
Surtax removal:				
P_1/Y_1	1.00/ 16.28	1.15/ 15.28	1.18/ 15.14	1.11/ 15.37
P_2/Y_2	1.00/ 25.30	1.22/ 23.08	1.25/ 22.85	1.14/ 23.54
P_3/Y_3	1.00/ 2.77	1.16/ 2.59	1.19/ 2.56	1.14/ 2.58
P_4/X_4	1.00/ 3.22	0.97/ 3.29	0.97/ 3.29	0.95/ 3.27
P_5/X_5	1.00/ 17.87	1.00/ 17.99	1.00/ 18.03	0.99/ 17.79
P_6/X_6	1.00/104.29	0.94/108.40	0.94/108.28	0.93/107.59
P_7/X_7	1.00/ 3.14	1.02/ 3.13	1.03/ 3.13	1.00/ 3.12
P_8/X_8	1.00/ 4.87	1.09/ 4.67	1.11/ 4.67	1.03/ 4.77
P_9/X_9	1.00/ 54.49	1.01/ 54.58	1.02/ 54.58	0.99/ 54.31
P_{10}/X_{10}	1.00/ 16.76	0.97/ 17.11	0.98/ 17.12	0.96/ 16.97

Table 6.4 *(cont.)*

	Observed equilibrium	Case		
		1	2	3
P_{11}/X_{11}	1.00/ 13.88	0.88/ 14.89	0.89/ 14.83	0.85/ 14.92
P_{12}/X_{12}	1.00/ 33.74	1.00/ 33.94	1.00/ 34.01	1.00/ 33.56
P_L	1.00	1.00	1.00	1.00
P_K	1.00	1.33	1.36	1.21
R	37.17	25.29	25.95	23.01
Shift factor	—	−0.17	−0.37	0.38
ΔNNP^a (Paasche)	—	1.30	0.66	0.39
ΔNNP^b (Laspeyres)	—	2.36	1.86	1.16
Equal yield:				
P_K	1.00	1.05	1.09	0.89
R	37.17	37.12	37.45	36.36
Tax rate	—	0.84	0.81	0.97

Note: Sector 1, agriculture; 2, real estate; 3, crude oil and gas; 4, mining; 5, contract construction; 6, manufacturing; 7, lumber and wood products; 8, petroleum and coal products; 9, trade; 10, transportation; 11, communication and public utilities; 12, services.
^{a} $ billion; calculated at new (i.e., nondistortionary) prices.
^{b} $ billion; calculated at old (i.e., observed) prices.

6.3 Appendix: Harberger's model of partial capital taxation

Working with the two-sector model of the economy described in this chapter, Harberger determines the change in the capital allocation and in the equilibrium price of capital resulting from the imposition of a surtax on the return to capital in one sector (X). He assumes that the demand for each product X and Y depends upon the level of consumer income and on relative prices. However, since the government is assumed to spend the tax revenue in the same manner as consumers would when faced with existing prices, only relative commodity prices affect aggregate demand (this is a local approximation that ignores income loss due to inefficiency of the taxation.) Working then with the assumption that the quantity demanded of X depends only on P_X and P_Y, Harberger differentiates this function to obtain

$$\frac{dX}{X} = E \frac{d(P_X/P_Y)}{(P_X/P_Y)},$$ (A6.1)

where E is the compensated price elasticity of demand for X. Given that $P_X \equiv P_Y \equiv 1$, a local approximation of (A6.1) gives

Table 6.5. *Shoven's estimated Fisher index of the production loss from distortionary U.S. capital income taxation*

2 sectors			12 sectors		
S_X	S_Y	\$ billion	$S_{1,2,3}$	$S_{4\text{-}12}$	\$ billion
-1.00	-1.00	1.49	-1.00	-1.00	2.11
-1.00	-0.50	1.19	—	—	—
-1.00	-0.25	1.00	—	—	—
-0.75	-0.25	0.97	-0.75	-0.25	1.47
-0.50	-0.50	0.99	—	—	—
-0.50	-0.25	0.89	—	—	—
-0.25	-0.25	0.69	-0.25	-0.25	0.92

Note: Consumer demand elasticities $= 1.0$; fixed factor supplies.
Source: From Shoven (1976), © 1976 by the University of Chicago, used by permission.

$$\frac{dX}{X} = E(dP_X - dP_Y). \tag{A6.2}$$

The production function of sector X,

$$X = F(K_X, L_X), \tag{A6.3}$$

is assumed to be continuous, differentiable, and homogeneous of degree one.

Taking a total derivative through (A6.3), one obtains

$$dX = \frac{\partial F(K_X, L_X)}{\partial K_X} dK_X + \frac{\partial F(K_X, L_X)}{\partial L_X} dL_X. \tag{A6.4}$$

Dividing both sides by X, this can be written as

$$\frac{dX}{X} = \left(\frac{\partial F(K_X, L_X)}{\partial K_X} K_X \middle/ X \right) \frac{dK_X}{K_X} + \left(\frac{\partial F(K_X, L_X)}{\partial L_X} L_X \middle/ X \right) \frac{dL_X}{L_X} \tag{A6.5}$$

or

$$\frac{dX}{X} = f_K \frac{dK_X}{K_X} + f_L \frac{dL_X}{L_X}, \tag{A6.6}$$

where f_K, f_L may be interpreted as the relative factor shares in sector X.

By the definition of S_Y, the elasticity of substitution between labor and capital in sector Y, we have

$$\frac{d(K_Y/L_Y)}{(K_Y/L_Y)} = S_Y = \frac{d(P_K/P_L)}{(P_K/P_L)}. \tag{A6.7}$$

A local approximation of (A6.7) yields

$$\frac{dK_Y}{K_Y} - \frac{dL_Y}{L_Y} = S_Y(dP_K - dP_L).$$ (A6.8)

In expression (A6.8), dP_K is the change in the price of capital relevant for production decisions in sector Y; that is, the change in the price of capital net of the tax. For sector X, the relevant change in the price of capital is the gross change $dP_K + T$. Thus, the equation analogous to (A6.8) for sector X is

$$\frac{dK_X}{K_X} - \frac{dL_X}{L_X} = S_X(dP_K + T - dP_L).$$ (A6.9)

The price of labor is taken to be the numeraire, the price in terms of which other prices are expressed; as such, it is taken to be unity both in the presence and absence of the tax:

$$dP_L = 0.$$ (A6.10)

By the assumption of full employment of all factors, the relations

$$dK_Y = -dK_X,$$ (A6.11)

$$dL_Y = -dL_X$$ (A6.12)

are obtained.

The production function of sector Y,

$$Y = G(K_Y, L_Y),$$ (A6.13)

is also assumed to be continuous, differentiable, and homogeneous of the first degree. These properties, along with competition in the factor markets, guarantee that factor payments just exhaust revenue:

$$P_Y Y = P_L L_Y + P_K K_Y.$$ (A6.14)

Taking a total derivative of each side of (A6.14) and appealing to a local approximation yields

$$P_Y dY + Y dP_Y = P_L dL_Y + L_Y dP_L + P_K dK_Y + K_Y dP_K.$$ (A6.15)

The equation analogous to (A6.4) for sector Y is

$$dY = \frac{\partial G(K_Y, L_Y)}{\partial K_Y} dL_Y + \frac{\partial G(K_Y, L_Y)}{\partial K_Y} dK_Y.$$ (A6.16)

Noting that competition implies the marginal product of labor in Y is (P_L/P_Y) and of capital (P_K/P_Y), (A6.16) may be written as

$$dY = \frac{P_L}{P_Y} dL_Y + \frac{P_K}{P_Y} dK_Y$$

or

$$P_Y dY = P_L dL_Y + P_K dK_Y. \tag{A6.17}$$

Subtracting this result from (A6.15), we have

$$Y dP_Y = L_Y dP_L + K_Y dP_K. \tag{A6.18}$$

Dividing both sides by Y and recalling that the initial prices of both factors and outputs are assumed to be unity, one obtains

$$dP_Y = g_L dP_L + g_K dP_K, \tag{A6.19}$$

where g_L, g_K are the relative factor shares in sector Y. Performing a similar procedure for sector X results in the relation

$$dP_X = f_L dP_L + f_K(dP_K + T). \tag{A6.20}$$

Equations (A6.20), (A6.19), and (A6.10) can be substituted into (A6.2), giving

$$\frac{dX}{X} = E[f_K(dP_K + T) - g_K dP_K]. \tag{A6.21}$$

By similarly substituting (A6.20), (A6.11), and (A6.12) into (A6.8) and substituting (A6.12) into (A6.9), one has

$$\frac{K_X(-dK_X)}{K_Y K_X} - \frac{L_X(-dL_X)}{L_Y L_X} = S_Y dP_K \tag{A6.22}$$

and

$$\frac{dK_X}{K_X} - \frac{dL_X}{L_X} = S_X(dP_K + T). \tag{A6.23}$$

By equating the right-hand sides of equations (A6.21) and (A6.6) and rearranging terms in (A6.22) and (A6.23), the following system of three equations is derived:

$$\begin{aligned} E f_K T &= E(g_K - f_K) dP_K + f_L \frac{dL_X}{L_X} + f_X \frac{dL_X}{K_X}, \\ 0 &= S_Y \cdot dP_K - \frac{L_X}{L_Y} \frac{dL_X}{L_X} + \frac{K_X}{L_Y} \frac{dL_X}{K_X}, \\ S_X T &= -S_X \cdot dP_K - \frac{dL_X}{L_X} + \frac{dK_X}{K_X}. \end{aligned} \tag{A6.24}$$

The solution for dK_X, which is required in order to evaluate the efficiency loss of the capital income taxation distortion, can be achieved by applying Cramer's rule to (A6.24). That is,

$$dK_X = K_X \cdot T \frac{\begin{vmatrix} E(g_K - f_K) & f_L & Ef_K \\ S_Y & -(L_X/L_Y) & 0 \\ -S_X & -1 & S_X \end{vmatrix}}{\begin{vmatrix} E(g_K - f_K) & f_L & f_K \\ S_Y & -(L_X/L_Y) & K_X/K_Y \\ -S_X & -1 & 1 \end{vmatrix}}$$

(A6.25)

or

$$dK_X = K_X \cdot T \frac{-E\left[g_K S_X \dfrac{L_X}{L_Y} + f_K S_Y\right] - S_X S_Y f_L}{E(g_K - f_K)\left(\dfrac{K_X}{K_Y} - \dfrac{L_X}{L_Y}\right) - S_Y - S_X\left(\dfrac{f_L K_X}{K_Y} + \dfrac{f_K L_X}{L_Y}\right)}.$$

(A6.26)

Similarly, the system of equations (A6.24) can be solved for dP_K, yielding

$$dP_K = \frac{Ef_K\left(\dfrac{K_X}{K_Y} - \dfrac{L_X}{L_Y}\right) + S_X\left(\dfrac{f_L K_X}{K_Y} + \dfrac{f_K L_X}{L_Y}\right)}{E(g_K - f_K)\left(\dfrac{K_X}{K_Y} - \dfrac{L_X}{L_Y}\right) - S_Y - S_X\left(\dfrac{f_L K_X}{K_Y} + \dfrac{f_K L_X}{L_Y}\right)} T.$$

(A6.27)

7

A general equilibrium model of U.S. tax policies

In this chapter we describe how a more recent and larger-scale model of the U.S. economy and tax system has been used by Ballard, Fullerton, Shoven, and Whalley (BFSW) to analyze a range of tax policy options. The model differs from that described in the previous chapter in many respects: It is more disaggregated (19 industries and 15 consumer goods), incorporates a series of consumer groups stratified by income range, includes all major existing taxes in the United States, and, importantly, is extended to a dynamic setting through a sequenced equilibrium approach. The data and parameters used in this model are described in BFSW (1985) and are not repeated here; this chapter provides an overview of model structure and results from a sample of the model applications. A more formal statement of model structure appears in the appendix to this chapter.

7.1 Main characteristics of the BFSW general equilibrium tax model

The BFSW general equilibrium tax model of the United States can be regarded as a higher-dimensional extension of the Harberger tax model presented in Chapter 6.[1] Taxes enter as *ad valorem* distortions of factor use, production decisions, and consumer purchases. The model generates sequences of equilibria through time; the equilibria are connected through savings decisions that imply growth in the capital-services endowment between periods. The model is calibrated to 1973 benchmark data that is assumed to lie on a balanced growth path for the economy.

The production side of the model includes 19 profit-maximizing industries that use labor and capital according to constant elasticity of substitution (CES) or Cobb–Douglas production functions. Substitution

---

[1] The model description given here draws on Section 2 of Fullerton (1978).

elasticities are chosen for each industry as the central figures in Caddy's (1976) survey of the literature, and range from 0.6 to 1. To obtain each industry's payments for labor and capital,[2] BFSW use data from the *Survey of Current Business* (U.S. Department of Commerce 1976) and unpublished data from the Commerce Department's National Income Division. Base-year quantities are derived according to the convention that a unit of each primary factor is that amount earning $1.00 net of taxes in the 1973 benchmark year. A fixed-coefficient input–output matrix is derived from Bureau of Economic Analysis tables.

The *ad valorem* tax on each industry's use of capital comprises the corporation income tax, state corporate franchise taxes, and local property taxes. The social security tax and contributions to workers' compensation are modeled as an *ad valorem* tax on industry's use of labor. Various federal excise taxes and indirect business taxes are modeled as output taxes; a different tax rate applies to each of the 19 industries. State and local sales taxes apply to each of the 15 consumer goods in the model. The 19 producer goods can be used directly by government, for export, or for investment; these producer goods can also be translated into the 15 consumer goods that enter consumer demand functions. This translation is made possible by a fixed-coefficient G matrix.[3] The G matrix is necessary because the Commerce Department production data include industries such as mining, electrical manufacturing, and trade, whereas the *Survey of Consumer Expenditures* (U.S. Department of Labor 1961) provides data on purchases of goods like furniture, appliances, and recreation.

Industry and government payments to buy labor and capital services are exactly matched by total household receipts from the supply of each factor. The Treasury Department's Merged Tax File provides information on labor and capital income for each of the 12 consumer classes, as well as tax payments and an estimate of the average marginal income tax rate τ_j for each group. These estimates range from a 1% average marginal rate for the lowest income class to a 40% rate for the highest income class. A progressive income-tax system is then modeled as a series of linear schedules, one for each group. Pensions, IRA plans, and Keogh plans are modeled as a 30% saving subsidy in order to capture the proportion of saving subject to such tax-sheltered treatment.

[2] Labor compensation includes all wages, salaries, commissions, and tips; capital earnings include net interest paid, net rent paid, and corporate profits, with adjustments for capital consumption and inventory valuation. Noncorporate profits were divided between labor and capital on the basis of full-time–equivalent hours and average wage for each industry. Some industries were averaged over several years to minimize the influence of transitory effects.

[3] The G matrix is derived from data in the February 1974 *Survey of Current Business*.

A "personal factor tax" is also modeled, designed to capture discrimination among industries by the personal income tax. Each industry is assigned a fraction f_i representing the proportion of capital income from industry i that is fully taxable at the personal level. This fraction is determined from proportions of capital income paid as noncorporate income, dividends, capital gains, interest, and rent.[4] At the industry level, capital income is taxed at rate τ, the overall capital-weighted average marginal personal income-tax rate. At the consumer level, rebates are given to groups having a marginal tax rate τ_j less than τ, while additional tax is collected from others. The personal factor tax acts as a withholding tax at the industry level, and corrections at the consumer level sum to zero. The model thus captures the favorable tax treatment given to industries with large noncorporate investment tax credits and to the housing industry.

The expanded income of each consumer group is given by transfer income plus endowments of capital and labor.[5] The latter is defined as 7/4 of labor income; 7/4 reflects BFSW's estimate that, in the benchmark year, 40 out of a possible 70 hours are worked. Consumer demands are based on budget-constrained maximization of the nested CES utility function:

$$U = U\left[H\left(\sum_{i=1}^{15} X_i, l\right), C_f\right]. \tag{7.1}$$

In the first stage, consumers save some income for future consumption C_f and allocate the rest to a subutility function H over present consumption goods X_i and leisure l. The elasticity of substitution between C_f and H is based on Boskin's (1978) estimate of 0.4 for the elasticity of saving with respect to the net-of-tax real rate of return. Saving in the model derives from consumer demands for future consumption under the expectation that all present prices, including the price of capital, will prevail in all future periods. Income for H is divided between the purchase of leisure l and the purchase of a bundle of 15 consumer goods. The composition of the consumer-good bundle derives from the maximization of a Cobb–Douglas function. The elasticity of substitution between leisure and consumer goods is based on an estimate of 0.15 for the elasticity of labor supply with respect to the net-of-tax wage.

[4] All dividends are 96% taxable, because of the 4% that fell under the $100 exclusion in 1973. All retained earnings are 73% taxable; this results from the value of the tax deferral and rate advantages for capital gains, as well as the taxation of purely nominal gains. Interest and rents are fully taxable except for the imputed net rent of owner-occupied homes, while the noncorporate investment tax credit also appears as a personal tax reduction that varies by industry.

[5] Portfolio effects are ignored because dividends, capital gains, interest, rent, and other types of capital income are summed to obtain capital endowments.

Consumer decisions regarding factor supplies are thus made jointly with consumption decisions. Demands for leisure and for savings will depend on all relative prices. Savings imply investment demand for producer goods, with proportions based on national accounting data for private investment and inventories.

Foreign trade also enters the model through a specification of export-demand and import-supply functions for the United States. No international factor flows enter the model, and trade is balanced. Literature estimates of trade elasticities are used to specify the model's parameters.

Specification of the government sector completes the model. Revenues from the various taxes described previously are used to finance transfers and the purchase of labor, capital services, and producer goods. Lump-sum transfers to each consumer group are based on Treasury Department data for social security, welfare, government retirement, food stamps, and similar programs. Government demands for factors and commodities are represented by a Cobb–Douglas demand system. In equilibrium, the government budget is balanced.

The procedures described in Chapter 5 are used by BFSW to generate a benchmark equilibrium data set in which values are separated into prices and quantities by assuming that a physical unit of each good and factor is the amount that sells for $1.00. Certain elasticity parameters are imposed exogenously, and the model's equilibrium conditions are used to generate remaining behavioral equation parameters that are consistent with the data set. Factor employments by industry are used to derive production function weights, and household expenditures are used to derive utility function weights and demand function weights. The resulting tax rates, function parameters, and endowments are used to solve the model, perfectly replicating the benchmark equilibrium. This calibration allows for a test of the solution procedure and ensures that the various agents' behaviors are mutually consistent with the benchmark data set.

The Merrill (1972) variant of Scarf's (1973) algorithm is used in each period to solve for a competitive equilibrium in which profits are zero and supply equals demand for each good and factor. Producer-good prices are calculated on the basis of factor prices and zero-profit conditions, while consumer-good prices are derived from producer-good prices through the G transition matrix. A complete set of prices, quantities, incomes, and allocations is calculated for every equilibrium.

The model's dynamic sequencing of single-period equilibria assumes first that the 1973 data set or benchmark equilibrium lies on a steady-state growth path. Observed savings behavior and the capital endowment are translated into an annual growth rate for capital (approximately 2.75%), growth that is also attributed to effective labor units. This exogenous growth rate for labor is split evenly between population growth and Harrod-neutral technical progress. The benchmark sequence of equilibria is then calculated by maintaining all tax rates and preferences, increasing labor exogenously, and allowing savings to augment capital endowments over time. By construction, this sequence will have constant factor ratios and constant relative prices.

Simulations of policy change are performed by altering tax rates while retaining preference parameters and the exogenous rate of labor growth. Saving and other behavior then conform to the specified elasticities; growth of capital diverges from the steady-state rate; and the economy approaches a new steady-state path with a new capital–labor ratio. Sequences are compared by discounting the H composites of instantaneous consumption through time with appropriate terminal conditions. Only leisure and present consumption are included in this welfare measure, because savings are reflected in later consumption. The sequence is discounted at a 4% rate. The welfare gain or loss of a tax change is taken as the sum of compensating variations over households.

7.2 Integration of the corporate and personal income taxes

It has long been recognized that the existence of separate taxes on corporate and personal income may reduce the efficiency of capital allocation. This recognition has given rise to proposals to integrate the two taxes in a variety of ways. This section summarizes the static and dynamic general equilibrium resource-allocation effects of four integration plans for the United States, an analysis that is based on the model described in Section 7.1.

The results indicate that total integration of personal and corporate taxes would yield an annual static efficiency gain of about $4–8 billion (in 1973 dollars). Partial integration plans yield fewer gains. The analysis also indicates that full integration may yield dynamic gains whose present value is at least $300 billion and perhaps as much as $700 billion. This is about 1.4% of the discounted present value of consumption and leisure in the U.S. economy. The plans also differ in their distributional effects. Both the distribution and efficiency results depend on the replacement taxes used to preserve government revenues.

A corporate tax that operates separately from the personal income tax is widely acknowledged to lead to a number of problems associated with the double taxation of corporate income (see McLure 1979): Dividends are paid out of corporate profits net of corporate taxes, and dividends are further taxed under the personal income tax. Retained earnings are also taxed twice, to the extent they are capitalized in higher share values. However, the capital gains resulting from retained earnings were not (until

1986) fully taxed by the personal income tax, and they are taxed on a deferred basis.

One problem with double taxation is that it may reduce overall rates of return and adversely affect capital accumulation. Another problem is that the deferral advantage given to retained earnings impairs the efficiency of capital markets. This is sometimes referred to as the "lock-in" effect. Firms can invest retained earnings in projects with a below-market yield, and their shareholders will still earn a higher net-of-tax return than if the funds were distributed as dividends and invested elsewhere.

A third problem with double taxation is that it creates a bias toward debt finance, since only equity returns are subject to corporate taxes; this bias may distort corporate financial policies. A fourth distortion is created to the extent that firms can choose whether or not to incorporate, as discussed in Ebrill and Hartman (1982). Finally, the corporate tax results in effective tax rates that are higher in some industries than others, because of special provisions in the corporate tax law and of the varying degrees to which industries are incorporated. Such tax-rate differentials further disrupt the efficient allocation of capital.

In the BFSW model, personal taxes combine with corporate taxes to raise effective tax rates in industries that are highly incorporated, but observed corporate taxes are still reduced by the extent to which each industry makes use of credits, deductions, and allowances. The model considers intertemporal and intersectoral distortions in the allocation of real capital, but does not include endogenous financial decisions or distortions in the choices among debt, retained earnings, or dividend policy.

Integration plans seek to remove or mitigate the adverse effects of the two separate tax systems by linking the personal income-tax liabilities of stockholders to the corporate tax liabilities of the firms. Four corporate tax–integration alternatives are evaluated, which differ in the extent to which they remove undesirable features of the separate corporate income tax.

Plan 1 – total integration: Under this alternative, the corporate income tax is eliminated and the personal income tax is modified to tax total shareholder earnings, rather than just dividends. When capital gains are realized, the tax basis is set at the original purchase price plus the retained earnings accumulated during the holding period. This feature avoids a double tax on retained earnings capitalized in higher stock prices. However, if the basis is not reset for inflation, capital-gains taxes will be assessed on purely nominal appreciation; this amounts to a levy on capital wealth. Such total integration, with and without inflation indexation of capital gains, is evaluated by BFSW.

Plan 2 – dividend deduction from corporate income–tax base: This alternative removes the double taxation of dividends simply by making them deductible from taxable corporate income. Capital-gains taxation of individuals is unaltered, and the corporate income tax is effectively converted into a tax on retained earnings. Unless differences in retention policies by industry were to disappear, the corporate tax would continue to result in some discrimination among industries. This plan would result in an incentive to pay out more dividends.

Plan 3 – dividend deduction from personal income–tax base: An alternative way of removing the double taxation of dividends is to allow a dividend deduction from the personal income tax rather than from the corporate income tax. Capital-gains taxation is again unaltered. As with Plan 2, differences in retention policies by industry will perpetuate the industrial discrimination caused by the corporate tax. Once again, however, corporations will have an incentive to pay out more dividends.

Plan 4 – dividend gross-up: This was the plan most actively discussed in the U.S. tax-reform debate during 1977, and is similar to the tax treatment of dividends in Canada. This plan seeks only a partial reduction of the double taxation of dividends. The taxable incomes of individual shareholders are "grossed up" by some proportion of the income taxes paid by corporations; the shareholders then receive a corresponding tax credit. Individuals whose personal tax rates are lower than the corporate tax rate will effectively receive a rebate. Individuals with higher personal tax rates will end up paying additional taxes at the personal level. Because of the partial nature of the credit, none of the distortions listed previously will be entirely removed.

Each of the four tax-integration plans just described must be represented in model-equivalent form for the purpose of analyzing its general equilibrium effects. Each plan implies a different set of capital tax rates by industry, as well as a different proportion of capital income from industry i that is taxable at the personal level.

Representing the plans in the model

Plan 1 – total integration: Under this plan, corporate taxes are eliminated from the numerator of the industrial capital tax–rate calculation. The personal income tax is changed to tax all earnings, rather than just dividends; this means that the fraction of retained earnings taxed at the personal level is set to 1. New parameters represent the fraction of capital income from each sector that is taxable at the personal level (calculated under this new capital-gains treatment). These changes imply new personal factor taxes and new capital tax rates by industry.

Plan 2 - dividend deduction from corporate income–tax base: This plan's corporate income–tax base is the undistributed profits of corporations, represented in model-equivalent terms by removing (for each industry) a portion of the corporate tax paid from the 1973 capital taxation figures and recalculating the capital tax rate. The portion of corporate tax removed is given by the ratio of dividends to net-of-tax corporate profits by industry (U.S. Department of Commerce 1976). Neither the fraction of industry income taxable at the personal level nor the personal income-tax functions change under this plan.

Plan 3 - dividend deduction from personal income–tax base: This plan removes dividends from the personal income–tax system. In model-equivalent terms, this plan is specified by considering the effect of dividend deductibility on the income taxes of households. The proportion of dividends taxable by the personal income tax is set to zero. Other adjustments are analogous to those made for Plan 1.

Plan 4 - dividend gross-up: This scheme gives stockholders an income-tax credit of 15% of the corporate taxes paid by those firms in which they own an interest. It is most satisfactorily modeled as a reduction in the corporate taxes of each industry by the amount of the credit; this amount is then treated as an increase in dividends in the calculation of the fraction of capital income taxable at the personal level. The new effective tax rates include 85% of corporate income taxes and the new personal factor taxes. The result is higher dividends relative to retained earnings, and consumers experience an increase in taxable capital income.

Table 7.1 presents results on the static efficiency effects of the four alternative integration plans. Table 7.2 reports the static distributional effects. In Table 7.3 we present calculations of dynamic effects.[6]
To obtain the static measures of efficiency changes displayed in Table 7.1, BFSW first calculate the changes in national income plus leisure, valued at prices before and after the policy change. Paasche and Laspeyres quantity indexes (rather than compensating or equivalent variations) are used,

[6] The figures in Tables 7.1 and 7.3 are presented in billions of 1973 dollars. It may be useful to give some idea of the value of a 1973 dollar. The Commerce Department's GNP deflator stood at 105.8 in 1973 (with the 1972 value set to 100.0); by 1985, the GNP deflator had risen to 250. Thus, if the structure of the economy were unchanged in the intervening 11 years, the welfare gain figures in Tables 7.1 and 7.2 would have to be increased by about 150% in order to bring them up to 1985 levels.

Table 7.1. *Static welfare effects of corporate and personal tax integration: change in annual real expanded national income (billions of 1973 dollars)*

Plan	Tax replacement			
	Lump-sum scaling	Multiplicative scaling	Additive scaling	VAT scaling
Plan 1: Full integration with indexing	9.671	2.192	2.695	4.917
Plan 1: Full integration without indexing	7.855	4.234	4.381	5.291
Plan 2: Dividend deduction from corporate income tax[a]	3.580	0.063	0.230	0.985
Plan 2: Dividend deduction from corporate income tax, with extreme-behavior assumption[a]	8.061	4.230	4.388	5.380
Plan 3: Dividend deduction from personal income tax[a]	4.068	2.873	2.928	1.841
Plan 3: Dividend deduction from personal income tax, with extreme-behavior assumption[a]	4.539	2.903	2.965	3.390
Plan 4: Dividend gross-up	3.450	2.455	2.486	2.719
Equal capital tax rates on industry[b]		10.912		

Notes: Real expanded national income incorporates the change in the valuation of leisure through induced variations in labor supply. The numbers reported are the geometric means of Paasche and Laspeyres index numbers, for each tax replacement, as described in the text.

[a] The standard simulations for dividend deduction plans 2 and 3 assume that corporate financial policies do not change. In particular, the new parameters representing the fraction of capital income from each sector that is taxable at the personal level are calculated with the old levels of dividends and retained earnings as weights for the fraction of dividends taxable by the personal income tax and the fraction of retained earnings taxed at the personal level. However, these dividend deduction plans might encourage greater distribution of corporate profits. The extreme-behavior assumption uses the sum of dividends and retained earnings as the weight on the fraction of dividends taxable by the personal income tax, with no weight on the fraction of retained earnings taxed at the personal level.

[b] This result is for complete equalization of capital tax rates by industry. The property tax, corporate franchise tax, corporate income tax, and personal factor tax are included in this equalization. This result is presented for comparison purposes.

Table 7.2. *Percentage changes in expanded real income after income taxes and transfers, by income class, for various tax-integration plans*

Income of consumer group (1973 dollars)	Equal capital tax rates on industry[b]	Plan 1 Full integration with indexing (additive scaling)	Plan 1 Full integration with indexing (multiplicative scaling)	Plan 2[a] Dividend deduction from corporate income tax (multiplicative scaling)	Plan 2[a] With extreme behavior (multiplicative scaling)	Plan 3[a] Dividend deduction from personal income tax (multiplicative scaling)	Plan 3[a] With extreme behavior (multiplicative scaling)	Plan 4 Dividend gross-up (multiplicative scaling)
0–2,999	1.763	1.935	3.981	2.393	3.632	0.270	0.291	0.897
3,000–3,999	1.329	1.210	2.939	1.767	2.647	0.283	0.311	0.685
4,000–4,999	1.063	0.592	2.045	1.239	1.863	0.258	0.285	0.519
5,000–5,999	1.055	0.624	1.946	1.166	1.789	0.272	0.296	0.504
6,000–6,999	1.118	0.595	1.830	1.061	1.693	0.284	0.317	0.488
7,000–7,999	1.036	0.431	1.468	0.839	1.406	0.269	0.296	0.425
8,000–9,999	0.920	0.244	1.033	0.587	1.070	0.238	0.253	0.344
10,000–11,999	0.961	0.478	0.991	0.523	1.031	0.274	0.294	0.336
12,000–14,999	1.035	0.527	0.888	0.420	0.945	0.283	0.311	0.325
15,000–19,999	0.938	0.741	0.608	0.214	0.686	0.312	0.338	0.266
20,000–24,999	1.012	1.310	0.809	0.223	0.730	0.426	0.486	0.296
25,000–	0.651	6.501	3.970	1.125	1.330	1.992	2.515	0.656

Notes: Expanded real income includes leisure, valued at the household net-of-tax wage rate. Numbers shown are the arithmetic means of percentage changes to income based on Paasche and Laspeyres price indexes.
[a] See footnote *a*, Table 7.1.
[b] See footnote *b*, Table 7.1.

Table 7.3. *Dynamic welfare effects of corporate and personal tax integration: present value of equivalent variations over time (billions of 1973 dollars)*

Plan	Tax replacement			
	Lump-sum scaling	Multiplicative scaling	Additive scaling	VAT scaling
Plan 1: Full integration with indexing	695.0 (1.394)	310.6 (0.623)	418.2 (0.839)	559.6 (1.122)
Plan 1: Full integration without indexing	473.5 (0.950)	288.2 (0.578)	339.7 (0.681)	408.6 (0.819)
Plan 2: Dividend deduction from corporate income tax[a]	259.8 (0.521)	57.6 (0.115)	114.5 (0.230)	188.6 (0.378)
Plan 2: Dividend deduction from corporate income tax, with extreme-behavior assumption[a]	492.9 (0.989)	295.8 (0.593)	351.0 (0.704)	424.0 (0.850)
Plan 3: Dividend deduction from personal income tax[a]	263.7 (0.529)	208.1 (0.417)	222.4 (0.446)	238.4 (0.478)
Plan 3: Dividend deduction from personal income tax, with extreme-behavior assumption[a]	315.7 (0.633)	236.1 (0.475)	256.9 (0.515)	286.8 (0.575)
Plan 4: Dividend gross-up	179.0 (0.359)	128.8 (0.258)	142.3 (0.285)	160.8 (0.323)
Equal capital tax rates on industry[b]		544.8 (1.093)		

Notes: We consider eleven equilibria, five years apart, in order to project annual consumption values over the fifty intervening years. For consumption beyond year fifty, we have an appropriate treatment of the terminal conditions. The dynamic equivalent variations are analogs of static concepts applied to the consumption sequence over time, assuming the first-period discount factor is unchanged.

The numbers in parentheses represent the gain as a percentage of the present discounted value of welfare (consumption plus leisure) in the base sequence. The value is $49 trillion for all comparisons, and only accounts for a population the size of that in 1973.
[a] See footnote *a*, Table 7.1.
[b] See footnote *b*, Table 7.1.

because consumers may assess the utility contribution of savings inaccurately owing to their myopic expectations. Instead of showing both the Laspeyres and Paasche indexes, we merely report the geometric mean of the two.

The main static effect of corporate tax integration is that capital stock is allocated more efficiently among the industrial sectors. To arrive at some idea of the magnitude of these changes, BFSW focus on eight industries. Four of these (agriculture, petroleum refining, real estate, and government enterprises) had low rates of capital tax under the 1973 law. The other four (chemicals and rubber, metals and machinery, transportation equipment, and motor vehicles) had high capital taxes. The differences are due largely to differences in the degree of incorporation in these industries.

When the corporation income tax is removed, capital in industries that were previously more heavily taxed becomes cheaper. Table 7.4 shows how capital is reallocated among industries. Seven industries end up using less capital (in the first-period equilibrium) under corporate tax integration than they used in the base case: agriculture, mining, crude petroleum and gas, petroleum refining, real estate, services, and government enterprises. Approximately 6.5% of the total capital stock is reallocated from these seven industries to the other twelve. Table 7.4 shows that the outputs of industries that were previously treated more favorably increase in price as a result of the tax change. It is not surprising that such price changes lead to changes in the prices of consumer goods. Two consumer goods have large increases in their relative prices: housing as well as gasoline and other fuels. Consumer goods with the largest decreases in relative prices include nondurable, nonfood household items; motor vehicles; appliances; and clothing and jewelry.

Overall taxes on capital are reduced as a result of corporate-tax integration, so the net return to capital rises sharply. Capital also earns a higher net retu.n because it is allocated more efficiently. In the base sequence of equilibria, all prices are equal to unity in all periods (by our units convention and the assumption that the benchmark equilibrium lies on a steady-state growth path). In the first equilibrium period under full corporate tax integration, the relative price of capital rises to 1.208 (we normalize by setting the price of labor equal to 1.0). However, the price of capital falls from that point on, because more saving occurs under integration than in the base case. In the first equilibrium period, the higher net rate of return to capital leads to a 14.5% increase in savings. By the second equilibrium period, which occurs five years after the first period, the relative price of capital drops to 1.188. In the third period it reaches 1.171, in the fourth 1.151, and so on. By the tenth equilibrium period, the price of capital services stands at 1.111, dropping to 1.107 by the eleventh and final period. Notice that decreases in the relative price of capital become smaller over time, as the economy approaches a new steady-state growth path asymptotically.

The distributional effects reported in Table 7.2 depend upon both the sources and uses of each consumer's budget. As indicated, the price of capital rises in the simulated equilibrium. Low-income consumers spend a large proportion of their income on goods produced by lightly taxed,

Table 7.4. *Changes resulting from full corporate tax integration for selected industries, in first equilibrium period*

Industry	Capital tax rates		Relative output prices[a]		Percentage of total capital stock used by given industry	
	Before integration	After integration	Before integration	After integration	Before integration	After integration
Industries currently lightly taxed						
Agriculture	0.54	0.46	1.0	1.059	15.4	13.5
Petroleum refining	0.46	0.44	1.0	1.060	4.8	4.5
Real estate	0.63	0.56	1.0	1.084	36.1	32.7
Government enterprises	0.26	0.26	1.0	1.051	4.4	3.8
Industries currently heavily taxed						
Chemicals	1.87	0.60	1.0	0.943	2.0	2.8
Metals and machinery	1.72	0.67	1.0	0.959	5.4	6.9
Industries heavily taxed						
Transport equipment	23.50	4.88	1.0	0.936	0.04	0.10
Motor vehicles	1.29	0.47	1.0	0.941	2.5	3.2

[a] Price of labor = 1.0.

capital-intensive industries such as agriculture and real estate. For example, the poorest group spends 19.9% of its net money income on food and 21.8% on housing, while the richest group spends 14.6% on food and 12.5% on housing. Therefore, the uses side of consumer budgets has some regressive effects on income distribution under corporate tax integration.

On the sources side, the distributional impact of any policy change is driven by the fact that the capital–labor ratio of income is bowl-shaped across the 12 consumer groups. That is, the lowest-income group and the highest-income group have factor endowments that are more heavily weighted by capital. The higher net price of capital leads to a *U*-shaped pattern of gains by consumer groups when corporate tax integration is simulated (see the "Plan 1" column in Table 7.2).

Plan 1 removes only part of the industrial discrimination in the taxation of capital income, because property taxes remain as differential capital taxes by industry. Property taxes are particularly important in the agriculture and real estate industries. Interindustry discrimination is reduced enough to provide a $4 billion annual static welfare gain in each year (Table 7.1, in 1973 dollars) for those cases with either multiplicative or additive scaling for revenue neutrality or inflation indexation of capital-gains taxes. Without this correction for inflation, the efficiency gains are lower. Table 7.3 shows that dynamic gains are sensitive to the yield-preserving replacement tax considered. Additive scaling of the personal income tax yields a $418 billion gain; multiplicative scaling a $311 billion gain. The discounted present value of the future income stream for the 1973 population is about $49 trillion in 1973 dollars.[7]

Under Plan 2, dividends are treated like interest for tax purposes, and we first assume that corporations continue to retain the same portion of income. Reduction of the corporate income–tax base causes some leveling of capital tax rates and results in a small increase in annual welfare. Dynamic gains under multiplicative scaling of tax rates are $58 billion. Under lump-sum replacement, dynamic gains are $260 billion. We also consider the extreme case where all corporate earnings are distributed; the corporate income tax would thus be effectively eliminated. The static gain for such a tax replacement is around $8 billion per year under lump-sum replacement, $4 billion under additive or multiplicative scaling, and $5 billion under a sales-tax replacement. The dynamic gains are comparable

---

[7] The sensitivity of these dynamic results to the replacement tax can be explained by the positive correlation between income and the proportion of income saved. Since multiplicative scaling collects more tax revenue from high-income groups, it creates a greater distortion in their intertemporal choices. Less saving occurs, and the new balanced growth path has a lower capital–labor ratio than with other kinds of replacement.

to the gains under full integration. These welfare gains are substantially above those calculated using the assumption of fixed dividend–retention policies.

Under Plan 3, the reduced tax on dividends again implies lower tax rates on heavily incorporated industries and a leveling of all rates in general. Static welfare gains are about $3 billion per year. With multiplicative scaling, dynamic gains are $208 billion. Under lump-sum replacement, the gains here are about $264 billion, about the same as under Plan 2. The multiplicative results reflect the importance of the deduction from the upwardly scaled income tax. As might be expected, Table 7.2 shows that Plan 3 has less progressive effects than Plan 2, since dividend income is all taxed at the corporate rate instead of at progressive personal tax rates.

Under extreme financial policy behavior, where firms no longer retain earnings, both the static and dynamic gains are somewhat larger. Less corporate income is subject to the personal income tax. The difference between results with and without the extreme-behavior assumption is less than for Plan 2, because the personal income–tax deduction does less to eliminate interindustry discrimination than does the corporate income–tax deduction for dividends. The distributional effects for the extreme-behavior case of Plan 3 are generally regressive, although the middle groups all have similar relative improvements. This pattern is similar to that for the case in which we assume no change in financial policies.

All plans that decrease the corporate income tax on dividends only can be termed "partial integration" plans. The fourth plan might be called a "partial partial" plan, because it reduces only part of the tax on dividends. The static welfare gain is $2.5 billion per year when personal tax rates are scaled upward in order to maintain real government expenditure. Dynamic gains under multiplicative scaling are $129 billion; under additive scaling, $142 billion; and under VAT (value-added tax) replacement, $161 billion. Here again, the spread between dynamic welfare gains is less than that with full integration, because this plan involves smaller revenue loss than full integration. Multiplicative scaling makes up most revenue from high-income, high-saving consumers, and it thus reduces future capital stocks and incomes. The dynamic lump-sum and additive cases show that the dividend gross-up does substantially less to improve interindustry resource allocation than other plans.

As a basis for comparison, we also report the effects of complete equalization of capital tax rates by industry. In this case all tax discrimination on capital use among industries is eliminated by using a single tax rate for all industries, and taxing equally all capital income at the personal level. Capital tax rates are set to a common rate, providing government with enough revenue to maintain its real purchases. The resulting efficiency gains are larger than those of the four integration plans. These gains represent the maximum possible increase in expanded national income from the elimination of interindustry capital tax distortions.

7.3 Replacing the personal income tax with a progressive consumption tax

For many years there has been interest in the progressive consumption tax as an alternative to the federal personal income tax. This interest is reflected in *Blueprints for Basic Tax Reform,* published in 1977 by the U.S. Department of the Treasury's Office of Tax Analysis (and hereafter referred to simply as *Blueprints*), as well as tax-reform documents in other countries, such as the Meade Report (Meade 1978) in the United Kingdom.

In this section we report on use of the BFSW model to evaluate changing the U.S. tax system to a progressive consumption tax. Since the model incorporates a labor–leisure choice, where leisure is an untaxed commodity, results reflect the fact that both the consumption tax and the income tax are distortionary. The BFSW model has been used to quantify the relative efficiency of these two second-best tax systems.

The main concern is with intertemporal distortions; consequently, all simulations use the dynamic model. The dynamic sequences describe transitions between the base-case steady-state growth path and the new steady-state paths that result from various policy changes. By comparing capital-labor ratios in the base case and the revised case at various points in time, BFSW establish about how long the economy takes to approach its new steady-state capital–labor ratio.

In order to evaluate the efficiency of adopting a consumption tax as the major broadly based U.S. tax source, BFSW consider eight alternative plans that differ in rate structure and in the accompanying tax changes. The features of each plan are shown in Table 7.5.

Plan 1, consumption tax, would simply raise the fraction of sheltered savings in the federal personal tax from 30% to 80%. With the current sheltering of the imputed return to housing, this would effectively remove all savings from the tax base. This plan could be effected by greatly liberalizing the provisions governing savings vehicles such as Keogh plans and Individual Retirement Accounts. Plan 2, integration of corporate and personal income taxes, includes full integration of capital gains. Plan 3 is the consumption tax (80% of savings deductible) combined with corporate tax integration. Plan 4 corresponds most closely to a pure consumption tax, in that all income is taxed (including the imputed income from housing), while all saving is deductible. The corporate income tax is eliminated with this plan also.

Table 7.5. *Tax alternatives considered in the analysis of consumption tax options*

Description	Fraction of saving deduction from taxation	Preferential treatment of income from housing capital at industry level	Fraction of dividends taxable	Fraction of nominal capital gains taxable at personal level	Separate corporate income tax
0. Current U.S. system	0.3	Yes	0.96	0.25	Yes
1. Consumption tax	0.8	Yes	0.96	0.25	Yes
2. Corporate tax integration with indexation of capital gains	0.3	Yes	1.0	1.0	No
3. Consumption tax with integration	0.8	Yes	1.0	1.0	No
4. Pure consumption tax with integration	1.0	No	1.0	1.0	No
5. Partial consumption tax	0.55	Yes	0.96	0.25	Yes
6. Full savings deduction with housing preference	1.0	Yes	0.96	0.25	Yes
7. Pure income tax without integration	0.0	No	1.0	1.0	Yes
8. Pure income tax with integration	0.0	No	1.0	1.0	No

Plans 5 and 6 represent possible policy outcomes, although they do not correspond to particular proposals. Plan 5 represents a partial movement toward a consumption tax, where the 55% deduction for savings represents a point halfway between the 1973 tax system and the 80% deduction of Plan 1. In Plan 6, all saving is deductible, and the existing preferences on income from housing capital are retained.

Plans 7 and 8 investigate whether the 1973 U.S. federal income tax system (which is about halfway toward a consumption tax) is better or worse than a pure income tax. A pure income tax would remove the special treatment of capital gains and of the imputed income to homeowners who occupy their own homes. Plan 7 also eliminates the tax shelters offered by pension funds and other retirement savings vehicles. While savings would be taxed more heavily, many of the interindustry distortions of the present tax system would be eliminated. Plan 8 goes further and removes the corporate income tax as well.

The present value of equivalent variations over time is calculated for each of the 12 consumer groups in the BFSW model, using the same procedure as that used to analyze corporate and personal tax integration. Individual results are summed over the 12 groups, and are presented in Table 7.6.

The consumption tax (Plan 1) leads to an efficiency gain of $616 billion if the revenue shortfall caused by the additional deduction for savings is recovered via a lump-sum tax. The gain is reduced to $537 billion if marginal tax rates are increased in a multiplicative manner, and to $556 billion if an additive surtax is applied to the marginal rates. With sales-tax scaling, the gain is $564 billion. In Table 7.6, the figures in parentheses represent the efficiency gain of each plan as a fraction of the present value of future expanded national income (estimated at $49 trillion). The consumption tax yields gains ranging from 1.08% to 1.24% of this present value, or from 1.58% to 1.81% when leisure is excluded from the present value of national income. A more important comparison is between these gains and the present value of revenue raised by the income tax in the base case; efficiency gains from adopting a consumption tax range from 11.6% to 13.4% of base-case income-tax revenues.

Some results regarding corporate income–tax integration are presented in row 2 of Table 7.6 (these results were shown before, in Table 7.3). They indicate that such integration promises a gain for the economy of about the same order of magnitude as that shown for the consumption tax. This present-value gain, as estimated by BFSW, is roughly $695 billion (1973 dollars) with lump-sum replacement taxes. When the lost revenue is regained by increases in distortionary taxes, the gains range from $310 billion to $560 billion.

Table 7.6. *Dynamic welfare effects in present value of equivalent variations over time (billions of 1973 dollars)*

Tax replacement	Types of scaling to preserve tax yield			
	Lump-sum	Multiplicative	Additive	VAT
1. Consumption tax	615.8 (1.235)	536.9 (1.077)	556.1 (1.115)	573.6 (1.150)
2. Corporate tax integration with indexation of capital gains	695.0 (1.394)	310.6 (0.623)	418.2 (0.839)	559.6 (1.122)
3. Consumption tax with integration	1303.6 (2.614)	836.0 (1.677)	976.1 (1.958)	1080.6 (2.167)
4. Pure consumption tax with integration	1431.6 (2.871)	1175.5 (2.357)	1246.2 (2.499)	1254.9 (2.517)
5. Partial consumption tax (55% savings deduction)	299.0 (0.600)	259.3 (0.520)	267.1 (0.536)	280.6 (0.563)
6. Full savings deduction with housing preference	877.3 (1.759)	789.2 (1.583)	806.7 (1.618)	792.2 (1.589)
7. Pure income tax without integration	−544.6 (−1.092)	−238.0 (−0.477)	−317.8 (−0.637)	−447.5 (−0.897)
8. Pure income tax with integration	236.8 (0.475)	152.8 (0.306)	177.0 (0.355)	210.8 (0.423)

Notes: The numbers in parentheses represent the gain as a percentage of the present discounted value of consumption plus leisure in the base sequence. This number is $48.978 trillion for all comparisons, and accounts for only the initial population.

In the first equilibrium period under the 80% deduction for savings (with additive replacement), the price of capital actually drops to 0.988, compared with a labor price of 1.0. This result can be explained by the relative factor intensities in the production of consumer goods and capital goods. In the first period, the consumption tax (with additive replacement) leads to a 32.8% increase in the quantity of savings; these savings are used directly for investment. It turns out, however, that investment is more labor-intensive than the other components of aggregate demand. In the base case, the total value added in all industries consists of 82% labor and 18% capital. If we weight the base-case industry labor intensities by the quantities of investment goods produced in each industry, we find that investment goods consist of 91.6% labor and only 8.4% capital.[8] The increase in savings generates an indirect increase in the relative demand for labor and thus an indirect decrease in the relative price of capital.

After the first period, the price of capital continues to fall as capital deepening occurs. By the second equilibrium, the relative price of capital drops to 0.952. It continues to drop, and by the eleventh equilibrium (fifty years into the future) it reaches 0.831.

Another effect of corporate tax integration is the large sectoral reallocation of capital and the large degree of relative price changes among sectors. This phenomenon does not appear in the first equilibrium under the consumption tax, because the price of capital is still close to unity. In the first period, the largest relative price change for consumer goods is only 0.6%. However, as capital deepening causes the price of capital to drop farther, larger changes in relative prices occur. In this case, such capital-intensive industries as agriculture and real estate show price decreases and quantity increases; this pattern is the opposite of that emerging from simulations of corporate tax integration.

Plan 3 combines the features of Plans 1 and 2, and BFSW's estimates indicate that the efficiency improvement is almost precisely additive. This combination of tax changes was advocated in *Blueprints*. The plan offers an efficiency gain of $976 billion, even with an additive surcharge to marginal rates. The additive surcharge is substantial, since both the consumption tax and corporate tax integration reduce revenues. In the first period, marginal tax rates are increased by 8.6%. The additive surcharge falls to 4.0% by the eleventh equilibrium. This gain of $976 billion is well over 60% of national income for 1973; nearly 2% of the total present value

---

[8] This difference is caused primarily by two industries: construction and metals and machinery. Some 98.5% of value added in the construction industry comes from labor; metals and machinery is 92.1% labor. Together, these two industries account for 73.4% of the total amount of investment.

of national income and leisure; and about 15% of the present value of revenue collected from the corporate and personal income tax in the base case.

The effect of Plan 3 on the price of capital is a mixture of the effects discussed for the consumption tax and corporate tax integration separately. The relative price of capital rises in the first period to 1.186. However, it falls below unity by the fifth period (twenty years after the policy change). By the eleventh equilibrium, the price of capital stands at 0.884.

Plan 4 treats housing as any other investment and taxes its return, but allows deductions for all net savings (including housing): In any particular year there is no necessary equivalence between the income from housing and investment in housing, so the efficiency results are not the same for Plans 3 and 4. Furthermore, Plan 4 better captures the industrial neutrality of a policy combining a consumption tax with corporate tax integration. The efficiency surplus of Plan 4 relative to the current tax system is roughly $1.43 trillion with lump-sum revenue replacement, $1.18 trillion with multiplicative marginal rate surcharges, and $1.25 trillion with additive marginal rate surcharges. When revenues are replaced with increased sales taxes, the gain is about $1.25 trillion.

At first, Plan 4 induces a reallocation away from the real estate industry and the housing commodity; over time, however, the deduction for net savings in housing has a stimulating effect on the sector. In the base case, 8.2% of total domestic demand for the 19 producer goods goes into the real estate industry, and consumers spend 14% of their net money income on housing. In the first period under Plan 4, these figures drop to 6.5% and 10.5%, respectively. By the fifth equilibrium (twenty years into the sequence) these sectors have recovered somewhat, so that the corresponding figures are 7.3% and 12.0%. The recovery continues, but these sectors never reach the shares they had in the base case.

The adoption of Plan 5, which is a move halfway toward a consumption tax from the current system, would result in efficiency gains roughly half those estimated for Plan 1. The decrease in the price of capital and the increase in savings are roughly half of that when 80% of savings are deductible.

Plan 6 exempts all savings from taxation and leaves the housing preference unchanged; it thus results in a net subsidy to savings. However, the total efficiency gain is even larger under this plan than with an 80% deduction for savings, because the subsidy to savings offsets somewhat the distortionary effects of the corporate tax.

The gains for multiplicative scaling are typically smaller than those for additive scaling, because multiplicative scaling implies greater increases in the tax rates of high-income consumers. Since these individuals are already the most highly taxed, multiplicative scaling causes greater distortions in their labor–leisure choice. Generally speaking, efficiency losses increase with the square of the tax rate, so we would expect very high tax rates on some to be more distorting than somewhat higher rates for all. However, high-income consumers also have higher propensities to save, so the savings deduction benefits these groups most. As a consequence, even though it is less efficient, multiplicative scaling may be viewed as necessary to maintain vertical equity and the relative tax burdens of different income groups when savings deductions are increased.

The results of Table 7.6 regarding Plans 7 and 8 indicate that we could move to a pure income tax with no loss in efficiency, but only if we also integrate the corporate and personal income taxes. The tax base actually increases under Plan 7, because the imputed income from housing is included and existing savings deductions are eliminated. Consequently, the tax-rate structure is lowered in order to maintain government revenues. As a result, the usual relationship between the change in efficiency under lump-sum, multiplicative, and additive replacement is reversed. When we increase taxes in order to maintain revenue yield, a lump-sum change is always the best way to raise the required revenue. However, under Plan 7, a lump-sum decrease in taxes is not as good for the economy as a reduction in the distortionary income-tax rates.

Table 7.6 shows that Plan 7 is a losing proposition, despite the tax reductions that are necessary to maintain equal revenue yield. Moving to a pure income tax alone, without corporate tax integration, results in a $545 billion loss if there is a lump-sum tax reduction. Even with a multiplicative reduction in income-tax rates, the loss is still almost $240 billion. These losses arise primarily because the intertemporal distortions of the 1973 system are worsened. The improvement in the interindustry allocation of capital (resulting mainly from taxing the return to owner-occupied housing) is more than offset by the deterioration in intertemporal efficiency.

Plan 8 is a comprehensive income-tax plan involving corporate tax integration. The revenue losses from integration outweigh the revenue gains from taxing the imputed income from owner-occupied housing and eliminating savings deductions. Thus, tax increases are needed to preserve revenue. Plan 8 involves a substantial reduction in intertemporal efficiency. The net effect is a welfare improvement – but a smaller one than most of the other plans investigated. Lump-sum replacement yields an efficiency gain of about $237 billion. If the equal-yield replacement taxes are distortionary, the increase in welfare ranges from $153 billion to $211 billion.

A host of other tax changes have also been evaluated using this model, as discussed by BFSW. A summary of tax-policy applications using other models is presented in Shoven and Whalley (1984).

7.4 Appendix: Structure of the BFSW tax model[9]

Value added and intermediate production

As in the Harberger model, there are two primary factors of production – capital and labor – each of which is homogeneous, mobile among sectors, and internationally immobile. Capital K is owned by the 12 consumer groups and by government. We denote endowments by K_j ($j = 1, \ldots, 12$) and K_g. Capital can be used in any of the 19 producer industries or in the general government sector. These uses of capital are denoted by the i subscript, K_i ($i = 1, \ldots, 20$). Only consumers have endowments E_j ($j = 1, \ldots, 12$) of labor, but – due to the consumption of leisure – their actual labor supplies are L_j ($j = 1, \ldots, 12$). This factor can be used in any of the 20 sectors (including government) as labor L_i ($i = 1, \ldots, 20$), or can be retained by consumers for leisure l_j ($j = 1, \ldots, 12$). For each consumer, then, we have $E_j = L_j + l_j$. In total, we have

$$E = \sum_{j=1}^{12} E_j = \sum_{i=1}^{20} L_i + \sum_{j=1}^{12} l_j = L + l. \tag{A7.1}$$

We define each of these factors in service or rental units per period. When a unit of capital services is rented out for one period, the owner receives a price P_K that is net of factor taxes and depreciation. In addition to the rental prices P_L and P_K, which are paid to factor owners, producers are required to pay *ad valorem* taxes at rates t_{Li} and t_{Ki}. These taxes differ by sector. The user of the ith factor thus faces gross-of-tax factor costs of P_{Li}^* and P_{Ki}^*, which respectively equal $P_L(1 + t_{Li})$ and $P_K(1 + t_{Ki})$.

Capital and labor produce value added according to a constant elasticity of substitution (CES) value-added function of the form

$$\text{VA} = \phi[\delta L^{(\sigma-1)/\sigma} + (1+\delta)K^{(\sigma-1)/\sigma}]^{\sigma/(\sigma-1)} \tag{A7.2}$$

for each industry, where ϕ and δ are parameters for production scale and input weighting (respectively) and σ is the elasticity of substitution. For expositional simplicity, we have suppressed the i subscripts of all variables and parameters in these expressions.

The model uses a 19×19 fixed-coefficient input–output matrix A, with columns giving the intermediate input requirements per unit of output. The industry outputs are represented as Q_i ($i = 1, \ldots, 19$). In the standard version of the single-period submodel, we do not allow for substitution between intermediate inputs and value added.

A single output is produced by each industry, under constant returns to scale. Producer behavior is characterized by cost minimization for each

---

[9] This appendix is based on Chapter 3 of BFSW (1985).

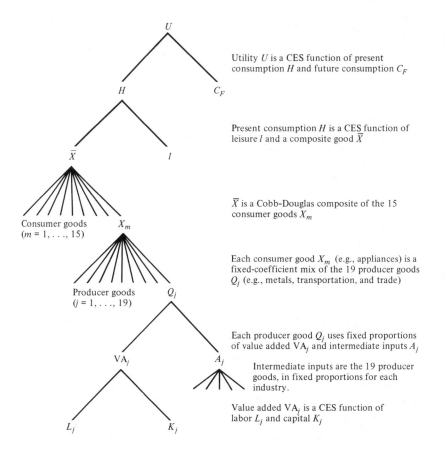

Figure A7.1. The structure of consumption and production in the model.

unit of output. Minimization of factor costs $(P_L^* L + P_K^* K)$, subject to the constraint that $VA = 1$ in (A7.2), yields the factor demands per unit of value added. For each industry, these demands are:

$$R_L = \phi^{-1} \left[(1-\delta) \left(\frac{\delta P_K^*}{(1-\delta) P_L^*} \right)^{1-\delta} + \delta \right]^{\sigma/(1-\sigma)}; \qquad (A7.3)$$

$$R_K = \phi^{-1} \left[\delta \left(\frac{(1-\delta) P_L^*}{\delta P_K^*} \right)^{1-\delta} + (1-\delta) \right]^{\sigma/(1-\sigma)}. \qquad (A7.4)$$

Consumer goods X_m ($m = 1, \ldots, 15$) are produced from producer goods Q_i ($i = 1, \ldots, 19$) through the fixed-coefficient Z matrix shown in the lower right of Figure A7.1. Each coefficient z_{im} gives the amount of producer goods i needed to produce one unit of consumer good m. For example, a unit of "alcoholic beverages" will include outputs from three industries: food and tobacco; transportation, communications, and utilities; and trade.

Different *ad valorem* tax rates can be imposed on each industry's intermediate purchases from other industries. State and local motor vehicle-registration fees, for example, are modeled as a tax on intermediate use of the motor vehicle industry's output, t_{MV_i} ($i = 1, \ldots, 19$). Each industry also pays an output tax at rate t_{Q_i} on its own output, regardless of where the output is used.

Because of perfect competition, producers make zero profits after making payments for factors, factor taxes, intermediate inputs, motor-vehicle input taxes, and output taxes. The zero-profit conditions also apply to production of consumer goods. Cost-covering consumer-good prices are given by

$$P_m = \sum_{i=1}^{19} z_{im} P_i \quad (m = 1, \ldots, 15). \tag{A7.5}$$

The expenditure matrix is shown in the upper right of Figure A7.1. When consumers purchase consumer goods X_m, they must pay additional *ad valorem* taxes. Sales taxes on the purchase of each good are given at the rates t_m ($m = 1, \ldots, 15$), and the gross-of-tax prices paid by consumers are $P_m^*(1 + t_m)$.

Household savings, labor supply, and commodity demands

Within a single period, individuals make savings decisions based on expectations about the resulting increment to future consumption. In the BFSW model, expectations are myopic in the sense that individuals expect all current prices, including the return to capital, to remain constant through all future periods. Because of this assumption, the savings of individuals can be calculated knowing only current prices.[10]

Savings decisions are based on the maximization of a nested utility function, where the outer nest is defined over present consumption and the expected future-consumption stream made possible from savings. Bequests are excluded, as is any explicit life-cycle structure.

Consider the general case of a consumer faced with choosing between consumption today (H) and consumption in future periods ($C_1, C_2, \ldots$). This consumer choice problem can be represented as the maximization of

---

[10] Ballard and Goulder (1982a, b) have investigated the effect of giving consumers foresight into the movements of relative prices over time. When a capital-deepening tax change is introduced, consumers will save less if they have foresight, because they see that the return to capital will decrease over time. The results of our simulations change somewhat, depending upon the expectational structure, but the magnitude of the change is not great.

$$U = U(H, C_F), \tag{A7.6}$$

subject to a budget constraint. Here, H is a composite of leisure and present-consumption goods, and C_F is a composite of the future-consumption stream $(C_1, C_2, \dots)$. Specific functional forms for H and C_F are described shortly. Implicit in these forms is a rate-of-time preference between H and C_F. In the calculations below, C_F is assumed to be the annual consumption of a perpetual annuity made possible by savings in the current period.

In a more complete model of life-cycle behavior, households would calculate the discounted present value of resources over their remaining lifetimes. In the BFSW model, by contrast, households concern themselves only with the allocation of current income between consumption and savings. Other applied general equilibrium models[11] have been developed with life-cycle consumption features.

The structure of the BFSW nested CES/Cobb–Douglas utility functions is depicted in Figure A7.1. Each consumer starts with a budget I that equals the rental value of capital and labor endowments (whether sold or retained as leisure), plus transfers, minus taxes. We refer to I as "expanded" income, to differentiate it from observed money income. Because of the nested CES form, consumer decisions can be divided into stages. In the first stage, the consumer divides I into present consumption H (costing P_H, as described subsequently) and future consumption C_F. Next, the consumer decides how to divide present consumption H into consumption of leisure time (costing P_l) and a composite consumption commodity $\bar{X}$ (costing $\bar{P}$). When we subtract the values of savings and leisure from I, the result is earned income available for present consumption of goods. Since the composite good $\bar{X}$ has a composite price $\bar{P}$, expenditure on consumption goods is $\bar{P}\bar{X}$. In the final utility nest shown in Figure A7.1, individuals divide these expenditures among the 15 consumer goods X_m $(m = 1, \dots, 15)$ according to a Cobb–Douglas function. Consumers face gross-of-tax prices P_m^* $(m = 1, \dots, 15)$ on these consumer goods. (Figure A7.1 also shows how each consumer good is a combination of 19 producer goods, and how each producer good is a combination of primary factors and intermediate inputs.)

It is assumed that consumers use their savings to purchase an investment portfolio, referred to as the savings good S. The implicit assumption is that consumer groups own real capital and rent it directly to the ultimate users in industry and the government. When individuals save, they add to their stocks of real capital. The model therefore assumes that the

---

[11] See Summers (1981) and Auerbach, Kotlikoff, and Skinner (1983) for numerical life-cycle models incorporating tax effects.

household sector buys investment goods with their savings. This savings–investment commodity S is actually a composite of the 19 industry outputs; these outputs go into the composite in fixed proportions that are given by the observed 1973 total investment purchases from each industry.

The savings commodity can be interpreted as a composite of newly produced capital goods, since savings are invested immediately. The price of savings, P_S, can also be interpreted as the composite price of investment goods. The capital goods purchased with savings will yield a flow of capital services in the future. This flow can, in turn, be sold for future consumption. Each unit of S is assumed to yield γ units of capital services in each future period, and each of these capital-service units is expected to earn P_K per period. (Because $P_K = 1$ in the benchmark year, γ is the initial real after-tax rate of return.) The capital income in each future year finances planned future consumption, which is expected to cost $\bar{P}$. Therefore, $P_K \gamma S = \bar{P} C_F$. If we multiply both sides of this equality by P_S and rearrange, we have

$$P_S S = \frac{P_S P}{P_K \gamma} C_F \qquad (A7.7)$$

for each consumer; that is, the value of savings matches the discounted present value of expected future consumption. The parameter γ denotes the physical service flow per unit of capital goods purchased. We specify γ exogenously. A given value of saving, $P_S S$, earns a return of $P_K \gamma S$ in every future period. Therefore, the endogenous after-tax rate of return is $P_K \gamma / P_S$, which we denote by r. Since the price $\bar{P}$ of consumption goods is not expected to change, r is also the expected real rate of return.

The consumer's budget constraint is given by

$$I = P_H H + P_S S, \qquad (A7.8)$$

where I is current expanded income after taxes and transfers, $P_S S$ is the value of savings, and P_H is the price of composite present consumption H. Using (A7.7), the consumer's maximization problem can be written as

$$\max U[H, C_F] \quad \text{s.t.} \quad I = P_H H + \frac{P_S P}{P_K \gamma} C_F. \qquad (A7.9)$$

Each consumer group has its own parameters and values in the CES form of this utility function, but we suppress indexes for expositional simplicity. The consumer utility function is

$$U = [\alpha^{1/\sigma_2} H^{(\sigma_2-1)/\sigma_2} + (1-\alpha)^{1/\sigma_2} C_F^{(\sigma_2-1)/\sigma_2}]^{\sigma_2/(\sigma_2-1)}, \qquad (A7.10)$$

where α is a weighting parameter and σ_2 is the elasticity of substitution between H and C_F. Constructed maximization of this utility function yields

$$H = \frac{\alpha I}{P_H^{\sigma_2} \Delta_2} \tag{A7.11}$$

and

$$C_F = \frac{(1-\alpha)I}{(P_S P / P_K \gamma)^{\sigma_2} \Delta_2}, \tag{A7.12}$$

where

$$\Delta_2 = \alpha (P_H)^{1-\sigma_2} + (1-\alpha) \left(\frac{P_S P}{P_K \gamma} \right)^{1-\sigma_2}. \tag{A7.13}$$

We discuss P_H subsequently. Using (A7.7), the demand for C_F can be translated into the demand for saving:

$$S = \frac{(1-\alpha)I}{P_S^{\sigma_2} [\bar{P}/P_K \gamma]^{(\sigma_2-1)} \Delta_2}. \tag{A7.14}$$

After saving $P_S S$, consumers have $I - P_S S$ to spend on consumption of H. In the second stage, they maximize

$$H = [(1-\beta)^{1/\sigma_1} \bar{X}^{(\sigma_1-1)/\sigma_1} + \beta^{1/\sigma_1} l^{(\sigma_1-1)/\sigma_1}]^{\sigma_1/(\sigma_1-1)} \tag{A7.15}$$

subject to

$$I - P_S S = \bar{P}\bar{S} + P_l l, \tag{A7.16}$$

where β is a weighting parameter and σ_1 is the elasticity of substitution between $\bar{X}$ and l. The price of leisure, P_l, is taken to be the after-tax return to labor of each group. Since a unit of labor earns P_L after factor taxes, $P_l = P_L(1-\tau_j)$, where τ_j is the j'th consumer's personal marginal tax rate. Constrained maximization of the subutility function H provides the demand functions

$$\bar{X} = \frac{(1-\beta)(I - P_S S)}{\bar{P}^{\sigma_1} \Delta_1} \tag{A7.17}$$

and

$$l = \frac{\beta(I - P_S S)}{P_l^{\sigma_1} \Delta_1}, \tag{A7.18}$$

where

$$\Delta_1 = (1-\beta)\bar{P}^{(1-\sigma_1)} + \beta P_l^{(1-\sigma_1)}. \tag{A7.19}$$

We discuss the construction of $\bar{P}$ shortly.

After spending $P_l l$ on leisure, consumers have $I - P_S S - P_l l$ to spend on the consumption components of $\bar{X}$. In the third stage, they maximize a Cobb–Douglas form for the subutility function

$$\bar{X} = \prod_{m=1}^{15} X_m^{\lambda_m} \tag{A7.20}$$

subject to

$$I - P_S S - P_l l = \sum_{m=1}^{15} X_m \cdot P_m^*. \tag{A7.21}$$

The λ_m exponents in (A7.20) are the Cobb–Douglas expenditure shares. Constrained maximization of the subutility function $\bar{X}$ provides the demand functions

$$X_m = \frac{\lambda_m (I - P_S S - P_l l)}{P_m^*} \quad (m = 1, \ldots, 15). \tag{A7.22}$$

An important property of the nested Cobb-Douglas and CES utility functions is that the indirect utility functions and expenditure functions can be easily derived. For example, in the Cobb–Douglas case just described, the indirect utility function is obtained by substituting the demand functions (A7.22) into the direct utility function (A7.20). If I_X is used to denote $I - P_S S - P_l l$, then

$$\bar{X} = \prod_{m=1}^{15} \left(\frac{\lambda_m I_X}{P_m^*} \right)^{\lambda_m}. \tag{A7.23}$$

The Cobb–Douglas function is defined such that the sum of the 15 exponents λ_m is unity. Thus we have

$$\bar{X} = I_X \prod_{m=1}^{15} \left(\frac{\lambda_m}{P_m^*} \right)^{\lambda_m}. \tag{A7.23'}$$

The indirect utility function in this case expresses subutility $\bar{X}$ as a function of income, prices, and preference parameters. From here, it is easy to solve for the expenditure function, which is the income solution of the indirect utility function:

$$I_X = \bar{X} \cdot \prod_{m=1}^{15} \left(\frac{P_m^*}{\lambda_m} \right)^{\lambda_m}. \tag{A7.24}$$

The expenditure function gives the income necessary to reach a given level of utility under a given configuration of prices.

Note that we can rewrite (A7.21) as

$$I_X = \bar{X}\bar{P}. \tag{A7.25}$$

Combining (A7.24) and (A7.25), we see that

$$\bar{P} = \prod_{i=1}^{15} \left(\frac{P_m^*}{\lambda_m} \right)^{\lambda_m}. \tag{A7.26}$$

The expenditure function has been used to create an index of the composite price $\bar{P}$ from the individual prices P_m^*. An especially convenient property of this type of price index, for both the Cobb–Douglas and CES functions, is that the composite price can be calculated without knowing the actual quantities X_m; this property simplifies calculations considerably.

Similar procedures can be used to derive the expenditure functions for the CES nests of the utility functions. The function H is a composite of $\bar{X}$ and l, and the composite price is

$$P_H = [(1-\beta)\bar{P}^{(1-\sigma_1)} + \beta P_l^{(1-\sigma_1)}]^{1/(1-\sigma_1)}. \tag{A7.27}$$

If I_H is used to denote $I - P_S S$, the income available for expenditure on H, we have the expenditure function

$$I_H = P_H H. \tag{A7.28}$$

As with the Cobb–Douglas nest, the quantity of a composite good multiplied by the composite price equals the expenditure on the good.

The function U is a composite of H and C_F, and its composite price is

$$P_U = \left[\alpha P_H^{(1-\sigma_2)} + (1-\alpha)\left(\frac{P_S P}{P_K \gamma}\right)^{(1-\sigma_2)}\right]^{1/(1-\sigma_2)}. \tag{A7.29}$$

The overall indirect utility function is $U = I/P_U$, and the overall expenditure function is $I = P_U \cdot U$.

In order to detail the discriminatory aspects of the personal and corporate tax systems, BFSW first calculate each industry's capital income net of corporate income tax, corporate franchise tax, and property tax. Denote these figures by CAP_i ($i = 1, \ldots, 19$). The government's payments for privately owned capital are represented by CAP_{20}. The sum of this capital income is received by the model's 12 consumer classes. Therefore

$$\sum_{i=1}^{20} CAP_i = \sum_{j=1}^{12} CAP_j, \tag{A7.30}$$

where CAP_j is the capital income received by the jth consumer class.

Each consumer class has a marginal tax rate on all capital and labor income, denoted by τ_j ($j = 1, \ldots, 12$). We can then calculate τ, the weighted average marginal tax rate on capital income:

$$\tau = \frac{\sum_{j=1}^{12} CAP_j \tau_j}{\sum_{j=1}^{12} CAP_j}. \tag{A7.31}$$

For each of the 19 industries and government we define a fraction f_i, which is the proportion of that sector's capital income subject to full taxation of personal income. This fraction will differ across industries for a number of reasons, including the variance in dividend-retention policies and differences in the degree to which unincorporated capital qualifies for the investment tax credit.

In order to capture intersectoral differences in the taxation of capital income at the personal level, BFSW employ a construct called the "personal factor tax" PFT_i $(i = 1, ..., 20)$. Total capital tax in each industry is the sum of corporate taxes, property taxes, and the personal factor tax. For each sector, total personal factor taxes paid are given as

$$PFT_i = f_i CAP_i \tau \quad (i = 1, ..., 20), \tag{A7.32}$$

where the personal factor tax rate on CAP_i is $f_i \tau$.

It is then possible to define net capital income $NCAP_i$ as capital income net of the corporate taxes, property taxes, and the personal factor tax on capital income in that industry:

$$NCAP_i = CAP_i - PFT_i = CAP_i(1 - f_i \tau). \tag{A7.33}$$

The average fraction of CAP_i that is fully taxable by the personal income tax is

$$\bar{f} = \frac{\sum_{i=1}^{20} CAP_i f_i}{\sum_{i=1}^{20} CAP_i}. \tag{A7.34}$$

If CAP and NCAP are defined as the sums of CAP_i and $NCAP_i$ over the 20 sectors, then the previous two equations imply

$$NCAP = CAP(1 - \bar{f}\tau). \tag{A7.35}$$

This expression provides an average conversion from capital income net of corporate and property taxes to capital income net of all taxes.

Although consumers in fact receive CAP_j $(j = 1, ..., 12)$ and pay their own personal income taxes, BFSW model the personal income tax on capital income as if it were paid at the industry level. However, because tax at rate τ has been paid on an average $\bar{f}$ of household j's capital income CAP_j, there must be a correction for differences among marginal rates at the personal level. The personal factor tax at the industry level can be viewed as a withholding tax. For consumer j with capital income of CAP_j, the amount of tax paid at the industry level is $\tau \bar{f} CAP_j$. However, consumer j should actually pay a tax of $\tau_j \bar{f} CAP_j$, so consumers for whom τ_j exceeds τ must pay additional taxes at the personal level (in addition to the personal factor tax withheld at the industry level). Those for whom τ_j falls below τ receive rebates. Thus the correction at the personal level is

$$\Gamma_j = (\tau_j - \tau)CAP_j \bar{f}. \tag{A7.36}$$

Because τ is the capital-weighted average of the marginal tax rates, the sum of these corrections at the personal level is zero. Since $NCAP_j = CAP_j(1 - \bar{f}\tau)$, the personal tax correction can also be described as

$$\Gamma_j = (\tau_j - \tau) \text{NCAP}_j \frac{\bar{f}}{1 - \bar{f}\tau}. \tag{A7.37}$$

This rearrangement is necessary because our endogenously determined rental price P_K is defined as the amount earned by each unit of capital, net of all taxes. Net capital income $P_K K_j$ is used for NCAP$_j$ in (A7.37) for our model calculations.

Many transfer payments are not subject to the income tax; in the BFSW model it is assumed that all transfers are tax-exempt. Labor income is fully taxable. The formula for income taxes paid by group j is therefore

$$T_j^I = B_j + \tau_j P_L L_j + (\tau_j - \tau) P_K K_j \frac{\bar{f}}{1 - \bar{f}\tau}. \tag{A7.38}$$

The intercept of each linear tax function B_j is negative, reflecting the fact that marginal tax rates exceed average tax rates. While marginal changes in income are taxed at the appropriate marginal rate for each group, this marginal rate does not change as income changes. Expanded income I_j equals transfers plus labor and capital income, plus the value of leisure, minus income taxes. Since $E_j = L_j + l_j$, we have

$$I_j = T_j^R - B_j + E_j P_L (1 - \tau_j) + P_K K_j \left[1 - (\tau_j - \tau) \frac{\bar{f}}{1 - \bar{f}\tau} \right], \tag{A7.39}$$

where T_j^R are lump-sum transfers. Transfer payments are held constant in real terms by a price index on each consumer group's consumption purchases. When the value of leisure, $P_l l_j$, is subtracted from this expression, we have

$$I_j - P_l l_j = T_j^R + P_L L_j + P_K K_j - T_j^I. \tag{A7.40}$$

The price of leisure, P_l, is equal to $P_L(1 - \tau_j)$.

Government receipts and expenditures

Government activities are divided into two broad categories. Some publicly supplied goods and services are offered free of charge, and are referred to as general government activities. Other goods and services are subject to user charges, even though the charges may not cover costs (e.g., postal services and some utilities); these are treated as government enterprises, industry 19.

Expenditures by government other than those for public enterprises are an element of final demand. The government is modeled as if it were a single consumer, with a Cobb–Douglas utility function defined over all

19 producer goods, capital, and labor.[12] These government expenditures do not enter the utility functions of consumers as public goods. When tax rates are changed for a simulation, the equal-yield feature ensures that enough tax revenue is obtained from an alternative source so that government expenditures at the new equilibrium prices leave the government with the same utility level as in the old equilibrium. Consequently, we need only be concerned with changes in consumer utility when calculating the total welfare change. The government obtains income by collecting taxes and by renting out its endowment of capital services. It makes redistributive transfer payments to consumers in a lump-sum fashion; data for Social Security, food stamps, Aid to Families with Dependent Children, and similar programs is used to determine the amounts of these transfers. The transfers are held constant in real terms, using a Laspeyres price index for each consumer group. The government uses the remaining revenues to buy producer goods at prices P_i ($i = 1, \ldots, 19$), to buy labor at the gross-of-tax price $P_L(1 + t_L^G)$, and to buy capital at the gross-of-tax price $P_K(1 + t_K^G)$.

The tax rate paid for labor is based on Social Security and railroad retirement taxes paid by the government and its employees. When the government pays these taxes on its use of labor, it pays the taxes to itself; consequently, the income effects cancel out. However, the price effects correctly measure the opportunity cost to government of hiring additional labor.

The tax rate on capital used by government, t_K^G, is more problematic. Government in the United States does not typically pay corporate income taxes or property taxes. If t_K^G is modeled as only the personal tax on that capital income, the government's tax rate on K would be substantially less than the private sector's tax rate. The benchmark equilibrium would imply a misallocation of capital in favor of government use. Any reduction in the capital taxes faced by the private sector would imply a reallocation from the government sector to the private sector. Since the gross-of-tax capital price in the private sector reflects the marginal product of capital, this capital flow from the public to the private sector would imply welfare gains.

It is probably undesirable to contaminate in this way the calculation of welfare effects of distorting taxes. Therefore, in the BFSW model the entire government sector faces a price for capital that is equal to $P_K(1 + \phi)$, where ϕ is the weighted average tax rate on capital used in industry. Then, if the

---

[12] This formulation allows government to purchase quantities that depend at least somewhat on output prices, but in any case it does not greatly affect model results pertaining to structural tax reform.

industry tax rates were to change, the government's price would change accordingly. For example, if industry tax rates were reduced through corporate tax integration then the price of capital used in government would not change relative to the price faced by producers. Thus capital would not flow from the government to the private sector.[13]

The external sector

The foreign trade activity of the United States is treated in a simple manner, so as to close the model.[14] In the standard BFSW model, commodities are not distinguished by their origin; that is, U.S.-produced cars and imported cars are considered to be identical. Foreign trade introduces a difference between the demands of consuming groups in the United States (broadly defined to include business investment and government purchases) and the demands for products faced by U.S. domestic industries. We can represent this distinction by introducing a vector of imports and a vector of exports, using the producer-good classifications of the model. These vectors account for differences between the demands of U.S. groups and the demands facing U.S. industries.

The demand for U.S. exports by foreigners has a negative price elasticity whereas the supply of imports to the United States has a positive price elasticity. The relative prices of traded goods are determined endogenously in the model. Trade balance is assured, since the export-demand and import-supply functions satisfy budget balance.

For each of the 19 producer goods, we specify foreign export-demand and import-supply functions. These functions incorporate parameters that determine constant price elasticities of import supply and export demand,

$$M_i = M_i^0 (P_{M_i}^W)^\mu \quad (0 < \mu < \infty, \, i = 1, \ldots, 19) \quad \text{and}$$
$$E_i = E_i^0 (P_{E_i}^W)^\nu \quad (-\infty < \nu < 0, \, i = 1, \ldots, 19),$$

(A7.41)

[13] If the government acts to maximize social welfare, it would recognize that each unit of capital taken out of the private sector reduces general welfare by the gross-of-tax price paid by the private purchasers of capital. When government uses another unit of capital, it gives up not only P_K but also the tax revenue paid by a private producer if that unit of capital were used in the private sector. If the government realizes this and acts to maximize social welfare, it would charge itself a shadow price equal to $P_K(1+\phi)$.

[14] For modeling and results of several alternative trade and international capital-flow specifications in this context, see Chapter 11 of BFSW (1985). The treatment of foreign trade in this chapter is based on Whalley and Yeung (1984). Alternatives include use of the Armington assumption (that imports differ from domestically produced goods) and the possibility of imbalanced commodities through international capital flows. The capital flows might be in capital goods or in capital services.

where M_i and E_i are import supply and export demand, M_i^0 and E_i^0 are constants, $P_{M_i}^W$ is the world price of imports, and $P_{E_i}^W$ is the world price of U.S. exports. These equations imply that the ith commodity can be both imported and exported. This phenomenon of crosshauling is evident from trade statistics, even with highly disaggregated data, and it underlies much of the literature on interindustry trade (see Grubel and Lloyd 1975). There are many reasons for this phenomenon. One explanation asserts that foreign commodities are qualitatively different from domestic goods. For example, U.S. and foreign cars are close but not perfect substitutes; this explanation was offered by Armington (1969). Crosshauling can also be explained by reference to geography and transportation costs. For example, it may be perfectly sensible for the United States to export Alaskan oil to Japan and at the same time import the identical product through ports on the East Coast and the Gulf of Mexico, given the cost of delivering Alaskan oil to the eastern United States.

In order to close the system and solve the general equilibrium model, we add the trade-balance constraint

$$\sum_{i=1}^{19} P_{M_i}^W M_i = \sum_{i=1}^{19} P_{E_i}^W E_i. \tag{A7.42}$$

If we substitute for M_i and E_i from equation (A7.41) into equation (A7.42), we have

$$\sum_{i=1}^{19} P_{M_i}^W M_i^0 (P_{M_i}^W)^\mu = \sum_{i=1}^{19} P_{E_i}^W E_i^0 (P_{E_i}^W) \nu. \tag{A7.43}$$

Define the relationship between U.S. and world prices through an exchange rate term e as $P_{E_i}^{US} = e P_{E_i}^W$ and $P_{M_i}^{US} = e P_{M_i}^W$. Of course, the model is a real trade model and has no financial exchange-rate variables, but this construct enables us to write foreign import-supply and export-demand functions as functions of U.S. prices rather than of world prices. In the model, U.S. prices are determined endogenously. If we substitute these U.S. prices into (A7.43), we have

$$e = \left(\frac{\omega_2}{\omega_1} \right)^{1/(\nu - \mu)}, \tag{A7.44}$$

where

$$\omega_1 = \sum_{i=1}^{19} (P_{M_i}^{US})^{\mu+1} \quad \text{and} \quad \omega_2 = \sum_{i=1}^{19} (P_{E_i}^{US})^{\nu+1}. \tag{A7.45}$$

Finally, substituting these results into equation (A7.41) yields

$$M_i = M_i^0 (P_{M_i}^{US})^\mu \left(\frac{\omega_2}{\omega_1} \right)^{\mu/(\mu-\nu)} \quad \text{and} \quad E_i = E_i^0 (P_{E_i}^{US})^\nu \left(\frac{\omega_2}{\omega_1} \right)^{\nu/(\mu-\nu)}. \tag{A7.46}$$

This gives us an import-supply and export-demand function for each commodity in terms of U.S. prices. Note that ω_1 and ω_2 are themselves functions of U.S. import and export prices. Equations (A7.46) can be thought of as foreign import-supply and export-demand functions, written as functions of U.S. prices, and incorporating a zero trade balance. Thus, although equations (A7.41) specify import and export behavior, the μ and ν parameters are not supply and demand elasticities that incorporate trade-balance conditions. To derive expressions for import-supply and export-demand elasticities that do satisfy trade balance, consider a simplified two-commodity case where each country exports one item and imports the other. Let us say that the foreigner demands our exports of good 1. Then, suppressing the US superscript and substituting equations (A7.45) into the export equation (A7.46), we have

$$E_1 = E_1^0 (P_{E_1})^\nu. \tag{A7.47}$$

It is simple to differentiate with respect to P_{E_1} and obtain the own-price elasticity of export demand:

$$\epsilon_E^{FD} = \frac{\nu(\mu+1)}{\mu-\nu}. \tag{A7.48}$$

Similarly, we can find the own-price elasticity of import supply as

$$\epsilon_M^{FS} = \frac{-\mu(1+\nu)}{\mu-\nu}. \tag{A7.49}$$

We would like to restrict μ and ν so that the export-demand curve slopes downward and the import-supply curve slopes upward. These conditions will be met if $\mu \geq 0$ and $\nu \leq -1$.

In the two-good case, (A7.48) and (A7.49) can be used to set values for μ and ν that are consistent with econometric estimates of ϵ_E^{FD} and ϵ_M^{FS}. A similar procedure is followed by BFSW in specifying parameter values for their model with 19 commodities.

Dynamic sequencing of static equilibria

Thus far we have discussed the economic model and the data (based on 1973) with which we can calculate a static general equilibrium for the U.S. economy. However, tax-policy evaluations based on single-period, static equilibria can be misleading. In particular, meaningful welfare calculations can be based neither on H, the utility of present consumption in 1973, nor on U, the overall utility measure that includes expected consumption in later years.

First, consider a welfare measure based on H and also a tax change that increases the net return to savings. If consumers respond to increased incentives for saving, then the utility H from current consumption will fall.

Only over time will the additional savings provide deepening of capital sufficient to allow higher future consumption. Thus a policy that looks harmful in the short run can provide substantial welfare gains in the long run.

Second, consider a welfare measure, based on U, from 1973. This utility function includes expected future consumption for each household group. The expectations are myopic in that consumers in the BFSW model assume that the current price of capital will remain unchanged in the future.[15] Thus a tax change that raises the net rate of return also raises expectations about the amount of future consumption that can be obtained from a given amount of current savings. Actual deepening of capital will lower the net return; thus expected future consumption overstates actual future consumption. Expected utility U therefore overstates the utility from actual consumption.

Myopic expectations turn out to be correct only if the economy is on a balanced growth plan; they are incorrect in any transition to a higher or lower capital–labor ratio, but become more accurate as the economy settles down to a new steady-state path. Consequently, it is appropriate to look explicitly at the future path of the economy. In so doing, BFSW base their welfare measures on current consumption H from each year in a sequence of static equilibria. Preferences based on U and expected future consumption are used only insofar as they generate actual consumption and savings for any particular year.

The first equilibrium in every sequence corresponds to the 1973 benchmark year. It would be possible to calculate one equilibrium for every year in the future for (say) 100 years; however, computational expenses increase with the number of equilibria to be calculated. Therefore, BFSW calculate equilibria that are five or ten years apart, and usually calculate enough equilibria to look fifty years beyond 1973. For example, they frequently calculate a sequence of equilibria representing the years 1973, 1983, 1993, 2003, 2013, and 2023.[16]

---

[15] In fact, the price of capital can change substantially over time, as shown in Chapters 9 and 10 of BFSW (1985).

[16] When making dynamic welfare calculations (as discussed under the next heading), values of certain variables are needed for every year, even though an equilibrium calculation is usually not made for every year. In order to calculate the intermediate-year values for these variables, BFSW assume that the path between equilibria is characterized by smooth exponential growth. For example, assume that the value of function H has been calculated for 1973 and 1983. If the growth rate between the two years is assumed to be constant then we must have $H_{1983} = H_{1973}(1+\text{GR})^{10}$, where GR is the growth rate. We can then solve for GR as

$$\text{GR} = \left[\frac{H_{1983}}{H_{1973}}\right]^{1/10} - 1.$$

Then, for the intermediate years, H can be calculated as

$$H_{1973+t} = H_{1973}(1+\text{GR})^{t}.$$

The equilibria in any sequence are connected to each other through capital accumulation. Each single-period equilibrium calculation begins with an initial capital-services endowment. Savings in the current period will augment the capital-services endowment available in the next period. Moving through a sequence of equilibria, the capital stock grows owing to savings. When the capital endowment grows at the same rate as the effective labor force, the economy is on a balanced growth path.

In fact, BFSW assume (in a base-case sequence) that the economy is on a steady-state, balanced growth path in 1973. This assumption is crucially important. Just as the assumption that the economy is in equilibrium in 1973 is central to the development of the static version of the model, so the assumption of a base-case balanced growth path is central to the development of the dynamic version.

To be more precise, a steady-state growth path is defined as one where tax policy is unchanging and

$$\frac{\dot{E}}{E} = \frac{\dot{K}}{K} = n, \tag{A7.50}$$

where

E = labor endowment,
$\dot{E}$ = increase in labor endowment,
K = capital endowment,
$\dot{K}$ = increase in capital endowment, and
n = growth rate of effective units of labor.

Moreover, the growth of effective labor units is separated into components that reflect population growth and Harrod-neutral technical change (increase in productivity of existing labor). Thus,

$$n = (1+h)(1+g) - 1, \tag{A7.51}$$

where

g = growth rate of natural units of labor, and
h = growth rate of output per worker hour.

On the steady-state path, all relative prices remain constant. Tax-policy changes will alter the steady-state path and set the economy on a transition path (which may be rather lengthy). Eventually the economy approaches a new steady state. Figure A7.2 illustrates the transition for a tax-policy change that results in increased savings. Without the change, consumption per capita grows at a constant rate. With the change, consumption is at first lower than it would otherwise have been; however, consumption will then rise at a faster rate as a result of the greater amount of capital accumulation. The level of consumption under the new regime eventually surpasses the level under the old set of taxes, and consumption

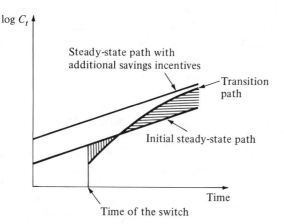

Figure A7.2. The transition for a tax-policy change that stimulates savings.

approaches a new balanced growth path asymptotically. By calculating a sequence of equilibria, the transition can be studied in detail.

Parameters for the dynamic version of BFSW's model are chosen as follows. First, the amount of savings and the size of the capital stock are observed in the benchmark year. This gives the rate of growth of capital; the effective labor force is then assumed to grow at the same rate.

When all endowments and incomes increase at the rate n, and when demand functions in income are homogeneous of degree one, the government's tax receipts also grow proportionately. Transfer income will grow at the same rate because consumers are each given a share of government revenue in the benchmark. The only problem is presented by progressive personal income taxes. This problem is solved by scaling the (B_j) intercept of each linear tax schedule by the steady-state growth rate n. With a larger negative intercept and larger incomes subject to the same marginal tax rate, each consumer will experience a constant average rate of tax as income grows through time. The personal income tax remains progressive, however, in the sense that high-income consumers still have higher average and marginal tax rates than low-income consumers.

Comparison of dynamic sequences

In this section we describe the BFSW procedures for evaluation of alternative sequences of equilibria.

A well-known concept in static welfare analysis is the compensating variation, defined as the amount of additional income at new prices that would be necessary in order to allow a consumer to reach the old level of utility. The equivalent variation is defined as the amount of additional income at old prices that would enable a consumer to reach the new utility level.

We can derive the static compensating and equivalent variations for the H utility function (the CES composite of current consumption and leisure). The H function might be called an evaluation function, distinguishing it from the overall utility function U used to determine savings behavior. The H function is the appropriate one to use in dynamic welfare evaluations. Because savings are used to buy future consumption, to include savings in our evaluation of current-period utility would constitute double counting.

The first step in deriving compensating and equivalent variations is to solve for the expenditure function that corresponds to H. Each household constraint is

$$I = P_H H + P_S S. \tag{A7.52}$$

In (A7.52), I is expanded income (defined previously). When we subtract $P_S S$ (the amount of savings spent), the remainder is income available for current consumption and leisure; let us call this I_H. Substitution implies that

$$I_H = H \cdot P_H. \tag{A7.53}$$

The evaluation function H is a combination of goods and leisure, similar to a utility function. For present purposes, however, it is also useful to think of H as a composite commodity, a physical combination or aggregation of goods and leisure. Each unit of H costs P_H, defined previously as a composite of prices for goods and leisure. The expenditure function is $H \cdot P_H$, a function of the required utility level and prices.

Assume we have old values H^O, I_H^O, P_H^O and new values H^N, I_H^N, P_H^N. The compensating variation for any single period is defined as the additional income required to obtain old utility levels at new prices:

$$CV = H^O P_H^N - H^N P_H^N = (H^O - H^N) P_H^N. \tag{A7.54}$$

It is customary to reverse the sign of this welfare measure, so that the CV is positive for a welfare gain. In similar fashion, we can write the equivalent variation as

$$EV = (H^N - H^O) P_H^O. \tag{A7.55}$$

These measures can be applied to any consumer in any period, since the simulation procedure involves calculating each consumer's income and utility in each time period under each tax regime. A problem arises, however, in trying to sum a stream of compensating or equivalent variations, because these are measured in prices of different years from different sequences. Fortunately, the benchmark sequence is on a steady-state path, so its prices remain stable with no tax change. Thus a natural choice is to measure welfare gains in benchmark prices, equal to actual 1973 prices. For the ith period, then, the constant-dollar difference between revised-case consumption and benchmark consumption is $(H_i^N - H_i^O)P_H^O$. If we use PV to denote a present value operator, then the present value of this stream of welfare gains is

$$\text{PVWG} \equiv \text{PV}[(H_i^N - H_i^O)P_H^O] = P_H^O \cdot [\text{PV}(H_i^N) - \text{PV}(H_i^O)], \qquad \text{(A7.56)}$$

since P_H^O is a constant. Also, because $(H_i^N - H_i^O)P_H^O$ is just the EV for period i in unchanged prices, this measure might be interpreted as the present value of equivalent variations. This is the measure used in the chapters that follow to report all welfare gains. For aggregate welfare gains, BFSW use the sum of PVWG across consumers.

In order to analyze tax-policy changes, it is often important to use an assumption of equal revenue yield. This is true in the dynamic case as well as in the static case. In the dynamic case, however, there are several standards of yield equality. A strong form of yield equality is invoked by BFSW, who require government to collect the same revenue in each period of the revised sequence as collected in the corresponding period of the base sequence. This requirement can cause some problems, most notably with a switch from an income tax to a consumption tax. Since the consumption-tax base is less than the income-tax base for at least the first few periods, unchanged rates of tax would provide substantially reduced revenue in those periods. The strong form of yield equality implies that, in the initial periods, the tax rates must be substantially higher with a consumption tax. These higher tax rates exacerbate the already distorted choice between work and leisure. As time goes on, however, the economy will grow faster under the consumption tax because it leads to faster capital accumulation.

PART III

Policy applications

8

Global trade models

In this chapter the four-region and seven-region models of world trade due to Whalley (1985) are described, along with a series of results that illustrate their application. Although closely related, the two models use different levels of aggregation and different functional forms. The first part of the chapter details the specification of production and demand in these models, the way protection policies are represented, how equilibrium conditions are characterized, and how each of the models is used in counterfactual equilibrium analysis. The second part of the chapter describes two applications. The first is an analysis of alternative tariff-cutting formulas proposed in the Tokyo Round of multilateral trade negotiations in the General Agreement on Tariff and Trade (GATT) during the 1970s; the other evaluates North–South trade and the impact of protectionist trade policies.

The two general equilibrium models used by Whalley are oriented toward quite different issues of trade liberalization. The four-region model uses 1973 data for the European Economic Community (EEC), the United States, Japan, and the "Rest of the World" (hereafter "RoW"). This was the first of two models constructed to analyze the impact of changes in trade policies among developed countries participating in the then-current trade negotiations under the GATT. This four-region model contains a more detailed classification of commodities (33) than the seven-region model, and more detail among households within each of the regions. Its shortcoming is the crude specification of the rest of the world, which is modeled as a single trading area even though it accounts for a substantial portion of trade and income. The model is well suited for analysis of trade-protection issues affecting major developed trading areas. However, for

This chapter is based upon Chapters 3, 8, and 11 of Whalley (1985).

other issues such as trade policies affecting less developed countries, the model is less satisfactory.

The seven-region model was developed as an outgrowth of the four-region model to allow for a more thorough analysis of North-South (developed-less developed; see Section 8.4) trade issues. The seven regions identified are the EEC, the United States, Japan, other developed countries (ODCs), the Organization of Petroleum-Exporting Countries (OPEC), newly industrialized countries (NICs), and less developed countries (LDCs). Data for 1977 is used. Because of the larger number of regions, fewer commodities (six) are considered for each trading area in order to keep the model tractable. Significantly less detail than in the four-region model is incorporated among household types on the demand side in each region. On the other hand, the seven-region model allows more flexibility in the specification of functional forms. Both models require inputs of elasticity values (and, importantly, trade elasticities reflecting import- and export-demand functions), as is true of other applied models. Both are also calibrated to their respective benchmark equilibrium data sets using the techniques discussed in Chapter 5.

The two models are structurally similar. Both specify demand and production functions in each region. Regions are linked through foreign trade, which in turn is affected by trade-protection policies (tariffs and nontariff barriers). The models examine equilibrium solutions involving demand-supply equalities for all goods and factors in the model, zero-profit conditions for each industry, and external sector balance for each region. Changes in trade-protection policies in any one (or all) of the regions change the equilibrium solution, affecting equilibrium behavior in all regions. With both models, the impacts of policy change (who gains and who loses, and by how much) are appraised by comparing equilibria before and after the policy change. More details on model structure, parameterization methods, and parameter estimates used are given in Whalley (1985).

Figures 8.1 and 8.2 show the main features of the models. Both are based on a world commodity price system, with producers receiving world prices and consumers paying world prices plus tariffs, nontariff barriers, and any applicable domestic taxes. Investment and other capital-account transactions are part of the external-sector activity that connects regions. Constant elasticity of substitution (CES) production functions are used; CES combined with LES (linear expenditure system) demand functions are used.

8.1 Basic structure of the models

These four- and seven-region models are most easily thought of as higher-dimensional analogs of traditional two-sector general equilibrium models, which have been used extensively in international trade theory. These models are associated with the work of Meade (1955), Johnson (1958), Jones (1965), and Kemp (1964), among others. In their present form these models have been extended both in dimensionality and in detail from their use in pure theory, but their essential structure remains.

In both models each region has a production structure described by industry production functions, which include both primary factors (capital and labor) and intermediate products as inputs. Fixed endowments of capital and labor are assumed for each region. Each region also has a system of market demand functions and a set of trade and domestic tax policies.

Commodities are treated as heterogeneous across regions (the Armington assumption) even though they may have similar characteristics. For instance, Japanese, European, and American automobiles are treated as qualitatively different, although a higher degree of substitutability between comparable (rather than noncomparable) products can be specified through the functional forms used. Most commodities in both models are traded internationally, but some nontraded goods are identified. Factors are mobile across industries within regions but are internationally immobile. Market demands within any region satisfy Walras's law for the region; that is, the value of demand by any region equals the value of incomes accruing to that region. This condition holds at any of commodity and factor prices, and thus global demands (summed across regions) also satisfy a global version of Walras's law. No transport costs are considered. Trade and tax policies operate as *ad valorem* distortions from international prices, which are defined as prices received by sellers of goods on international markets.

Equilibrium in both models is given by a set of international goods and factor prices for each region, so that demands equal supplies for all goods and factors, no industry in any region does any better than break even, and each region is in external-sector balance. The zero-profit equilibrium condition implies that, in equilibrium, capital receives the same rate of return in all industries in each region. These equilibrium conditions are the same irrespective of the policies in place, although the particular equilibrium changes as policies change.

A key feature of the models is the separate treatment of goods and factors in each region. For expositional purposes, we assume that there are N goods, two factors (K and L), and Q^r agents in each of R regions, where the index r denotes the rth region. The world consists of NR goods, $2R$ factors, and Q agents. Factors are nonproduced commodities for which there are no final demands, but which are endowed to the consumers of each region.

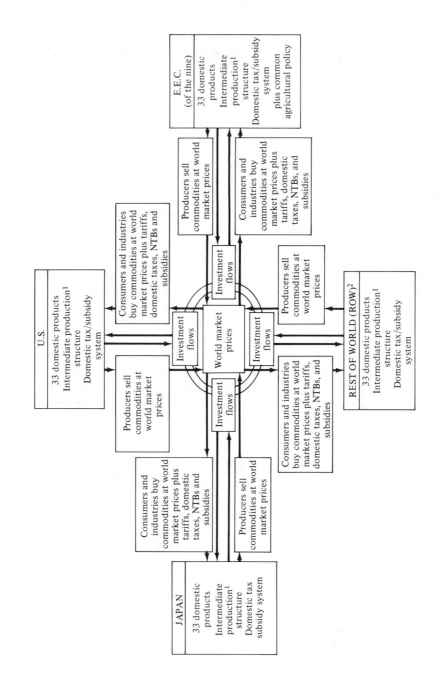

Production functions for each good specify input requirements of both factors and other goods. A requirement of fixed input per unit production is assumed for a composite of factors and for a composite of intermediate goods defined over the available production sources. Foreign and domestic steel, for instance, can be substituted for each other in meeting a fixed steel requirement per automobile. Factor input requirements are represented by value-added functions defining substitution possibilities over capital and labor in each industry. Intermediate input requirements are represented by coefficient functions specifying substitution possibilities across production sources (e.g., the substitution possibilities between domestically produced steel and steel imported from other regions).

If G_i^r is the output of good i in region r, Y_i^r is the value added in producing good i in region r, and H_{ji}^r is the use of composite good j in producing good i in region r, then these production functions can be written as

$$G_i^r = \min\left(\frac{Y_i^r}{a_{\mathrm{VA}i}^r}, \frac{H_{1i}^r}{a_{1i}^r}, \dots, \frac{H_{ji}^r}{a_{ji}^r}, \dots, \frac{H_{Ni}^r}{a_{Ni}^r}\right), \tag{8.1}$$

where $a_{\mathrm{VA}i}^r$ is the fixed value-added requirement per unit of output of good i and $a_{1i}^r, \dots, a_{Ni}^r$ are the fixed composite-good requirements in region r per unit production of good i.

The value-added and intermediate-substitution possibilities are represented by the equations

$$Y_i^r = F_i^r(K_i^r, L_i^r) \tag{8.2}$$

and

$$H_{ji}^r = H_{ji}^r(H_{ji_r}^1, \dots, H_{ji_r}^R), \tag{8.3}$$

Figure 8.1. Schematic outline of four-region general equilibrium model of world trade (adapted from Brown and Whalley 1980). Equilibrium involves a set of world market prices such that demand equals supply for all goods and factors, no industry makes positive profits (those in operation break even), and each region is in zero trade balance (including investment flows, dividends and interest, and transfers).
Notes: 1. This incorporates intermediate substitution between similar inputs differentiated by country of origin: e.g., a fixed steel requirement per car produced in the United States might be specified, but this can be met by a substitutable mix of domestically produced steel and steel imported from the various trading areas. 2. The rest of the world is specified "schematically," and no strong claims to realism are made. An arithmetic average of comparable parameters in three major trading areas is used. The factor endowments in the rest of the world are selected to reflect the relative capital abundance of the three major trading areas. The capital–labor ratio in the rest of the world is considered to be, in aggregate, 1/5 of that in the combination of the three major trading areas, with a ratio of 1:10 for manufacturing.

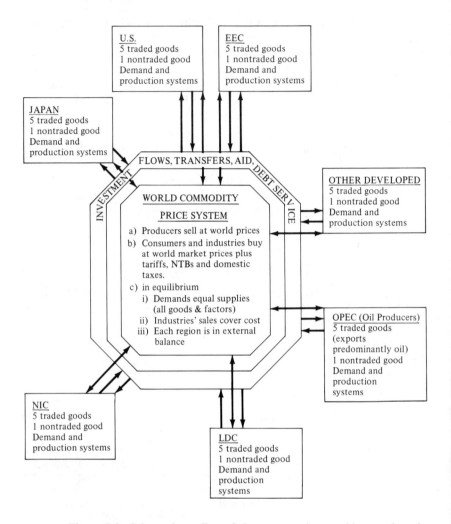

Figure 8.2. Schematic outline of the seven-region world general equilibrium model.

where K_i^r and L_i^r are the capital and labor used in production of good i in region r, and where $H_{ji_r}^1, \ldots, H_{ji_r}^R$ are the amounts of good j (supplied by regions $1, \ldots, R$) used to produce good i in region r. In both models, (8.2) and (8.3) are represented by CES functions, but with differing specifications of substitution possibilities. These take the form of nested functions, which allow for hierarchical chains of substitution –

first between elements within composites and subsequently between composites.

Final demand functions for all agents in all regions in both models are derived from utility maximization. If X_{ir}^q is the amount of good i from region r demanded by agent q, then demands are derived from

$$\max U^q(X_{11}^q, ..., X_{N1}^q, ..., X_{1r}^q, ..., X_{ir}^q, ..., X_{NR}^q)$$

$$\text{s.t.} \sum_{r=1}^{R} \sum_{i=1}^{N} P_{ir}^q X_{ir}^q = I^q, \tag{8.4}$$

where P_{ir}^q is the price paid by agent q for good i from region r. If P_{ir} denotes the international price of good i produced in region r, then P_{ir}^q differs from P_{ir} by the taxes, tariffs, and other deviations from world prices due to the trade policies captured by the model. The four-region model uses two-stage CES utility functions for each agent in (8.4); the seven-region model uses four-stage CES and LES functions.

The income of agent q, I^q, is defined as income from ownership of factors, plus transfers received from governments, less direct taxes paid:

$$I^q = \sum_{r=1}^{R} P_{K_r} \bar{K}_r^q + P_{L_r} \bar{L}_r^q + R_r^q - T^q. \tag{8.5}$$

The variables P_{K_r} and P_{L_r} define the selling prices of factors in region r; $\bar{K}_r^q$ and $\bar{L}_r^q$ are the ownership by agent q of capital and labor used in region r, R_r^q are transfers received by agent q from region r, and T^q are taxes paid by agent q. The sum over r for capital income includes the ownership of factors located abroad.

If (for now) we ignore tariffs, taxes, and transfers from government in this system, then $P_{ir}^q = P_{ir}$ for all q and $R_r^q = T^q = 0$. In this special case, a general equilibrium for the international economy is given by a set of goods prices $(P_{11}, ..., P_{N1}, ..., P_{1r}, ..., P_{1R}, ..., P_{NR})$ and factor prices $(P_{K_1}, P_{L_1}, ..., P_{K_r}, P_{L_r}, ..., P_{K_R}, P_{L_R})$ such that demand–supply equalities hold for goods and factors; that is, in goods markets,

$$G_i^r = \sum_{e=1}^{R} \sum_{j=1}^{N} H_{ij_e}^r + \sum_{r=1}^{R} \sum_{q=1}^{Q^r} X_{ir}^q \quad (i=1,...,N; r=1,...,R), \tag{8.6}$$

gross output of good i — intermediate demands for good i — final demands for good i

and in factor markets,

$$\sum_{i=1}^{N} K_i^r = \sum_{r=1}^{R} \sum_{q=1}^{Q^r} \bar{K}_r^q \quad (r=1,...,R); \tag{8.7}$$

Policy applications   204

$$\sum_{i=1}^{N} L_j^r = \sum_{r=1}^{R} \sum_{q=1}^{Q^r} \bar{L}_r^q \quad (r=1,\dots,R).$$ (8.8)

factor   factor
use by   ownership
industries   by agents

Zero-profit conditions hold for all industries in all regions; that is,

$$P_{ir} G_i^r = \sum_{j=1}^{N} \sum_{e=1}^{R} P_{je} H_{ji_r}^e + P_{K_r} K_i^r + P_{L_r} L_i^r$$

value of   intermediate costs   capital costs   labor costs
sales of   of producing good   of producing   of producing
good i i in region r good i in   good i in
produced   region r region r
in region r

$$(i=1,\dots,N; \; r=1,\dots,R). \quad (8.9)$$

In equilibrium, external sector balance also holds for each region; that is,

$$\sum_{i=1}^{N} E_{ir} + \sum_{e \neq r} \sum_{q=1}^{Q^r} P_{K_e} \bar{K}_e^q = \sum_{i=1}^{N} \sum_{e \neq r} M_{ie}^r + \sum_{e \neq r} \sum_{q=1}^{Q^e} P_{K_r} \bar{K}_r^q,$$ (8.10)

value of   capital income from   value of   capital income
exports by   abroad received   imports by   paid abroad
region r by region r region r by region r

where

$$E_{ir} = \sum_{e \neq r} \sum_{j=1}^{N} P_{ir} H_{ij_e}^r + \sum_{e \neq r} \sum_{q=1}^{Q^e} P_{ir} X_{ir}^q;$$

$$M_{ie}^r = \sum_{j=1}^{N} P_{ie} H_{ij_r}^e + \sum_{q=1}^{Q^r} P_{ie} X_{ie}^q.$$

The representation of an equilibrium is more complex if trade policies and taxes are incorporated, but the same three equilibrium conditions will still apply. An additional property is that government budget balance will hold in each region, because of Walras's law and external sector balance. This structure essentially parallels that presented by Shoven and Whalley (1974), who provide a proof of such an equilibrium's existence as well as techniques that can be used in computation.

Both the four- and seven-region models deviate from the framework of Shoven and Whalley (1974) in explicitly dividing the list of products into goods and factors. An important property resulting from this structure is that an equilibrium can be characterized for the whole model by a set of factor prices alone, rather than both factor and goods prices. This method of reducing the effective dimensions for the four- and seven-region models substantially reduces the cost of numerically computing an equilibrium solution for each of the models, and provides an important simplification in structure. The dimension-reduction procedure in these models works the same as that described for a single economy in Chapters 2 and 3.

The demand and production functions used in the four-region model, with their hierarchical nesting structure, are set out in Figure 8.3. On the production side, two internationally immobile but intersectorally mobile factors of production (capital and labor) are considered for each region. These are used in production processes that have constant returns to scale. These factors can be combined in a substitutable mix to provide the value-added requirement per unit of output for each industry. Substitution possibilities between capital and labor in each industry are described by CES functions.

Final demand functions in the four-region model are derived from two-level nested CES utility functions. At the lower level of the nesting, substitution occurs between comparable domestic and imported products (e.g., U.S. and Japanese cars); at the higher level, between composites of similar products (e.g., cars and other products). The CES functions used involve a separate CES subfunction for each composite good in the demand system and for each agent in each region. As for the production side, the substitution elasticities specified between comparable products directly affect import price elasticities of demand.

For the seven-region model, the structure of the substitution possibilities on the demand and production sides is as outlined in Figure 8.4; the range of substitution possibilities is wider. In contrast with the four-region model, which uses homothetic preferences, the capability exists for using nonhomothetic preferences through LES functions. These enable income elasticities for import-demand functions to differ from unity. In addition, further levels of nesting operate on the demand side, with substitution first taking place between variouis types of imports to form a composite import before substitution takes place between import composites and domestic products. This third level of substitution, between domestic products and imported composites, determines the price elasticity of demand for imports in a way similar to that at the lower level of substitution in the four-region model. The fourth level of substitution, between imports by region of production, forms a composite import for each product type in the importing region and determines export-price elasticities of that region's own import demands.

Demand-substitution elasticities in the second level play a role similar to that of higher-level substitution elasticities in the four-region model. The first level of substitution enables different substitution elasticities between groups of composites, with a separately specified substitution elasticity among these groups. This additional flexibility was built into the model so that composite products could eventually be divided into energy

DEMAND

Final Demand Functions

Each agent in each region has a 2-level CES utility function. Demands are generated by maximizing utility subject to the agent budget constraint.

CES Nesting Structure

Higher level 33 composite products

Lower level 4 types in each composite, subscripted by region of production
(except for nontraded goods)

PRODUCTION

Value Added Functions

Each industry in each region has a CES value added function with capital and labor services as substitutable primary inputs.

Intermediate Production

Each industry in each region has fixed-coefficient intermediate requirements in terms of composite goods. Fixed requirements of composites can be met by a substitutable mix of comparable domestic and imported goods. CES functions are used at this level for each fixed composite requirement.

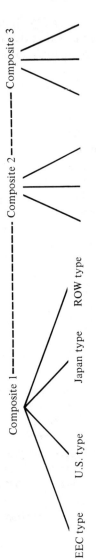

Composite 1 ———————— Composite 2 ——————— Composite 3

EEC type   U.S. type   Japan type   ROW type

Figure 8.3. Demand and production functions in the four-region model.

and nonenergy groups, allowing a price elasticity of energy demand to be incorporated separately. Potential uses of the seven-region model in the analysis of global energy trade have thus far not been developed, and this extra level of nesting plays little role in the applications of the seven-region model reported here.

The production side of the seven-region model uses a structure similar to that adopted in the four-region model, but the same extended nesting structure is used as on the demand side. Fixed coefficients are specified in each industry in terms of composite goods; input requirements may be met by a substitutable mix of comparable domestic and imported products. In contrast with the four-region model, for which single-stage CES functions are used, two-stage CES intermediate-requirement functions operate. Substitution first occurs between comparable import types to generate a composite import for each product; the second level of substitution occurs between composites of imports and domestic products. As on the demand side, the first-level substitution elasticities primarily affect price elasticities of demand faced by exporting regions; the second-level substitution elasticities primarily affect import-price elasticities.

Treatment of trade-protection policies

Three separate categories of trade-protection policies are incorporated in the two models, all of which affect trade flows. The categories are tariffs, nontariff barriers, and domestic taxes and subsidies.

Tariffs operate in each model in *ad valorem* form, and act as taxes on products imported from abroad. Tariffs have the effect of protecting domestic industries, since (behind the tariff wall) products can be sold domestically at gross-of-tariff prices. Revenues raised accrue to the government in the importing region, whose total revenues (including those from other sources) finance both real expenditures by government and transfers to persons.

The data used for tariff rates by product and by region draw on a compilation for 1976 produced by the U.S. Special Trade Representative's (STR) office during the Tokyo Round negotiations, which in turn was based on GATT data. This source is used to give tariff rates by product both for the United States and for each of its major trading partners. Since detailed tariff data is not readily available for the rest of the world for use in the four-region model, a simple linear average across EEC, U.S., and Japanese rates is used. For the seven-region model, tariffs on trade between the United States and the LDCs in the STR compilation are supplemented by additional estimates of *ad valorem* tariff rates for a number of developing countries.

PRODUCTION

Value-added functions
Each industry in each region has a CES value-added function with capital and labor services as primary inputs.

Intermediate substitution
Fixed-coefficient intermediate requirements technology, but with each fixed coefficient expressed in terms of composites only (i.e. a fixed machinery requirement per unit of manufacturing).

Each fixed-coefficient input requirement met by cost-minimizing bundle of domestic and import composites obtained from CES substitution functions.

CES hierarchy
(For each fixed coefficient in terms of composites; e.g., machinery requirement per unit of manufacture.)

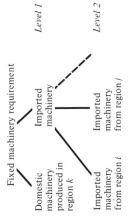

Fixed machinery requirement

Level 1
Domestic machinery produced in region k — Imported machinery

Level 2
Imported machinery from region i — Imported machinery from region j

DEMAND

Final demand functions
In each region, 1 4-level CES/LES functional form is used.

CES hierarchy

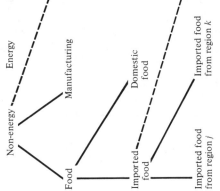

Non-energy — Energy

Manufacturing

Food

Domestic food

Imported food

Imported food from region j — Imported food from region k

Level 1
Substitution between categories (e.g., energy/non-energy)

Level 2
Substitution within categories among composite goods (e.g., among components of non-energy)

Level 3
Substitution between domestic and import composites (e.g., between domestic and imported food)

Level 4
Substitution between import types in import composites (e.g., between imported food from regions k and j)

LES hierarchy
Minimum requirements for each import composite at Level 3 used. These allow income elasticities for import demands to differ from unity.

Nontariff barriers (NTBs) are represented in both models in *ad valorem* tariff-equivalent form, in order to ease problems of computing equilibria relative to models with the explicit quantity and other constraints frequently implied by NTBs. This treatment allocates all rents and revenues from these trade barriers to the government in the importing regions, even though this does not actually happen with some of the trade-policy instruments classified as NTBs. Quotas and other quantity constraints create rents that accrue to the government only if quotas are sold or auctioned. In practice, quotas are usually issued by governments free of charge; rents from the quotas accrue to recipients of quotas, who may be either importers or exporters. In allocating revenues from NTBs to governments in this way, the models depart from what many might consider a realistic description of what happens in practice. This treatment also neglects the rent-seeking incentives that quotas can generate (Krueger 1974). The main justifications for this approach are the simplification gained and the paucity of data on the full range of quantity constraints. Further, the income effects involved are only a small portion of government and household revenues.

A long list of policies fit within the NTB category; the best-known policies are quotas, licensing restrictions of various kinds, valuation procedures, health and sanitary regulations, and the use of standards and other methods to restrict trade. It is difficult to quantify these nontariff barriers. The *ad valorem*–equivalent approach used by Whalley relies on data compiled from United Nations Conference on Trade and Development (UNCTAD) sources that estimate the significance of these barriers by a residual method; see especially Roningen and Yeats (1976) and Yeats (1977, 1979). Although some difficulties arise in the interpretation of these estimates, they appear to be the best available.

A further feature of this treatment of NTBs is the assumption that the *ad valorem* equivalents remain unchanged when other trade policies (such as tariffs) change, even though relative prices will also be affected. With a quantity constraint, the *ad valorem* equivalent implied by the constraint is that equivalent distortion needed to meet the constraint as part of a full equilibrium solution. However, the equilibrium solution depends on more than the quantity constraint alone, because if other policies were altered and the equilibrium price changed then the *ad valorem* equivalent would need to be revised. In actual use of the models, these effects usually are relatively small.

A final set of policies that affect trade involve domestic taxes and subsidies. These are incorporated in *ad valorem*–equivalent form for all regions

Figure 8.4. Hierarchy of substitution possibilities in the seven-region model. *Source: Trade Liberalization Among Major World Trading Areas,* MIT Press, 1985.

in both models. For the developed countries, this category includes income, corporate, property, sales and excise, and social security taxes. For OPEC, NICs, and LDCs in the seven-region model, income, property, and social security taxes are excluded since they are relatively unimportant, but export-promotion subsidies are included. A number of trade-policy issues related to taxation have arisen over the years, such as the trade impact of the destination-based rather than origin-based value-added tax in the EEC. The treatment of domestic taxes and subsidies in the models allows some of these issues to be analyzed.

8.2 Regional classifications: trade, commodity, and agent disaggregation

In Table 8.1, data on gross national product (GNP) and population are presented for the seven regions for 1977. The U.S. and EEC GNPs are close in size, and the Japanese GNP is approximately 40% as large. Out of a total gross world product in 1977 of approximately $8 trillion, the EEC and the United States in combination account for a little less than half (each somewhat less than $2 trillion). The GNP of ODCs is slightly larger, and Japan's GNP is around $700 billion. The gap in incomes between developed and developing countries is evident from the fact that the Japanese and LDC GNPs are of comparable orders of magnitude even though the population ratio is 1:24. The LDCs have over 50% of the world's population, but account for less than 10% of the gross world product.

A notable feature in the four-region model is the size of trade with the RoW. Although the EEC, the United States, and Japan are major participants in world trade, each has a trading partner that is more important than the other two major trading areas. For the EEC this partner is other European countries, for the United States it is Canada, and for Japan it is other Pacific Basin countries (South Korea, China, Taiwan, Hong Kong, Australia, and Singapore). Trade in the seven-region model is more equally dispersed, although ODCs have more trade than any of the other regions. A notable feature is the small size of trade between NICs and LDCs. Most trade is either North–North (involving the EEC, the United States, Japan, and ODCs) or North–South (vertical trade between LDCs and NICs on the one hand, and among developed countries of the North on the other); South–South trade between developing countries is small.

Trade, although central to the two models, does not exhaust the external-sector transactions in the two models; investment flows, interest, dividends and royalties, aid, and other financial transactions also enter the picture. In the main, these transactions are incorporated into the models to yield external-sector balance conditions without the adjustment of observed

Table 8.1. *GNP, population, and GNP per capita, by region, for 1977*

	GNP[a]	Approximate population	GNP per capita[a]
EEC	$1,629 billion[b]	0.3 billion	$6,283
U.S.	1,897 billion	0.2 billion	8,751
Japan	737 billion	0.1 billion	6,511
ODCs[c,d]	2,024 billion	0.5 billion	3,848
OPEC[c]	303 billion	0.3 billion	1,000
NICs[c]	461 billion	0.4 billion	1,306
LDCs[c]	773 billion	2.4 billion	325
World	7,824 billion	4.2 billion	1,863

[a] In 1977 U.S. dollars.
[b] 1 billion = 10^9.
[c] These regions are part of the Rest of the World in the four-region model.
[d] Other developed countries.

trade data that would otherwise be necessary. This additional data is not reported, since it is less essential in gaining an overview of the coverage and the main links in the models.

The levels of commodity detail used in the two models are given in Table 8.2. The choice of these classifications reflects a balance among the desire to capture the major distorting influences of trade policies to be analyzed, the level of detail that can be handled computationally in solving the models, and the availability of data. The same commodity classifications appear on the producer and consumer sides of both models. This treatment models margins (such as retail and wholesale trade) as separate products at both the producer and the consumer level, and is not wholly satisfactory because consumer products include margins whereas producer products do not. Data limitations prevent a more complete treatment of margins.

Since commodities are treated as heterogeneous by region, the 33 commodities in the four-region model represent a relatively fine level of detail in commodity classification compared to other models used in the applied general equilibrium literature. Four of the 33 commodities are treated as nontraded. These commodities are excluded from the model for the RoW, giving 128 commodities in total. In the seven-region model, 42 products are considered. Although slightly more commodity detail could be handled in this model, a further constraining feature is the availability of data –

Table 8.2. *Commodity classifications used in the trade models*

Commodities included	SITC divisions
4-region model (33 commodities)	

Agriculture

1. Meats, dairy products	Div 00, Div 02, Div 94, 011, 012
2. Cereals	Div 04–045
3. Other agricultural products, fruits, vegetables, oil seeds, nuts, animal feed, crude animal and vegetable materials; silk, wool, cotton, jute, and vegetable fibers	Div 05–051, 054, Div 22, Div 29, Div 08, 261, 262, 263, 264, 265
4. Forestry, fisheries	031

Mining

5. Coal	321, 4
6. Oil, natural gas	331, Div 34
7. Metallic, nonmetallic, other	Div 27, 181, 285, 286, 283

Manufacturing (nondurable goods)

8. Tea, sugar, coffee, spices, cocoa	Div 06, Div 07
9. Alcoholic drinks	112
10. Other foods, animal and vegetable oils and fats, misc. foods, prep. fruits and veg., prep. cereals, beverages, prep. meat and fish	Div 09, Div 41, Div 42, Div 43, 111, 0–48, 052, 053, 055, 013, 032, 046, 047
11. Tobacco	Div 12
12. Apparel, textile products	266, 267, Div 65, Div 84, Div 21, Div 61, Div 85
13. Paper, printing, publishing	Div 25, Div 64
14. Pharmaceuticals and toiletries	Div 54, Div 55
15. Other chemical and allied products	Div 51, Div 52, Div 53, Div 56, Div 57, Div 59
16. Petroleum, coal products	Div 32 less 321, 4, 332
17. Rubber, plastics	Div 23, Div 58, Div 62

Manufacturing (durable goods)

18. Lumber, wood, furniture	Div 24, Div 63, Div 82
19. Primary and fabricated metals, stone, glass	Div 66, Div 67, Div 68, Div 69, 282, 284
20. Machinery except electrical	Div 71
21. Electrical machinery	Div 72
22. Transport vehicles	Div 73

Table 8.2 *(cont.)*

Commodities included	SITC divisions
23. Scientific and precision instruments	Div 86, Div 95, Div 96
24. Miscellaneous manufacturing	Div 83, Div 89, Div 93
Construction and services 25. Construction	
26. Water transportation	
27. Other transportation and communications	Div 91
28. Housing services	
29. Electricity, gas, water	Div 35, Div 81
30. Wholesale and retail trade	
31. Finance, insurance, real estate	
32. Other services	
33. Government services	
7-region model (6 commodities)	
1. Agriculture and food	0+1
2. Mineral products and extractive ores	2+4
3. Energy products (including oil)	3
4. Nonmechanical manufacturing	5, 6, 8, 9
5. Machinery and transport equipment (including vehicles)	7
6. Construction, services, and other nontraded	None

especially data on bilateral trade flows by commodity for the regional classification used here.

Table 8.3 reports the demand-side disaggregation by agent in the two models. In the case of the seven-region model, a simple treatment is adopted in which one single agent is considered for each region. The single agent incorporates investment, government, and household consumption demands. In the four-region model, not only are these separate sectors identified in each region, but further disaggregation of the household sector is incorporated. For the United States and Japan, income classifications are used to group households; for the EEC, data for separate countries is used. The original motivation for the use of increased household

Table 8.3. *Demand-side disaggregation by agent in the models*

4-region model			
U.S.	EEC	Japan	7-region model
Government sector: 1 agent	Government sector: 1 agent	Government sector: 1 agent	1 demand-side agent in each region: EEC U.S. Japan ODCs OPEC NICs LDCs
Corporate sector: 1 agent	Corporate sector: 1 agent	Corporate sector: 1 agent	
Household sector: 10 households stratified by the following net-of-tax household income ranges, as given in the 1960–1 data[a]	Household sector: 1 agent considered for each of France, W. Germany, U.K., Italy, Ireland, Denmark, Belgium and Luxembourg, Netherlands	Household sector: 16 households stratified by the following net-of-tax household income ranges (in thousands of yen), as given in the 1973 Japanese family income and expenditure survey	
–$999 $1,000–$1,999 $2,000–$2,999 $3,000–$3,999 $4,000–$4,999 $5,000–$5,999 $6,000–$7,499 $7,500–$9,999 $10,000–$14,999 $15,000–		–¥400 ¥400–¥600 ¥600–¥800 ¥800–¥1,000 ¥1,000–¥1,200 ¥1,200–¥1,400 ¥1,400–¥1,600 ¥1,600–¥1,800 ¥1,800–¥2,000 ¥2,000–¥2,500 ¥2,500–¥3,000 ¥3,000–¥3,500 ¥3,500–¥4,000 ¥4,000–¥4,500 ¥4,500–¥5,000 ¥5,000–	

[a] *Survey of Consumer Expenditures 1960–1* (Bureau of Labor Statistics). When the data for the four-region model was compiled, this was the most recent complete set of consumer income and expenditure data for the United States. Data for 1973 have since been collected by the BLS (U.S. Department of Labor 1978).

disaggregation in the four-region model stems from earlier concerns about designing a model capable of analyzing the impacts of changes in trade-protection policies on the distribution of personal income. As Whalley (1985) emphasizes, in most cases these impacts turn out to be extremely small, so in the subsequent construction of the seven-region model a more aggregated approach was used in which this detail was ignored.

8.3 Tariff-cutting proposals in the Tokyo Round

The four-region model has been used by Whalley (1985) to evaluate the effects of alternative tariff-cutting proposals made in the Tokyo Round, the seventh in a series of negotiated rounds conducted under the GATT since 1947. Major participants spent a significant amount of time trying to agree on a single guiding formula to be used by all parties in making multilateral tariff cuts. The analyses reported here use the four-region model to evaluate the various formulas proposed by the major national delegations, to assess whether or not they were in the interest of the region proposing the cut, and to calculate gains and losses from each proposal. The four-region rather than the seven-region model is used because of its superior commodity detail.

The formula approach to multilateral tariff cutting under the GATT appeared first in the Kennedy Round, which preceded the Tokyo Round. The Trade Reform Act of 1964, which authorized U.S. participation in this round of negotiations, gave full presidential authority for a 50% proportional cut in tariff rates to be made as part of a balanced multilateral tariff-reduction package. The subsequent negotiations concentrated on sector-by-sector exemptions from the general 50% proportional cut, but the proportional-cut approach was accepted from the start as the guiding general formula.

After the conclusion of the Kennedy Round, it was widely believed in Europe that proportional tariff reductions were advantageous to the United States because U.S. tariff rates were more dispersed than European rates. (For instance, the United States has significantly higher tariffs on textiles and footwear than does the EEC.) The European argument was that a nonlinear (or harmonization) formula that would cut high tariffs more than low tariffs would be advantageous to Europe. Some Europeans also argued, on grounds of economic efficiency, that disparities in tariff rates should be reduced. A nonlinear cutting formula comes closer to achieving such a goal than a linear formula. Thus, one of the first items on the agenda at the Tokyo Round in 1974 was agreement on a general guiding formula for all tariff cuts.

The major formulas proposed during the earlier stages of the Tokyo Round are listed in Table 8.4. These proposals are somewhat curious in structure, and it appears that there was relatively little input from economic modeling in their selection. Indeed, it is not clear that perceived national gain was always the primary determinant of the proposals.

The U.S. proposal involved a straight proportional cut for tariffs above a threshold of approximately 6.5%, and a nonlinear cut for tariffs below

Table 8.4. *Major multilateral tariff-cutting proposals made in the Tokyo Round of GATT*

U.S. proposal

$T_N = 0.4T_0$ if $T_0 > 0.067$

$T_N = 0.5T_0 - 1.5T_0^2$ if $T_0 < 0.067$

EEC proposal (four iterative cuts)

$$T_N = T_0 - 2T_0^2 + 2T_0^3 - T_0^4 - (T_0 - 2T_0^2 + 2T_0^3 - T_0^4)^2$$
$$- [T_0 - 2T_0^2 + 2T_0^3 - 2T_0^4 - (T_0 - 2T_0^2 + 2T_0^3 - T_0^4)^2]^2$$

Japanese proposal (applied to post–Kennedy Round and not current tariffs)

$T_N = 0.3T_0 + 0.035$ if $T_0 > 0.05$

$T_N = T_0$ if $T_0 < 0.05$

Canadian proposal[a] (all countries adopt reduced U.S. tariffs)

$T_N = 0.4T_0^{US}$ if $T_0 > 0.05$

$T_N = 0.0$ if $T_0 < 0.05$

Swiss proposal (compromise formula)

$T_N = AT_0/(A + T_0)$, where A is a constant (a representative value is 0.14)

Note: T_N = post-cut tariff; T_0 = pre-cut tariff.
[a] The Canadian proposal was in fact restricted to the sector-by-sector negotiations and was proposed primarily in the context of tariffs on pulp and paper, but it has been considered here as an alternative general formula.

the threshold. This proposal was made in the spirit of providing a simple proposal akin to the proportional-reduction approach of the Kennedy Round. The Europeans proposed a four-way iterative cut, which was to have the effect of reducing higher tariffs proportionally more than low tariffs. This formula reflected the European belief that a simple proportional cut was advantageous to the United States. To apply this European proposal to an existing tariff rate of (say) 20%, one would cut the 20% tariff rate by 20% in the first round. The resulting 16% rate would then be cut by 16%, and so on. This procedure would be applied four times to produce the final tariff rate. The Europeans justified this proposal on the grounds that harmonizing tariff rates would move the global economy closer to a common tariff structure. They suggested that this approach was in line with the objectives of the 1957 Treaty of Rome, and with the general movement in Europe to harmonize all policies.

The Japanese rejected both these formulas. They suggested that post–Tokyo Round tariff rates simply be calculated as a flat tariff of 3.5% plus one-third of the old tariff. The key feature of the Japanese proposal was the stipulation that the old tariffs used should be post–Kennedy Round tariffs, rather than those rates in operation when cuts were first implemented. Since the Japanese had made substantial unilateral reductions in tariffs between the end of the Kennedy Round and the initiation of the Tokyo Round, this formula would have had significantly smaller effects on Japanese tariffs than on those of other countries.

These three major participants viewed each other's tariff-cutting proposals with some suspicion, and as a result "compromise" proposals were also discussed. One of the more interesting of these was the Canadian proposal, which was actually made in the context of more limited sector negotiations but which (for the purpose of present discussion) can be considered as a general formula. Under the Canadian approach, all countries would have adopted a common harmonized tariff set at 40% of the U.S. tariff, with the provision that all tariff rates less than 5% would be set equal to zero. This proposal contrasts with the usual Canadian perspective that protection for Canada is desirable. Since Canada has higher tariffs than many other major industrialized countries, it is perhaps a little surprising that Canada should propose an approach to tariff reduction in which Canada would receive larger tariff cuts than its trading partners. As the majority of Canadian trade is with the United States, an offsetting feature from the Canadian perspective is the zero tariff replacing any existing tariffs that are less than 5%. Important Canadian exports to the United States are lumber and energy products, many of which attract U.S. tariffs in the region of 3%–4%. Thus, the Canadian approach could be defended on grounds of national interest as a suggested compromise proposal, one likely to attract U.S. support while having the net effect of eliminating the small tariffs Canada faced on major export items.

The compromise actually adopted was the Swiss proposal of a non-linear cut intermediate between the EEC and the U.S. proposals, involving the ratio of the product of the tariff rate and a constant to their sum. The traditional view of Swiss neutrality, combined with the perception that the Swiss formula was intermediate between the EEC and U.S. proposals, seems to have been partly responsible for the adoption of this formula. With its adoption, negotiations moved to the next stage of agreeing on the constant term to be used in the formula.

To provide some sense of how these formulas translate into tariff cuts, their impacts on different initial tariff rates are presented in Table 8.5. Precut tariff rates of 5%, 10%, 15%, and 20% are used, and the new tariff-cut rates are reported. A major feature illustrated by this table, one not apparent from Table 8.4, is the difference in the average depth of the

Table 8.5. *Results of applying tariff-cutting formulas listed in Table 8.4 to illustrative tariff rates*

	Ad valorem rate before application of proposed formulas			
	5%	10%	15%	20%
U.S. proposal	2.1	4	6	8
EEC proposal	4.1	7.0	8.9	10.3
Japanese proposal	5	6.5	8	9.5
Canadian proposal	0	4	6	8
Swiss proposal	3.7	5.8	7.2	8.2

cuts involved; the U.S. proposal involves a significantly deeper cut than the EEC proposal. On the other hand, the nonlinearity of the EEC cut is clearly apparent, since a 5% tariff would be cut only to 4.1% while a 20% tariff would be cut to 10.3%. The Swiss proposal appears as a clear intermediate case between the European and American proposals.

To analyze the effects of multilateral adoption of these alternative formulas to guide tariff cuts with the four-region model, it is necessary to represent each formula in model-equivalent form; this has been done as described in Table 8.6. The seven different types of tariff cuts correspond to the five formulas listed in Table 8.4, with two versions of the Japanese and Canadian formulas. Tariff cuts apply to all regions in the model, including the RoW.

The two Japanese cases reflect the impact of using post–Kennedy Round rather than current tariff rates. Under the "Japan 1" cut, the Japanese formula is mechanically applied to tariffs in all regions; under the "Japan 2" cut, the formula is applied to tariffs in all regions but Japan receives only half of the full cut. Two different versions are also used for the Canadian cut. In the first version, the Canadian formula is mechanically applied to all tariffs in all regions. However, the possibility exists that this formula can increase tariffs in some regions. With the "Canada 2" cut, the formula is applied with the provision that, if the resulting tariff on any commodity in any region is higher than the original tariff, the original tariff is left unchanged.

A further set of issues in implementing these tariff cuts in the model relates to commodity coverage. In the past, tariff-cutting negotiations in the GATT have concentrated on manufacturing products, and this was also true of the Tokyo Round. This has been a source of contention for LDCs in that agricultural products and other products (including textiles)

Table 8.6. *Model representation of tariff cuts*

U.S. cut	Application of U.S. formula proposal to tariffs in all regions
EEC cut	Application of EEC formula proposal to tariffs in all regions
Japan 1 cut	Application of Japanese formula proposal to tariffs in all regions
Japan 2 cut	Application of Japanese formula proposal to tariffs in all regions, but Japan receives only half of the full cut
Canada 1 cut	Application of Canadian formula proposal to tariffs in all regions
Canada 2 cut	Application of Canadian formula proposal to tariffs in all regions, but commodities for which the tariff increases are left unchanged
Swiss cut	Application of Swiss formula proposal to tariffs in all regions

Note: Commodity coverage of tariff-cutting formulas in four-region model: commodities 5–24 are included (broadly, manufacturing plus mineral ores), except textiles (12); coffee, tea, sugar, spices, cocoa (8), and tobacco in Japan only (11).

on which major nontariff barriers operate are effectively removed from the GATT negotiating process.

The commodity coverage in the model formulas is also indicated in Table 8.6. In the four-region model the manufacturing and mineral-ore products (commodities 5–24) are included, with special exceptions made for textiles, which are taken out of the cuts altogether. Coffee, tea, sugar, spices, and cocoa are also exempted. The exclusion of textiles reflects the implicit agreement among developed countries to exclude textiles even at the negotiating stage. Further exclusions include tobacco in Japan. This tariff is set at high rates and was not part of the negotiations in the Tokyo Round.

Whalley (1985) evaluates the welfare and terms-of-trade effects of the tariff-cutting formulas in Table 8.4, using the four-region model. In Table 8.7, the welfare effects of these cuts are reported as equivalent variations in billions of 1973 dollars. Terms-of-trade effects appear as a percentage change in each region's terms of trade, with positive entries indicating improvement.

Table 8.7 considers cases where the formula cut applied to the EEC, the United States, and Japan also applied identically to the RoW. Rest of the World comprises ODCs (such as Canada, non-EEC European countries, and Australia) that participate fully in GATT tariff reductions, along with developing and less-developed countries that do not. Whalley also considers other analyses with the alternative of only a half cut applying

Table 8.7. *Welfare and terms-of-trade effects of alternative tariff-cutting formulas with full cut in RoW: four-region model*

Formula							
	U.S.	EEC	Japan 1	Japan 2	Canada 1	Canada 2	Swiss
Welfare impact[a]							
EEC	+3.5	+1.7	+1.6	+1.6	+5.4	+5.5	+2.3
U.S.	+0.6	+0.9	+1.0	+1.0	+1.0	+1.4	+0.9
Japan	+1.1	+0.3	+0.3	+0.3	+1.5	+1.6	+0.5
RoW	−2.6	−1.2	−1.4	−1.4	−4.1	−4.1	−1.7
Total	+2.6	+1.7	+1.6	+1.5	+3.8	+4.3	+2.0
Percentage change in terms of trade							
EEC	+1.2	+0.5	+0.5	+0.5	+1.8	+1.8	+0.7
U.S.	−0.5	+0.3	+0.5	+0.4	−0.6	−0.2	+0.2
Japan	+0.4	−0.2	−0.3	−0.2	+0.5	+0.2	−0.1
RoW	−1.7	−1.0	−1.1	−1.1	−2.7	−2.8	−1.3

[a] Equivalent variations in billions of 1973 dollars.

in the RoW; this difference in treatment of the RoW has a substantial impact on results.

In Table 8.7, the United States is a relatively small gainer from the various tariff cuts in comparison with the EEC, and the RoW loses consistently. The smaller U.S. gains reflect the fact that the United States is a major exporter of agricultural products, and has less to gain from the liberalization of trade in manufactures that follows from GATT tariff reductions. As a fraction of GNP, the United States typically gains less than Japan.

Results across the various formulas yield some interesting implications in terms of national interest and the motives in promoting particular formulas. For instance, the U.S. proposal would give the EEC twice as much of a welfare gain as the EEC's own proposal. This is because the EEC gains most from deeper tariff cuts, whether they are linear or nonlinear, and the U.S. cut is a deeper cut. In fact, under only one other national proposal (the Japanese) would the EEC countries gain less than under their own proposal.

This perverse ranking of national well-being and proposal origin shows up also in the cases of the United States and Japan. Both the United States and Japan gain least under their own proposals. This suggests a somewhat paradoxical view of the policy process under the GATT: that negotiating groups come together in Geneva to bargain fiercely for their own proposals, even though other proposals are (from a nationalistic viewpoint) preferable.

Another prominent feature of Table 8.7 is that in all cases the RoW loses while the developed world gains. This welfare loss for the RoW is reflected in the deterioration of its terms of trade. The reason for this effect is that tariff cuts are limited to manufactures and raw materials while no trade-policy reductions occur for agricultural products. In addition, existing tariffs on raw materials are low. The RoW is a large exporter of agricultural products and raw materials. The net effect of tariff reductions in the three developed-country regions is to expand world trade in manufactures and inflict a terms-of-trade loss on the rest of the world, since the relative terms of trade between manufactures and agriculture move against agriculture. Table 8.7 thus supports the view often expressed by LDCs that trade liberalization under the GATT is a vehicle through which rich countries are able collectively to improve their terms of trade with poor countries.

8.4 The North–South debate and the terms of trade

Whalley has used the seven-region trade model to analyze the implications of trade protection in the North and other factors on North–South terms of trade. Much of the recent debate on global aspects of trade policy has focused not on the GATT and trade between developed countries, but on the relationship between developed ("northern") countries and developing ("southern") countries – in particular, the terms of trade.

Aside from naive unequal-exchange doctrines, several arguments have surfaced as to why existing North–South arrangements produce terms of trade that are unfair to the South. One is the Singer–Prebisch thesis (Singer 1950, Prebisch 1962), which suggests an inevitable long-term deterioration in the terms of trade of the South; a second is that protectionist policies in the North adversely affect the terms of trade faced by the South; a third theory is the possibility of "immiserizing" growth, which has been prominent in theoretical literature for over two decades; yet another is the requirement that foreign aid be used primarily to buy imports from the North.

Empirical literature on the North–South terms of trade has concentrated on the first of these arguments. Spraos (1980), for instance, concludes that before World War II the net terms of trade moved against exports of primary products in favor of exports of manufactures, although not by the margin originally suggested by Prebisch. Since the war, it appears that terms of trade have moved in favor of primary products (even excluding oil). Michaely (1980) highlights some of the dangers of identifying primary exports exclusively as exports of LDCs, since developed countries are also major exporters of primary products. He proposes and calculates an income index for each traded commodity at a three-digit SITC level, and concludes that the terms of trade of "poor" nations show a clear improvement between 1952 and 1970. There is little literature on the other arguments, partly because a numerical model of world trade patterns is needed in which the terms of trade are endogenously determined. Whalley applied the seven-region model to these issues with this purpose in mind.

The Singer–Prebisch thesis asserts that there is an inevitable long-term deterioration in the terms of trade of the South. This thesis follows primarily from statistical observations (most involving the United Kingdom's trade in manufactures and nonmanufactures) of a long-term deterioration in the terms of trade of agricultural and raw-material exports of developing countries relative to imports of manufactures from the 1870s up to World War II. As noted above, recent evidence casts doubt on whether this trend remains characteristic of the postwar period and on whether it is still reasonable to characterize all developing countries as heavy exporters of agriculture and raw materials.

A number of explanations of the Singer–Prebisch thesis exist. One is that high income elasticities of import demand in the South coupled with low income elasticities in the North imply that growth in the world economy leads to a deterioration in the Southern terms of trade. This position is sometimes defended by claiming that Southern exports are necessities (i.e., enter Northern import demands with low income elasticities) whereas Northern exports are luxuries (i.e., enter Southern import demands with high income elasticities). Another explanation sometimes offered is that the South is growing in absolute size more rapidly than the North. While growth rates of per-capita GNP are lower, significantly higher population growth leads to higher absolute GNP growth. The faster-growing region, other things being equal, will suffer a deterioration in its terms of trade.

A more extreme case of the second of these themes is Bhagwati's (1958) idea of immiserizing growth. In Bhagwati's paper and in subsequent literature, the theme stressed is that it is possible for a country to grow and simultaneously suffer a terms-of-trade deterioration that leaves the country worse off than before its growth. The usual case is where growth occurs in factor endowments and the country faces a low export-price elasticity in trade. In this case the terms-of-trade deterioration can be sharp enough to give a net loss.

In the regional classification used in the seven-region model, the South has slow growth in GNP per capita, but has higher total GNP growth because of sharply higher population growth. Other things being equal, the literature on immiserizing growth suggests that a terms-of-trade deterioration is to be expected in the fastest-growing region. The size of the deterioration, rather than the possibility of being made worse off through growth, is what we analyze here.

The role of tariffs and nontariff barriers in the North in inflicting terms-of-trade losses on the South is also a theme raised continually in debates on trade between developed and developing countries. The key protection issues involve the role of the Multifiber Arrangement in textile trade and the role of agricultural protection via NTBs, which is especially important in the EEC and Japan. With textiles in particular, the Northern protection is by quotas, the revisions of which do not keep pace with real growth rates in world trade. This issue is complicated by the rules governing allocation of quotas, and an argument can be made that producers in LDCs gain from the quotas because of the rents they receive from being allocated quotas at no charge. This question is not fully addressed by the seven-region model (since quota protection in the North is modeled in *ad valorem*–equivalent form), and the model treatment does not encompass Wolf's (1983) view of textile protection that producers in both developing and developed countries gain at the expense of consumers in developed countries.

A further issue related to North–South terms of trade involves both aid itself and the tying of aid to purchases of exports from the donating developed countries. What evidence there is (much of it anecdotal) suggests that two-thirds or more of foreign aid may either be directly tied to purchases of imports from the donating country or be explicit aid in kind. This specific redistribution is clearly advantageous to donating countries with regard to cash transfers, since a larger fraction than would otherwise obtain is used to repurchase imports. A common view is that aid in this form probably leads to more advantageous terms of trade to the North than might prevail with an unconstrained income transfer.

In Table 8.8, results using the central-case elasticity specification of Whalley (1985) in the seven-region model are reported for the abolition of tariffs and nontariff barriers in the North (regions 1–4), in the South (regions 5–7), and finally in the world (all regions). The abolition of tariffs and nontariff barriers in the North produces an annual welfare gain for LDCs and NICs of approximately $30 billion, with these two regions accounting for the majority of the worldwide welfare gain. These welfare changes are collinear with the terms-of-trade effects, with the terms of trade of NICs and LDCs improving by 9%.

This annual gain to the South from the removal of protection in the North is approximately 50% more than the aid flow from the North to the South. That is, the North–South aid mechanism generated approximately

Table 8.8. *Impacts of removal of Northern and Southern trade protection in the seven-region model*

	Abolition of tariffs and NTBs in		
	North (regions 1-4)	South (regions 5-7)	All regions
Annual welfare impacts, central-case model specification[a]			
1. EEC	−0.8	+38.2	+35.5
2. U.S.	−1.6	+12.9	+9.3
3. Japan	−1.4	+21.4	+20.8
4. ODCs	−4.1	+4.7	−1.8
5. OPEC	+5.7	+7.0	+8.3
6. NICs	+13.2	−31.8	−21.0
7. LDCs	+17.0	−28.4	−18.7
Total	+28.0	+24.0	+33.1
Percentage change in terms of trade			
1. EEC	−3.1	+14.9	+12.7
2. U.S.	−2.2	+2.5	+1.5
3. Japan	−5.1	+24.0	+23.1
4. ODCs	−3.7	−2.0	−4.7
5. OPEC	+4.8	−0.1	+1.7
6. NICs	+8.5	−29.6	−23.0
7. LDCs	+9.5	−33.6	−29.3

[a] Equivalent variations in billions of 1977 dollars.

$20 billion of aid to the South in 1977, which was more than offset by a terms-of-trade loss inflicted through protectionist policies imposed in the North. Such a finding clearly supports the South's position that gains are available to the South from the removal of protection in the North.

However, the effects of trade protection in the North must also be considered alongside the impacts of trade protection in the South, where *ad valorem*-equivalent protection is significantly higher. Removal of protection in the South yields substantial gains to the North and losses to the South. The worldwide gain from removal of Southern tariffs and nontariff barriers is in the nieghborhood of $24 billion, but approximately $60 billion of losses are inflicted on the South along with $80 billion of gains to the North. This result dramatizes the neglect of Southern trade barriers in the North–South debate, where the focus has been almost exclusively on ways of improving the South's position.

On the basis of these results, a possible response by the North to pressure from the South for removal of Northern trade protection might be that trade liberalization in the North should be accompanied by liberalization in the South. Indeed, since both developed and developing countries inflict losses on each other through their relative protective stances, it should be possible to design a global liberalization package in which all would gain. However, such an arrangement would be extremely difficult to negotiate and administer owing to the large number of countries involved.

These results also argue that the South as a region will not gain by liberalizing its trade policies, in spite of the arguments often made by development economists that trade liberalization is a desirable policy option for many if not most LDCs. Although individual countries in the South may well gain from trade liberalization if the region as a whole does not liberalize, simultaneous moves by all countries in the region to liberalize will be detrimental to the South because of the adverse terms-of-trade impacts. Because of its importance for the trade-policy stance adopted by developing countries, we must qualify this conclusion by noting its dependence on factors being excluded from the model – for instance, rent seeking associated with protection in the South.

The last column in Table 8.8 describes effects of the joint abolition of all tariffs and nontariff barriers in all regions. Here the worldwide gain of \$33 billion is smaller than the sum of the gains reported in the subcases in the table. In terms of worldwide protection, the South is the significant terms-of-trade gainer because of the higher protection that prevails in the South; this more than offsets the size differential between regions. This suggests that the South would lose from global trade liberalization. However, the North could achieve further gains from a more restrictive trade-policy regime than the one currently in effect. Thus, to portray the South as a net loser from global trade liberalization may be misleading, in that current protection levels, rather than a set of optimal tariffs, provide the comparison point.

Table 8.9 considers various other modifications to protectionist policies in the North. In Case 1, tariffs in the North are replaced by a mean-preserving equal-rate tariff on all products. Results here indicate that the high tariffs in the North on certain items (particularly textiles) are significant to developing countries, and slightly more so to LDCs than to NICs. Case 2 considers the situation where all Northern countries remove NTBs on agricultural imports from all regions, including developed-country regions. Because of the importance of agricultural exports to LDCs and NICs, the gain to the developing-country regions is significant:

Table 8.9. *Impacts of various modifications to Northern trade policies*

	Case 1[a]	Case 2[b]	Case 3[c]
Welfare impacts[d]			
EEC	−0.1	−0.4	−2.2
U.S.	+0.1	−0.2	−1.5
Japan	+0.6	−0.8	−0.3
ODCs	−0.4	−0.4	−2.2
OPEC	−1.5	+0.9	+0.3
NICs	+1.6	+5.3	+7.0
LDCs	+1.9	+6.7	+9.4
Total	+2.2	+11.1	+10.5
Percentage change in terms of trade			
EEC	−0.0	−0.8	−1.4
U.S.	−0.1	−0.8	−1.3
Japan	+0.5	−2.8	−1.4
ODCs	−0.1	−1.0	−1.2
OPEC	−1.0	+1.0	+0.3
NICs	+0.9	+3.6	+4.8
LDCs	+1.1	+3.8	+5.5

[a] All countries in North replace existing tariffs by a mean-preserving equal-rate tariff on all products.
[b] All countries in North remove NTBs on agricultural imports.
[c] All countries in North remove NTBs on imports of agricultural products from NICs and LDCs only.
[d] Equivalent variations in billions of 1977 dollars.

the terms-of-trade improvement is approximately 3.5%. Case 3 illustrates that the gain to developing countries is larger where the removal by the North of NTBs on agricultural imports is restricted to imports from NICs and LDCs. The terms-of-trade improvement in this case is approximately 5%, with an annual gain to these regions of $16 billion.

Several other issues beyond trade protection have been under discussion in the literature in recent years. Table 8.10 reports cases where the terms-of-trade effects associated with differential growth rates in the North and South are analyzed using the seven-region model. Although these analyses are motivated by the literature on immiserizing growth, strict immiserization due to growth does not occur in the model. A terms-of-trade deterioration does occur in the faster-growing region, but the purpose of these

Table 8.10. *Differential growth rates and North–South terms of trade*

Annual GNP growth[a]						
EEC	U.S.	Japan	ODCs	OPEC	NICs	LDCs
3.3%	2.8%	4.8%	4.1%	3.5%	5.2%	4.5%

Percentage change in terms of trade

Homothetic case, central-case specification

	After 5 years	After 10 years	After 20 years
EEC	+3.4	+6.9	+14.0
U.S.	+3.5	+7.0	+14.0
Japan	−3.3	−6.7	−13.0
ODCs	−2.9	−5.7	−11.1
OPEC	+0.9	+1.8	+3.5
NICs	−4.4	−9.0	−17.2
LDCs	−3.1	−6.1	−12.1

Nonhomothetic cases, after 10 years
Import income elasticities:

Regions 1–4	1.5	0.5	0.75
Regions 5–7	1.5	1.5	1.25
EEC	+6.8	+6.7	+6.4
U.S.	+6.7	+6.9	+6.6
Japan	−6.2	−6.4	−5.9
ODCs	−5.5	−5.6	−5.9
OPEC	+1.7	+1.8	+1.8
NICs	−8.9	−9.0	−8.8
LDCs	+6.1	−6.0	−5.9

[a] Averages for 1969–78, by region; computed from *World Bank Atlas* data.

calculations is to investigate the strength of this effect and not to establish the existence of immiserization per se.

The annual growth rates of GNP by region used in these calculations are taken from the *World Bank Atlas* and are reported in Table 8.10. The North, on average, is slower-growing in GNP terms than the South. The higher rate of Southern GNP growth reflects not higher growth of GNP per capita but rather significantly higher population growth. These growth rates are used as the differential annual rates of growth for both factor endowments in each region in the model, even though in practice growth is not balanced. This treatment corresponds to the approach used in the theoretical literature on immiserizing growth.

The impact of differential growth on the terms of trade is reported in Table 8.10 for both homothetic and nonhomothetic preferences. As expected from the literature on this issue, faster-growing regions suffer a deterioration in their terms of trade. In the homothetic cases, after 10 years the EEC and the United States have a 7% appreciation in their terms of trade and the South has a deterioration of approximately 7%. This 10-year deterioration is slightly smaller than that in the Southern terms of trade resulting from protectionist trade policies in the North. Thus, ten years of differential North–South growth might be roughly comparable in its significance for the North–South terms of trade to the annual terms-of-trade effects of protection in the North. The results in the nonhomothetic cases are little different from those in the corresponding homothetic case. These cases are motivated partially by indications in the literature that income elasticities in world trade exceed unity, and partially by the rationalization of the Singer–Prebisch thesis that with differential income elasticities in import demands there will be an inevitable deterioration in Southern terms of trade.

Another issue concerns the impact of foreign aid on North–South terms of trade. Table 8.11 shows model results for an abolition of annual North–South aid flows and also for a doubling of the same flows. Because of the complexities of incorporating partial or full tying of aid, the model treats all aid as untied cash transfers; this explains the striking conclusion that donor countries have a substantial secondary burden of aid. However, the reason for this result suggests that untying foreign aid would lead to major gains for the South (and for LDCs in particular). In the model, recipients of aid use most of the transferred cash to purchase their own products rather than to purchase imports from aid donors. This occurs because the expenditure patterns by product within all regions are dominated by purchases of the regions' own products. As a result, the secondary burden of aid borne by donors is substantial. In the case of an abolition of aid flows from the North to the South, the welfare loss to LDCs is $47 billion while the direct cash loss to LDCs from abolition of aid is only $20 billion. Correspondingly, a doubling of aid flows from North to South increases welfare of the LDCs by $40 billion, whereas the incremental aid flow would be only $20 billion. The terms-of-trade effects reported in Table 8.11 confirm the substantial secondary burdens.

The crucial issue with these calculations is thus the representation of aid as untied. If aid flows are smaller than the commodity imports to which they are tied, and if all funds are fungible, then tying aid should have no effect. Using tied aid to buy imports means that other domestic

Table 8.11. *Model analyses of changes in aid mechanisms*

	Abolition of aid from North to South	Doubling of aid from North to South	1977 net aid flows
Welfare impacts[a]			
EEC	+15.0	−13.5	−7.4
U.S.	+6.9	−6.5	−4.9
Japan	+4.1	−3.5	−3.0
ODCs	+5.0	−4.5	−2.0
OPEC	+11.4	−10.5	−6.1
NICs	−7.8	+7.4	+2.6
LDCs	−47.3	+40.9	+20.8
Total	−12.6	+9.7	
Percentage change in terms of trade			
EEC	+3.1	−2.8	
U.S.	+0.7	−0.8	
Japan	+2.1	−1.9	
ODCs	−0.1	−0.1	
OPEC	+2.6	−2.3	
NICs	−2.9	+2.7	
LDCs	−1.2	+12.1	

[a] Equivalent variations in billions of 1977 dollars.

income need no longer be used to purchase these imports, and thus the tying of aid is ineffective. On the other hand, many complaints are voiced by LDCs about aid-tying provisions, and Table 8.11 clearly suggests that the potential secondary benefits to LDCs from an untying of aid are substantial.

9

Single-country trade modeling

In analyzing trade and other policy questions from a single-country (rather than a global) perspective, a common modeling strategy is to build single-country models along with a simple specification of behavior in the rest of the world (model closure). This is typically done by specifying a system of export-demand and import-supply functions that the single country is assumed to face in its transactions with the rest of the world. In this chapter we outline how this approach can be implemented and discuss some applications of the technique.

9.1 Model closure through foreign export demand and import supplies

In some applied general equilibrium models (Boadway and Treddenick 1978; Deardorff and Stern 1981; Dervis et al. 1982; Dixon et al. 1982), a system of simple export-demand and import-supply functions is used to represent external-sector behavior so as to "close" what is otherwise a single-country model. These models were outlined briefly in Chapter 4; they separate traded from nontraded goods and use the so-called Armington assumption, which treats similar domestically produced and imported goods as qualitatively different. The procedure is used primarily to account for the phenomenon of "crosshauling" that appears in the international trade data to which these models are calibrated.

The precise structure of the external sector tends to vary somewhat from model to model, although the broad characteristics are similar. The models cited in the previous paragraph all have exchange-rate variables appearing in their external sectors. It is common in these models for results to be presented for policy simulations in which changes in exchange rates are reported as if financial variables have real effects. This contradicts the neutrality of money in conventional general equilibrium analysis.

230

Boadway and Treddenick (1978) present an especially clear explanation of their external-sector closure procedure, and it is useful to use their discussion to illustrate some issues common to all these models. Their focus is on the domestic impacts of variations in Canadian tariff policy. They construct a model for Canada with substantial industrial and commodity detail involving either Cobb–Douglas or CES functions for both primary and intermediate production. The data base for the model is provided by Canadian input–output tables. Boadway and Treddenick comment on the need for a simple way of closing their domestic economy model by incorporating the external sector, and outline a partial equilibrium system that can be appended to the more elaborate general equilibrium specification of the domestic economy.

They first describe a closure system for a model where homogeneous products appear, presenting a subsystem in which foreigners are assumed to have import-supply and export-demand functions of constant price elasticity. A zero–trade-balance condition applies. They suggest that this is an especially convenient system, since elasticities can be chosen either to correspond to empirical estimates or to allow for polar cases such as price-taking behavior. Because of the crosshauling in trade data, their computations use the Armington assumption of product heterogeneity, and specification of the external sector differs from that discussed in the earlier part of their paper. They assume foreign demand functions of constant price elasticity, and treat Canada as a taker of world prices for imported goods. This assumes a perfectly elastic foreign import-supply function, although foreign and domestic goods are not perfect substitutes. The elasticity of substitution between comparable domestic and foreign goods controls the degree to which the Canadian price system is governed by world prices. An external-sector balance condition involving an exchange-rate variable closes the system.

Somewhat similar subsystems to that used by Boadway and Treddenick appear in Dervis et al. (1982) and Dixon et al. (1982). In all cases the Armington assumption of product heterogeneity is used along with foreign export-demand functions of constant price elasticity, domestic price-taking behavior with respect to world import prices, and an external-sector balance condition. Deardorff and Stern's (1981) model differs in that the submodels of the separate economies are linked through an international price system. Each country's export-demand function is given by the sum of import demands for the country's exports across all other countries. The Armington assumption of product heterogeneity is used, and exchange-rate variables affect domestic-currency import and export prices.

These external-sector closure procedures thus have a number of common features. First, external-sector equation systems are described in some models as giving a capability of separately incorporating foreign export-demand and import-supply elasticities while simultaneously meeting an external-sector balance condition. Secondly, an exchange-rate variable frequently appears, giving the impression of a financial factor that affects real variables of the system in long-run equilibrium, even though real models (with no monetary sector specified) are used. Thirdly, common procedure is to use the Armington assumption of product heterogeneity to model price-taking behavior by country with respect to all or some of the imported goods, while foreigners' demand functions for domestic exports incorporate some degree of price elasticity.

The closure approach discussed by Boadway and Treddenick (1978) for a general equilibrium model in which no Armington assumption appears (products are homogeneous between countries) is helpful in illustrating some of the issues in the design of a closure rule. This approach can be represented by the following system of foreign export-demand and import-supply functions:

$$E = E_0 \left(\frac{\mathbf{p}_E}{e} \right)^{\eta} \quad (-\infty < \eta < 0), \tag{9.1}$$

$$M = M_0 \left(\frac{\mathbf{p}_M}{e} \right)^{\mu} \quad (0 < \mu < \infty), \tag{9.2}$$

where $\mathbf{p}_E$ and $\mathbf{p}_M$ are denominated in home-country currency and are the home-country prices paid for exports by foreign purchasers and received for imports supplied by foreign producers. The variables $\mathbf{E}$ and $\mathbf{M}$ are vectors of exports and imports (respectively), and E_0 and M_0 are base-year exports and imports. Elasticities η and μ are described as export-demand and import-supply price elasticities (respectively), explaining the restrictions on η and μ in (9.1) and (9.2). The exchange rate between domestic and foreign currency is given by e. The ratios $\mathbf{p}_E/e$ and $\mathbf{p}_M/e$ represent foreign country (world) prices, and thus enter the functions expressed by (9.1) and (9.2). A balance-of-payments condition,

$$\mathbf{p}_M \mathbf{M} = \mathbf{p}_E \mathbf{E}, \tag{9.3}$$

closes the system.

In computing an equilibrium for a larger general equilibrium model of a domestic economy with this form of external-sector closure, domestic prices are determined as cost-covering prices from zero-profit conditions. Using the equation system (9.1)–(9.3), together with some form of solution for e (iterative or otherwise), $\mathbf{M}$ and $\mathbf{E}$ are determined and hence market excess demands for all commodities in the model can be calculated. The equilibrium vectors $\mathbf{p}_M$ and $\mathbf{p}_E$ are calculated as those guaranteeing that excess demands equal zero for all commodities.

The external-sector system actually used by Boadway and Treddenick in their analysis of Canadian tariff policy does differ from this specification, as indicated earlier. However, with the system they adopt, different calculations are performed on the effects of policy changes for alternative values of η, which they interpret as the export-price elasticity. In each case, impacts on the exchange rate are reported and interpreted.

Two issues arising immediately with this specification are the role of the exchange-rate term (since it can be removed by simple substitution) and the interpretation of the parameters μ and η, which have an alternative elasticity interpretation to that apparently offered by this system. These issues derive from the fact that the three-equation system (9.1)–(9.3), in the two-good case where M and E are scalars, specifies a foreign offer curve of constant elasticity. This single elasticity parameter determines both the import-supply and export-demand elasticities. Since a real trade model does not involve an exchange-rate term, the system of equations is overidentified.

This can be illustrated by substituting (9.1) and (9.2) into (9.3). The exchange-rate term can be solved for as:

$$e = \left(\frac{M_0}{E_0}\right)^{1/(\mu-\eta)}. \tag{9.4}$$

Using this solution for e enables (9.1) and (9.2) to be rewritten as:

$$\mathbf{E} = E_0 \mathbf{p}_E^{-1} \cdot \left(\frac{M_0}{E_0}\right)^{-\eta/(\mu-\eta)} \cdot \mathbf{p}_M^{-(\mu+1)\eta/(\mu-\eta)} \cdot \mathbf{p}_E^{\mu(\eta+1)/(\mu-\eta)}; \tag{9.5}$$

$$\mathbf{M} = M_0 \mathbf{p}_M^{-1} \cdot \left(\frac{M_0}{E_0}\right)^{-\mu/(\mu-\eta)} \cdot \mathbf{p}_M^{-(\mu+1)\eta/(\mu-\eta)} \cdot \mathbf{p}_E^{\mu(\eta+1)/(\mu-\eta)}. \tag{9.6}$$

Equations (9.5) and (9.6) describe a system of excess demand functions in which the prices $\mathbf{p}_M$ and $\mathbf{p}_E$ appear but the exchange rate e is absent. It should be noted that, unlike conventional excess demand functions, the sign of $\mathbf{E}$ and $\mathbf{M}$ cannot change; the direction of trade assumed by choice of E_0 and M_0 remains unaltered irrespective of the equilibrium prices determined by the remainder of the model to which the subsystem (9.1)–(9.3) is appended.

More importantly, the system of (9.5) and (9.6) does not have the same properties as those suggested by equations (9.1)–(9.3). Equations (9.5) and (9.6) can be termed "trade-balance–compensated" import-supply and export-demand functions. The export-demand elasticity ξ_E^{FD}, with respect to the endogenously determined home-country export price $\mathbf{p}_E$, is not η as suggested by (9.1) but rather

$$\xi_E^{FD} = \frac{\partial \mathbf{E}}{\partial \mathbf{p}_E} \cdot \frac{\mathbf{p}_E}{\mathbf{E}} = \frac{\eta(1+\mu)}{(\mu-\eta)}, \tag{9.7}$$

and the import-supply price elasticity ξ_M^{FS}, with respect to the home-country import price $\mathbf{p}_M$, is not μ but rather

$$\xi_M^{FS} = \frac{\partial \mathbf{M}}{\partial \mathbf{p}_M} \cdot \frac{\mathbf{p}_M}{\mathbf{M}} = \frac{-\mu(1+\eta)}{(\mu-\eta)}. \tag{9.8}$$

For this import-supply elasticity to have the appropriate sign, the restriction should be $\eta \le -1$ rather than $\eta \le 0$ as in (9.1). This difference in interpretation arises because the elasticities in (9.7) and (9.8) are measured with respect to the home country's prices rather than world prices.

The values of the two elasticities in (9.7) and (9.8) are constrained by the trade-balance condition (9.3).[1] These are not independent parameters but are jointly determined by the single elasticity of the offer surface. For the case where E and M are scalars, we can define the elasticity of the foreign offer curve, ξ^{OC}, as:

$$\xi^{OC} = \frac{M}{E} \cdot \frac{dE}{dM}, \tag{9.9}$$

which implies that

$$\xi^{OC} = \frac{\xi_E^{FD}}{\xi_E^{FD}+1} = \frac{\xi_M^{FS}+1}{\xi_M^{FS}}; \tag{9.10}$$

it follows from both (9.7) and (9.8) that

$$\xi^{OC} = \frac{\eta}{1+\eta} \cdot \frac{1+\mu}{\mu}. \tag{9.11}$$

Thus, specifying an equation subsystem (9.1)–(9.3) is equivalent in the two-good case to the specification of a foreign offer curve of constant elasticity. The elasticities of export-demand and import-supply functions with respect to home-country prices are derived from the elasticity of the offer curve, as shown in (9.10). The critical parameter in this case is neither μ nor η taken alone, but the product $[\eta/(1+\eta)] \cdot [(1+\mu)/\mu]$. If $\eta < -1$ and $\mu > 0$ then it follows that $1 < \xi^{OC} < \infty$, and if η is specified close to -1 then ξ^{OC} approaches ∞ independently of μ. A large positive value of μ and a large negative value of η causes ξ^{OC} to approach 1. An offer curve with elasticity 1 is a straight line through the origin, that is, the case of a small price-taking economy.

In calculations with their model, Boadway and Treddenick specify three values of μ as 1, 10, and 25, interpreting these values as export-price

---

[1] Econometricians do not typically incorporate the restrictions implied by trade balance when they estimate export-demand and import-supply elasticities. This issue is explored in Mansur (1982).

Table 9.1. *Relationship of home-country export demand elasticity to η and μ*

η	μ	ξ_E^{FD}
-10	1	-1.8
-10	10	-5.5
-10	25	-7.4
-25	1	-1.9
-25	10	-7.8
-25	25	-13

Note: ξ_E^{FD} denotes home-country price elasticity of foreign export demand.

elasticities. For the system of equations (9.1)–(9.3), these values are not the home-price elasticities since the values of μ can have this interpretation only if μ and η are both 1. In other cases, solutions using (9.7) and (9.8) are obtained, as shown in Table 9.1.

Thus, if a system of the form described by equations (9.1)–(9.3) were used to represent the external sector for a two-good general equilibrium model, the equation system could be misleading in creating an appearance of monetary nonneutralities, as well as in potentially misspecifying intended elasticity values. For the n-good case, trade balance also implies similar cross-equation restrictions. Although the algebra is not as simple as in the preceding presentation, the general point still applies: Trade balance needs to be explicitly recognized in specifying combinations of export-demand and import-supply elasticities.

9.2 External-sector closure using a formulation of fixed and endogenous prices

Although the system outlined in Section 9.1 has the virtue of simplicity, a more common formulation is to model the economy under investigation as facing fixed world prices for imports while simultaneously facing a foreign demand function for exports with constant own-price elasticity. Domestic and foreign goods are imperfect substitutes in domestic demand functions. An external-sector balance condition completes the system. Unlike the specification of Section 9.1, prices of imports are not endogenously determined in the larger model but given as data from outside the model. The Armington assumption commonly used in these models treats imports as different from goods produced domestically, to account for crosshauling in trade data.[2]

We can extend the equation system presented in Section 9.1 to capture such a formulation. The foreign export-demand equation is unchanged:

$$\mathbf{E} = E_0 \left(\frac{\mathbf{p}_E}{e} \right)^{\eta} \quad (-\infty < \eta < 0), \tag{9.12}$$

where $\mathbf{p}_E$ is the home-country price of exports.

The foreign import-supply function is constructed to guarantee that any amount will be supplied at a fixed (exogenously determined) world price. To close the system we therefore need to consider the domestic import-demand function, which (for now) we also consider to be of constant elasticity. It should be noted that this specification is typically part of a more complex domestic general equilibrium system containing specific substitution parameters to capture our notion of domestic and foreign goods as imperfect substitutes.

This formulation yields an external-sector equation subsystem consisting of (9.12) plus:

$$\mathbf{M} = \mathbf{M}^S = \mathbf{M}^D, \tag{9.13}$$

$$\mathbf{M}^D = M_0 (e \cdot \mathbf{p}_M)^{\mu} \quad (-\infty < \mu < 0), \tag{9.14}$$

$$\mathbf{p}_M = \bar{\mathbf{p}}_M, \tag{9.15}$$

where $\mathbf{M}^S$ and $\mathbf{M}^D$ denote foreign import supply and domestic import demand (respectively) and $\mathbf{p}_M$ denotes the world price of imports, which is fixed at $\bar{\mathbf{p}}_M$. We note that $\mathbf{p}_M$ has a different interpretation than in Section 9.1; here it denotes a world rather than a domestic price. Also, μ now represents the elasticity of the domestic import-demand function, rather than of the foreign import-supply function as in Section 9.1, and a different sign restriction on μ now applies.

The system is completed by a balance-of-payments condition as in Section 9.1, but this condition changes slightly due to the fact that $\mathbf{p}_M$ denotes a world price:

$$\bar{\mathbf{p}}_M \mathbf{M} = \frac{\mathbf{p}_E}{e} \cdot \mathbf{E}. \tag{9.16}$$

As before, e can be removed through substitution:

$$e = \left(\frac{E_0}{M_0} \right)^{1/(\mu+\eta+1)} \cdot \mathbf{p}_E^{(\eta+1)/(\mu+\eta+1)} \bar{\mathbf{p}}_E^{-(\mu+1)/(\mu+\eta+1)}, \tag{9.17}$$

---

[2] This specification is used by Boadway and Treddenick (1978) in their reported calculations, and is common to the other models referenced.

yielding the reduced forms

$$\mathbf{M} = M_0 \left(\frac{E_0}{M_0} \right)^{\mu/(\mu+\eta+1)} \cdot \mathbf{p}_E^{\mu(\eta+1)/(\mu+\eta+1)} \cdot \bar{\mathbf{p}}_M^{(\mu\cdot\eta)/(\mu+\eta+1)} \qquad (9.18)$$

and

$$\mathbf{E} = E_0 \left(\frac{E_0}{M_0} \right)^{-\eta/(\mu+\eta+1)} \cdot \mathbf{p}_E^{(\mu\cdot\eta)/(\mu+\eta+1)} \cdot \bar{\mathbf{p}}_M^{(\mu+1)\eta/(\mu+\eta+1)} \qquad (9.19)$$

as well as reduced-form elasticities that are identical to each other:

$$\frac{\partial \mathbf{E}}{\partial \mathbf{p}_E} \cdot \frac{\mathbf{p}_E}{\mathbf{E}} = \frac{\mu\cdot\eta}{\mu+\eta+1} \qquad (9.20)$$

and

$$\frac{\partial \mathbf{M}}{\partial \bar{\mathbf{p}}_M} \cdot \frac{\bar{\mathbf{p}}_M}{\mathbf{M}} = \frac{\mu\cdot\eta}{\mu+\eta+1}. \qquad (9.21)$$

Thus, in a similar vein to the argument in Section 9.1, the specification of parameters for (9.12) and (9.14) could be misleading in that it creates the impression of specifying separate export- and import-demand elasticities (η and μ), whereas (9.20) and (9.21) involve a single elasticity parameter. It should be noted that the import elasticity (9.21) is not an independent supply elasticity as in Section 9.1, but rather a reduced-form elasticity reflecting domestic import demands and the trade-balance condition. Also, as in Section 9.1, no real exchange-rate effects enter the system.

A further characteristic of this system is that, in the two-good case, a complete foreign offer curve is not specified by the system (9.12)–(9.15). The reduced-form system (9.18) and (9.19) determines the equilibrium values of **M** and **E** for both domestic and foreign sectors of the model, provided that export prices are consistent with zero-profit conditions. Equations (9.18) and (9.19) passively meet the equilibrium conditions necessary for both domestic and foreign economies for any set of prices specified. Unlike the formulation in Section 9.1, the system (9.12)–(9.15) does not define a foreign offer curve but makes a locus of external-sector equilibria. Instead of two intersecting offer curves as in traditional trade theory, offer curves of both domestic and foreign countries are constructed so as to satisfy external-sector equilibrium conditions at any set of prices; that is, the curves lie one on top of the other. This formulation thus runs counter to conventional trade theory.

In typical applied general equilibrium models, the domestic portion of the general equilibrium system does not usually contain import-demand functions of constant elasticity, but uses other functions for complete domestic demand systems; Cobb–Douglas and CES forms are particularly common. Even in these cases, the same problems arise as with the formulation just outlined.

Suppose we consider the foreign export-demand function to be as in (9.12), namely,

$$E = E_0 \left(\frac{p_E}{e} \right)^{\eta} \quad (-\infty < \eta < 0), \tag{9.22}$$

but allow the domestic import-demand function to be part of a system of Cobb–Douglas demand functions (for domestic and foreign goods) that are derived from utility maximization. For simplicity we may assume a pure trade formulation with no production, where the only source of domestic income is the sale of a fixed endowment $\bar{E}$ of the exportable commodity. This gives an import-demand function

$$M^D = \frac{\alpha(p_E \bar{E})}{\bar{p}_M \cdot e}, \tag{9.23}$$

where α is the Cobb–Douglas weight on the imported good in the utility function. Use of the balance-of-payments condition (9.16) yields

$$e = \left(\frac{E_0}{\alpha \bar{E}} \right)^{1/\eta} \cdot p_E, \tag{9.24}$$

from which we obtain

$$E = \alpha \bar{E} \quad \text{and} \quad M = \frac{(\alpha \bar{E})^{(\eta+1)/\eta} \cdot E_0^{-1/\eta}}{\bar{p}_M}. \tag{9.25}$$

As a reduced form, this system differs sharply from the specification intended. The notable characteristic of (9.25) is that η from (9.22) does not appear in the export function. The reason is that Cobb–Douglas demand functions must satisfy a domestic version of Walras's law, and this (together with the balance-of-payments condition) yields (9.25) independently of the value of η in (9.22).

9.3 External-sector closure using a price-taking formulation for all tradables

An alternative procedure to the external-sector closure outlined in Sections 9.1 and 9.2 is to assume that the domestic economy faces fixed world prices for all traded goods. This involves abandonment of the Armington assumption of product heterogeneity and adoption of an assumption of product homogeneity among countries. Domestic prices are endogenously determined in this system, with an "exchange-rate" variable determined to give external-sector balance. The exchange-rate variable is in fact the relative price between a composite of traded and nontraded goods.

The role of the exchange rate in this formulation can be seen most simply by considering a price-taking pure exchange economy engaging in international trade. More than two goods are required to present this model, and our notation and presentation differ somewhat from the preceding two sections.

We consider N commodities where the first n_0 are traded goods and the remainder, $n_{0+1}, \ldots, N$, are nontraded goods; $n_0 \leq N$. The economy faces fixed world prices for the traded goods. We define the vector of prices $\mathbf{p} = (p_1, \ldots, p_N)$ as the vector of domestic prices, and define a set of domestic market demand functions $D_i(\mathbf{p})$ $(i = 1, \ldots, N)$ that are nonnegative, continuous, homogeneous of degree zero in the domestic prices $\mathbf{p}$, and satisfy a domestic version of Walras's law:

$$\sum_{i=1}^{N} p_i D_i(\mathbf{p}) = \sum_{i=1}^{N} p_i Z_i, \tag{9.26}$$

where the vector $\mathbf{Z} = (Z_1, \ldots, Z_N)$ defines the domestic economywide endowments of the N commodities.

We suppose the world prices of traded goods $\mathbf{p}^W = (p_1^W, \ldots, p_{n_0}^W)$ to be given and fixed. For convenience, we consider these to be normalized to sum to unity; that is,

$$\sum_{i=1}^{n_0} p_i^W = 1.$$

Equilibrium is characterized in this model by a vector of domestic prices $\mathbf{p}^*$ such that demand–supply equalities hold for each nontraded good, where relative domestic prices of traded goods are the same as the fixed relative world prices, and a zero–trade-balance condition applies.

From the homogeneity of degree zero of domestic demand functions, we can arbitrarily normalize domestic prices to sum to an arbitrary constant. Furthermore, we can impose the restrictions implied by the fixed relative world prices of traded goods by considering only domestic price vectors $(\lambda p_1^W, \ldots, \lambda p_{n_0}^W, p_{n_0+1}, \ldots, p_N)$, where $p_1^W, \ldots, p_{n_0}^W$ are given world prices of traded goods. The normalization rule on $\mathbf{p}$ is satisfied if we consider vectors $(\lambda, p_{n_0+1}, \ldots, p_N)$ whose elements sum to unity. The notation $\mathbf{p}(\lambda)$ denotes the vector $(\lambda p_1^W, \ldots, \lambda p_{n_0}^W, p_{n_0+1}, \ldots, p_N)$.

An equilibrium may be formally characterized by a vector $\mathbf{p}^*(\lambda^*) = (\lambda^* p_1^W, \ldots, \lambda^* p_{n_0}^W, p_{n_0+1}^*, \ldots, p_N^*)$ such that:

(i) demands equal supplies for nontraded goods,

$$D_i(\mathbf{p}^*(\lambda^*)) - Z_i \leq 0 \quad (= 0 \text{ if } p_i^* > 0), \quad i = n_0 + 1, \ldots, N; \tag{9.27}$$

and

(ii) zero trade balance holds for traded goods,

$$\sum_{i=1}^{n_0} p_i^W(D_i(\mathbf{p}^*(\lambda^*)) - Z_i) = 0. \qquad (9.28)$$

In such a formulation, λ plays the role of a relative price between traded and nontraded goods. Existence of an equilibrium in such a model follows directly from a small modification to the Gale–Nikaido mapping employed by conventional proofs that use Brouwer's theorem.[3] The relevance of this model to the discussion here, however, is that a parameter such as λ implicitly appears in some of the formulations adopted by the applied models just mentioned. The implication of this discussion is that, in using these models, the "real" exchange rate should not be equated with a financial exchange rate.

An external-sector formulation using this approach clearly differs from the formulations presented in Sections 9.1 and 9.2, and some comments on their relative merits are in order. A simplifying feature of the closure procedure outlined in this section is that no specification of elasticities in the rest of the world is involved, since the external-sector closure involves a single parameter that sets the relative prices of traded and nontraded goods. In a two-good case, the foreign offer curve is a straight line whose slope is given by the world prices of traded goods. The domestic offer curve will have some elasticity to it, depending on the specification of the domestic portion of the model constructed. The intersection of foreign and domestic offer curves determines equilibrium quantities traded. An obvious disadvantage of this procedure is that the price-taking assumption will be unpalatable for work on large countries (e.g., the United States). Also, this formulation is unable to accommodate crosshauling in trade statistics.

9.4 Domestic policy analysis in an open price-taking economy

The approach outlined in Section 9.3 has been used by Lenjosek and Whalley (1986) to evaluate the impacts of Canadian energy policies in the early 1980s. Unlike multipurpose applied general equilibrium models, their model is sparse in detail, its main features being designed to highlight the key elements of equilibrium structure relevant to the policy issues at hand: controls on energy prices and foreign ownership of petroleum and natural gas leases. The price-taking assumption also substantially simplifies computation in their model.

Lenjosek and Whalley use the assumption that Canada is an international price-taker in both energy and other products to determine cost-covering factor prices from given world prices of goods. Using these factor

---

[3] See Mansur and Whalley (1982), where this proof is given as part of a decomposition computational algorithm for international-trade general equilibrium models.

prices, full-employment conditions for factors then determine industry production levels. Once domestic demands are calculated, excess demands (imports and exports) for goods are known. Since the rest of the world is assumed sufficiently large to accommodate Canadian excess demands in goods at unchanged goods prices (subject to Walras's law), demand–supply equalities need only hold in domestic factor markets.

This approach allows for further structural elements to be introduced as required. These include a system of energy price controls, energy import subsidies generated by energy consumption taxes such that no net revenues or losses are realized by the government, and the presence of nontraded goods. The major restriction of this approach is the requirement that the number of factors equal the number of traded goods produced domestically, but Lenjosek and Whalley claim that, for the policy issues analyzed, the resulting model is not in any way unsuitable because of this restriction.

The advantage of this approach is that implementation is much simpler than with the modeling methods for the small open economy summarized in Sections 9.1 and 9.2. The traditional approach uses an Armington formulation and allows elasticities of substitution between similar domestic and foreign commodities to become large in order to approximate a small open economy. In contrast, the approach of Lenjosek and Whalley sharply reduces the dimension of the equilibrium problem: first, by assuming internationally homogeneous rather than heterogeneous (Armington) products; second, by removing the need to satisfy demand–supply equalities for goods, since the large foreign economy accommodates any domestic imbalance. Furthermore, no fixed point or other computational algorithm is required to solve the model. The simplicity of their approach also allows other complications, such as foreign ownership of factors and the complexities of differing policy regimes, to be more easily introduced than in the case of more traditional treatments. Thus, as a manageable and quickly implementable approach to equilibrium policy-evaluation modeling in a small open economy, Lenjosek and Whalley provide a useful procedure.

To illustrate this approach, consider an N-good, N-factor, static general equilibrium model of an economy that we treat as a taker of goods prices on world markets.[4] In their model of Canada, Lenjosek and Whalley (1986) specify three goods-producing industries: manufacturing, nonmanufacturing (including services), and energy (oil and natural gas). The three

---

[4] A more complex dynamic formulation, in which the country involved is a taker of a price path for all goods (with energy prices obeying Hotelling's rule), could also be used. We ignore dynamic issues here, both to simplify the presentation and to keep the numerical model more manageable.

factors of production are capital services, labor services, and resources. To simplify the exposition, we initially ignore all complications arising from government intervention through price controls and taxes; these are discussed later.

Production in each industry is described by the two-level, fixed-coefficient, value-added production system

$$Y_i = \min\left\{\frac{v_i}{a_{vi}}, \frac{H_{ki}}{a_{ki}}; \ (k=1,...,N)\right\} \quad (i=1,...,N), \quad (9.29)$$

where Y_i is the gross output of industry i, v_i is the value added in industry i, a_{vi} is the value-added requirement per unit of output i, H_{ki} is the use of good k in industry i, and a_{ki} is the requirement of good k per unit of output of good i.

Lenjosek and Whalley consider fixed-coefficient intermediate production, but allow for substitution between primary factors in meeting each industry's value-added requirements. Value added for industry i is given by the CES function

$$v_i = \beta_i \left(\sum_{j=1}^{N} \gamma_{ij} F_{ij}^{(\sigma_i - 1)/\sigma_i} \right)^{\sigma_i/(\sigma_i - 1)} \quad (i=1,...,N), \quad (9.30)$$

where β_i is a units parameter, γ_{ij} are the share parameters on the factor inputs in industry i, and F_{ij} are the amounts of factor j used by industry i. The use of factor j per unit of output i, F_{ij}/Y_i, is denoted by f_{ij}.[5] The variable σ_i defines the elasticity of factor substitution in industry i.

Net output for each industry, N_i, is

$$N_i = Y_i - \sum_{k=1}^{N} a_{ik} Y_k \quad (i=1,...,N). \quad (9.31)$$

On the demand side, Q consumers are assumed, each of which has a utility function (for convenience, also assumed to be CES) represented by

$$U^q = \left\{ \sum_{i=1}^{N} \alpha_i^q C_i^{q(\sigma^q - 1)/\sigma^q} \right\}^{\sigma^q/(\sigma^q - 1)} \quad (q=1,...,Q), \quad (9.32)$$

where C_i^q is consumption of good i by consumer q, α_i^q are share parameters for consumer q, and σ^q is consumer q's elasticity of substitution in preferences.[6]

Commodity prices are denoted as p_i ($i=1,...,N$) and factor prices as w_j ($j=1,...,N$). These can be normalized to sum to unity if so desired,

---

[5] In the specific model used for Canada, only the resource factor input enters the energy industry; that is, $F_{ij} = 0$ ($i=1,2, j=3$).

[6] A more general multistaged CES function could be used in which more than one elasticity appears.

$$\sum_{i=1}^{N} p_i + \sum_{j=1}^{N} w_j = 1,$$

since factor demands are homogeneous of degree zero in p_i and w_j. Since the f_{ij} reflect the outcome of cost minimization they are written as $f_{ij}(\mathbf{w})$, where $\mathbf{w}$ denotes the vector $(w_1, \ldots, w_N)$. The economywide endowment of each of the factor inputs is $\bar{F}_j$. Any foreign ownership of any factor is denoted by $\bar{F}_j^R$. Domestic ownership of each factor, $\Sigma_{q=1}^{Q} \bar{F}_j^q$, equals $\bar{F}_j - \bar{F}_j^{R}$.[7]

Maximizing (9.32) subject to each domestic consumer's budget constraint yields the domestic commodity demands

$$C_i^q = \frac{\alpha_i^{q^{\sigma^q}} I^q}{p_i^{\sigma^q} \sum_{k=1}^{N} \alpha_k^{q^{\sigma^q}} p_k^{(1-\sigma^q)}} \quad (i=1,\ldots,N;\ q=1,\ldots,Q), \qquad (9.33)$$

where consumer q's income I^q is given by the value of q's factor endowment; that is, $I^q = \sum_{j=1}^{N} w_j \bar{F}_j^q$.

Given fixed world prices $\bar{p}_i$ of goods, a domestic equilibrium in this model is characterized by a vector $\mathbf{w}^* = (w_1^*, \ldots, w_N^*)$ such that two sets of conditions hold:

(i) demands equal supplies for factors,

$$\sum_{i=1}^{N} f_{ij}(\mathbf{w}^*) Y_i^* = \bar{F}_j \quad (j=1,\ldots,N), \qquad (9.34)$$

and

(ii) zero-profit conditions hold in domestic industries,

$$\bar{p}_i = \sum_{k=1}^{N} a_{ki} \bar{p}_k + \sum_{j=1}^{N} f_{ij}(\mathbf{w}^*) \cdot w_j^* \quad (i=1,\ldots,N). \qquad (9.35)$$

At such an equilibrium, domestic commodity excess demands (foreign trades) are given by

$$X_i^* = \sum_{q=1}^{Q} C_i^{q*} + \sum_{k=1}^{N} a_{ik} Y_k^* - Y_i^* \quad (i=1,\ldots,N). \qquad (9.36)$$

Summing the domestic consumers' budget constraints and using the zero-profit conditions, it follows that

$$\sum_{i=1}^{N} \bar{p} X_i^* = 0; \qquad (9.37)$$

that is, trade balance holds.

---

[7] In the model of Canada, there is foreign ownership of resources but no foreign ownership of either capital or labor; that is, $\Sigma_{q=1}^{Q} \bar{F}_j^q = \bar{F}_j$ $(j=1,2)$.

At such an equilibrium, domestic excess demands for goods are accommodated by the foreign country considered to be large enough that buying or selling the required quantities at the given world prices will not affect global equilibrium. Other than this willingness to buy or sell any quantities of goods at fixed world prices (subject to trade balance), no further characteristics of foreign behavior need be specified.

Solving this model for an equilibrium is considerably easier than for the traditional general equilibrium model. From the first-order conditions for cost minimization in each industry,

$$f_{ij}(\mathbf{w}) = \frac{v_i}{Y_i} \frac{\gamma_{ij}^{1/(1-\sigma_i)}}{\beta_i} \left\{ \left[\sum_{l \neq j} \left(\frac{\gamma_{il}}{\gamma_{ij}} \right)^{\sigma_i} \left(\frac{w_l}{w_j} \right)^{(1-\sigma_i)} \right] + 1 \right\}^{\sigma_i/(1-\sigma_i)}$$

$$(i = 1, \ldots, N; \; j = 1, \ldots, N). \quad (9.38)$$

Using these solutions for the $f_{ij}(\mathbf{w})$ in the zero-profit conditions (9.35) provides a system of N equations involving N unknown factor prices. Given the commodity prices, the equilibrium factor prices w_j^* satisfying (9.35) can then be solved for. If the values of w_j^* corresponding to the given goods prices $\bar{p}_i$ yield goods and factor prices that do not sum to unity then goods and factor prices can be rescaled so that they lie on a unit simplex, since both demands and the solutions to cost minimization are homogeneous of degree zero in goods and factor prices. Any normalization of prices can be used, as only relative goods and factor prices are relevant in the model.

Given the equilibrium factor prices, the equilibrium values of gross outputs Y_i^* satisfying (9.34) can be determined. Further, consumer incomes I^{q*} and hence consumer demands C_i^{q*} can also be solved for by using the equilibrium factor prices in (9.33). Equilibrium domestic excess demands for goods (imports and exports) are given by (9.36). Implementing this basic approach requires no computational algorithm. Provided the system of nonlinear equations (9.38) can be solved for the w_j^*, a fixed point solution procedure is not necessarily required to determine an equilibrium.

The key feature making this approach operational is that there are the same number of traded goods as factors, so (9.35) can be solved. However, specialization in production is not ruled out, in which case the model can become underdetermined unless extra goods are added. Such additions typically indicate a poorly specified numerical model, with production sets that yield large supply responses when prices change (unrealistically large supply elasticities). In the case of energy price controls, Lenjosek and Whalley choose values of substitution elasticities in energy production that are approximately consistent with literature estimates, so specialization does not occur for the policy changes considered.

Lenjosek and Whalley's analysis of the effects of Canadian energy policy involves a number of extensions to the model presented here. Producer and consumer energy price controls, and the degree of foreign ownership of energy resources, must be specified. Factor and excise taxes on energy industries and products must be incorporated. The model also needs to be generalized in order to incorporate the "blended-price mechanism" actually used in Canada (a zero-revenue system of taxes on domestic energy consumers and subsidies for energy imports). Modifications to accommodate the existence of nontraded goods are a further extension that can be made.

Under a government-declared system of producer and consumer energy price controls set below world energy prices, an approach similar to that just described can be used to determine a domestic equilibrium. However, modifications to the basic approach are needed. We denote the (given) world price of any good as $\bar{p}_i$, and the controlled domestic producer and consumer prices by $\bar{p}_i^p$ and $\bar{p}_i^c$. Consumer prices are net of excise taxes.

Determining a domestic equilibrium in this case involves using $\bar{p}_i^p$ rather than $\bar{p}_i$ on the left-hand side of (9.35), and $\bar{p}_k^p$ rather than $\bar{p}_k$ in the summation term on the right-hand side in (9.35). The latter reflects the assumption that $\bar{p}_k^p$ is the controlled price applying to domestic intermediate users of the kth good. As before, (9.35) and (9.38) can be used to determine equilibrium values for the factor prices w_j^* satisfying the zero-profit conditions modified to include controlled producer rather than world prices. Equation (9.34) is again used to determine gross industry output Y_i^*.

The major change relative to the previous section arises in the way (9.33) is used to generate consumer demands. Controlled consumer prices, controlled producer prices, and world prices all differ. A subsidy or tax, at a rate equaling the difference between domestic and world prices, is required if a price-controlled good is imported or exported, respectively. Consumer income is affected in both cases. This occurs through either an income loss due to lump-sum taxes needed to finance the subsidy, or an income gain as export taxes are returned to consumers through lump-sum transfers.

Denoting these transfers T as

$$T = \sum_{i=1}^{N} (\bar{p}_i - \bar{p}_i^c)\left(\sum_{q=1}^{Q} C_i^q\right) - \sum_{i=1}^{N} (\bar{p}_i - \bar{p}_i^p)\left(Y_i - \sum_{k=1}^{N} a_{ik}Y_k\right), \qquad (9.39)$$

the income term in the demand functions equation (9.33) must be written as

$$I^q = \sum_{j=1}^{N} w_j \bar{F}_j^q - T^q, \qquad (9.40)$$

where $T^q = \alpha^q T$. The terms α^q sum to unity and determine the share of consumer q in the lump-sum tax or transfer.

The term T plays the same role in this system as the revenue term in the analysis of general equilibrium in the presence of taxes (Shoven and Whalley 1973). As with taxes, a simultaneity is created with price controls in the evaluation of demands. Until consumer demands are known, the revenues created by (or required to sustain) controlled prices are unknown. Equally, the size of such revenues depends on the values, of demands. This simultaneity is accommodated in the same way that Shoven and Whalley accommodate the revenue simultaneity from taxes, namely, by making T endogenous to the model.

Thus, given world prices and controlled domestic producer and consumer prices, an equilibrium is characterized by a vector $\mathbf{w}^* = (w_1^*, \ldots, w_N^*)$ and a value T^* such that (9.34) and (9.35) hold. In addition, (9.39) holds and the equilibrium demands are given by (9.33), where the income term is modified as in (9.40).

Solving this version of the model for a domestic equilibrium is slightly more complex than for the simpler model just described, owing to the endogeneity of T. It is no longer possible to solve the model directly, from the given world goods prices through the factor prices to the excess demands for goods, since a value T must be assumed in order to make the calculations. Typically, this will not be the equilibrium value T^*, so a fixed point or other computational algorithm is required to solve for an equilibrium. However, a 1-dimensional simplex (T, λ) can be used, where λ is a scalar applying to the world goods prices $\bar{p}_i$ and to controlled producer and consumer prices $\bar{p}_i^p$ and $\bar{p}_i^c$. If price controls apply only to a subset of goods, this same procedure can be used. (In the model of Canada, price controls apply only to energy products.)

Canadian energy price controls in the early 1980s differed slightly from the preceding description of price controls, in that the controlled producer and consumer prices were not independent of each other. Instead, a blended-price mechanism was used under which subsidies on imports were fully financed by a tax on domestic consumers. The blended consumer price was set so that world prices for imports and controlled prices for domestic production were blended into a single consumer price at zero net cost to government.

Introducing this blended-price system into the approach described previously requires only that p_E^c (the controlled consumer energy price net of excise taxes) now be endogenously determined, while T becomes exogenous (set equal to zero through the government zero-revenue requirement). For any given world energy price $\bar{p}_E$ and controlled producer energy price $\bar{p}_E^p$, the consumer energy price p_E^c will be endogenously determined so that, in equilibrium, $\bar{T} = 0$;

$$\bar{T} = (\bar{p}_E - p_E^c)\left(\sum_{q=1}^{Q} C_E^q\right) - (\bar{p}_E - \bar{p}_E^p)\left(Y_E - \sum_{k=1}^{N} a_{Ek}Y_k\right). \qquad (9.41)$$

The case of blended prices bears the same relationship to the case of prespecified controlled consumer and producer prices as the equal–tax yield equilibria (considered by Shoven and Whalley 1977) bears to general equilibria under prespecified tax rates. In the case of equal–tax yield equilibria, tax rates are endogenous and the revenue requirement exogenous; the reverse is true in the case of prespecified tax rates.

To solve the model for a blended-price equilibrium for energy, both $\bar{p}_E^p$ and $\bar{p}_E$ are prespecified. For any given consumer energy price p_E^c, the model could be solved for a domestic equilibrium using the procedures outlined in Section 9.3. However, a computational problem arises in that the zero-revenue requirement (that $T = 0$) will typically not be satisfied for an initial, arbitrarily chosen value of p_E^c. Thus, as with the case of consumer and producer price controls just described, a fixed point or other computational algorithm is required to find a domestic equilibrium (although, once again, the dimension of the equilibrium problem is relatively small). In our case of a single controlled consumer energy price, the 1-dimensional simplex (p_E^c, λ) can be used, where λ is a scalar applying to the given world price $\bar{p}_E$ and to the controlled producer price $\bar{p}_E^p$. In this case, p_E^c rather than T is endogenously determined.

The model discussed thus far has N traded goods and N primary factors. Although this feature is necessary in order to solve for equilibrium factor prices from the given world goods prices, the procedure can be augmented by also including an arbitrary number of nontraded goods. This feature was not incorporated by Lenjosek and Whalley in their 1986 analysis of Canadian energy policies, because the required coding changes were significant and because only second-order effects from such incorporation were anticipated. For other applications of this approach, such as analyzing the effects of a tariff change, the addition of nontraded goods would be an important extension; we therefore discuss it next.

Suppose there are G nontraded goods whose prices are denoted by p_i^N $(i = 1, ..., G)$. Each nontraded goods industry has production functions as described by (9.29) and (9.30), and the nontraded goods appear as part of consumer demands (equation (9.33)). Since the goods are not traded, there are no foreign demands and consequently the domestic economy is not a price-taker for these commodities.

To determine a domestic equilibrium in the presence of nontraded goods, (9.35) can be solved both for the values of factor prices $\mathbf{w}^*$ and the values of nontraded goods prices $\mathbf{p}^{N*}$ satisfying the zero-profit conditions for the traded goods industries. With all endogenous prices calculated in this way, consumer demands for nontraded goods can be determined from (9.33) and the per-unit factor demands in nontraded goods industries calculated from (9.39); this enables the total factor requirements of nontraded goods industries to be determined. These are then subtracted from the economywide endowments $\bar{F}_j$, and a so-modified version of equation (9.34) is used to determine the equilibrium domestic production of traded goods. The rest of the approach that treated just traded goods remains unchanged.

The general approach has been applied by Lenjosek and Whalley (1986) to a numerical model of Canada, benchmarked to a 1980 micro-consistent equilibrium data set, to analyze the impacts of changes in Canadian energy policies. To specify parameter values for functions used in the model, they follow the calibration procedure outlined in Mansur and Whalley (1984) that requires exogenous specification of key elasticity parameters prior to calibration to a benchmark data set.

The data set used by Lenjosek and Whalley is based on a number of different source materials. The broad aggregates, such as net domestic product (NDP), are consistent with national accounts totals. The detail by industry and commodity relies heavily on the 1972 Canadian micro-consistent data set reported in St-Hilaire and Whalley (1983), which are aggregated and updated to 1980. Owing to the importance of the energy industry and the resource input to the calculations, all data relating to this industry is calculated separately; data from Petroleum Monitoring Agency Canada (1982) and Statistics Canada (various years) is used for this purpose. Adjustments are also required to the foreign trade data in order to attain zero trade balance in the benchmark data set.

In addition to the benchmark equilibrium data, a series of other parameter values are required to complete the specification of the model, including those reflecting price controls and elasticities. As a result, computation is dramatically simplified. Extensions of the basic model – to incorporate the distorting effects of price controls, taxes, tariffs, and other policy interventions – are relatively straightforward; extensions to incorporate nontraded goods can also be accommodated.

The effects of Canadian policies on energy prices, in terms of national welfare, depend on two separate effects. On the one hand, consumer and producer prices set below world prices result in overconsumption and underproduction of energy, and a consequent welfare loss. On the other hand, producer prices of energy set below world prices reduce the factor returns accruing to owners of Canadian resources, many of whom are foreigners. Lenjosek and Whalley's results portray the rent-transfer effect against foreigners as the dominant effect of these energy policies. Removing price controls is a change that worsens national welfare, since the increased rents transferred to foreigners more than outweigh welfare gains.

9.5 Trade-policy analysis in price-taking developing countries

The approach outlined in Section 9.3 is also used by Clarete and Whalley (1988) to explore the interaction of trade policies with other domestic distortions in the Philippines, using a numerical general equilibrium model of a small open economy. The purpose of their exercise is to explore the ways in which domestic distortions in developing countries can change the traditional analysis of such trade policies as tariffs. The domestic distortions examined are rent-seeking activities associated with import quotas, and those involved with rural–urban migration processes.

The model consists of N sectors producing T trade goods and NT homegoods, where $N = T + NT$. World prices are given for traded goods. Each producer uses K variable factors and a fixed factor in production.

Production in each industry is represented by a Cobb–Douglas value-added function defined on both the variable and the sector-specific factors. Denoting X_j as the output of sector j, F_{ij} as sector j's use of the variable factor i, and $\bar{Z}_j$ as the fixed factor in sector j, these functions can be written as

$$X_j = B_j \prod_{i=1}^{K} F_{ij}^{\alpha_{ij}} \bar{Z}_j^{(1-\theta_j)} \quad \text{for all } j, \tag{9.42}$$

where θ_j and α_{ij} are Cobb–Douglas exponents and B_j is a units parameter. Intermediate inputs enter production in fixed proportion to output, denoted by the coefficients a_{ij}, representing the requirement of good i in producing one unit of good j.

Under profit maximization, the supply function corresponding to (9.42) is

$$X_j = \left[B_j p_j^{\theta_j} \prod_{i=1}^{K} \left(\frac{\alpha_{ij}}{w_i} \right)^{\alpha_{ij}} \right]^{1/(1-\theta_j)} \quad \text{for all } j, \tag{9.43}$$

where p_j and w_i are the domestic prices of good j and factor i, respectively. The price elasticity of supply for good j is $\theta_j/(1-\theta_j)$. Because θ_j is the total share of variable factors in the value added originating in sector j, the supply of good j is more elastic the more important are variable factors relative to the fixed factor.

From a modeling perspective, supply elasticities introduced in this way (through sector-specific factors) also provide a natural strategy for avoiding the problem of complete specialization when modeling small countries. As is well known from trade theory, this problem can easily occur in a Samuelson trade model, which has more traded goods than factors. Moreover, even if absent in a base-case equilibrium, a small shift in policy can lead to a large and discrete supply response, possibly producing complete specialization. By making supply curves rise through factor specificity, these problems are removed.

In the model, the return to sector-specific factors is obtained by deducting total intermediate and factor costs from total sales. Denoted by M, this amount is

$$M = \sum_{j=1}^{N} p_j X_j - \sum_{j=1}^{N}\sum_{i=1}^{K} w_i F_{ij} - \sum_{j=1}^{N}\sum_{i=1}^{N} p_i a_{ij} X_j. \tag{9.44}$$

Since the consumer sector is endowed with these sector-specific factors, the rent accruing to these factors appears as part of household income.

Consumer demands are also assumed to be Cobb–Douglas, with the demand for good j given by

$$C_j = \frac{\gamma_j Y}{p_j}, \tag{9.45}$$

where Y is the total household income and γ_j is the share of commodity j in total expenditure.

Since the model includes homegoods and internationally immobile factors, an equilibrium solution must include the relative price between tradables and nontradables. In a small open economy without homegoods, the given world prices fully characterize a domestic equilibrium. Any excess demands are absorbed by the much larger rest of the world, and trade balance is satisfied by Walras's law. In the presence of nontraded goods, however, the relative price between tradables and nontradables is endogenous. In equilibrium, any excess demands for nontradables must be fully absorbed domestically by appropriate adjustments of their prices relative to those of traded goods.

The relative price of traded and nontraded goods is calculated using the Hicks aggregation theorem (Diewert 1978, Hicks 1939), which states that if the prices of a basket of goods are proportional then the goods in the basket can be regarded as one commodity with its own price. As a result, tradables in this framework can be aggregated at their fixed world prices to form a Hicksian composite good. The demand C_T and supply X_T of this good are

$$C_T = \sum_{j=1}^{T} \bar{p}_j X_j \quad \text{and} \quad X_T = \sum_{j=1}^{T} \bar{p}_j (C_j + \mathrm{ID}_j), \tag{9.46}$$

where $\bar{p}_j$ is the given world price and ID_j is the total intermediate demand for good j; that is,

$$\mathrm{ID}_j = \sum_{i=1}^{N} a_{ji} X_i.$$

The price of the composite good r_T is the relative price of tradables and nontradables, or the real exchange rate (Dervis et al. 1982, Dornbusch 1973, Whalley and Yeung 1985). The expenditure on the composite good is

$$r_T C_T = r_T \sum_{j=1}^{T} \bar{p}_j (C_j + \mathrm{ID}_j),$$

and the value of production is

$$r_T X_T = r_T \sum_{j=1}^{T} \bar{p}_j X_j.$$

It follows from the Hicks theorem that the domestic price of tradable good j is $p_j = r_T \bar{p}_j$.

This treatment of the Hicksian composite good closes the external sector of the model. The excess demand function for this aggregate commodity is (by definition) the total net imports of residents. In equilibrium, then, trade balance holds when the market for this commodity clears; that is, residents sell enough goods and services to nonresidents to pay for their imports.

Under this treatment, relative domestic prices of traded commodities are equal to the given relative world prices. Because of this model feature, larger impacts of changes in trade policies will be produced than using the alternative Armington (1969) assumption that regards imports and domestic products as imperfect substitutes for each other. The latter approach fails to fully transmit trade-related disturbances to domestic prices, resulting in smaller impacts on consumption and production at home.

To incorporate tariffs into the model, Clarete and Whalley (1988) introduce a government that collects both tariffs and export taxes before redistributing the revenues to the consumer in a lump-sum fashion. Denoting t as the vector of *ad valorem* tariff rates, where $t_j > 0$ (< 0) if j is importable (exportable), and denoting E_j as the net import of good j, we define the tariff revenue TR of the government as

$$\text{TR} = r_T \sum_{j=1}^{T} \bar{p} t_j E_j. \tag{9.47}$$

A problem encountered in all general equilibrium modeling of distortions is the simultaneity between the revenues generated by distortions and demands (see Shoven and Whalley 1972). In order to deal with this in the present model, we treat government transfers to consumers, L, as endogenous. In any evaluation of consumer demands, the government distributes L to the consumer, who then calculates his or her income (consisting of transfers from the public sector and the value of endowments of variables and sector-specific factors). Given this income, the consumer then evaluates demands, based on which tariff revenues can be computed. In full equilibrium, the income received by the household sector from the government exactly matches the revenues actually collected.

Denoting Y as income and $\overline{FS}_i$ as the endowment of variable factor i,

$$Y = \sum_{i=1}^{K} w_i \overline{FS}_i + M + L = \sum_{j=1}^{N} p_j C_j, \tag{9.48}$$

where the second equality implies that the household sector spends its entire income, satisfying Walras's law.

The excess demand system characterizing the model is derived as follows. Substituting (9.44), (9.46), and (9.47) into (9.48), we obtain:

(i) $C_j + \mathrm{ID}_j - X_j$ for all homegoods;
(ii) $F_i - \overline{FS}_i$ for all variable factors;
(iii) $C_T - X_T$ for the composite traded good; and
(iv) $\mathrm{TR} - L$ for government revenues.

If all these excess demands equal zero, an equilibrium for the model will have been found. There are as many excess demands to be solved as there are prices of homegoods and variable factors, plus two; and equal numbers of endogenously determined prices and excess demands. Such an equilibrium can easily be found using a fixed point or other algorithm.

Besides tariffs, nontariff barriers also appear in the model. Import quotas are commonly imposed in developing countries, both as a short-term response to disturbances in the current account and also as a way of protecting domestic industries from foreign competition. During periods of rising world prices for important exportables, where domestic prices are controlled by the government, exports of these commodities are typically restricted to meet domestic shortages through export bans and other devices.

In the present model, only import quotas are explicitly included, since these are quantitatively more important in the Philippine case than are export controls. We assume that the government imposes binding quotas on imports through a licensing system. Under these arrangements, importables become more expensive due to the scarcity induced by the quota system. Inefficiencies result as producers allocate more resources to produce import substitutes, while consumers reduce their demands for importables in response to higher prices. The economic rents created accrue to producers, who sell these importables to consumers at a premium.

To incorporate import quotas in the model, we require that importers purchase a license from the government for every unit of quota-restricted imports they bring into the country. We assume that there is a market for licenses for each restricted importable good. Importers demand licenses, and the government supplies a fixed amount of licenses equal to the permitted quota. The cost of a license reflects the scarcity premium consumers are willing to pay for the importable. The proceeds to the government from selling licenses to importers define revenues from the quota system, and are part of total income. Denoting $\bar{Q}_j$ as the level of quota on import j, and T' as the set of tradables with binding quotas, the revenues from quotas are defined as

$$\mathrm{QR} = \sum_{j \in T'} (p_j - r_T \bar{p}_j (1 + t_j)) \bar{Q}_j. \tag{9.49}$$

The inclusion of import quotas in the model in this way introduces one additional excess demand function for each restricted importable. Under the quota system, the excess demands for restricted importables are absorbed by the rest of the world only to the extent permitted by the quota. Thus, the domestic prices of these goods must be adjusted until the domestic supply and the quota match the domestic demand in these markets, or until an equilibrium import premium (the equilibrium price of the import license) is found. Thus, for all tradables with binding trade quotas, $(C_j + \mathrm{ID}_j - X_j - \bar{Q}_j - E_j) - L = 0$.

This model extension assumes that import quotas are auctioned by the government, implying that economic rents from import licensing are income transfers among agents in the economy and generate no economic waste from rent seeking. However, in our modeling approach we can also feature rent-seeking activities and assume that import licenses are allocated through administrative discretion.

Competitive rent-seeking activities are known to be a significant source of economic inefficiency (Krueger 1974). These activities use real resources to seek out rights to quotas and other rent-generating licenses. If perfect competition is assumed, agents will use real resources to acquire licenses until the amount of rents generated by them is dissipated by the cost of rent seeking. Resources used in rent seeking produce no incremental output and are thus wasted.

The amount of this waste depends on how the rent-seeking activity is specified. Little is known about the extent of rent seeking in practice, and about how it actually takes place in developing countries. Not all economies that use quotas necessarily exhibit large degrees of rent seeking. The popular perception is that rent seeking is widespread in South Asia, but less prevalent in Latin America despite the widespread use of quotas there. The claim often made is that Latin American countries have monopoly importers, and so competition for licenses is largely excluded.

The conventional approach in empirical work on rent seeking and trade policy has been to follow Krueger's assumption of full and competitive rent seeking (e.g., Blomqvist and Mohammad 1984; Hamilton, Mohammad, and Whalley 1985; Mohammad and Whalley 1984). Under this approach, factors are drawn from economically productive uses and devoted to unproductive rent seeking until the rents are dissipated.

Following Hamilton et al. (1985), the version of our Phillippine model that incorporates rent seeking assumes the value of resources used in rent seeking to be proportional to the value of rents created, with the proportion reflecting the relative economywide endowments of each factor input. Factor demands include both the amounts of factors used productively and those employed in rent seeking. Denoting FRS_i as the amount of variable factor i allocated for rent seeking,

$$FRS_i = \frac{\overline{FS}_i}{\sum_{i=1}^K w_i \overline{FS}_i} QR. \tag{9.50}$$

Accordingly, the excess demand function for variable factor i becomes $(F_i + FRS_i - \overline{FS}_i)$. The income of the consumer excludes rents from quotas that are lost in rent seeking.

A final feature that Clarete and Whalley incorporate in extending the basic model is the presence of rural–urban migration, widely observed in developing countries. A predetermined rural–urban wage differential is often thought to explain the phenomenon (Harris and Todaro 1970). In response to a higher wage in urban sectors, labor migrates from rural areas to the cities until the expected urban wage – that is, the urban wage multiplied by the probability of being employed in the city – is equal to the free-market wage in rural sectors. Letting ρ be the urban employment rate, $1/\rho$ workers will move and compete for every job offered in the city.

In this model formulation, the total labor endowment of the economy (including those unemployed) is valued at the free-market wage in the rural sector, since all migrants expect to receive at least the rural wage while employed in the urban sector. Denoting UR and RL as the sets of industries in urban and rural sectors (respectively), the superscripts U and R as urban and rural, and L as labor,

$$\sum_{i \in UR} w_L^U L_i^U + \sum_{i \in RL} w_L^R L_i^R = w_L^R \overline{L}. \tag{9.51}$$

Since $w_L^U = w_L^R/\rho$ and

$$\rho = \frac{\sum_{i \in UR} L_i^U}{\sum_{i \in UR} L_i^U + UE},$$

where UE stands for the unemployed labor in the urban areas, the total wage bill can be restated as $w_L^R(\sum_{i \in UR} L_i^U + \sum_{i \in RL} L_i^R + UE)$. Hence the excess demand function for labor is $(LD + UE - \overline{L})$, where LD is total productively employed labor. This excess demand function must include any amount of labor used in rent seeking. In determining an equilibrium in this model formulation, the rural wage is adjusted to clear the labor market.

With these modifications, Clarete and Whalley's basic model can therefore be extended to incorporate a series of institutional arrangements common in developing countries, each potentially important to the evaluation of trade-policy impacts. These extensions to the model allow consideration of how these factors, either singly or cumulatively, interact with more traditionally analyzed trade policies (such as *ad valorem* tariffs and export taxes) to either modify or amplify the effects usually associated with such distortions. Clarete and Whalley apply their model to

Philippine data to investigate the strength of interactions between trade policies and domestic distortions; they use a Philippine benchmark equilibrium data set for 1978, performing counterfactual equilibrium analysis for a range of policy changes.

Their results clearly indicate that interactions between trade policies and other domestic distortions are significant. An interesting result is that, in the presence of import quotas and rent seeking, removal of tariffs (even for a price-taking small open economy) typically worsens welfare. This is because, in the presence of quotas, tariffs serve to reduce quota values and hence lower the costs of rent seeking. Thus, removing tariffs is typically undesirable. Even the lifting of export taxes has the same effect, since the real exchange rate appreciates, increasing the premium value from quotas. The social cost of trade distortions (including quotas) in the presence of rent seeking and the Harris–Todaro labor-market distortions is approximately double their cost when these factors are ignored. The implication of Clarete and Whalley's analysis is that these interactions must be fully considered in numerical trade-policy analysis for developing countries.

10

Analysis of price controls

Applied general equilibrium analysis has been used to investigate policy issues ranging beyond the areas of taxation and international trade. In this chapter we describe some studies of price controls.

10.1 General equilibrium with price-intervention policies

We begin by discussing a computational general equilibrium framework for analysis of the distorting effects of price-intervention policies. Examples include evaluation of agricultural price-maintenance schemes (such as the EEC Common Agricultural Policy), interest-rate ceilings, and the like, where government policies specify target ceiling or minimum prices for particular products or sectors. Under such policies, equilibrium is achieved through government price-support programs or government marketing agencies. Our discussion follows that presented by Imam and Whalley (1982).

We first consider cases where the government legislates product-specific minimum or ceiling prices. The government enforces minimum prices by requiring agents involved to purchase minimum-priced commodities from a government marketing agency. At a market price below the minimum price, the government purchases the commodity at the market price and resells at the higher price. Proceeds acquired by the government from these transactions are redistributed to consumers. With ceiling prices, the government buys at a higher market price and sells at the lower ceiling price; losses are covered by lump-sum taxation. Unlike the price-support mechanism discussed subsequently, the government neither accumulates nor holds stocks of commodities under these mechanisms.

These formulations are closely related to Shoven and Whalley's (1973) analysis of general equilibrium with taxation. Here, the differentials between market prices and minimum or ceiling prices are endogenously determined instead of being prespecified. Revenues accruing to government through the administration of minimum prices play the same role as tax revenues, and the same augmented price–revenue simplex can be used both to compute and prove existence of an equilibrium. With consumer ceiling prices, endogenous subsidy rates are involved and revenues are needed by government to cover losses. Consumer subsidies are not considered by Shoven and Whalley, and the analysis here illustrates how their framework can be applied to the subsidy case.

We consider an economy with n commodities, initial economywide endowments of these commodities being denoted by the vector $\mathbf{W} = (W_1, \ldots, W_n)$, where $W_i \geq 0$ and is strictly positive for at least one i. Following Shoven and Whalley (1973), we define government revenues as R and assume (for simplicity) that all revenues are redistributed to consumers. The term R is nonnegative for the minimum-price case; a transformation used to determine R in the subsidy case is explained shortly. Since revenues enter consumer incomes, the demand side of the economy is represented by the market demand functions $\xi_i(\mathbf{p}, R)$ $(i = 1, \ldots, n)$, which are continuous and nonnegative functions of both the market prices $\mathbf{p}$ ($\mathbf{p} = p_1, \ldots, p_n$) and revenue R. These functions are assumed to be homogeneous of degree zero, and satisfy Walras's law.

The production side of the economy is characterized by an activity matrix A, each column of which represents a feasible activity that can be operated at any nonnegative level of intensity. We consider M activities, the notation a_{ij} denoting the output of good i in activity j. Inputs are denoted by negative and outputs by positive entries in the matrix A. Joint production is permissible; the matrix A also includes n activities representing the possibility of free disposal of any commodity; for convenience, these are taken to be the first n activities. We assume that A satisfies the boundedness condition that the set of $\mathbf{X}$ such that $A\mathbf{X} + \mathbf{W} \geq 0$ is contained in a bounded set, where $\mathbf{X}$ denotes any vector of nonnegative activity levels.

We consider minimum and ceiling prices expressed in terms of a price index $\bar{P}(\mathbf{p})$, which is a function of the market prices p_i and is homogeneous of degree one in $\mathbf{p}$. The term $\bar{P}(\mathbf{p})$ is strictly positive if $p_i > 0$ for at least one i. Minimum or ceiling prices are considered to be policy objectives of government that involve the selection of parameters[1] $\lambda_i \geq 0$

---

[1] The policy parameters λ_i considered here are differentiated only by commodity. It is possible to extend the analysis so as to incorporate further differentiation. With minimum producer prices, λ_{ij} would give the parameter for commodity i when purchased by consumer j. Further differentiation of this form may be important in certain policy applications (e.g., minimum wages for regions, ceiling food prices for the poor), but is not pursued here in order to avoid notational complexity.

$(i = 1, ..., n)$. These parameters define the minimum or ceiling prices $\hat{p}_i$ for any given vector of market prices:

$$\hat{p}_i = \lambda_i \bar{P}(\mathbf{p}) \quad (i = 1, ..., n). \tag{10.1}$$

Minimum consumer prices

In this case we denote market prices by the vector $\mathbf{p}$ and consumer prices by the vector $\mathbf{p}^c$, some components of which may be regulated. Consumers are required to pay $\mathbf{p}^c$ for any purchase they make; producers pay or receive $\mathbf{p}$; owners of endowments receive $\mathbf{p}$. The term R defines government proceeds from administering the minimum prices.

As in the Shoven and Whalley tax formulations, Walras's law is stated in this case as[2]

$$\sum_{i=1}^{n} p_i^c \xi_i(\mathbf{p}, R) = \sum_{i=1}^{n} p_i W_i + R. \tag{10.2}$$

An equilibrium is defined as a vector $(\mathbf{p}^*, \mathbf{X}^*, R)$ of prices, activity levels, and revenue (with associated minimum prices $\mathbf{p}^{c*}$) such that:

(i) demands equal supplies (including disposals),

$$\xi_i(\mathbf{p}^*, R^*) = W_i + \sum_j a_{ij} X_j^* \quad (i = 1, ..., n); \tag{10.3}$$

and

(ii) no activity makes positive profits, with those in use breaking even:

$$\begin{aligned} \sum_i p_i^* a_{ij} &\leq 0 \\ &= 0 \text{ if } X_j^* > 0 \end{aligned} \quad (j = 1, ..., m). \tag{10.4}$$

A property of such an equilibrium, which follows from Walras's law, is that

$$R^* = \sum_{i=1}^{n} (p_i^{c*} - p_i^*) \xi_i(\mathbf{p}^*, R^*). $$

Minimum producer prices

In this case consumers pay $\mathbf{p}$ and owners of endowments receive $\mathbf{p}$, but producers are required to pay $\mathbf{p}^p$. For any commodity i, $p_i^p = \max(p_i, \lambda_i \bar{P}(\mathbf{p}))$. Demand functions are $\xi(\mathbf{p}, R)$ and satisfy Walras's law, which is written as

---

[2] This statement assumes that any consumer initially owning commodities to which a minimum price applies must sell the entire endowment at prices p_i and repurchase for consumption at prices p_i^c. In the same way that the Shoven–Whalley consumer tax model can alternatively be applied to purchases net of endowments, a similar modification is possible here.

$$\sum_{i=1}^{n} p_i \xi_i(\mathbf{p}, R) = \sum_{i=1}^{n} p_i W_i + R. \tag{10.5}$$

In this case, we need to restrict minimum prices to inputs in order to prove existence; an input is defined as a commodity i for which $a_{ij} \leq 0$ for all j. The reason for this limitation is that with minimum output prices it is possible to choose a technology such that positive profits must be made at any set of specified prices. We exclude this possibility here by considering only inputs, but such a limitation should not be necessary in policy-evaluation work. Equilibrium involves demand–supply equalities as in (10.3), as well as zero-profit conditions as in (10.4) but with profits evaluated at $\mathbf{p}^{p*}$ rather than at $\mathbf{p}^*$.

Ceiling consumer prices

In this case we once again denote market prices by the vector $\mathbf{p}$ and regulated ceiling consumer prices by the vector $\mathbf{p}^c$; producers pay $\mathbf{p}$, owners of endowments receive $\mathbf{p}$. For any commodity, $p_i^c = \min(p_i, \lambda_i \bar{P}(\mathbf{p}))$.

We redefine R to be the lump-sum taxes collected by government to cover losses involved in administering the ceiling-price program. In this case R represents an income withdrawal from the private sector to cover government losses, rather than recycled revenues as in the preceding cases. Walras's law becomes

$$\sum_{i=1}^{n} p_i^c \xi_i(\mathbf{p}, R) = \sum_{i=1}^{n} p_i W_i - R, \quad \text{where } R \leq \sum_{i=1}^{n} p_i W_i. \tag{10.6}$$

In another formulation, inputs have sector-specific rather than economy-wide minimum prices. This alternative formulation follows the Harris–Todaro (1970) analysis of urban–rural migration. Inputs are subject to minimum prices only if they are employed in a particular portion of the economy (e.g., the urban sector). Once made, decisions by owners of inputs to sell in sectors cannot be changed. Asset owners equate the expected return in the regulated sector of the economy (the minimum price multiplied by the probability of employment) to the free-market price.[3] Unlike our preceding analysis, no government monopoly agency is necessary to sustain equilibrium. An equilibrium probability of employment in the minimum-price sector supports equilibrium.

---

[3] With repeated drawings for the right to be employed at the higher price from the pool of input owners wishing to sell, such an equilibrium is sustainable over time. Alternatively, one can think of input owners receiving one-way tickets to the higher-priced sectors of the economy, preventing their return of unemployed inputs to the free-market sector. The probabilistic equilibrium condition would be satisfied in this case in an ex ante sense, with no ex post return possible should their particular inputs be unemployed.

Input prices in the minimum-price sectors are defined as follows:

$$\hat{p}_i = \max(p_i, \lambda_i \bar{P}(\mathbf{p})) \quad (i = 1, \dots, n), \tag{10.7}$$

where λ_i describe minimum-price policy parameters. We assume that the division of the economy into minimum-price and nonminimum-price sectors is fixed and also described by a simple partition of the set of available activities.

We treat owners of resources as expected-income maximizers, so that in equilibrium the free-market price p_i equals the expected price received in the minimum-price sector:

$$p_i = \phi(\hat{p}_i, p_i) \cdot \hat{p}_i \quad (I = 1, \dots, n), \tag{10.8}$$

where $\phi(\hat{p}_i, p_i)$ defines the probability of the ith input being employed in the minimum-price sector, conditional on seeking employment in that sector. We define this probability as S_i, where, from (10.8), $S_i = p_i / \hat{p}_i$.[4] The variable S_i equals unity for all nonminimum-price commodities. If $p_i = \hat{p}_i$ then $S_i = 1$, implying full employment of the ith input. We therefore rewrite (10.8) as

$$p_i = S_i \hat{p}_i \quad (i = 1, \dots, n). \tag{10.9}$$

As before, the production side is characterized by an activity-analysis matrix A with M activities, but these activities are partitioned. Activities $1, \dots, M_1$ characterize the nonminimum-price sector and activities $M_1 + 1, \dots, M$ the minimum-price sector.

The demand side of the model is represented, as before, by a set of market demand functions that are nonnegative, continuous, and homogeneous of degree zero in an $(n+1)$-dimensional vector $(\mathbf{p}, T)$, where $\mathbf{p}$ defines the vector of free-market prices and T is an income-correction term (defined subsequently) that is homogeneous of degree one in p.

The income correction T incorporated into the demand functions plays a similar role to the revenue augmentation in the Shoven–Whalley tax analysis. In the present case, incomes depend on the allocation of inputs between sectors, which in turn depends on demands. We break this simultaneity through the income-correction term T. Incomes are determined

---

[4] In the Harris–Todaro (1970) formulation of labor-market migration, this probability is defined as the ratio of employed (NE) to total labor (NT) in the minimum-wage sector:

$$\phi = \phi\left(\frac{NE}{NT}\right); \quad \phi' > 0.$$

In their formulation, $NE/NT = \psi(p_i/\hat{p}_i)$ with $\psi' > 0$, and thus S_i is a specific interpretation of ϕ.

by valuing endowments of inputs at prices $\hat{p}_i$. The term T is subtracted from household incomes, and in equilibrium equals the lost income from unemployment in the minimum-price sector plus valuation at p_i (rather than at $\hat{p}_i$) in the nonminimum-price sector. Thus, Walras's law in this framework is written as

$$\sum_{i=1}^{n} p_i \xi_i(\mathbf{p}, T) = \sum_{i=1}^{n} \hat{p}_i W_i - T. \tag{10.10}$$

An equilibrium under this formulation is defined by the vectors $(\mathbf{p}^*, \mathbf{X}^*, T^*)$ such that

$$\xi_i(\mathbf{p}^*, T^*) = \sum_{j=1}^{M_1} a_{ij} X_j^* + \frac{1}{S_i^*} \sum_{j=M_1+1}^{M} a_{ij} X_j^* + W_i \quad (i = 1, \ldots, n);$$

$$\begin{aligned} \sum_{i=1}^{n} p_i^* a_{ij} &\leq 0 \\ &= 0 \text{ if } X_j^* > 0 \end{aligned} \quad (j = 1, \ldots, M_1), \tag{10.11}$$

$$\begin{aligned} \sum_{i=1}^{n} \hat{p}_i^* a_{ij} &\leq 0 \\ &= 0 \text{ if } X_j^* > 0 \end{aligned} \quad (j = M_1+1, \ldots, M),$$

where S_i^* and p_i^* follow from the previous definitions. The term

$$\frac{1}{S_i^*} \sum_{j=M_1+1}^{M} a_{ij} X_j^*$$

in the demand–supply equalities reflects the total requirements of the ith commodity (input), including unemployment in the minimum-price sector.

In equilibrium, it follows from Walras's law that

$$T = -\sum_{i=1}^{n} \sum_{j=1}^{M} (\hat{p}_i^* - p_i^*) a_{ij} X_j^* - \sum_{i=1}^{n} \sum_{j=M_1+1}^{M} \frac{1 - S_i^*}{S_i^*} \hat{p}_i^* a_{ij} X_j^*.$$

The price interventions just described allow legislated minimum or ceiling prices (for either consumers or producers) to be achieved through government price regulations. These forms of minimum-price intervention by government do not correspond to the more familiar idea of minimum- or ceiling-price supports through market intervention.

To capture this notion, Imam and Whalley (1982) also consider target minimum prices that control government purchase interventions in the market. They consider specific rules that trigger interventions; the formulation of Walras's law allows income to be transferred to the public from the private sector to finance price-support intervention. Given that economywide minimum prices apply to producers as well as to consumers, target minimum prices must once again be restricted to inputs in order to guarantee that these prices are achievable in equilibrium.

Imam and Whalley consider target minimum prices $\hat{p}_i$ defined in terms of the composite good:

$$\hat{p}_i = \lambda_i \bar{P}(\mathbf{p}) \quad (i = 1, ..., n). \tag{10.12}$$

These target prices control government price-support interventions, which are defined by those quantity purchases G_i that are functions of the vector $\mathbf{p}$. They consider a specific function for the G_i that (in the case where target minimum prices are restricted to inputs) guarantees existence of a market equilibrium in which market prices are greater than or equal to target minimum prices.

The $G_i(\mathbf{p})$ are defined as

$$G_i(\mathbf{p}) = W_i \left[\max \left\{ \frac{\hat{p}_i - p_i}{\hat{p}_i}, 0 \right\} \right] \tag{10.13}$$

and satisfy the restriction that

$$\sum_{i=1}^{n} p_i G_i \le \sum_{i=1}^{n} p_i W_i, \tag{10.14}$$

so that at any price vector sufficient income can be withdrawn from the private sector to finance planned government purchases. This leads to a statement of Walras's law that

$$\sum_{i=1}^{n} p_i(\xi_i(\mathbf{p}) + G_i) = \sum_{i=1}^{n} p_i w_i. \tag{10.15}$$

To achieve target ceiling prices, government intervention is necessary. This case is almost identical to that of ceiling consumer prices with a government marketing agency; the only difference is that producer subsidies on outputs are paid directly, rather than having the marketing agency purchase and resell at a loss.

Target ceiling prices for outputs $\hat{p}_i$ are defined as

$$\hat{p}_i = \lambda_i \bar{P}(\mathbf{p}) \quad (i = 1, ..., n). \tag{10.16}$$

Producer subsidies per unit level of intensity are

$$S_j = \max \left[\sum_i (p_i - \hat{p}_i) a_{ij}, 0 \right] \quad (j = 1, ..., M). \tag{10.17}$$

Imam and Whalley illustrate their approach using four numerical examples; these are specified in Table 10.1. They consider an illustrative two-good, two-factor, two-consumer economy with CES demands and production. Parameters for the functions, along with the endowment

Table 10.1. *Parameter values used in numerical examples by Imam and Whalley (2 sectors, 2 consumers)*

CES production functions

$$Y_i = A_i[(1-\delta_i)K_i^{-\rho_i} + \delta_i L_i^{-\rho_i}]^{-1/\rho_i}, \quad \sigma_i = 1/(1+\rho_i)$$

A_1	A_2	δ_1	δ_2	σ_1	σ_2
1.0	1.0	0.6	0.3	2.0	0.5

CES demands

$$X_i^j = \frac{b_{ij}I^j}{P_i^{Ej}\sum_k b_{kj}P_k^{(1-Ej)}}$$

(i refers to goods, j refers to consumers)

b_{11}	b_{21}	b_{12}	b_{22}	E_1	E_2
0.3	0.7	0.6	0.4	1.2	0.7

Policy regimes
Case 1: No policy intervention
Case 2: Minimum output price on good 1; set at 1.5 of P^a
Case 3: Sector-specific minimum wage; set at 0.8 of P
Case 4: 25 percent output tax on good 1

Factor endowments

	Consumer 1	Consumer 2
Capital	100	0
Labor	0	50
Revenue share	0.5	0.5

---

[a] P denotes the price index used to define minimum or ceiling price interventions. We use an arithmetic sum of capital and labor prices.
Source: From Imam and Whalley (1982), used by permission of Elsevier Science Publishing Company.

specification, are listed in the table. Four cases are considered: a no-policy intervention equilibrium (case 1); a minimum-output price on good 1 (case 2); a sector-specific minimum wage (case 3); and a 25% output tax on good 1 (case 4). The last case is included to stress the close relationship between these equilibria and tax equilibria.

Characteristics of the equilibria including relative prices, quantities, utility levels of consumers, and (in case 3) the unemployment rate are reported in Table 10.2.

10.2 General equilibrium analysis of wage and profit controls

A further application is the use of a computational general equilibrium framework for evaluating welfare costs associated with economywide

Table 10.2. *Results from Imam and Whalley's numerical examples*

	Case 1	Case 2	Case 3	Case 4
Price of good 1	1.468	2.243[a]	1.674	1.463
Price of good 2	1.295	1.298	1.336	1.298
Wage rate	1.000	1.000	1.223[b]	1.000
Rental rate	0.497	0.500	0.528	0.500
Demand for good 1	30.733	24.239	27.525	27.238
Demand for good 2	42.174	49.544	32.386	46.168
Utility of consumer 1	20.386	21.856	20.492	21.282
Utility of consumer 2	18.225	16.744	16.572	17.497

[a] 2.243 is the minimum price; the free price is 1.470.
[b] 1.223 is the minimum wage; the free wage is 1.000.
Source: From Imam and Whalley (1982), used by permission of Elsevier Science Publishing Company.

price controls. Price controls have been used since earliest recorded history. They have been employed in all ages by governments all over the world, during war and peace, in response to all manners of threats (both real and imaginary). Despite this long history, other than traditional commodity-specific partial equilibrium analysis, most empirical literature on price controls still concentrates on macroeconomic issues such as the impact of inflation and unemployment. This is surprising, since the main attack on price controls is usually in terms of their efficiency losses and associated resource misallocation. A paper by Nguyen and Whalley (1986) seeks to reorient empirical literature on the effects of these controls. They provide a framework that can be used to address the issue of how large these economic inefficiencies are, and who wins and who loses from them.

Their approach is based on the well-known general equilibrium models of distortions due to Harberger (1962) and Shoven and Whalley (1973). Their point of departure is the use of an equilibrium mechanism in the presence of price controls that involves endogenously determined search costs, costs that yield additional welfare losses under price controls beyond those associated with more traditional tax or tariff models. The lesson is that, in an economy with price controls, the greater the difference between controlled prices and market-clearing prices the costlier it is for buyers and sellers to find each other and transact. The differences between actual buying and selling prices are endogenously determined to clear markets; these differences involve real resource costs rather than revenues raised and recycled by the government, and thus contribute directly to the social costs of the controls.

This formulation differs from models of the Harberger type, since the wedge between buying and selling prices is no longer prespecified. As a result, existing models of distortions are not suitable for analyzing the effects of price controls in a general equilibrium framework. Nguyen and Whalley's model is in fact closer to those used to analyze the effects of distortions in developing countries, which involve resource waste or socially valueless transactions as part of the equilibrium concept; examples include Krueger's (1974) rent-seeking model and the Harris–Todaro (1970) model of urban–rural migration.

Their model also differs from those in the literature on fixed-price equilibria (e.g., Benassy 1975 and Drèze 1975) that employ quantity constraints as an equilibrating mechanism in the presence of (downward) price rigidities. This body of literature has been mainly motivated by the objective of providing a theoretical bridge between general equilibrium theory and Keynesian macroeconomics, rather than by the desire to address micro policy issues such as evaluation of the welfare effects of price controls. In this model, prices are fixed by government decree instead of simply being institutionally rigid.

Also, the analytic structure of Nguyen and Whalley's model is more complex than that of traditional distortion-ridden general equilibrium models. In the presence of price controls, endogenous search activity is generated on either the demand or supply side of each market, but not on both since only one of excess supply or excess demand can occur in any one market. Because of the complexities introduced by this one-side-of-market condition, we limit our computational analysis to only two sectors and use a traditional goods-and-factor general equilibrium model. Furthermore, since with fixed prices for goods and factors it is possible to construct an activity that automatically makes positive profits, we limit our analysis to price controls either on goods or on factors (wages and profits).

Nguyen and Whalley illustrate their approach using a small-dimensional numerical model of the 1972 Canadian economy. They assume that price controls fix prices at their equilibrium values at the date controls are imposed. Resource-allocation problems therefore arise only as subsequent changes occur, which in a free-market environment would change relative prices. Simulation results are presented of the welfare costs of price controls operating in the presence of different scenarios of sectoral productivity growth. We outline their approach to analyzing the impacts of price controls in a traditional two-sector general equilibrium framework for the two cases of factor price (or wage and profit) controls and goods price controls.

Factor price controls

In this formulation, Nguyen and Whalley assume that the government controls wages and profits at non–market-clearing levels $(\hat{w}, \hat{r})$. Under such controls, in equilibrium there will be real resource costs associated with transactions by agents on the constrained side of each factor market. In effect, a dual price system acts as a surrogate equilibrating mechanism that clears factor markets in the presence of government price controls. Transactions costs are thus endogenously determined, in contrast to the usual assumption of fixed-transactions technology (see Foley 1970 and Hahn 1971) in the literature on general equilibrium with transactions costs.

Under wage and profit controls, buyers of factors face buying prices (w^b, r^b) gross of any transactions costs they may bear, while sellers face selling prices (w^s, r^s) net of transactions costs. As a result, there are real resource losses (per unit transacted) associated with the endogenously determined wedges of $w^b - \hat{w} \geq 0$ and $r^b - \hat{r} \geq 0$ (on the buying side) and $\hat{w} - w^s \geq 0$ and $\hat{r} - r^s \geq 0$ (on the selling side). These differ from the tax wedges in Harberger models in that the latter do not involve real resource costs.

More formally, the production side of the economy is characterized by linearly homogeneous production functions

$$X = F(L_x, K_x) \quad \text{and} \tag{10.18}$$

$$Y = G(L_y, K_y), \tag{10.19}$$

where L_x, K_x, L_y, K_y are factors used by sectors X and Y, respectively. Cost minimization at the factor buying prices (w^b, r^b) results in the following derived factor-demand functions (per unit of output):

$$l_x = l_x(w^b, r^b); \tag{10.20}$$

$$l_y = l_y(w^b, r^b); \tag{10.21}$$

$$k_x = k_x(w^b, r^b); \tag{10.22}$$

$$k_y = k_y(w^b, r^b). \tag{10.23}$$

Zero-profit conditions are given by

$$p_x = w^b l_x + r^b k_x = p_x(w^b, r^b) \quad \text{and} \tag{10.24}$$

$$p_y = w^b l_y + r^b k_y = p_y(w^b, r^b). \tag{10.25}$$

The demand side of the economy is characterized by the demand functions

$$X^d = X^d(p_x, p_y, w^s, r^s) \quad \text{and} \tag{10.26}$$

$$Y^d = Y^d(p_x, p_y, w^s, r^s). \tag{10.27}$$

In the one-consumer case, these functions are derived from consumer utility maximization, subject to the budget constraint

$$p_x X^d + p_y Y^d = w^s \bar{L} + r^s \bar{K}, \tag{10.28}$$

where $\bar{L}, \bar{K}$ denote aggregate factor endowments of the economy. The same approach can easily be extended to the multiconsumer case.

Equations (10.20)–(10.23), (10.26), and (10.27) yield aggregate factor demands

$$L = L_x + L_y = l_x X^d + l_y Y^d \quad \text{and} \tag{10.29}$$

$$K = K_x + K_y = k_x X^d + k_y Y^d. \tag{10.30}$$

Market excess demands for factors differ from those used in the traditional two-sector goods-and-factor general equilibrium model, being defined as

$$Z_l = (w^b/\hat{w})L - (w^s/\hat{w})\bar{L} \quad \text{and} \tag{10.31}$$

$$Z_k = (r^b/\hat{r})K - (r^s/\hat{r})\bar{K}, \tag{10.32}$$

since the endogenously determined transactions costs in each market must be included. These costs are denominated in units of the commodities being transacted. The terms $(w^b/\hat{w})L$ $(\geq L)$ and $(r^b/\hat{r})K$ $(\geq K)$ denote factor demands *gross of transactions costs* under price controls: total factor demands L, K plus the transactions costs borne by buyers. The terms $(w^s/\hat{w})\bar{L}$ $(\leq \bar{L})$ and $(r^s/\hat{r})\bar{K}$ $(\leq \bar{K})$ denote the factor supplies *net of transactions costs* under price controls: total factor supplies $\bar{L}, \bar{K}$ net of the transactions costs borne by sellers. If no transactions costs are involved, $w^b = w^s = \hat{w}$ and $r^b = r^s = \hat{r}$; in this case (10.31) and (10.32) degenerate to the more usual market excess demand functions for factors, $Z_l = L - \bar{L}$ and $Z_k = K - \bar{K}$, that characterize the two-sector model.

Given that (10.24) and (10.25) guarantee the fulfillment of zero-profit conditions, and given that (10.29) and (10.30) involve factor requirements that meet goods-market demands, a general equilibrium in the presence of factor price controls is given by the factor prices $(w^{b*}, r^{b*}, w^{s*}, r^{s*})$ such that

$$Z_l(w^{b*}, r^{b*}, w^{s*}, r^{s*}) = 0 \quad \text{and} \tag{10.33}$$

$$Z_k(w^{b*}, r^{b*}, w^{s*}, r^{s*}) = 0, \tag{10.34}$$

where, in addition,

either $w^{b*} = \hat{w}$ and $w^{s*} < \hat{w}$ or $w^{b*} > \hat{w}$ and $w^{s*} = \hat{w}$, and   (10.35)

either $r^{b*} = \hat{r}$ and $r^{s*} < \hat{r}$ or $r^{b*} > \hat{r}$ and $r^{s*} = \hat{r}$.   (10.36)

Conditions (10.33) and (10.34) clear the factor markets in the sense that market demands for any factor, *gross* of any transactions costs on the buying side, equal the market supply of that factor, *net* of any resource losses from transactions costs on the selling side. Conditions (10.35) and (10.36) require that in any factor market there can be resource losses on either the buying side or the selling side, but not on both. This is because controls in any market can result in either excess demand or excess supply, but not both at the same time. This one-side-of-market condition is a nontrivial extension of the traditional two-sector general equilibrium model.

To find an equilibrium solution, controlled prices $\hat{w}, \hat{r} > 0$ are normalized so that $\hat{w} + \hat{r} = 1$, and buying and selling factor prices are defined as

$$w^b = \max(\hat{w}, v) \geq \hat{w} \quad \text{and} \tag{10.37}$$

$$w^s = \min(\hat{w}, v) \leq \hat{w}; \tag{10.38}$$

$$r^b = \max(\hat{r}, 1 - v) \geq \hat{r} \quad \text{and} \tag{10.39}$$

$$r^s = \min(\hat{r}, 1 - v) \leq \hat{r}, \tag{10.40}$$

where $0 \leq v \leq 1$ is an unknown variable to be determined. This construction allows demands (10.20)–(10.23) and excess demands (10.31) and (10.32) to be redefined in terms of the unknown variable v:

$$Z_l = \max\{1, v/\hat{w}\} L(s) - \min\{1, v/\hat{w}\} \bar{L} \quad \text{and} \tag{10.41}$$

$$Z_k = \max\{1, (1-v)/\hat{r}\} K(s) - \min\{1, (1-v)/\hat{r}\} \bar{K}. \tag{10.42}$$

Substituting equations (10.24), (10.25), (10.29), (10.30), (10.31), and (10.32) into the budget constraint (10.28), we obtain Walras's law

$$\hat{w} Z_l + \hat{r} Z_k = 0. \tag{10.43}$$

This implies that whenever one factor market clears, so does the other. Therefore, to determine the equilibrium solution v^*, we need only solve either the equation $Z_l(v^*) = 0$ or the equation $Z_k(v^*) = 0$. Equilibrium buying and selling prices $(w^{b*}, w^{s*}, r^{b*}, r^{s*})$ calculated from v^* using (10.37)–(10.40) automatically satisfy the one-side-of-market conditions (10.35) and (10.36), since – no matter what value v^* has – there can be only two possibilities:

> either $v^* \leq w^*$, in which case $w^{b*} = \hat{w}$, $w^{s*} \leq \hat{w}$ and $1 - v^* \geq r^*$, $r^{b*} \geq \hat{r}$, $r^{s*} = \hat{r}$; or $v^* \geq \hat{w}$, in which case $w^{b*} \geq \hat{w}$, $w^{s*} = \hat{w}$ and $1 - v^* \leq \hat{r}$, $r^{b*} = \hat{r}$, $r^{s*} \leq \hat{r}$.

The value v^* can easily be found using a fixed point algorithm or other computational algorithm.

Goods-price controls

With price controls applying to outputs, prices are fixed at $(\hat{p}_x, \hat{p}_y)$. In this case transactions costs are borne by agents on the constrained side of goods markets, rather than factor markets. These costs are represented by the price wedges $(p_x^b - \hat{p}_x, p_y^b - \hat{p}_y)$ for buyers (consumers) and $(\hat{p}_x - p_x^s, \hat{p}_y - p_y^s)$ for sellers (producers). Factor prices (w, r) are completely flexible. The relevant equations for the supply side of the model are:

$$l_x = l_x(w, r); \tag{10.44}$$

$$l_y = l_y(w, r); \tag{10.45}$$

$$k_x = k_x(w, r); \tag{10.46}$$

$$k_y = k_y(w, r); \tag{10.47}$$

$$p_x^s = wl_x + rk_x; \tag{10.48}$$

$$p_y^s = wl_y + rk_y; \tag{10.49}$$

$$L = L_x + L_y = l_x X + l_y Y; \tag{10.50}$$

$$K = K_x + K_y = k_x X + k_y Y. \tag{10.51}$$

Equations (10.44)–(10.47) are factor demands per unit of output, (10.48) and (10.49) represent zero-profit conditions, and (10.50) and (10.51) are total factor demands. On the demand side, we have the consumer-goods demand functions

$$X^d = X^d(p_x^b, p_y^b, w, r) \quad \text{and} \tag{10.52}$$

$$Y^d = Y^d(p_x^b, p_y^b, w, r), \tag{10.53}$$

which are derived from constrained utility maximization. Excess demands are defined as follows:

(a) in factor markets,

$$Z_l = L - \bar{L} \quad \text{and} \tag{10.54}$$

$$Z_k = K - \bar{K}; \tag{10.55}$$

(b) in goods markets,

$$Z_x = (p_x^b/\hat{p}_x)X^d - (p_x^s/\hat{p}_x)X \quad \text{and} \tag{10.56}$$

$$Z_y = (p_y^b/\hat{p}_y)Y^d - (p_y^s/\hat{p}_y)Y. \tag{10.57}$$

With price controls in goods markets, the excess demands for goods measure the differentials between *gross* demands (i.e., goods demands including transactions costs borne by buyers) and *net* supplies (i.e., output supplies net of transactions costs borne by sellers). Walras's law implies that

$$\hat{p}_x Z_x + \hat{p}_y Z_y + w Z_l + r Z_k = 0. \tag{10.58}$$

A general equilibrium in this case is defined by the set of prices (p_x^{b*}, $p_x^{s*}, p_y^{b*}, p_y^{s*}, w^*, r^*$) such that:

(a) in factor markets,

$$Z_l = 0 \quad \text{and} \tag{10.59}$$

$$Z_k = 0; \tag{10.60}$$

(b) in goods markets,

$$Z_x = 0 \quad \text{and} \tag{10.61}$$

$$Z_y = 0; \tag{10.62}$$

(c) and, in addition,

either $p_x^{b*} = \hat{p}_x$ and $p_x^{s*} < \hat{p}_x$ or $p_x^{b*} > \hat{p}_x$ and $p_x^{s*} = \hat{p}_x$,

$$\tag{10.63}$$

and

either $p_y^{b*} = \hat{p}_y$ and $p_y^{s*} < \hat{p}_y$ or $p_y^{b*} > \hat{p}_y$ and $p_y^{s*} = \hat{p}_y$.

$$\tag{10.64}$$

Computing such an equilibrium is more difficult in this case than for factor market controls, since reducing this system of excess demands to functions of a single parameter is not possible. Nonetheless, it is still possible to apply fixed point algorithms or other computational algorithms to this case, although it rapidly becomes more complex as the number of commodities increases beyond two.

Nguyen and Whalley (1986) use a small-dimensional numerical example to illustrate their approach to the analysis of the welfare costs of price controls. Their data is taken from the 1972 Canadian benchmark equilibrium data set (compiled by St-Hilaire and Whalley 1983). They consider two sectors (X for manufacturing and Y for nonmanufacturing) and two factors (capital and labor). To consider distributional effects of price controls, they also consider three broad income groups:

1. low-income group (less than \$8,000 in 1972);
2. middle-income group (between \$8,000 and \$18,000 in 1972); and
3. high-income group (above \$18,000 in 1972).

In this data set, the basic information is drawn from a number of sources (e.g., input–output tables, national income accounts, household income and expenditure data, taxation statistics, foreign trade statistics, and flows of funds). These are all adjusted for mutual consistency. The final result is a micro-consistent data set in which demands equal supplies for all products, zero-profit conditions hold for all industries, and all agents satisfy their budget constraints – that is, the conditions characterizing a general equilibrium for the economy.

Nguyen and Whalley determine demand and production parameters directly from the consumer and producer equilibrium conditions, using the calibration procedures outlined in Chapter 5. The parameter values so calculated will reproduce the benchmark equilibrium data set as an equilibrium solution to the model in the no–price control case.

After calibration, the model is used to evaluate the welfare costs of fixing either factor or goods prices at preassigned values, allowing changes to occur over time such that, were it not for the presence of price controls, the equilibrium prices would also change. Simulations are carried out for a period of 20 years for each of a series of cases. With factor-price controls, wages and profits are assumed frozen at initial competitive equilibrium levels. Productivity changes are introduced into the economy through changes in the normalizing constant in the production function for one of the two sectors. Equilibrium buying and selling prices $(w^{b*}, r^{b*}, w^{s*}, r^{s*})$ are then calculated for each year in the simulation.

10.3 Price controls and black markets

The underground economy is regarded by most economists as an inevitable consequence of government intervention in the overground economy, be it through tax policies, regulatory activity, or other measures. The so-called black market is thought to be growing in most regions of the globe, including the market-oriented OECD countries, centrally planned economies of the Soviet type, and developing countries (see, e.g., Ericson 1984 and Frey 1983). In fact, many different types of underground activity exist, each reflecting quite different institutional arrangements. The tax system of most OECD countries encourages tax-free transactions to take place underground; inappropriate allocations of inputs under Soviet-style economic plans encourage illegal underground trades between enterprises; and, in developing countries, price and quantity controls on foodstuffs, raw-material inputs, foreign exchange, and many other items encourage black-market trading.

It is the last of these types of underground activity that provides the focus for this section, where we describe the analysis contained in another paper by Nguyen and Whalley (1985) that is closely related to work by

Mohammad and Whalley (1984) on the international terms of trade. Black markets are widely viewed as both endemic and widespread in the Third World, and are in part a response to price controls on official (or white) markets. The observation that motivates the 1985 paper of Nguyen and Whalley is that, in practice, both black and white markets coexist together. If this is so, there must be an equilibrium structure that links them. They develop an analytical equilibrium formulation of linked black and white markets, illustrate how such an equilibrium can be computed, and explore some of the implications of linkage using Indian data. Unlike some previous work on underground activity (particularly that on tax evasion by Allingham and Sandmo 1972, Srinivasan 1973, and others) that explores single-agent optimizing behavior given incentives for evasion, Nguyen and Whalley (1985) stress the equilibrium structure that links legal and illegal activities.

Their formulation of linkage involves white markets on which binding government price controls apply, and black markets where penalties apply for those caught transacting. Buyers must choose between buying on white markets at controlled prices and incurring search or queueing costs, or on black markets without queueing costs but at higher prices. Sellers must choose between selling on white markets at controlled prices, or on black markets at higher prices but with a probability of detection and fine. In equilibrium, with risk-neutral behavior, effective buying prices (gross of search costs) will be the same across black and white markets for any product. Similarly, expected selling prices (net of expected penalties) must be equalized. If both black and white markets clear, then, across the linked markets, demands must equal supplies for all products.

A prominent feature of this approach is the endogenously determined transactions costs, which reflect differences between effective consumer buying prices and producer selling prices on official markets. These are real resource costs, additional to those usually associated with taxes, tariffs, and other more traditional distortions. One implication is that, in the presence of price controls on white markets, government "anticorruption" drives designed to reduce the size of black markets are undesirable. If such initiatives involve increased fines or heightened surveillance of black marketeers, the result is to increase the differential between effective buying and selling prices on white markets, generating increased wasteful search activity on white markets. The first-best policy is either to eliminate price controls on white markets or remove penalties for transacting on black markets. Given the presence of controls, attempts to restrict black markets are typically Pareto worsening.

To illustrate how interlinkage between black and white markets operates, consider an economy with n goods and n factors; the reason for restricting the number of goods to the number of factors will be more fully explained in what follows. Nguyen and Whalley assume that the government imposes price controls $\bar{\mathbf{p}} = (\bar{p}_1, \ldots, \bar{p}_n) > 0$ on all goods at below–market-clearing levels. In the presence of these controls, black markets develop because consumers cannot achieve their desired consumption plans by transacting on white markets alone, and producers are induced to sell at higher black-market prices.

It is also assumed that the government pursues enforcement efforts designed to detect and fine black marketeers. Further, Nguyen and Whalley assume that enforcement is only applied to the supply side of any market; penalties or fines are levied only on producers, not consumers. The rationale for this assumption is that it is easier for the government to detect and prosecute firms than consumers, since the former typically have larger volumes of transactions. Producers must therefore decide whether to sell goods on white markets at lower controlled prices $\bar{p}$, or on black markets at higher prices $\mathbf{p} = (p_1, \ldots, p_n)$ but with the risk of prosecution and fines. Nguyen and Whalley assume risk-neutral behavior by producers, and so (in equilibrium) the expected price received by a producer selling on either market must be the same.

On the demand side, consumers decide whether to buy goods on black markets at the higher prices $\mathbf{p}$, or on white markets at lower controlled prices $\bar{p}$ but with endogenously determined transactions (or search) costs. The greater the difference between black-market and controlled prices, the costlier it becomes for consumers to find a producer willing to sell at the lower white-market price. These transactions costs adjust so as to clear white markets. In equilibrium, the expected prices paid by buyers on either market, gross of transactions costs, must be the same.

More formally, the structure of their model is as follows. Each sector j is characterized by a linearly homogeneous production function

$$y_j = F_j(R_j) \quad (j = 1, \ldots, n), \tag{10.65}$$

with output supply y_j and factor requirements $R_j = (R_{j1}, \ldots, R_{jn})$. Cost minimization at the factor prices $\mathbf{w} = (w_1, \ldots, w_n)$ yields derived factor-demand functions per unit of output,

$$\frac{R_{ji}}{y_j} = r_{ji}(\mathbf{w}) \quad (i, j = 1, \ldots, n). \tag{10.66}$$

In equilibrium, zero-profit conditions will hold for production and sales in both black and white markets. These conditions are given by

$$p_j = \sum_{i=1}^{n} w_i r_{ji}(\mathbf{w}) + f_j \rho_j \quad (j = 1, \ldots, n); \tag{10.67}$$

$$\bar{p}_j = \sum_{i=1}^{n} w_i r_{ji}(\mathbf{w}) \quad (j = 1, \ldots, n).$$ (10.68)

The first term on the right-hand side of (10.67) and (10.68) is the cost of producing one unit of output. The second term on the right-hand side of (10.67) is the expected cost of selling on black markets, where ρ_j is the probability of being detected (per unit of production) and f_j is the fine imposed if caught.

We assume that ρ_j is an increasing function of the relative size of black-market sales to total sales (on both black and white markets) of good j. That is,

$$\rho_j = \rho_j(s_j) \text{ with } \rho' > 0 \quad (j = 1, \ldots, n)$$ (10.69)

and

$$s_j = \frac{y_j^b}{y_j^b + y_j^w} \quad (j = 1, \ldots, n),$$ (10.70)

where y_j^b, y_j^w, s_j are (respectively) black-market sales, white-market sales, and the relative size of the black market in good j. The argument is that the bigger the relative size of the black market the more attention it draws from the government enforcement agency, and hence the higher the probability of black-market sellers being caught. Fines collected by the government are assumed to be redistributed to consumers as transfers.

For simplicity, the demand side of the economy is characterized either by a single consumer or by many consumers with identical homothetic preferences. There are fixed aggregate factor endowments $\mathbf{\bar{R}} = (\bar{R}_1, \ldots, \bar{R}_n) > 0$. Government transfers T accrue to consumers who determine commodity demands on the basis of utility maximization. For each good j, consumers decide whether to buy at the higher price p_j on the black market, or to buy at price $\bar{p}_j$ on the white market and bear the transactions costs. In equilibrium, consumers are indifferent as to which market is used.

The equilibrium conditions linking black and white markets from the demand side are

$$p_j = \bar{p}_j(1 + g_j) \quad (j = 1, \ldots, n),$$ (10.71)

where g_j is the transactions cost per unit of good j purchased on white markets.

Real resources used in transacting on white markets are denominated in terms of the good being transacted. The search-cost input requirement per unit of good j bought on white markets is assumed to be given by

$$g_j = \frac{p_j}{\bar{p}_j} - 1 \quad (j = 1, \ldots, n);$$ (10.72)

that is, transactions (search) costs increase with the differential between black- and white-market prices.

Denoting demands for good j on black and white markets as x_j^b and x_j^w (respectively), consumer utility functions are defined over the total consumption of each good,

$$x_j = x_j^b + x_j^w \quad (j = 1, \dots, n), \tag{10.73}$$

since consumers do not differentiate between goods bought on black or white markets. The consumer problem is to maximize utility subject to the following budget constraint:

$$\sum_{j=1}^n p_j x_j^b + \sum_{j=1}^n \bar{p}_j (1 + g_j) x_j^w = \sum_{i=1}^n w_i \bar{R}_i + T. \tag{10.74}$$

The left-hand side of (10.74) denotes total expenditures on black markets at black-market prices and on white markets at controlled prices, plus endogenous white-market transactions costs. The right-hand side denotes consumer incomes from factor endowments and government transfers; the latter arise as fines collected by government on black markets are recycled to consumers.

Equations (10.71), (10.73), and (10.74) thus give the equivalent budget constraint

$$\sum_{j=1}^n p_j x_j = \sum_{i=1}^n w_i \bar{R}_i + T. \tag{10.75}$$

Utility maximization, subject to the budget constraint (10.75), yields consumer demands

$$x_j = x_j(\mathbf{p}, \mathbf{w}, T) \quad (j = 1, \dots, n). \tag{10.76}$$

Given that (10.67) and (10.68) guarantee the existence of zero-profit conditions for producers on either black or white markets, and given that (10.71) ensures that black-market buying prices equal white-market buying prices gross of transactions costs, a general equilibrium in the presence of both black and white markets can be defined as the quadruplet $(\mathbf{p}^*, \mathbf{w}^*, s^*, T^*)$ such that four sets of conditions hold:

(i) demands equal supplies in factor markets,

$$\sum_{j=1}^n r_{ji}(\mathbf{w}^*) y_j = \bar{R}_i \quad (i = 1, \dots, n); \tag{10.77}$$

(ii) demands equal supplies for goods in black markets,

$$x_j^b = y_j^b \quad (j = 1, \dots, n); \tag{10.78}$$

(iii) demands (gross of transactions costs) equal supplies for goods in white markets,

$$(1+g_j)x_j^w = y_j^w \quad (j=1,\dots,n); \tag{10.79}$$

and

(iv) government transfers equal fines collected,

$$T^* = \sum_{j=1}^n f_j \rho_j(s_j^*)y_j^b. \tag{10.80}$$

Equations (10.77) and (10.78) are standard market-clearing conditions with factor prices and black-market prices as the equilibrium mechanism, while (10.79) uses the endogenously determined transactions costs on white markets as the equilibrating mechanism in the presence of price controls. Substituting definitions (10.70) and (10.71) into (10.79) gives the equivalent equilibrium conditions on white markets:

$$\frac{p_j}{\bar{p}_j}\cdot x_j^w = (1-s_j)y_j \quad (j=1,\dots,n). \tag{10.81}$$

Finally, (10.80) recycles government revenues collected as fines on producers caught trading in black markets, in a fashion similar to general equilibrium tax models (e.g., Shoven and Whalley 1973).

It is when computation of interlinked black- and white-market equilibria is considered that the reasons for requiring the number of goods and factors to be equal in their model becomes apparent. Output prices are fixed at $\bar{\mathbf{p}}$ on white markets, and zero-profit conditions (10.68) must hold. To be operational, this approach requires the same number of goods and factors in the trade-model traditions of Samuelson (1953) and Gale and Nikaido (1965). The zero-profit conditions yield a system of n nonlinear equations in n unknown factor prices $\mathbf{w}^*$. Once equilibrium factor prices $\mathbf{w}^*$ are found, equilibrium output supplies $\mathbf{y}^*$ can be determined from factor market equilibrium conditions (10.77), but again it is necessary to have the same number of goods and factors for the system of linear equations (10.77) to be solvable.

Substituting (10.68) and (10.69) into the black-market zero-profit conditions (10.67), equilibrium black-market prices can be expressed as a function solely of the size of each black market:

$$p_j = \bar{p}_j + f_j\rho_j(s_j) = p_j(s_j) \quad (j=1,\dots,n). \tag{10.82}$$

As a result, consumer demands (10.76) and per-unit transactions costs on white markets (10.81) can be expressed in terms of the vector of proportional black-market size and government transfers:

$$x_j = x_j(\mathbf{p}(s), \mathbf{w}, T) = x_j(s, T) \quad (j = 1, \ldots, n); \tag{10.83}$$

$$g_j = \frac{p_j(s_j)}{\bar{p}} - 1 \quad (j = 1, \ldots, n). \tag{10.84}$$

Since consumers do not differentiate between goods bought on black and white markets, we can represent total excess demands (summed across both black and white markets) from (10.76) and (10.79) as

$$z_j = x_j(s, T) + g_j x_j^w - y_j \quad (j = 1, \ldots, n), \tag{10.85}$$

or equivalently from (10.81) as

$$z_j = x_j(s, T) - \frac{s_j p_j + (1 - s_j)\bar{p}_j}{p_j} \cdot y_j \quad (j = 1, \ldots, n). \tag{10.86}$$

The problem of computing an interlinked black- and white-market equilibrium can therefore be reduced to that of solving a system of $n + 1$ nonlinear equations involving total excess demands for goods and a government budget imbalance in $n + 1$ unknowns (s, T):

$$z_j(s, T) = 0 \quad (j = 1, \ldots, n); \tag{10.87}$$

$$T - \sum_{j=1}^{n} f_j \rho_j(s_j) s_j y_j = 0. \tag{10.88}$$

This system is similar to that used in general equilibrium tax models (e.g., Shoven and Whalley 1973), except that here the extended unit simplex is defined over the endogenously determined size of each black market and revenues from fines. Using this representation of the equilibrium problem, computation can proceed by applying either a fixed point algorithm or a more traditional Newton or Gauss–Seidel method.

Nguyen and Whalley illustrate their approach with some numerical calculations for India. India is widely thought to be one of the most heavily regulated of the larger economies in the developing world, and one in which issues of policy toward the black market are prominent. Nguyen and Whalley apply the same type of approach as in Chapter 5: calibrating a model to a micro-consistent benchmark equilibrium data set, followed by counterfactual equilibrium analysis.

11

Conclusion

In this volume, we have tried to convey how general equilibrium analysis can be applied to policy and other issues, and how we have made such applications in some of our work. We have not tried to be comprehensive in our coverage of work by others; nor have we emphasized approaches different from our own, though readers should be aware that they exist.

What constitutes operationality of any theoretical approach in any discipline is a highly subjective matter. What is operational to one is not so to another, and vice versa. However, our emphasis on operationalizing general equilibrium analysis stresses that the techniques and applications summarized in this volume clearly demonstrate the capability to solve equilibrium models of large dimensionality, and in a fashion sufficiently rapid for use in policy-based and other analysis. This is in contrast to contributions in the original debate on the feasibility of large-scale equilibrium computation, a debate initiated by Barone in 1907 and continued through the 1920s and 1930s with von Mises, Robbins, Hayek, and Lange.

Many years ago, Schumpeter characterized Walras as providing the Magna Carta of economics, implicitly doubting that the Walrasian approach could be used in any satisfactory way to generate meaningful analysis of actual economywide economic behavior. Robbins subsequently suggested that applying general equilibrium analysis in a meaningful way required the solution of millions of equations in millions of unknowns. He did not, however, ask the question of what the appropriate model ought to be prior to the solution of an equilibrium system mimicked by a central planner. How would a range of issues be treated, including foreign trade, public expenditures, market structures, and others? As a result, despite the demonstration in this book of operational equilibrium techniques, issues of applicability remain. These all pose challenges for users of existing models and builders of new models.

First, there is model choice. It is clear to us that, in any analysis of economic policy making, the choice of model is as crucial in determining results as is developing a numerical specification once the model has been chosen. Clear demonstrations in the modeling literature show that conclusions from numerical models change by changing key assumptions. Model choice precedes computation, and computation gives no clear guidance as to the appropriate choice of model.

Second, there are questions of parametric specification, including procedures used for calibration. Calibration procedures are now widely emphasized in applied equilibrium systems, in part because of the large dimensionalities involved. The calibration approach generally finds a receptive audience among those who feel that modern econometrics – by overemphasizing the statistical component and downplaying the economic component of modeling – has produced models that are too simplistic in terms of their economic content. On the other hand, modeling work based on calibration (described in Chapter 5) generally has no statistical content whatsoever, and therefore validation of calibrated models is very much an issue.

Indeed, the challenge that calibration poses to econometric models intensifies the issue: With enough freedom over the parameters and functional forms in an applied general equilibrium model, it is generally possible to build a model that will exactly replicate any chosen data set. Models may be complex, but exact calibration is still possible. There are typically many such models that can be calibrated to a given data set, but this large variety provides no basis for choice between models.

Third, after questions of model choice and validation of models come issues concerning elasticity values. These are perhaps the weakest of all the parameter values used in current applied equilibrium models. Unfortunately, we see empiricism in economics as heavily driven by hypothesis testing rather than parameter generation, and this is reflected in the current literature where estimates of elasticity parameters are relatively few. Hence, applied general equilibrium models are often viewed with discomfort by econometricians because the underlying parametric specifications are weak.

Despite all these problems, we obviously feel that the approach set out in this volume is useful. We think the attempt to operationalize a large body of existing theory, developed through the 1950s and 1960s and devoted largely to nonconstructive proofs of the existence of equilibrium, is beneficial in the long run. We also believe that the insights generated on policy issues by using techniques of this kind, if quantified in the appropriate way, can help raise the level of policy debate. The use of any model of social process is not without problems, but done in an intelligent and focused way and in the context of contemporary debates on policy issues, the rewards can be large.

As work continues on applied equilibrium modeling, we foresee a series of possible future developments. One is the choice between large-scale general purpose models and more focused, smaller-scale, issue-specific models. Much of the work described here relies on large-scale equilibrium systems that have a multipurpose capability. Our sense is that such capabilities, when used for specific issues, are at once too simplistic (in the areas relevant to issues at hand) and too specific (in modeling details not pertinent to these issues). The focus of some research in this area has thus switched increasingly toward smaller-scale, issue-specific models. The problem with smaller models is that they are less realistic and, to an outside audience, lacking in credibility when compared to larger models. Nonetheless, one can generate large numbers of small-scale and issue-specific models simply by building a new model every time an issue is to be analyzed; we think this choice likely to arise increasingly in future modeling work.

Ultimately, it is up to readers and users of model results to ask themselves whether they think that the applied general equilibrium approach is the right way to analyze issues of concern to them, and, if it is, whether a numerical structure developed along the lines laid out in this book can help them. We hope the conclusion will be positive and the demonstration attempted here convincing enough for such work to be carried forward.

REFERENCES

Adelman, I., and S. Robinson (1978) *Income Distribution Policy in Developing Countries: A Case Study of Korea.* Stanford, CA: Stanford University Press.

Allingham, M. G. (1973) *Equilibrium and Disequilibrium: A Quantitative Analysis of Economic Interaction.* Cambridge, MA: Ballinger.

Allingham, M. G., and A. Sandmo (1972) "Income Tax Evasion: A Theoretical Analysis." *Journal of Public Economics* 1, 323–38.

Armington, P. S. (1969) "A Theory of Demand for Products Distinguished by Place of Production." International Monetary Fund *Staff Papers* 16, 159–76.

Arrow, K. J. (1951) *Social Choice and Individual Values.* New York: Wiley.

Arrow, K. J., and G. Debreu (1954) "Existence of an Equilibrium for a Competitive Economy." *Econometrica* 22, 265–90.

Arrow, K. J., and F. H. Hahn (1971) *General Competitive Analysis.* San Francisco: Holden-Day.

Arrow, K. J., H. B. Chenery, B. S. Minhas, and R. M. Solow (1961) "Capital–Labor Substitution and Economic Efficiency." *Review of Economics and Statistics* 43, 225–50.

Atkinson, A. B. (1970) "On the Measurement of Inequality." *Journal of Economic Theory* 2, 244–63.

Auerbach, A. J., L. J. Kotlikoff, and J. Skinner (1983) "The Efficiency Gains from Dynamic Tax Reform." *International Economic Review* 24, 81–100.

Bacharach, M. (1971) *Biproportional Matrices and Input–Output Change.* Cambridge: Cambridge University Press.

Ballard, C. L., and L. H. Goulder (1982a) "Expectation in Numerical General Equilibrium Models." Research Paper No. 31, Stanford Workshop in the Microeconomics of Factor Markets, Department of Economics, Stanford University.

Ballard, C. L., and L. H. Goulder (1982b) "Tax Policy and Consumer Foresight: A General Equilibrium Simulation Study." Discussion Paper No. 940, Institute of Economic Research, Harvard University.

Ballard, C. L., D. Fullerton, J. B. Shoven, and J. Whalley (1985) *A General Equilibrium Model for Tax Policy Evaluation.* Chicago: University of Chicago Press.

Ballentine, G., and W. R. Thirsk (1979) "The Fiscal Incidence of Some Community Experiments in Fiscal Federalism: Technical Report." Community Services Analysis Division, Canada Mortgage and Housing Corp., Ottawa: Minister of Supply and Services.

Benassy, J. P. (1975) "Neo-Keynesian Disequilibrium Theory in a Monetary Economy." *Review of Economic Studies* 42, 503-23.

Berndt, E. R. (1976) "Reconciling Alternative Estimates of the Elasticity of Substitution." *Review of Economics and Statistics* 58, 59-69.

Bhagwati, J. N. (1958) "Immiserizing Growth: A Geometrical Note." *Review of Economic Studies* 25, 201-5.

Blomqvist, A., and S. Mohammad (1984) "Controls, Corruption, and Competitive Rent-Seeking in LDC's." CSIER Working Paper 8418C, University of Western Ontario.

Boadway, R. W. (1974) "The Welfare Foundations of Cost-Benefit Analysis." *Economic Journal* 84, 926-39.

Boadway, R. W., and N. Bruce (1984) *Welfare Economics.* Oxford: Blackwell.

Boadway, R. W., and J. Treddenick (1978) "A General Equilibrium Computation of the Effects of the Canadian Tariff Structure." *Canadian Journal of Economics* 11, 424-6.

Boskin, M. J. (1978) "Taxation, Saving, and the Rate of Interest." *Journal of Political Economy* 86 (Part 2), S3-S27.

Bovenberg, L., and J. Keller (1983) "Dynamics in Applied General Equilibrium Models." Internal Report, Voorburg: Netherlands Central Bureau of Statistics.

Brown, F., and J. Whalley (1980) "General Equilibrium Evaluations of Tariff-Cutting Proposals in the Tokyo Round and Comparisons with More Extensive Liberalization of World Trade." *Economic Journal* 90, 838-66.

Burns, M. E. (1973) "A Note on the Concept and Measure of Consumer's Surplus." *American Economic Review* 63, 335-44.

Caddy, V. (1976) "Empirical Estimation of the Elasticity of Substitution: A Review." Mimeo, Melbourne, Australia: Industries Assistance Commission.

Clarete, R., and J. Whalley (1988) "Interactions between Trade Policies and Domestic Distortions in a Small Open Developing Country." *Journal of International Economics* 24, 345-58.

Clements, K. W. (1980) "A General Equilibrium Econometric Model of an Open Economy." *International Economic Review* 21, 469-88.

Deardorff, A. V., and M. Stern (1981) "A Disaggregated Model of World Production and Trade: An Estimate of the Impact of the Tokyo Round." *Journal of Policy Modelling* 3, 127-52.

Debreu, G. (1959) *Theory of Value.* New York: Wiley.

Debreu, G., and H. E. Scarf (1963) "A Limit Theorem on the Care of an Economy." *International Economic Review* 4, 235-46.

Denison, E. F. (with J. P. Poullier) (1967) *Why Growth Rates Differ.* Washington, DC: The Brookings Institution.

Dervis, K., J. de Melo, and S. Robinson (1982) *General Equilibrium Models for Development Policy.* Cambridge: Cambridge University Press.

Diewert, W. E. (1978) "Hicks' Aggregation Theorem and the Existence of a Real Value-Added Function." In M. Fuss and D. M. McFadden (eds.) *Production Economics: A Dual Approach to Theory and Applications,* v. 2. Amsterdam: North-Holland.

Dixon, P. B. (1978) "Economies of Scale, Commodity Disaggregation and the Costs of Protection." *Australian Economic Papers* 17, 63-80.

Dixon, P. B., B. R. Parmenter, J. Sutton, and D. P. Vincent (1982) *ORANI: A Multisectoral Model of the Australian Economy.* Amsterdam: North-Holland.

Dornbusch, R. (1973) "Devaluation, Money and Non-traded Goods." *American Economic Review* 63, 871-81.

Drèze, J. H. (1975) "Existence of an Exchange Equilibrium Under Price Rigidities." *International Economic Review* 16, 301-20.

Dupuit, J. (1844) "De la Mesure de L'Utilité des Travaux Publics." *Annales des Ponts et Chaussees* 8 (2nd series). English translation in K. J. Arrow and T. Scitovsky (1969) *Readings in Welfare Economics.* Homewood, IL: Irwin, pp. 225–83.

Ebrill, L., and D. G. Hartman (1982) "On the Incidence and Excess Burden of the Corporation Income Tax." *Public Finance* 37, 48–58.

Ericson, R. E. (1984) "The 'Second Economy' and Resource Allocation Under Central Planning." *Journal of Comparative Economics* 8, 1–24.

Fisher, I. (1927) *The Making of Index Numbers: A Study of Their Varieties, Tests and Reliability,* 3rd ed. New York: Houghton Mifflin.

Foley, D. K. (1970) "Economic Equilibrium with Costly Marketing." *Journal of Economic Theory* 2, 276–91.

Frey, B. S. (1983) "Politics, Economics, and the Underground Economy." In K. R. Monroe (ed.) *The Political Process and Economic Change.* New York: Agathon Press.

Fullerton, D. (1978) "A General Equilibrium Taxation Model with Applications and Dynamic Extensions." Ph.D. thesis, University of California, Berkeley.

Fullerton, D., J. B. Shoven, and J. Whalley (1983) "Replacing the U.S. Income Tax with a Progressive Consumption Tax: A Sequenced General Equilibrium Approach." *Journal of Public Economics* 20, 3–23.

Gale, D. (1955). "The Law of Supply and Demand." *Mathematica Scandinavia* 3, 155–69.

Gale, D., and H. Nikaido (1965) "The Jacobian Matrix and Global Univalence of Mappings." *Mathematische Annalen* 159, 81–93.

Ginsburgh, V. A., and J. L. Waelbroeck (1981) *Activity Analysis and General Equilibrium Modelling.* Amsterdam: North-Holland.

Gordon, R. H. (1981) "Taxation of Corporate Capital Income: Tax Revenues vs. Tax Distortions." Working Paper Series No. 687, Massachusetts: National Bureau of Economic Research Inc.

Goulder, L. H., J. B. Shoven, and J. Whalley (1983) "Domestic Tax Policy and the Foreign Sector: The Importance of Alternative Foreign Policy Formulations to Results from a General Equilibrium Tax Analysis Model." In M. S. Feldstein (ed.) *Behavioral Simulation Methods in Tax Policy Analysis.* Chicago: University of Chicago Press.

Grubel, H. G., and P. J. Lloyd (1975) *Intra-Industry Trade: The Theory and Measurement of International Trade in Differentiated Products.* New York: Wiley.

Gunning, J. W., G. Carrin, and J. Waelbroeck (with J. M. Burniaux and J. Mercenier) (1982) "Growth and Trade of Developing Countries: A General Equilibrium Analysis." Discussion Paper 8210, CEME, Université Libre de Bruxelles.

Hahn, F. H. (1971) "Equilibrium with Transactions Costs." *Econometrica* 39, 417–39.

Hamilton, B., S. Mohammad, and J. Whalley (1985) "Applied General Equilibrium Analysis and Perspectives on Growth Performance." CSIER Working Paper 8524C, University of Western Ontario.

Hamilton, B., and J. Whalley (1985) "Tax Treatement of Housing in a Dynamic Sequenced General Equilibrium Model." *Journal of Public Economics* 27, 157–75.

Hansen, T. (1969) "A Fixed Point Algorithm for Approximating the Optimal Solution of a Concave Programming Problem." Cowles Foundation Discussion Paper No. 277, Yale University.

Harberger, A. C. (1959) "The Corporation Income Tax: An Empirical Appraisal." *Tax Revision Compendium* 1 (House Committee on Ways and Means, 86th Congress, First Session), 231–40.

Harberger, A. C. (1962) "The Incidence of the Corporation Income Tax." *Journal of Political Economy* 70, 215–40.

Harberger, A. C. (1966) "Efficiency Effects of Taxes on Income from Capital." In M. Krzyzaniak (ed.) *Effects of Corporation Income Tax.* Symposium on Business Taxation, Wayne State University, Detroit: Wayne State University Press.

Harris, J. R. (1984) "Applied General Equilibrium Analysis of Small Open Economies with Scale Economies and Imperfect Competition." *American Economic Review* 74, 1016–32.

Harris, J. R., and M. P. Todaro (1970) "Migration, Unemployment and Development: A Two-Sector Analysis." *American Economic Review* 60, 126–42.

Heckscher, E. (1949) "The Effect of Foreign Trade on the Distribution of Income." In H. S. Ellis and L. A. Metzler (eds.) *Readings in the Theory of International Trade.* Homewood, IL: Irwin.

Hicks, J. R. (1939) *Value and Capital.* Oxford: Clarendon Press.

Imam, H., and J. Whalley (1982) "General Equilibrium with Price Intervention Policies: A Computational Approach." *Journal of Public Economics* 18, 105–19.

Johansen, L. (1960) *A Multi-Sectoral Study of Economic Growth.* Amsterdam: North-Holland.

Johnson, H. G. (1957). "Factor Endowments, International Trade and Factor Prices." *Manchester School* 25, 270–83.

Johnson, H. G. (1958) *International Trade and Economic Growth: Studies in Pure Theory.* London: Allen and Unwin.

Jones, R. W. (1965) "The Structure of Simple General Equilibrium Models." *Journal of Political Economy* 73, 557–72.

Jorgenson, D. W. (1984) "Econometric Methods for Applied General Equilibrium Modelling." In H. E. Scarf and J. B. Shoven (eds.) *Applied General Equilibrium Analysis.* Cambridge: Cambridge University Press.

Kehoe, T., and J. Serra-Puche (1983) "A Computational General Equilibrium Model with Endogenous Unemployment: An Analysis of the 1980 Fiscal Reform in Mexico." *Journal of Public Economics* 22, 1–26.

Keller, W. J. (1980) *Tax Incidence: A General Equilibrium Approach.* Amsterdam: North-Holland.

Kemp, M. C. (1964) *The Pure Theory of International Trade.* Englewood Cliffs, NJ: Prentice-Hall.

Krueger, A. O. (1974) "The Political Economy of the Rent-Seeking Society." *American Economic Review* 64, 291–303.

Kuhn, H. W., and J. G. MacKinnon (1975) "The Sandwich Method for Finding Fixed Points." *Journal of Optimization Theory and Application* 17, 189–204.

Lemke, C. E., and J. T. Howson, Jr. (1964) "Equilibrium Points of Bi-Matrix Games." *SIAM Journal of Applied Mathematics* 12, 412–23.

Lenjosek, G., and J. Whalley (1986) "A Small Open Economy Applied to an Evaluation of Canadian Energy Policies Using 1980 Data." *Journal of Policy Modelling* 8, 89–110.

McLure, C. E., Jr. (1979) *Must Corporate Income be Taxed Twice?* Washington, DC: The Brookings Institution.

Manne, A. S., and P. Preckel (1983) "A Three-Region Intertemporal Model of Energy, International Trade, and Capital Flows." Operations Research, Stanford University.

Mansur, A. H. (1980) "On the Estimation of General Equilibrium Models." Mimeo, Department of Economics, University of Western Ontario.

Mansur, A. H. (1982) "Three Essays on Applied General Equilibrium." Ph.D. thesis, University of Western Ontario.

Mansur, A. H., and J. Whalley (1982) "A Decomposition Algorithm for General Equilibrium Computation with Application to International Trade Models." *Econometrica* 50, 1547–57.

Mansur, A. H., and J. Whalley (1984) "Numerical Specification of Applied General Equilibrium Models: Estimation, Calibration and Data." In H. E. Scarf and J. B. Shoven (eds.) *Applied General Equilibrium Analysis.* Cambridge: Cambridge University Press.

Meade, J. E. (1955) *The Theory of International Economic Policy.* London: Oxford University Press.

Meade, J. E. (1978) *The Structure and Reform of Direct Taxation.* Report of a Committee Chaired by Prof. J. E. Meade, London: Allen and Unwin.

Merrill, O. H. (1972) "Applications and Extension of an Algorithm that Computes Fixed Points of Certain Upper Semi-Continuous Point to Set Mappings." Ph.D. thesis, Department of Industrial Engineering, University of Michigan.

Michaely, M. (1980) "The Terms of Trade Between Rich and Poor Nations." Paper 162, Institute for International Economic Studies, University of Stockholm.

Miller, M. H., and J. E. Spencer (1977) "The Static Economic Effects of the U.K. Joining the EEC: A General Equilibrium Approach." *Review of Economic Studies* 44, 71–93.

Mohammad, S., and J. Whalley (1984) "Rent-Seeking in India: Welfare Costs and Policy Implications." *Kyklos* 37, 387–413.

Musgrave, R. A. (1959) *The Theory of Public Finance.* New York: McGraw-Hill.

Nerlove, M. (1967) "A Survey of Recent Evidence on CES and Related Production." *Studies in Income and Wealth* 31, *The Theory and Empirical Analysis of Production.* New York: National Bureau of Economic Research.

Nguyen, T., and J. Whalley (1985) "Coexistence of Equilibria on Black and White Markets." CSIER Working Paper 8523C, University of Western Ontario.

Nguyen, T., and J. Whalley (1986) "Equilibrium Under Price Controls with Endogenous Transactions Costs." *Journal of Economic Theory* 29, 290–300.

Nikaido, H. (1956) "On the Classical Multilateral Exchange Problem." *Metroeconomica* 8, 135–45.

Ohlin, B. (1933) *Interregional and International Trade.* Cambridge: Harvard University Press.

Petroleum Monitoring Agency Canada (1982) *Canadian Petroleum Industry: Monitoring Survey 1981.* Ottawa: Petroleum Monitoring Agency Canada.

Piggott, J. R. (1980) "A General Equilibrium Evaluation of Australian Tax Policy." Ph.D. dissertation, University of London.

Piggott, J. R. (1988) "General Equilibrium Computation Applied to Public Sector Issues." In P. Hare (ed.) *Surveys in Public Sector Economics.* Oxford: Blackwell.

Piggott, J. R., and J. Whalley (1977) "General Equilibrium Investigation of U.K. Tax-Subsidy Policy: A Progress Report." In M. J. Artis and A. R. Nobay (eds.) *Studies in Modern Economic Analysis.* Oxford: Blackwell, pp. 259–99.

Piggott, J. R., and J. Whalley (1985) *U.K. Tax Policy and Applied General Equilibrium Analysis.* Cambridge: Cambridge University Press.

Prebisch, R. (1962) "The Economic Development of Latin America and its Principal Problems." *Economic Bulletin for Latin America* 7, 1–22. (First published as an independent booklet by UN ECLA, 1950.)

Projector, D. S., and G. S. Weiss (1966) "Survey of Financial Characteristics of Consumers." Washington, DC: Federal Reserve Technical Papers.

Rosenberg, L. G. (1969) "Taxation of Income from Capital, by Industry Group." In A. C. Harberger and M. J. Bailey (eds.) *The Taxation of Income from Capital.* Washington, DC: The Brookings Institution.

Roningen, V., and A. J. Yeats (1976) "Non-Tariff Distortions of International Trade: Some Preliminary Empirical Evidence." *Weltwirtschaftliches Archiv* 112, 613–25.

Samuelson, P. A. (1953) "Prices of Factors and Goods in General Equilibrium." *Review of Economic Studies* 21, 1–20.

St-Hilaire, F., and J. Whalley (1983) "A Microconsistent Equilibrium Data Set for Canada for Use in Tax Policy Analysis." *Review of Income and Wealth* 29, 175–204.

Scarf, H. E. (1960) "Some Examples of Global Instability of the Competitive Equilibrium." *International Economic Review* 1, 157–72.

Scarf, H. E. (1967) "The Approximation of Fixed Points of a Continuous Mapping." *SIAM Journal of Applied Mathematics* 15, 1328–43.

Scarf, H. E. (with T. Hansen) (1973) *The Computation of Economic Equilibria*. New Haven: Yale University Press.

Serra-Puche, J. (1984) "A General Equilibrium Model for the Mexican Economy." In H. Scarf and J. B. Shoven (eds.) *Applied General Equilibrium Analysis*. Cambridge: Cambridge University Press.

Shoven, J. B. (1974) "A Proof of the Existence of a General Equilibrium with *ad Valorem* Commodity Taxes." *Journal of Economic Theory* 8, 1–25.

Shoven, J. B. (1976) "The Incidence and Efficiency Effects of Taxes on Income from Capital." *Journal of Political Economy* 84, 1261–83.

Shoven, J. B., and J. Whalley (1972) "A General Equilibrium Calculation of the Effects of Differential Taxation of Income from Capital in the U.S." *Journal of Public Economics* 1, 281–322.

Shoven, J. B., and J. Whalley (1973) "General Equilibrium with Taxes: A Computation Procedure and an Existence Proof." *Review of Economic Studies* 40, 475–90.

Shoven, J. B., and J. Whalley (1974) "On the Computation of Competitive Equilibrium on International Markets with Tariffs." *Journal of International Economics* 4, 341–54.

Shoven, J. B., and J. Whalley (1977) "Equal Yield Tax Alternatives: General Equilibrium Computational Techniques." *Journal of Public Economics* 8, 211–24.

Shoven, J. B., and J. Whalley (1984) "Applied General Equilibrium Models of Taxation and International Trade: An Introduction and Survey." *Journal of Economic Literature* 22, 1007–51.

Silberberg, E. (1972) "Duality and the Many Consumer's Surpluses." *American Economic Review* 62, 942–52.

Singer, H. W. (1950) "The Distribution of Gains Between Investing and Borrowing Countries." *American Economic Review, Papers and Proceedings* 40, 473–85.

Slemrod, J. (1983) "A General Equilibrium Model of Taxation with Endogenous Financial Behavior." In M. Feldstein (ed.) *Behavioral Simulation Methods in Tax Policy Analysis*. Chicago: University of Chicago Press, pp. 427–54.

Spraos, J. (1980) "The Statistical Debate on the Net Barter Terms of Trade Between Primary Commodities and Manufactures." *Economic Journal* 90, 107–28.

Srinivasan, T. N. (1973) "Tax Evasion: A Model." *Journal of Public Economics* 2, 339–46.

Statistics Canada (1967–81) *System of National Accounts, National Income and Expenditures Accounts: The Annual Estimates*. Catalog #13-201.

Statistics Canada (1981) *The Crude Petroleum and Natural Gas Industry*. Catalog #26-213.

Statistics Canada (1981) *System of National Accounts, Gross Domestic Product by Industry*. Catalog #61-213.

Statistics Canada (1982) *Canadian Statistical Review*. Catalog #11-003E (December).

Statistics Canada (1982) *Estimates of Labour Income*. Catalog #72-005 (October–December).

Statistics Canada (1982) *Fixed Capital Flows and Stocks*. Catalog #13-211.

Statistics Canada (1982) *System of National Accounts, Quarterly Estimates of the Canadian Balance of International Payments*. Catalog #67-001 (October–December).

Stern, R. M., J. Francis, and B. Schumacher (1976) *Price Elasticities in International Trade: An Annotated Bibliography*. London: Macmillan (for the Trade Policy Research Centre).

Stiglitz, J. E. (1973) "Taxation, Corporate Financial Policy, and the Cost of Capital." *Journal of Public Economics* 2, 1-34.

Summers, L. H. (1981) "Capital Taxation and Accumulation in a Life Cycle Growth Model." *American Economic Review* 71, 533-44.

U.S. Department of Commerce (1974) *Survey of Current Business* 54 (February).

U.S. Department of Commerce (1976) *Survey of Current Business* 56 (July).

U.S. Department of Commerce. Bureau of Economic Analysis (REA) (1976) "U.S. National Income and Product Accounts, 1973 to Second Quarter 1976." *Survey of Current Business* 56 (July).

U.S. Department of Labor. Bureau of Labor Statistics (1961) *Survey of Consumer Expenditures 1960-61.* BLS Report 3, Part C, pp. 237-8.

U.S. Department of Labor. Bureau of Labor Statistics (1978) "Consumer Expenditure Survey, 1972-73." In *BLS Bulletin 1985.* Washington, DC: Government Printing Office.

U.S. Department of the Treasury, Office of Tax Analysis (1977) *Blueprints for Basic Tax Reform.* Washington, DC: Government Printing Office.

Uzawa, H. (1963) "On a Two-Sector Model of Economic Growth: II." *Review of Economic Studies* 30, 105-18.

Van der Laan, G., and A. J. J. Talman (1979) "A Restart Algorithm for Computing Fixed Points Without an Extra Dimension." *Mathematical Programming* 17, 74-84.

Whalley, J. (1973) "A Numerical Assessment of the April 1973 Tax Changes in the United Kingdom." Ph.D. dissertation, Yale University.

Whalley, J. (1975) "A General Equilibrium Assessment of the 1973 United Kingdom Tax Reform." *Economica* 42, 139-61.

Whalley, J. (1982) "An Evaluation of the Recent Tokyo Round Trade Agreement Using General Equilibrium Computation Methods." *Journal of Policy Modelling* 4, 341-61.

Whalley, J. (1985) *Trade Liberalization Among Major World Trading Areas.* Cambridge, MA: MIT Press.

Whalley, J., and B. Yeung (1984) "External Sector Closing Rules in Applied General Equilibrium Models." *Journal of International Economics* 16, 123-38.

Wiegard, W. (1984) "The Algorithms of Scarf and Merrill for Numerically Solving General Equilibrium Models: An Introduction with Examples from Taxation Policy." Mimeo, University of Western Ontario.

Willig, R. D. (1976) "Consumer's Surplus Without Apology." *American Economic Review* 66, 589-97.

Wolf, M. (1983) "Managed Trade in Practice: Implications of the Textile Arrangements." In W. R. Cline (ed.) *Trade Policy in the 1980's.* Washington, DC: Institute for International Economics.

World Bank Atlas (1969-1978), annual issues. Washington, DC: World Bank.

Yeats, A. J. (1977) "Effective Protection for Processed Agricultural Commodities: A Comparison of Industrial Countries." *Journal of Economics and Business* 29, 31-9.

Yeats, A. J. (1979) *Trade Barriers Facing Developing Countries: Commercial Policy Measures and Shipping.* London: Macmillan.

INDEX

Note: Page numbers followed by *f* indicate figures; *t* following a page number indicates tabular material.

ad valorem taxes, 153, 154, 175–177, 176f, 207, 209–210
adjacent simplex, 65
agent disaggregation in trade model, 213–215, 214t
aggregation level in equilibrium models, 100–102, 101t
algorithms in computing equilibria
  fixed point, 42–44, 46–49, 48f
  Merrill's, 41, 42, 54–57, 54f, 56f, 58t
  modified Merrill's, 59, 60, 61t, 62
  modified Scarf's, 59–60, 60f, 62
  Scarf's, 37, 39–42, 49–54, 50f, 52t, 53f
  with taxes, 57, 59–62, 60f, 61t, 63t, 64, 64t
  Van der Laan and Talman's, 41, 64–66
approximate equilibrium price vector, 50
Armington assumption in trade models, 81, 230, 231, 232
Arrow, K. J., on elasticity of substitution in manufacturing, 119
Arrow–Debreu model, 1–2, 3
  vs. dynamic models, 128
  proof of, with no government policy intervention, 12–21, 14f, 15f
Atkinson measure of income inequality, 131, 132f
Australia
  tax models for (Piggott), 72t, 74t, 76t, 78
  trade models for, 83t, 84t, 100 (*see also specific model*)

Ballard–Fullerton–Shoven–Whalley tax model, 72t, 74t, 76t, 79, 153–193

  aggregation level in, 100–101, 101t
  characteristics of, 153–157
  integration of corporate and personal income taxes in, 157–168, 161–163t, 165t
  replacement of personal income tax with progressive consumption tax in, 168–174, 169t, 171t
  structure of, 175–193, 176f, 191f
  welfare measurement in, 129–130
Ballard–Goulder tax model, 79
Ballentine–Thirsk tax model, 72t, 74t, 76t, 78–79
base point in computing equilibria, 46, 48
benchmark equilibria/data sets, 103–105, 106–109, 110–113t, 114–115
Berndt, E. R., on elasticity estimates, 119
Bhagwati, J. N., on North–South trade, 222
black markets, price control analysis and, 271–277
Boadway–Treddenick trade model, 83t, 86t, 89t, 231–235, 235t
Bovenberg–Keller tax model, 79
Brouwer theorem, 13–16, 14f, 21, 41

Caddy, V., on elasticity estimates, 119, 120t
calibration, 103–118, 280
  benchmark equilibria in, 103–105, 106–109, 110–113t, 114–115
  deterministic calculation procedure in, 105–106
  elasticities in, 105
  parameter determination by, 115–118

Canada
  benchmark data sets for, 108–109,
    110–113t, 114–115
  price control analysis for, 265–271
  tax models for (Ballentine–Thirsk),
    72t, 74t, 76t, 78–79
  Tokyo Round proposals of, 217–219,
    216t, 218t, 219t
  trade models for, 83t, 231, 233,
    240–248 (*see also specific model*)
capital-energy-labor substitution
    elasticities, 123
capital flows in trade models, 92
capital-gains tax analysis, 157–168,
    161–163t, 165t
ceiling prices, effects of, 256–263, 263t,
    264t
"central tendency" tables for
    elasticities of substitution, 119–120,
    120t, 121, 122t
CES functions, *see* constant elasticity of
    substitution functions
Clarete–Whalley trade model, 248–255
closing rules in trade models, 81
closure of trade models
  with export-demand and import-
    supply, 230–235, 235t
  with price-fixing formulations, 235–238
  with price-taking formulations, 238–240
Cobb–Douglas functions
  in Ballard–Fullerton–Shoven–Whalley
    tax model, 153, 155, 156, 176f, 178,
    180–182, 184–185
  in calibration, 104, 105, 119
  in Clarete–Whalley trade model,
    249–250
  in Harberger model application, 137, 140
  in model design, 94–95, 95t, 96t, 97
  in single-country trade models, 237–238
commodities in models, 9–10, 11–12, 11f
  trade, 199, 211, 212–213t, 213
  see also specific model
compensating surplus in welfare impact
    measurement, 127–128, 127f
compensating variation in welfare impact
    measurement, 124–126, 124f
computing general equilibria, 37–68
  example of, 44, 45t, 46, 47t
  fixed point algorithms in, 42–44,
    46–49, 48f
  Merrill's algorithm in, 54–57, 54f, 56f,
    58t
  Newton methods in, 66–68
  pure exchange model, 37–42, 38f, 39f
  Scarf's algorithm in, 37, 39–42, 49–54,
    50f, 52t, 53f

tax inclusion in, 57–64, 60f, 61t, 63–64t
  Van der Laan and Talman's algorithm
    in, 64–66
constant elasticity of substitution
    functions, 44, 46
  in Harberger tax-model application,
    137, 139–140
  manufacturing, 118–120
  in model calibration, 104, 105, 116–118
  in model design, 94–95, 95t, 96t, 97
  in tax models, 153, 175, 181–182
  in trade models, 198, 202, 203, 205, 207
consumer side of model, 18–19
  modification for taxes, 24
consumption
  in dynamic models, 128–129
  in equilibrium models, 18–19
  in tax models, 177–184
consumption taxes
  in equilibrium models, 93
  replacement of income tax with,
    modeling of, 168–174, 169t, 171t
continuous mapping, 13–14, 15f, 40
contract curve in computing equilibria, 38
corporate taxes, integration with personal
    income taxes, modeling of, 157–168,
    161–163t, 165t
cost-covering commodity price ratio in
    two-sector models, 29–32, 31f
cost-minimizing factor input ratio in two-
    sector models, 29–32, 31f
cost-of-living index, true, 132
counterfactual equilibria, analysis of, 103,
    123–133, 124f, 126f, 127f, 130f, 132f
"crosshauling" in trade models, 230, 231

data sets, benchmark, 103–105, 106–109,
    110–113t, 114–115
Deardorff–Stern trade model, 82t, 85t,
    88t, 231
demand correspondence, 24
demand functions, 9–10
  elasticities, 120–121, 122t
  excess, in computing equilibria, 38
  functional forms and, 94–95, 96t, 97t
  parameter values for, 116
  in tax models, 72–73t, 74–75t
  in trade models, 82–83t, 203, 205, 206f,
    208f
Dervis–de Melo–Robinson trade model,
    83t, 87t, 90t, 91, 231
designing applied models, 71–102
  functional forms in, 94–95, 95–97t,
    97–98, 98f, 99f, 100
  level of aggregation in, 100–102, 101t
  structure in, 92–94

tax, 71, 72–77t, 78–80
trade, 80–81, 82–90t, 91–92
deterministic calculation procedure in
  model calibration, 105–106
developing countries
  black markets in, price controls and,
    271–277
  trade models for, 248–255 (*see also*
    Whalley seven-region trade model)
differential incidence analysis, 60–61, 62,
  63t, 64t
differential tax incidence, 60
dimension reduction in models, 32–33, 33f,
  43–44
dimensional simplex, 64–66
distribution, policy effects on, 130–131,
  130f, 132f
dividend taxation, analysis of, 157–168,
  161–163t, 165t
Dixon equilibrium computation method, 42
Dixon–Parmenter–Sutton–Vincent trade
  model, 84t, 87t, 90t, 231
double taxation, analysis of, 157–168,
  161–163t, 165t
Dupuit, J., on welfare impacts of policy,
  123
dynamic models
  tax, 188–193, 191f
  welfare impact measurement in, 128–130

Edgeworth box analysis, 9
elasticities, 95, 96t, 97, 97t, 98, 280
  in Boadway–Treddenick trade model,
    232–235, 235t
  in calibration, 105
  "central tendency" tables for, 119–120,
    120t, 121, 122t
  demand function, 120–121, 122t
  export-demand price, 121
  extraneous, specifying, 118–123, 120t
  import-demand price, 121
  labor-supply, 121
  leisure-goods substitution, 121
  migration from rural areas, 123
  production function, 118–120, 120t
  savings, 121, 123
  in tax models, 121
  in trade models, 81, 205, 207, 208f
  see also constant elasticity of
    substitution functions
endowments in equilibrium model, 9, 18
energy-capital-labor substitution
  elasticities, 123
energy policy analysis for Canada
  (Lenjosek–Whalley model), 240–248
equilibrium price vector, 20

equivalent surplus in welfare impact
  measurement, 127–128, 127f
equivalent variation in welfare impact
  measurement, 124–126, 124f
European Economic Community
  Tokyo Round proposals of, 215–221,
    216t, 218t, 219t, 220t
  trade models for, 83t (*see also* Whalley
    four-region trade model; *specific
    model*)
exchange rates in trade models, 91–92, 233,
  238–239
expenditure functions in equilibrium
  models, 93–94, 96t, 97t, 184–186
export-demand functions in trade models,
  230–235, 235t
export-demand price elasticities, 121
external-sector closure, *see* closure of trade
  models
external-sector data
  in benchmark data set, 109, 112t
  in tax model, 186–188

facet of dimensional simplex, 65
factor prices
  control of, 266–269
  equalization of, 32, 33f
  in equilibrium models, 67–68, 93
factor taxes in tax models, 57
financial flows account in benchmark data
  set, 113t
fines for black-market selling, 272, 273,
  274, 276
Fisher index in tax model, 146, 149t
fixed point algorithms in computing
  equilibria, 42–44, 46–49, 48f
fixed point theorems, 12–21, 14f, 15f
foreign aid in North–South trade
  evaluation, 223, 228–229, 229t
functional forms in equilibrium model
  design, 94–95, 95–97t, 97–98, 98f,
  99f, 100

Gale–Nikaido mapping, 14–16, 40
General Agreement on Tariff and Trade
  negotiations, Tokyo Round, model
  evaluation of, 215–221, 216t, 218t,
  219t, 220t
general equilibrium models
  benchmark equilibrium data sets for,
    106–109, 110–113t, 114–115
  calibration of, *see* calibration
  computing equilibria in, *see* computing
    general equilibria
  designing, *see* designing applied models
  elements of, 9

general equilibrium models *(cont.)*
    equilibrium existence proof in, 12–21, 14f, 15f, 21–28 (tax models)
    evaluation of results of, 123–133, 124f, 126f, 127f, 130f, 132f
    extraneous elasticity values in, 118–121, 120t, 122t, 123
    Harberger, *see* Harberger models
    normative content of, 34–35, 34f
    price controls analysis with, *see* price control analysis
    specifying, 103–106, 104f
    static, sequencing through time, 93
    structure of, 9–12, 10f, 11f
    tax, *see* tax models
    trade, *see* trade models
    two-good–two-factor, 42–44, 45t, 46
    two-sector, 28–34, 31–33f
Gini coefficient, calculation of, 130–131, 130f
Ginsburgh–Waelbroeck equilibrium computation method, 42
global (multicountry) trade models, 80–81, 82–83t, 85–86t, 88–89t, 91–92, 197–229
    four-region, *see* Whalley four-region trade model
    North–South trade-protection analysis with, 221–229, 224t, 226t, 227t, 229t
    regional classifications in, 210–211, 211t, 212–213t, 213–215, 214t
    seven-region, *see* Whalley seven-region trade model
    structure of, 198–210, 206f, 208f
    tariff-cutting proposal evaluation with, 215–221, 216t, 218t, 219t, 220t
    trade-protection policies in, 207, 209–210
goods-price controls, 269–271
Goulder–Shoven–Whalley tax models, 92
government
    expenditures by, 93–94, 184–186
    in general equilibrium model, 21–22, 25–28
    price distortion and, 34
    subsidies by, 256–259, 262
grid size in computing equilibria, 48
    in Merrill's algorithm, 54–55
    in Scarf's algorithm, 49, 51, 52t, 53–54
gross national product
    benchmark equilibrium data and, 108
    in trade models, 210, 211t, 227, 227t
Gunning–Carrin–Waelbroeck trade model, 82t, 85t, 88t

Hamilton–Whalley model
    aggregation level in, 100
    nested structures in, 97, 98f, 99–100, 99f

Hansen–Kuhn triangulation in computing equilibria, 46, 49
Harberger models, 94, 134–136, 135f
    of partial capital taxation, 148–152
Harberger tax-model application, 134–152
    basis for, 134–136, 135f
    calibration of, 136–137, 138t
    demand elasticities in, 137
    demand functions in, 140
    production functions in, 139
    results of, 141, 142–144t, 145–146, 147–149t
    shift factor in, 141, 142–144t, 145
Harris–Todaro model for urban–rural migration, 259–260
Harris trade model, 91
Heckscher–Ohlin trade model, 81
Hicks aggregation theorem, 250–251
Hicksian equivalent variations
    in computing equilibria, 62
    in welfare impact measurement, 124–130, 124f, 126f, 127f
household demand functions, parameter values for, 116
household savings in tax model, 177–184
housing, tax treatment of, 97, 98f, 99–100, 99f

Imam–Whalley model for price control analysis, 261–263, 263t, 264t
immiserizing growth concept in North–South trade, 221, 222, 223
import-demand price elasticities, 121
import quotas in trade models, 252–253
import supply functions in trade models, 230–235, 235t
income distribution
    policy effects on, 130–131, 130f, 132f
    price-control effects on, 270–271
income-outlay accounts, in benchmark data set, 113t, 114
income taxes
    in benchmark data set, 113t, 114
    in equilibrium models, 93
    Harberger tax-model application to, 136–137, 138–139t, 139, 142–144t, 145, 147–149t
    integration with corporate taxes, modeling of, 157–168, 161–163t, 165t
    replacement with progressive consumption tax, modeling of, 168–174, 169t, 171t
    in tax models, 57, 62, 64, 64t
indirect taxes in benchmark data set, 109, 112t, 114
indirect utility functions in equilibrium models, 96t, 97t

individual welfare effects of policy changes, 123–131, 124f, 126f, 127f
industrialized countries, trade model for, *see* Whalley seven-region trade model
initial simplex in computing equilibria
in Merrill's algorithm, 55–56, 58t
in Scarf's algorithm, 50, 51, 52t
initial vertex in computing equilibria, 54–55, 54f
investment in equilibrium models, 93
isoquants in equilibrium model, 11, 11f

Jacobian matrix in Newton methods, 42, 67–68
Japan
Tokyo Round proposals of, 217–220, 216t, 218t, 219t, 220t
trade models for, 83t, (*see also* Whalley four-region trade model; Whalley seven-region trade model; *specific model*)

Kakutani theorem, 13, 14f, 16–21, 41
Kehoe–Serra–Puche tax model, 78
Keller tax model, 72t, 74t, 76t, 78
Kennedy Round, 215, 216
Kreuger, A. O., on rent seeking, 253

labeling in computing equilibria
in Merrill's algorithm, 55, 56, 58t
in Scarf's algorithm, 51, 52t, 53
labor endowment in trade models, 254–255
labor-energy-capital substitution elasticities, 123
labor-supply elasticities in tax models, 121
labor supply in tax model, 177–184
Laspeyres price index, 131
Laspeyres quantity index, 131
leisure-goods substitution elasticities, 121
Lemke–Howson computation of equilibria, 39–40, 48
Lenjosek–Whalley trade model, 100, 240–248
licensing
for import quotas, 252–253
in trade models, 209
life-cycle behavior, consumption and, 178
linear expenditure system function
in model calibration, 104, 105
in model design, 94–95, 95t, 97, 97t
Lorenz curve of income distribution, 130–131, 130f

Manne–Preckel trade model, 82t, 85t, 88t
mapping, 12–21, 14f, 15f
continuous, 13–14, 15f, 40
Gale–Nikaido, 14–16, 40

point-to-point (Brouwer theorem), 13–16, 14f, 21, 41
point-to-set (Kakutani theorem), 13, 14f, 16–21, 41
marginal factor products in two-sector models, 29–30
market-augmented production response, 23–25
Merrill's algorithm for computing equilibria, 41, 42, 54–57, 54f, 56f, 58t
modified for tax inclusion, 41, 42, 54–57, 54f, 56f, 58t, 62
Mexico, tax models for, 73t (*see also specific model*)
Michaely, M., on North–South trade, 222
migration, rural–urban, 123, 254–255, 259–260
Miller–Spencer trade model, 83t, 85t, 88t
minimum prices, effects of, 256–259, 263, 263t, 264t
money-metric approach, 126
multicountry trade models, *see* global (multicountry) trade models
Multifiber Arrangement, North–South trade and, 223

Nash equilibrium in computing equilibria, 40
Nerlove, M., on elasticity estimates, 119
nested functions in equilibrium models, 97, 98f, 99–100, 99f, 205, 206f, 207
net national product, loss estimates of, in tax model, 145, 146, 147–148t
Netherlands, tax model for (Keller), 72t, 74t, 76t, 78
New Zealand, trade models for, 83t (*see also specific model*)
Newton methods in computing equilibria, 42, 66–68
Nguyen–Whalley model
for price controls in black market, 271–277
for wage-profit control analysis, 264–271
no-cycling argument in computing equilibria, 40, 41, 42
nonlinear equation solutions (Newton methods), 42, 66–68
nontariff barriers in trade models, 91, 209, 252
normative content of equilibrium models, 34–36, 35f
North–South trade protection debate, model analysis of, 221–229, 224t, 226t, 227t, 229t

ORANI model, aggregation level in, 100
Organization of Petroleum-Exporting
    Countries, trade model for, *see*
    Whalley seven-region trade model
own-price elasticities of demand functions,
    117–118

Paasche price index, 132
Paasche quantity index, 132
parameter values, determination through
    calibration, 115–118
Pareto optimal allocation, 34–36, 35f
payroll taxes in tax models, 57
personal sector in benchmark data set, 113t
Philippines, trade models for, 248–255
Piggott tax model, 72t, 74t, 76t, 78
Piggott-Whalley "central tendency" tables,
    119–120, 120t, 121, 122t
Piggott-Whalley tax model, 72t, 75t, 76t,
    78, 100, 101
pivoting theory in computing equilibria,
    39–40
point-to-point mapping (Brouwer
    theorem), 13–16, 14f, 21, 41
point-to-set mapping (Kakutani theorem),
    13, 14f, 16–21, 41
policy impacts
    distributional, 130–131, 130f, 132f
    price, 131–133
    quantity, 131–133
    welfare, 123–131, 124f, 126f, 127f
price(s), 9–12
    adjustment for computing equilibria, 39
    blended, in trade models, 246–247
    ceiling, effects of, 256–263, 263t, 264t
    distortion of, 34–36, 35f
    fixed, in trade models, 235–238
    intervention with, price control analysis
        and, 256–263, 263t, 264t
    minimum, effects of, 256–259, 263,
        263t, 264t
    policy impacts on, 131–133
    tax impact on, 22
    in two-sector models, 29–34, 31f, 33f
price-control analysis, 256–277
    with black markets, 271–277
    factor price controls in, 266–269
    goods-price controls in, 269–271
    with price-intervention policies,
        256–263, 263t, 264t
    with wage and profit controls, 263–271
price indexes
    in policy impact measurement, 131–133
    price controls and, 257–258
price-taking formulation in trade models,
    238–240

production in models, 11–12, 11f
    elasticities in, 118–120, 120t
    equilibria existence and, 16–17
    functional forms and, 95, 97
    market-augmented response of, 23–25
    single-country trade, 242, 249
    tax, 72–73t, 74–75t, 175–177, 176f
    tax-augmented response of, 23–24
    trade, 82–83t, 91, 201–203, 205, 206f,
        208f
    two-sector, 29
    units for, 115–116
profit control, price-control analysis with,
    263–271

quantity indexes in policy impact
    measurement, 131–133
quotas in trade models, 209, 223, 252–253

RAS adjustment method in benchmark
    data set preparation, 108, 114–115
rent seeking in trade models, 252–254
restart algorithms
    Merrill's, 41, 42, 54–57, 54f, 56f, 58t
    modified Merrill's, 41, 42, 54–57, 54f,
        56f, 58t, 62
    modified Van der Laan and Talman's,
        64–66
    Van der Laan and Talman's, 41
row-and-column sum (RAS) adjustment
    method in benchmark data set
    preparation, 108, 114–115
rural–urban migration, 123, 254–255,
    259–260

St-Hilaire–Whalley benchmark data sets,
    108–109, 110–113t, 114–115
sales taxes in tax models, 57
Samuelson trade models, 249
savings in tax models, 154, 156, 177–184
    elasticities in, 121, 123
Scarf's algorithm for computing equilibria,
    37, 39–42, 49–54, 50f, 52t, 53f
    modified for tax inclusion, 59–60, 60f, 62
sequenced equilibrium models, 93
Serra–Puche tax model, 73t, 75t, 76t, 78
shift factor in Harberger tax-model
    application, 141, 142–144t, 145
Shoven–Whalley models
    computing equilibria in, 44, 45t, 46,
        47t, 60
    tax, 73t, 75t, 76t, 78 (*see also*
        Harberger tax-model application)
simplex
    adjacent, 65
    dimensional, 64–66

initial, 50, 51, 52t
unit, *see* unit simplex in computing equilibria
simplicial subdivision in computing equilibria, 46
Singer–Prebisch thesis, on North–South trade, 221, 222
single-country trade models, 80–81, 83–84t, 86–87t, 89–90t, 91–92, 230–255
  Boadway–Treddenick, 231–235, 235t
  Canada, 231, 233, 240–248
  Clarete–Whalley, 248–255
  Deardorff–Stern, 231
  Dervis–de Melo–Robinson, 231
  Dixon–Parmenter–Sutton–Vincent, 231
  export-demand and import-supply closure of, 230–235, 235t
  Lenjosek–Whalley, 240–248
  Philippines, 248–255
  price-fixing closure methods for, 235–238
  price-taking formulation closure methods for, 238–255
Slemrod tax model, 73t, 75t, 76t, 79–80
South–North trade protection debate, model analysis of, 221–229, 224t, 226t, 227t, 229t
Spraos, J., on North–South trade, 221
stabilization policy analysis, *see* price-control analysis
subsidies, government, 256–259, 262
substitution functions
  in trade models, 205, 207, 208f
  see also constant elasticity of substitution functions
surplus in welfare impact measurement
  compensating, 127–128, 127f
  equivalent, 127–128, 127f
Switzerland, Tokyo Round proposals of, 217–218, 216t, 218t, 219t

target price control, 262–263, 263t
tariffs in models, 207, 209
  Boadway–Treddenick, 231–235
  Clarete–Whalley, 251–252
  equilibria existence in, 21, 26–28
  North–South trade evaluation and, 223–225, 224t, 226t
  Tokyo Round proposals for, evaluation of, 215–221, 216t, 218t, 219t, 220t
tax(es)
  ad valorem, 153, 154, 175–177, 176f, 207, 209–210
  avoidance in black market, 271, 272
  in computing general equilibria, 57–64, 60f, 61t, 63–64t

consumption, 93, 168–174, 169t, 171t
  double, analysis of, 157–168, 161–163t, 165t
  factor, 57
  income, *see* income taxes
  indirect, 109, 112t, 114
  minimum price situation and, 257
  payroll, 57
  price control and, 259, 263, 263t
  sales, 57
  in trade models, 207, 209–210
  value-added, in tax model, 175–177, 176f
tax-augmented production response, 23–24
tax models, 2–4
  aggregation level in, 100–102, 101t
  Ballard–Goulder, 79
  Ballentine–Thirsk, 72t, 74t, 76t, 78–79
  Bovenberg–Keller, 79
  computing equilibria in, 57, 59–62, 60f, 61t, 63t, 64, 64t
  consumer side of, 24
  elasticities in, 121
  equilibria existence in, 21–28
  Goulder–Shoven–Whalley, 92
  Harberger, *see* Harberger tax-model application
  housing consumption services in, 97, 98f, 99–100, 99f
  Kehoe–Serra-Puche, 78
  Keller, 72t, 74t, 76t, 78
  Piggott, 72t, 74t, 76t, 78
  Piggott–Whalley, 72t, 75t, 76t, 78, 100, 101
  price effects in, 22
  production side of, 22–24
  Serra-Puche, 73t, 75t, 76t, 78
  Shoven–Whalley, 73t, 75t, 76t, 78
  Slemrod, 73t, 75t, 76t, 79–80
  types of, 71, 72–77t, 78–80
  Whalley, 73t, 75t, 76t, 78
  see also Ballard–Fullerton–Shoven–Whalley tax model
terms of trade, North–South trade evaluation and, 226–227, 227t
textile industry protection, North–South trade and, 223
Third World countries, *see* developing countries
Tokyo Round tariff-cutting proposals, model evaluation of, 215–221, 216t, 218t, 219t, 220t
trade models, 4–5
  Armington assumption in, 81
  Boadway–Treddenick, 83t, 86t, 89t
  "crosshauling" in, 230, 231

trade models *(cont.)*
  Deardorff–Stern, 82t, 85t, 88t
  Dervis–de Melo–Robinson, 83t, 87t, 90t, 91
  for developing countries, 248–255
  Dixon–Parmenter–Sutton–Vincent, 84t, 87t, 90t
  exchange rates in, 91–92
  global, *see* global (multicountry) trade models
  Gunning–Carrin–Waelbroeck, 82t, 85t, 88t
  Harris, 91
  Heckscher–Ohlin, 81
  Manne–Preckel, 82t, 85t, 88t
  Miller–Spencer, 83t, 85t, 88t
  multicountry, *see* global (multicountry) trade models
  nesting structure in, 98, 99f, 100
  production side of, 91
  protective policies in, 91, 209, 221–229, 224t, 226t, 227t, 229t
  rural–urban migration in, 254–255
  Samuelson, 249
  single-country, *see* single-country trade models
  structure of, 9–12
  trade determinants in, 81, 91
  trade policy analysis with, 248–255
  types of, 80–81, 82–90t, 91–92
  Whalley, 83t, 86t, 89t
  Whalley–Yeung, 81, 91
trade patterns in trade models, 210–211
trade-protection policies
  in North–South trade, 221–229, 224t, 226t, 227t, 229t
  in trade models, 91, 209
transactions costs in price control analysis, 266–268, 269
transfers, lump-sum, in trade models, 245–246
Turkey, trade models for, 83t, *(see also specific model)*
two-sector general equilibrium models, 28–34, 31–33f

underground economy (black markets), price-control analysis and, 271–277
unit simplex in computing equilibria, 10, 10f
  artificial, in Merrill's algorithm, 54, 55
  mapping of, 12–21, 14f, 40
  in Merrill's algorithm, 54–57, 54f, 56f
  in Scarf's algorithm, 40–41, 46, 48, 48f, 49–51, 50f, 53
  two-dimensional, 54–57, 54f, 56f

United Kingdom
  tax models for, 72–73t, 120–121, 120t, 122t *(see also specific model)*
  trade models for, 83t, 100, 101 *(see also* Whalley seven-region trade model; *specific model)*
United States
  Harberger model applied to, *see* Harberger tax-model application
  tax models for, 72–73t, 100–101, 101t *(see also* Ballard–Fullerton–Shoven–Whalley tax model; Whalley four-region trade model; Whalley seven-region trade model; *specific model)*
  Tokyo Round proposals of, 215–221, 216t, 218t, 219t, 220t
urban areas, migration from rural areas, models for, 123, 254–255, 259–260
utility functions
  in calibration, 117
  in computing equilibria, 43, 45t
  in dynamic models, 128–129

value-added data
  in benchmark data set, 111t, 113t
  in tax model, 175–177, 176f
Van der Laan and Talman's algorithm in computing equilibria, 41, 64–66
variation in welfare impact measurement
  compensating, 124–126, 124f
  equivalent, 124–126, 124f
vertices in computing equilibria
  in Merrill's algorithm, 54–57, 54f, 56f, 58t
  in Scarf's algorithm, 46, 48, 48f, 49–50, 51, 52t, 53
  in Van der Laan–Talman's algorithm, 65–66

wage control, price-control analysis with, 263–271
wage–rentals ratio in two-sector models, 29, 32
Walras's law, 2, 10–11, 19, 38, 44, 279
  Pareto optimal allocation and, 35
  in price-control analysis, 258, 259, 261, 262, 270
  in trade models, 33–34, 199, 239, 250
welfare economics, theorems of, 34–36, 35f
welfare impacts
  of compensating surplus, 127–128, 127f
  of compensating variation, 124–126, 124f
  in dynamic models, 128–130
  of equivalent surplus, 127–128, 127f

of equivalent variation, 124–126, 124f
of policy changes, 123–131, 124f, 126f,
  127f
of tax changes, 62, 63t, 64, 64t
Whalley four-region trade model
  features of, 197–198, 200f
  regional classifications in, 210–211, 211t,
    212–213t, 213–214
  structure of, 198–199, 201–205, 206f,
    207, 209–210
  tariff-cutting proposal evaluation with,
    215–221, 216t, 218t, 219t, 220t
Whalley seven-region trade model
  features of, 197–198, 202f
  North–South trade protection analysis
    with, 221–229, 224t, 226t, 227t, 229t

regional classifications in, 210–211, 211t,
  213t, 213–215
structure of, 198–199, 201–205, 202f,
  207, 208f, 209–210
Whalley tax models, 73t, 75t, 76t, 78
Whalley trade models, 83t, 86t, 89t
Whalley-Yeung trade model, 81, 91
white market vs. black market, price
  controls and, 271–277

zero-profit conditions
  in black market analysis, 273–274, 275,
    276
  in tax models, 177
  in trade models, 33–34, 33f, 204
  in wage-profit control case, 266, 267, 271